INSIDE THE ISLAMIC REPUBLIC

MAHMOOD MONSHIPOURI

Editor

Inside the Islamic Republic

Social Change in Post-Khomeini Iran

OXFORD

UNIVERSITY PRESS

OXFORD
UNIVERSITY PRESS

Oxford University Press is a department of the
University of Oxford. It furthers the University's objective
of excellence in research, scholarship, and education
by publishing worldwide.

Oxford   New York
Auckland   Cape Town   Dar es Salaam   Hong Kong   Karachi
Kuala Lumpur   Madrid   Melbourne   Mexico City   Nairobi
New Delhi   Shanghai   Taipei   Toronto

With offices in
Argentina   Austria   Brazil   Chile   Czech Republic   France   Greece
Guatemala   Hungary   Italy   Japan   Poland   Portugal   Singapore
South Korea   Switzerland   Thailand   Turkey   Ukraine   Vietnam

Oxford is a registered trade mark of Oxford University Press
in the UK and certain other countries.

Published in the United States of America by
Oxford University Press
198 Madison Avenue, New York, NY 10016

Library of Congress Cataloging-in-Publication Data is available
Mahmood Monshipouri.
Inside the Islamic Republic: Social Change in Post-Khomeini Iran.
ISBN: 9780190264840

Printed in India on acid-free paper

CONTENTS

v

CONTENTS

LIST OF FIGURES AND TABLES

LIST OF FIGURES AND TABLES

ACKNOWLEDGEMENTS

The chapters in this volume are the culmination of two years of work organized primarily in two Working Group meetings held under the auspices of the Center for International and Regional Studies of Georgetown University's School of Foreign Services in Doha, Qatar. My heartfelt thanks go to the participants of the Working Group for their individual and collective intellectual contributions to the project as well as for presenting and submitting multiple drafts during several meetings in Doha, Qatar. Without the vigorous contributions of these extremely able collaborators, this volume never would have been completed. Over the past two decades, we have all benefited from the wisdom of our dear friend and colleague, Dr Mehran Kamrava, whose scholarship we applaud and friendship we treasure. Dr Kamrava provided not only the initial idea and suggestion to put this volume together but also the valuable camaraderie to see it through.

Grateful acknowledgment goes also to the Qatar Foundation for its support of research and other scholarly endeavors. While the final responsibility for the accuracy and intellectual worth of this volume remains mine as the editor of this volume, we all owe a debt of gratitude to the enormously capable staff of the Center for International and Regional Studies, namely Zahra Babar, Nerida Child Dimasi, Barb Gillis, Manata Hashemi, Suzi Mirgani, Nadia Talpur, and Dwaa Osman. Special words of thanks to Professors Rogaia Abusharaf and Luciano Zaccara, both from Georgetown University's School of Foreign Service in Qatar, who participated in these meetings and provided useful perspectives. We also would like to express our deep gratitude to anonymous external reviewers for providing us with most insightful remarks.

Finally, this book is dedicated to the men and women of Iran whose struggles for change, social justice, identity, and human rights has been steady, relentless, and imbued with hope and dreams of living a dignified life.

ABOUT THE CONTRIBUTORS

Arshin Adib-Moghaddam is Professor in Global Thought and Comparative Philosophies at the School of Oriental and African Studies, University of London, and Chair of the Centre for Iranian Studies at the London Middle East Institute. Educated at the Universities of Hamburg, American (Washington DC) and Cambridge, where he received his MPhil and PhD as a multiple scholarship student, he was the first Jarvis Doctorow Fellow in International Relations and Peace Studies at St Edmund Hall and the Department of Politics and International Relations, University of Oxford.

William Orman Beeman is Professor and Chair of the Department of Anthropology at The University of Minnesota, and the past President of the Middle East Section of the American Anthropological Association. He was formerly Professor of Anthropology and Director of Middle East Studies at Brown University. Best known as a Middle East specialist for more than thirty years, he has also worked in Central Asia, the Caucasus, Japan, China, and South Asia. He has served as consultant to the US State Department, the Department of Defense, the United Nations and the US Congress.

Manochehr Dorraj is a Professor of Political Science at Texas Christian University. He received his Ph.D. from the University of Texas at Austin. His areas of expertise are in Comparative Politics and International Relations in general and Developing Nations, Middle East and North Africa in particular. His publications include: *Iran Today: An Encyclopedia of Life in the Islamic Republic*, (New Haven: Greenwood Press, 2008); "Islam and human rights: ideals and practices" in Mahmood Monshipoori, ed., *Human Rights in the Middle East* (New York and London: Palgrave Macmillan, 2011); "Iran's regional foreign policy," in *Interpreting the Modern Middle East: An*

Introduction (Boulder, Co: Westview Press, 2010); co-editor of *Perspectives on Race, Ethnicity and Religion: Identity politics in America* (New York and London: Oxford University Press, 2010).

Bijan Khajepour completed his graduate studies in Management and Economy in Germany and the UK and his Doctorate of Business Administration at the International School of Management in Paris. He is a Managing Partner at Atieh International, the Vienna based international arm of the Atieh Group of Companies, a group of strategic consulting firms based in Tehran, Iran. Among his publications are contributions to the following books published in the US: *The Caspian Region at a Crossroad: Challenges of a New Frontier of Energy and Development* (2000), and *Security in the Persian Gulf: Origins, Obstacles, and the Search for Consensus* (2002). Dr Khajehpour is also an editorial board member of the Farsi Review, *Goftogu.*

Farzaneh Milani completed her graduate studies in Comparative Literature in 1979 at the University of California in Los Angeles. Her dissertation, *Forugh Farrokhzad: A Feminist Perspective*, was a critical study of the poetry of a pioneering Iranian poet. Milani has published over 100 articles, epilogues, forewords, and afterwords in Persian and in English. She has served as the Guest Editor for two special issues of *Nimeye-Digar, Persian Language Feminist Journal* (on Simin Daneshvar and Simin Behbahani), *IranNameh* (on Simin Behbahani), and *Iranian Studies: Journal of the International Society for Iranian Studies* (on Simin Behbahani). A former Director of Studies in Women and Gender, Milani is Professor of Persian Literature and Women Studies at the University of Virginia in Charlottesville. She was a Carnegie Fellow (2006–2007).

Mansoor Moaddel is a Professor of Sociology at University of Maryland-College Park. Dr Moaddel holds a Ph.D. from the University of Wisconsin with a major in Sociology and a minor in Economics. His dissertation was entitled, *A Sociological Analysis of the Iranian Revolution.* Dr Moaddel studies culture, ideology, political conflict, revolution and social change. His work currently focuses on the causes and consequences of values and attitudes of the Middle Eastern and Islamic publics. He teaches on the sociology of religion, ideology, revolution, Islam and the Middle East. He also teaches statistics and research methods. He has written many books, including *Values and Perception of the Islamic and Middle Eastern Publics: Findings from Values Surveys* (New York: Palgrave, 2007) and *Islamic Modernism, Nationalism, and Fundamentalism: Episode and Discourse* (Chicago: The University of Chicago Press, 2005).

Mohsen M. Mobasher teaches Anthropology and Sociology as an Associate Professor at the University of Houston-Downtown. Born in Tehran, Iran, he moved to Texas in 1978 as a teenager. He received his Ph.D. in Cultural Anthropology from the Southern Methodist University, Dallas, Texas where he specialized in immigration, ethnic economy, globalization, gender and migration, race and ethnic relations, and research methods. His publications include *Iranians in Texas: Migration, Politics, and Ethnic Identity* (2012) and *Migration, Globalization and Ethnic Relations: An Interdisciplinary Approach* (2003).

Mahmood Monshipouri is a faculty member of the Department of International Relations at San Francisco State University and a Visiting Professor at the University of California, Berkeley. He received his Ph.D. from University of Georgia in 1987. Monshipouri is author, more recently, of *Democratic Uprisings in the New Middle East: Youth, Technology, Human Rights, and US Foreign Policy* (Boulder, CO: Paradigm Publishers, 2014). His recent publications include: *Terrorism, Security, and Human Rights: Harnessing the Rule of Law* (Boulder, CO: Lynne Rienner Publishers, 2012); *Human Rights in the Middle East: Frameworks, Goals, and Strategies* (New York: Palgrave Macmillan Publishers, 2011); *Muslims in Global Politics: Identities, Interests, and Human Rights* (Philadelphia, PA: University of Pennsylvania Press, 2009).

Hamid Naficy is a Professor of Radio-Television-Film and the Hamad Bin Khalifa Al-Thani Professor in Communication at Northwestern University. He is a leading authority in cultural studies of diaspora, exile, and postcolonial cinemas and media and of Iranian and Middle Eastern cinemas. His areas of research and teaching include these topics as well as documentary and ethnographic cinemas. Naficy has published extensively on these and allied topics. His English language books are: *An Accented Cinema: Exilic and Diasporic Filmmaking*; *Home, Exile, Homeland: Film, Media, and the Politics of Place*; *The Making of Exile Cultures: Iranian Television in Los Angeles*; *Otherness and the Media: the Ethnography of the Imagined and the Imaged* (co-edited), and *Iran Media Index*. His latest work is the award-winning four-volume book, *A Social History of Iranian Cinema* (Duke University Press).

Arzoo Osanloo is an Associate Professor at the University of Washington's Law, Societies, and Justice Program and the Director of the Middle East Center. In addition, she holds adjunct positions in the School of Law, and the Departments of Anthropology, Comparative Religion, Near East Languages and Civilization and Women's Studies. She has a Ph.D. in Anthropology from Stanford and a J.D. from American University Washington College of Law. Formerly an immigration and asylum attorney, Professor Osanloo conducts research and teaches courses focusing on the intersection of law and culture, including human rights, refugee rights and identity, and women's rights in Muslim societies. Her book, *The Politics of Women's Rights in Iran* (2009), is published by Princeton University Press. She is currently working on a new project that considers the Islamic mandate of forgiveness, compassion, and mercy in Iran's criminal sanctioning system, jurisprudential scholarship and everyday acts among pious Muslims.

Djavad Salehi-Isfahani is Professor of Economics at Virginia Tech and a Nonresident Senior Fellow at the Global Economy and Development program at Brookings. In 2009, he became Dubai Initiative fellow at the Belfer Center for Science and International Affairs at Harvard University's John F. Kennedy School of Government. His expertise is in demographic economics, energy economics, and the economics of Iran and the Middle East. He received his Ph.D. in Economics from Harvard University in 1977. He is the co-author with Jacques Cremer of *Models of the Oil Market* (1991), editor of *Labor and Human Capital in the Middle East* (2001) which was selected as a Noteworthy Book for 2001 by the Princeton University Industrial Relations Program, and co-editor of *The Production and Diffusion of Public Choice* (2004). His current research interests are in labor markets and skill formation, population and development, and Middle Eastern economies, especially Iran.

Nahid Siamdoust is a research scholar at The Hagop Kevorkian Center for Near Eastern Studies at New York University, and teaches at NYU Steinhardt's Media, Culture and Communication Department. Before joining NYU, Siamdoust was a Faculty Associate at the University of Oxford, where she taught courses on the Middle East. She obtained her doctorate in Modern Middle Eastern Studies at St. Antony's College, University of Oxford, in 2013. She is the author of *Soundtrack of the Revolution: The Politics of Music in Iran* (Stanford University Press, forthcoming).

Mehdi Zakerian is a scholar of international law and international human rights. Dr. Zakerian holds a Ph.D. in International Relations from Islamic Azad University where he has been an Assistant Professor since 1999. As co-founder and presently Editor-in-Chief of the *International Studies Journal (ISJ)*, widely considered the most significant journal of international law and international politics in Iran, Zakerian promotes one of the few forums of academic dialogue in Iran to regularly publish and engage with colleagues from the West. Zakerian has penned over 100 publications including books, translations, book reviews and over seventy published articles, many focused on the implementation of international human rights standards in the context of an Islamic state.

INTRODUCTION

SOCIAL CHANGE IN POST-KHOMEINI IRAN

Mahmood Monshipouri

The dramatic transformation of Iranian society over the past two decades has led to renewed attention to the ways in which social interaction and cultural tradition have evolved. Iran is currently experiencing long-term processes of cumulative social change that have fostered various kinds of reactions and adjustments, including contentious politics and a wide variety of social movements bent on transforming the social realm. Internal challenges to long-held ways of defining power and status have intensified relations among different factions vying for control and access within the Islamic Republic.

Focusing on the complexity and interconnected patterns of change, Craig Calhoun argues that significant social disruptions—such as population growth, demographic transitions, capitalism, industrialization, modernity, and the spread of information and communications technologies—tend to have far-reaching repercussions. Given the pervasiveness of this process, dramatic change in one aspect of social life undoubtedly alters others.[1] It is in this sense that social change has caught up with the Islamic Republic. The striking intensity and speed with which change is occurring in Iran has far surpassed the ability of even the most entrenched regimes and establishments to come to grips with it. Although the Islamic Republic's success in exerting control

1

over the nature and direction of some aspects of social change has been clear, its attempts to curb the flow of information facilitated by modern technologies of communication have proven less so.

The inability of most formal Iranian political mechanisms to generate sustained economic growth and effective long-term socioeconomic planning reflects not only the country's oft-changing realities but also the enduring effects of mismanagement. Struggles for power among the competing factions within and outside of the governing institutions, especially in the post-Khomeini era, have completely overshadowed any systematic and meaningful attention to the economic, cultural, religious, and technological changes taking place in Iran. The persistent reliance of Iranian leaders on improvising policy decisions has led in the past to gross miscalculations and mismanagement. More broadly, these factors have led to cumulative uncertainties and policy failures in the wake of the dramatic socioeconomic, cultural, and political changes that the country has recently undergone, making it increasingly imperative to define and understand the broader contours of social and cultural change in Iran.

It is worth noting that Ayatollah Ruhollah Khomeini depicted the 1979 Revolution as an Islamic rather than an exceptionally Iranian one, conferring further legitimacy on it as an anti-imperialist and anti-West movement capable of spreading. Both symbolically and substantively, this move fueled pan-Islamism throughout the region and led to an increased disdain toward foreign influence. The impact of the Revolution was instant and heavily felt in the region.[2] The subsequent Iran-Iraq War (1980–1988), which was rooted in the Iraqi regime's belief that revolutionary Iran was attempting to trigger a Shi'ite uprising in Iraq, overshadowed the direction of the nation's socioeconomic and cultural change.

Indeed, the entire Khomeini era was dramatically overshadowed by the Iran-Iraq War. In 1980, a year after the Pahlavi dynasty crumbled, Iraqi President Saddam Hussein and his Ba'thist state became fearful of the populist implications of the Iranian revolution for his own regime, especially since Iraq was a Shiite-majority country. On 22 September 1980, Iraqi forces invaded Iran. One observer argues that there is no escaping the fact that the Shia movement and networks between Iran and Iraq were strong, spanning Qom and Mashad in Iran to Karbala and Najaf in Iraq.[3] The most widely shared explanation for the Iraqi invasion of Iran was that Saddam Hussein's regime felt threatened by the possible spillover of the Iranian Revolution into Iraq. Some experts have also argued that Iraqi leaders were intent on using the war as a way to maintain Arab unity and their pre-eminence in the Persian Gulf region.[4]

Other experts have pointed out that in the latter half of the war, following US attacks on Iranian oil platforms during the so-called "tanker war" and the accidental shooting down of an Iranian Air Bus aircraft by the USS *Vincennes*, which killed 290 civilians, Iranian leaders felt that this senseless violence had come to an end, agreeing to a cease-fire and finally adopting UNSCR Resolution 598 in 1987.[5] Still others have noted that the rivalries that underpinned the war and its somber legacy legacy demonstrated that neither side achieved its war aims and that this was truly a war without winners. In both countries, the war was used to legitimate the regimes that followed and prompted a stronger sense of national identity.[6]

Ironically, the war consolidated the Iranian regime's position, as it proved a very useful tool against internal opposition. Any criticism of the Islamic Republic and its leaders was denounced as treason, with severe penalties imposed on the convicted individual. Iran financed its war operations entirely from its own reserves, which created enormous economic hardship for its people, yet it also led to a sense of unity and self-reliance.[7]

The destruction wrought by the war allowed little space for normal life as most Iranians were badly hit by the economic stagnation and sociocultural restrictions it engendered. The long-term effects of that bloody and devastating conflict cast a dark shadow over many Iranians in the ensuing years. Khomeini's death in June 1989 ushered in a new era with a new emphasis for Iranian politics. Revolutionary fervor was replaced by a desperate and urgent need for national reconstruction and economic development.[8]

Thus the post-Khomeini era has been marked by a profoundly changed sociopolitical landscape in Iran. Since 1989, the internal dynamics of change in Iran—encompassing a panoply of socioeconomic, cultural, institutional, demographic, and behavioral factors—have led to a disruptive transition in both societal and governmental structures of power, as well as the ways in which Iranians have come to deal with the changing conditions of their society. Global trends in communication and information expansion have hastened burgeoning demands for women's rights and individual freedoms, as well as exacerbated festering tensions over cultural politics. These realities have rendered Iran a country of unprecedented—and a times paradoxical—changes.

This book intends to open up new ways of looking at Iran by upending and unpacking widely held but dubious assumptions about Iranian society, state, culture, and economy. Our aim is to promote critical engagement with social change in an evolving and modern Iran with an eye toward deepening normative analysis and inspiring action and results. A recurring theme in the literature on social change is that democratic reforms and socioeconomic development go hand-in-hand. While socioeconomic development does not automatically bring about democracy, political reforms alone will bear no results in the face of continuing structural problems. This reveals a general tendency in which political reforms typically raise democratic hopes but the subsequent lack of economic development quickly extinguishes them. In Iran, a middle class has developed that is digitally interconnected, tech-savvy, and acutely aware of profound changes that have transpired in the past three decades under the Islamic Republic. As a result, this middle class is leery of the regime, vehemently resists, and strongly resents the harsh social and political restrictions enforced by a small group of hardliners.

This book demonstrates how evolving identities, norms, and culture have shaped Iran's transformation in post-Khomeini era and how today's social forces such as ideas, knowledge, and rules have influenced what the Iranian state and its diverse structures regard as legitimate. The Islamic Republic has come under persistent pressure to concede the existence and importance of social facts as well as its citizens' evolving identities, interests, and subjectivities. Such clerical absolutist and totalitarian rule, blasé about social facts and observations, has ceased to be relevant a long time ago.

From ideological imperatives to pragmatic necessities

Khomeini's death and the rise of President Akbar Hashemi Rafsanjani (1989–1997) diminished the populist fervor of the early years of the Islamic Revolution. A national referendum abolished the post of prime minister and replaced it with a popularly elected president as head of the government. Although the Majlis (parliament) was important in promoting popular sovereignty in the post-Khomeini era, it failed to provide genuinely broad political participation. Parliamentary elections were manipulated by oversight committees that controlled access to the Majlis. Inter-factional disputes continued to present problems for the executive branch. The radicals in the legislature advocated for the nationalization of foreign trade and major industries, and sought land reform and progressive taxation.

The victory of the pragmatists demonstrated that Iran's devastated economy and practical needs had replaced vague political and ideological slogans. Rafsanjani's liberalization program (1989–1997) encountered many setbacks,

including low levels of private investment, low growth rates, budget bottle-
necks, and mounting foreign debt. Corruption and mismanagement of
resources also complicated these programs. The late 1990s "reform" era, characterized by the landslide victory of Mohammad Khatami in the 1997 presidential elections, ushered in the expansion of civil society, rule of law, women's
rights, and greater media freedom in the ensuing years.

Khatami's notable victory was also a firm rebuke to hardline clerics who had
dominated Iranian politics since the 1979 Revolution that had toppled the
pro-US Pahlavi regime. Khatami's supporters—mainly youth, women, intellectuals, and ethnic minorities—demanded greater social and political freedom and increased political pluralism. Khatami contributed significantly to
the growth of civil society in Iran by opening up the political climate, by
espousing the formation of different political parties by civil groups, and by
supporting the rule of law. He laid the groundwork for introducing transparency into the political texture of society via the institutionalization of law and
the multiparty system. Support for the rule of law has been widely regarded as
the key to the formation and expansion of civil society.

Khatami's ultimate goal of introducing an open and tolerant interpretation
of Islam and his broader understanding of Islamic philosophical tradition was
to show how reason and revelation could be reconciled. Khatami embraced a
notion of religious interpretation that was dynamic and prone to change.
Retrogressive religiosity, Khatami emphasized, was incapable of safeguarding
the sanctity of religion for it would fail to properly address the public demand
for change. The majority of Iranians, who seemed keen to maintain their attachment to the constructive features of the Islamic faith, responded positively to the
promise of greater freedom and transparency by the government.[9]

During Khatami's presidency, according to Human Rights Watch, the
country witnessed a substantial surge in the number of independent newspapers and journals, and an unprecedented increase in the number of Non-
Governmental Organizations (NGOs), both registered and unregistered,
including human rights groups. This opening was facilitated by a concurrent
rise in the number of Iranian internet users, particularly bloggers, which
allowed NGO activists to reach out to partners inside the country and
abroad.[10] During this time, approximately 8,300 officially registered NGOs
were operating in Iran. Many of these NGOs were later closed down during
Ahmadinejad's presidency.[11]

The dramatic social and political opening during Khatami's presidency can
be best illustrated by the increase in the number of political associations, from

thirty-five in 1997 to 130 by 2001. The number of professional and advocacy NGOs, including those of women's NGOs, increased to 230 by 2000 and 330 two years later. Youth and environmental organizations exceeded 2,500 after 2001. The Student's Office of Consolidation and Unity, an active organ of civil society and a barometer of democracy in Iran, began a news agency, Iranian Students News Agency (ISNA), and published a national newspaper called *Azar* and some 700 local newspapers while sponsoring some 1,437 cultural, scientific, and social associations.[12] In a backlash against these openings, between 1997 and 2002, 108 newspapers and periodicals were banned.[13]

Perhaps the most difficult challenge that Khatami faced was the country's sluggish economic development and reform. A key pressure point in the controversy over democratic reforms in the developing world more generally— but in the Middle East particularly—was the underestimation of the need for socioeconomic change alongside political reform. Democratic reforms are unlikely to be sustained over time if they are not shored up by social and economic development. This theory still holds and has yet to be discredited. Absent policies to tackle structural problems, the future of democratic reforms remains problematic.

This was especially true during the reformist era in Iran. Once in office, Khatami found himself faced with the onset of a global recession and a sharp decline in oil prices. He also faced persistent inflation, unemployment, and mismanagement. His economic policies were often based on small-scale initiatives that yielded no major results.[14] Although Khatami and his reform movement were credited with some initial steps toward enacting economic reforms, they failed to build and sustain broader public support in the long term. Their political tribulations persuaded much of the Iranian public that political reforms ranked higher than job creation on their priority list. This gross strategic miscalculation left the reformist camp vulnerable to a populist challenge, as the surprise 2005 election of Mahmoud Ahmadinejad demonstrated.[15]

In the meantime, radical vigilantes, threatened by reform and the expansion of civil society, changed tack, and did so by expanding their strategy of "defamation" in dealing with internal reformists who operate within Islamic legal bounds, to include disappearance and murder—a violent approach reminiscent of the killings of Iranian dissidents abroad. The defamation tactics included calculated attacks on major political and religious figures. As the defamation attacks continued, vigilante groups, known as the Ansar-e Hizbollah (the Partisans of the Party of God), "serve[d] as enforcers for conservative clerics."[16] Such assaults took the form of verbal and physical attacks on media figures, publications, and broadcasting networks; frequent and violent disruptions and the cancellation of public lectures by prominent cultural elites; acts of vandalism against the offices of opposing media and organizations and assaults against their leaders.

Blasting the reform and human rights campaign

During Khatami's presidency, the judiciary, which is accountable to Supreme Leader Ali Khamenei rather than the elected president, was at the center of many human rights violations. Many abuses were carried out by the so-called parallel institutions (*nahad-e movazi*)—that is, the plainclothes intelligence agents and paramilitary groups that violently attack peaceful protests, students, writers, and reformist politicians. These institutions also include illegal secret prisons and interrogation centers run by intelligence services. Groups such as Hezbollah and the Basij, working under the control of the Office of the Supreme Leader, are examples of such organizations.[17]

Khatami's reluctance to challenge the legitimacy of such organizations, and the theocratic constitution of the Islamic Republic more generally, increasingly undermined his support for civil society and the rule of law. Because of this, Khatami's rhetoric, as one expert notes, "went no further than advocating better management of the government."[18] This style of leadership severely limited Khatami's ability to spearhead the popular demand for democracy and promotion of civil society that his own election unleashed.

It should be mentioned, however, that in the first two years of Khatami's presidency, Iranian parliament enacted several laws significant to women. A law was passed that permitted female civil servants to retire after 20 years' service. Some 5,000 women were given a chance to run for 220,000 local council seats in cities, towns, and villages across the country. Nearly 300 women were elected to the local city councils. Many NGOs actively promoted women's rights in both rural and urban areas. Increasingly, Iranian women were drawn less to political arenas and more to the control of their lives within political, social, and economic institutions, irrespective of the ideological configuration of these institutions. Khatami's administration proved incapable of curbing the security apparatus, as the latter continued to act independently of the executive branch.

The slaying in late 1998 of five prominent secular critics of the Islamic government's conservative faction renewed fears of long-anticipated ideological and political turmoil and further related violence throughout the country.

The killing of Dariush Foruhar, former labor minister in the Bazargan government, and his wife, Parvaneh Eskandari, who belonged to the National Iranian People's Party—an outlawed but tolerated opposition party—and who lived under house arrest, spread shock waves among the reformists. In the ensuing weeks, the kidnapping and slayings of writers and social critics who had been openly critical of the ruling clerical establishment fueled fears of broader violence and chilled open dissent.

Iran faced and continues to face many structural obstacles en route to building a civil society. For these setbacks to be removed, there needs to be a balance between civil society and state organizations. Such a balance requires an independent judiciary, separation of powers, and a free press. The absence of these conditions in Iran is further confounded by the fact that ideological loyalties and commitments continue to determine the shape of political groups and the degree to which they can function within a safe environment.

The gap between Iranian politics and society was noticeable during the reform era. Although Iranian society has been exposed to modern ideas and constructions, Iranian politics has straddled and continues to navigate between autocratic and democratic tendencies. The result has been an intensified power struggle between two factions of the clerical regime with masses of ordinary people, secularists, and Islamic revisionists caught in the middle. A highly evolving and complex process, Iranian politics continues to grapple with the reality of civil society and the rule of law—elements without which no democratic system can function. Iranian society, on the other hand, is thoroughly impregnated with modern ideas such as civil society and internationally recognized human rights.

Islamic reformists are likely to play an important part in shaping the future, although change is going to be slow, gradual, and orderly. The most formidable challenge facing reformists is to promote civil society in light of the fact that civil society tends to be anti-statist by definition.[19] It is now a matter of time before democratic forces, both Islamic and secular, prevail over reactionary forces. Until then, the expansion of civil society is one of the means by which to safeguard and promote the individual's dignity, liberty, and autonomy vis-à-vis the absolutist tendencies of a theocracy.

In 2005, Mahmoud Ahmadinejad became the nation's new president. He banned Western music from Iran's radio and television stations. As the head of Iran's Supreme Cultural Revolutionary Council, Ahmadinejad promised to confront what he saw as a Western cultural invasion and to promote traditional Islamic values. His ban on media also included censorship of the content of films and music. These cultural restrictions were imposed at a time when Western music and films were widely available on DVD on the black market and when more than 3 million Iranian homes had satellite television. Many Iranians listened—and continue to listen—to the Voice of America and to watch CNN and BBC world news.

Today, there are more than 20 million internet users in Iran. An underground culture continues to dominate Iran's social and cultural life in the face of government-imposed restrictions. Modernization and information and communication technologies have drastically transformed and broadened the cultural life of many Iranians. Closing the borders and reverting to the conservative cultural control of the early years of the revolution has proven untenable.

The dramatic 2009 post-election protests in Iran—which arose in reaction to disputed election results that declared Ahmedinejad president for another term—rocked the foundation of the Islamic Republic. The so-called "Green Movement," reminiscent of the "color revolutions" in Ukraine and Georgia, posed a homegrown and popular threat to the country's power structure. The reach of social networking and digital communication diminished the effectiveness of the usual narrative of the conservative leadership, which blamed an externally directed conspiracy for the protests. Despite the fact the street protests in Tehran and other provinces of Iran faded away in the face of the government crackdown, the political cleavages within the ruling establishment continued. Moreover, the credibility of the Ahmadinejad administration sank so low that his government never recuperated in the ensuing four years from a cloud of doubt hanging over his presidency.

Islamic moderates within the Iranian political context can play an important part in shaping the future, although any change will hopefully be slow, gradual, and orderly. Hassan Rouhani's victory in Iran's 2013 presidential election was a clear protest vote against his predecessor's mismanagement of Iran's relations with the Western world. The Rouhani administration has thus far engaged in serious negotiations with the Western world within the context of the P5+1 talks (China, England, France, Russia, and the United States, plus Germany), reaching an interim deal with the West over its nuclear program, reduced regional conflict by declaring its preparation to participate in talks and mediations aimed at ending the Syrian crisis, and has prioritized Iran's economic recovery and the general wellbeing of the Iranian people above its nuclear program.

In the end, the fortune of Rouhani's presidency hinges upon his ability to come to grips with challenges such as Iran's strategic isolation in the region as well as managing its relations with the West over the nuclear standoff. Rouhani has acknowledged that he is willing to risk his political standing in order to clinch a nuclear deal, even as this means taking on the conservative forces in Iran who would prefer not to see an agreement.[20] Emphasizing that diplomacy with the Western world is the key to breaking Iran's isolation and that it is a "win-win" situation for both Iran and the West, the Rouhani administration has taken the view that beyond routing the Islamic State in Iraq and Syria (ISIS), Iran and the United States have other shared regional interests, including containing the spread of sectarianism, stability in Iraq and Afghanistan, and a possible rapprochement between Iran and its Arab neighbors and Turkey that have been so negatively impacted by disagreements over Syria's crisis, with Iran supporting the Bashar Assad regime and others vehemently opposing it.[21] Earlier indications point to the fact that Rouhani's presidency might provide the perspective necessary for breaking away from the outdated and futile approach of his predecessor.[22]

Organization of the book

This book is organized around four parts. Part One deals with the conceptualization of power and political authority, as well as the evolution of identity construction and the rise of technocratic leadership. Lacking the charismatic power of Khomeini and in the absence of a revolutionary fervor and ideology to steer the country's direction in the uncharted waters of the early revolutionary years, Khamenei faces a drastically different political milieu.

Nationalism, democracy, theocracy and identity construction

As Arshin Adib-Moghadam rightly observes in his chapter, while Khomeini ruled over a young state with budding bureaucratic structures and a diffuse political system without much institutional architecture, current Supreme Leader Khamenei oversees a state that is far more professionalized, with a rather more specialized and bloated public sector that is financially linked to the bureaucracy sustaining the state. Khamenei's moves have to be measured and strategic, as his power is channeled through the diverse power centers scattered throughout the Iranian body politic.

Increasingly, Khamenei's core task has become forging consensus at the same time that he has to control a diverse array of power blocs, economically powerful institutions, the national radio/television network, the Basij voluntary forces, and the Islamic Revolutionary Guard Corps. The Revolutionary Guard has become increasingly linked to the power of the *faqih* (the judicial leaders of Islamic law), but also inexorably connected with the economic and political power sustaining the Islamic Republic. The current transformation of the military has also encountered competing ideas from influential dissenters, from Abdol-Karim Soroush to Ayatollah Shabestari and Mohsen Kadivar, widening a pluralistic space that further challenges the Supreme Leader's sovereignty and legitimacy.

Since the 1979 Islamic Revolution, as William O. Beeman explains in his chapter, Western commentators have continually characterized the Iranian government as a theocracy, further declaring it to be non-democratic. Drawing on Michel Foucault's conception of "governmentality," this essay presents Iran's governmental structure as a blend of cultural elements unique to Iran. It is not theocratic, though it embodies models from religious history and religiously trained individuals who participate in leadership. Moreover, it contains many features that are common to other democratic governmental structures throughout the world, embodying a mix of directly elected and appointed offices. The core ideology for Iranian government is shown to be a concern for legitimacy, drawn from cultural models based on the inspirational historical figures of Shi'a Islam, and embodied in popular symbolism. But beyond this, the governmental structures of Iran are seen as expedient and practical as evidenced by the stability and longevity of transfers of office over more than three decades. There are practical limitations to this governmental structure that will likely result in change in the near future, but its basis is stable at present.

The reaction of the Iranian populace to Supreme Leader Khamenei's growing powers has been broadly negative as more Iranians have embraced the construction of new, "more open" identities. In his chapter, Mansoor Moaddel aptly captures these developments when he writes that the formation of the Islamic Republic and the forced Islamization of society were a major setback for the followers of liberal values and secular ideologies. Despite this reality, as Moaddel describes, decades of clerical absolutist rule have failed to create sustainable religious order in the country. The Iranian public appears to be less religious than the populations of many other Muslim-majority countries, and the trend in value orientations among Iranians appears to be toward individualism, equality, democracy, and national identity. On the national level, Moaddel concludes, liberal nationalism and anti-clerical secularism have grown diametrically opposed to the religious authoritarianism of the Islamic

Republic. Liberal nationalist values have been buttressed by people's global connectivity through access to the Internet and information and communication technologies.

Women, families, human rights and immigrants

Iranian women have played a significant role in nudging along the dynamics of social change in Iran. Following Khomeini's death in 1989, an overpopulation crisis compelled the state to rethink its previous stance against family planning. Subsequently, Iran's parliament passed a bill—however limited in its enforcement—that required court permission for divorce. For the most part, women's fortunes were inextricably connected to the promotion of the state's needs, interests, and agendas. Struggles for reform in legal and socioeconomic conditions conducive to women's presence in the public realm became fortified with their broad educational achievements. Similarly, participation in cultural arts, such as film and literature, provided crucial vehicles for maintaining the visibility of feminist agendas.[23]

Part Two of the book evaluates the role of women in pushing for reforms in law, engaging in struggles for political freedoms through the arts or culture, and facing the profound transformation in the family structure caused by socioeconomic change. This section also addresses broader human rights struggles—zeroing in on women's movements—for the protection and promotion of human dignity. The Iranian diaspora in the United States has gravitated toward gaining greater political power and visibility to assist in addressing prevailing discriminations against their communities. Their actions to redefine and protect their ethnic identity and rights have given them a newfound power base in a country where the rule of law governs.

While not denying that Iranian women face many setbacks in their attempts to achieve gender equality, they have achieved a degree of self-consciousness and self-expression that is unprecedented in modern times in Iran. Perhaps nowhere is change in the status of women more drastically visible than in the rising educational standards and achievements that have provided an impetus for peaceful, democratic change. Women's success in gaining more rights and changing gender-biased laws bears witness to the impact of female educational achievements.

These advances in socioeconomic and political contexts have also led to in an increasing emphasis on freedom and self-expression by women poets and writers, affecting the debate in both the social and political spheres. At the same time, women's struggles best exemplify social change by virtue of their embracing—as a matter of choice—modernity and globalism. These changing realities have emerged due to dramatic attitudinal changes among individuals, who tend to view themselves as rational, reasonable, and autonomous agents of change, as well as due to the spread of innovative information and communication technologies in the last few decades. To better understand the scope and scale of social change in post-Khomeini Iran, it is important to engage a new social paradigm, one that is capable of accurately describing the systemic, attitudinal, and structural characteristics of transformation in Iran since 1989.

Iranian women's ability to fight for their place in society has placed the state under enormous pressure to respond positively to such demands. The dramatic growth of the educational and professional capacity of Iranian women has become a social challenge for a country torn by a festering conflict between traditional and modern structures and contexts. Tensions remain over the system's lack of capacity to generate equilibrium between women's demands and their satisfaction.

This imbalance has increased the potential for a significant social problem in a society in which females constitute sixty-four percent of university graduates. Women have become a major presence in sports and social activities. The number of female laborers is growing steadily. More and more women are demanding full equality in pay and job opportunities and benefits. The increasing gap between women's expectations and the state's capabilities is becoming intolerable, with far-reaching implications and complications on the horizon. Increasingly, it has become difficult for Iranian women to find suitable marriage partners given the long-established tradition for women to marry a husband of their social status or above. Although no social institutions currently exist to translate this frustration into an organized resistance, this discontent is increasing and is bound to be a source of social friction in the near future.

In chapter four, Arzoo Osanloo points out that codification of the laws that derived from Islamic principles was also subject to jurisprudential doctrines. These doctrines have been flexible, fluid, and accommodating, debunking the notion that a law cannot be changed solely because it is based on a *Shari'a* understanding of Islamic principles. Legal scholars and activists on behalf of women have increasingly voiced their opinions through scholarship and public awareness campaigns, in part because of the role that the post-revolutionary state has assigned to women as signifiers of morality. The state, Osanloo argues, has elevated women's issues to a level where Iranian women can question the state's validity with an appraisal of how the state treats them.

Farzaneh Milani, in chapter five, examines the evolution of women's social context through literary movements, an important way in which Iranian women have expressed their identities and their claims. She describes an unprecedented flourishing of women's literature as an unexpected benefit of the 1979 Revolution. The Islamic Republic failed to silence prominent women writers and poets for a long time, although it banned most of them in the immediate aftermath of the revolution and succeeded in driving others into exile. Despite the multiplicity of problems that they face—including, but not limited to, sex re-segregation, social and economic hardships, the eight-year war with Iraq, censorship, and conformity to the Islamic Republic's interpretation of morality—women poets and writers have attained a stature previously reserved solely for men.

The accumulation of Persian literature, Milani reminds us in chapter five, is finally integrated in terms of the gender of its producers, consumers, and objects of representation. It is worth noting, however, that the literary universe of contemporary Iranian women writers is built on narratives of movement and containment. As well as shaping a new literary landscape, their themes are a radical socio-political upheaval of sorts. The major focus for women has been to challenge established familial and political hierarchies, religious traditions, and social conditions.

One of the most obvious changes transpiring since the 1979 Revolution is the transformation in the social structure of the Iranian family. In chapter six, Djavad Salehi-Esfahani looks at the past three decades, arguing that the country has seen a complete transformation of the Iranian family. At the time of the Islamic Revolution in 1979, Salehi-Esfahani notes, the average family lived in a home in a rural area with no running water and no accessible school beyond the primary grades. Neither husband nor wife could read or write. The wife would give birth to six or seven children on the average, with her main roles confined to cooking, cleaning, and struggling to keep her children alive.

The three decades of transformation since the revolution, Salehi-Isfahani maintains, have resulted in a narrowing gap between urban and rural residents and between men and women. The most striking aspect of this change is the narrowing gender gap in education. A generation ago, women had less than half the education of their husbands. Today, urban women are on average more educated than urban men, and in rural areas women have about the same level of education as men. Equality in education, coupled with the lower burden of fertility, has improved women's power within the family, helping channel family resources in the direction of child education.

Despite lower fertility and higher education leading to more balanced families, women still largely lack the opportunities to earn income that exist in the country for its male citizens. Women account for only one-fourth of the income-earning labor force, and their rate of unemployment is twice that of men. Barriers to women's employment are due in part to the lack of appropriate jobs for women, but there is also a powerful ideological barrier. These dramatic gains notwithstanding, women's struggle for political power is by no means assured. A recently amended family law requiring men to seek their wife's permission before taking a second wife has resulted in a conservative push-back on a number of fronts. There has been discussion in the parliament, for instance, to limit women's access to public universities, with some universities deciding on their own to block women's access to certain fields and subjects.

Monshipouri and Zakerian assert in chapter seven that Islamic and secular women alike began to reject their traditional confinement to the home and moved toward participation in the public sphere and socioeconomic activities. In doing so, they significantly contributed to the development of a broader civil society in Iran. Many NGOs have actively promoted women's rights in both rural and urban areas. Secular women have also created solidarity networks for mutual assistance. Lawyers and jurists provide legal advice. Through informal groups, they organize debates on such topics as *hijab*, motherhood, employment, feminism, and activism. The increasing number of third-generation feminists—that is, those who emphasize rationality over textual reinterpretations and dynamic jurisprudence—is bound to expand the ranks of opposition reformers. The potential costs for expressing themselves and organizing for their emerging demands have become less severe. There is always tension when the new and old collide, and disagreements among feminists (first, second, and third generations) will naturally continue. President Rouhani's support for broader social freedoms, including his strong advocacy for women's rights, made him a favorite candidate for change and won him the presidency.

In a carefully crafted image-building and symbolic move in his early days in office, Rouhani freed 80 political prisoners, including a prominent human rights lawyer and activist, Nasrin Sotoudeh, who had been imprisoned following protests over the disputed 2009 presidential elections. This has clearly led to a more relaxed social and political atmosphere under the presidency of Rouhani. Given the numerous domestic constraints that he faces, whether

Rouhani can play a sustained role in enhancing the country's human rights conditions and women's rights more particularly remains to be seen.

The struggle for human rights has also been followed outside of Iran via various other mechanisms and means. The large Iranian diaspora community that emerged after the 1979 Iranian Revolution is modernist in its outlook and openly at odds with the country's conservatives. Ironically but understandably, it should be noted that many young Iranians today dream of emigrating to the West.[24] For those who have become immigrants in the West, however, challenges are varied and many, especially in the post-9/11 period, which has seen alarming discrimination and threats against Muslims living in the West, particularly in the United States.

Mohsen Mobasher, in chapter eight, systematically examines the problems that Iranian-Americans face in the aftermath of 9/11. The initial feelings of vulnerability and helplessness, Mobasher points out, coupled with a better understanding of the US political system and their legal rights as US citizens, propelled many ordinary and prominent second-generation members of the Iranian community to find effective vehicles for political action and political mobilization across America, and to engage in political processes in their communities, including running for office. Mobasher observes that gradual political socialization—a deeper understanding of American culture, society, and language, and the availability of professional, legal, and human capital resources—coupled with an inherent sense of attachment to both American society and Iranian culture, has inspired many second-generation Iranian-Americans to be more politically active locally and nationally. The primary political aim of many of these activists is to protect the civil rights of naturalized Iranians in the United States and to reclaim, retain, and redefine the Iranian ethnic identity that has been under attack since the Islamic Revolution. Unlike their first-generation parents, who passively submitted to the sanctions and discriminatory practices in the United States during the 1979 hostage crisis, the young second-generation Iranian-Americans actively challenged the new post 9/11 discriminatory immigration sanctions that targeted Iranians and other Muslim groups through multiple channels.

Cinema and pop music

The contributors to Part Three pay special attention to the role that cinema, pop music, and art in general have in recent years played in spreading new ideas—sometimes challenging and in sync with dictates of temporal and special change but at other times in conformity with Islamic precepts, principles, and local norms. Of particular focus for the contributors to this section is how global impacts of art, cinema, and pop music have manifested in the emergence of a new cadre of post-revolutionary filmmakers and musicians and songwriters who courageously create under strict social and political conditions.

Iranian cinema has become an internationally recognized medium of expression for Iranian society. The Islamization of society in the immediate aftermath of the 1979 Revolution failed to contain the imagination of the new generation of filmmakers, who were dedicated to disconnecting their arts from the social and ideological restrictions of the state. These artists embraced the notion that filmmaking can free an artist from state ideology. Like other cultural and artistic features, cinema has come to define—and even help construct—a new identity for Iranians, both at home and internationally.

Hamid Naficy, in chapter nine, discusses the reasons for the global impact of art-house cinema. He also examines politics and aesthetics behind such impact. The Iranian art cinema, or as he dubbed it "art-house cinema," has deeply impressed Western critics and audiences for many reasons. Modernization of the industry involved wide-ranging activities, including infrastructure, the de facto banning of film imports, government financing, production, and wide-ranging censorship, rehabilitation of veteran Pahlavi-era new-wave directors, and the emergence of a new cadre of post-revolutionary filmmakers. These filmmakers included, among others, women and ethnic minority directors.

The state's involvement intensified for a time after the revolution to the point of a de facto takeover of all means of film production and distribution, but privatization ultimately prevailed, making room for independent directors and, subsequently, underground filmmakers. There were certain characteristics of their themes that further contributed to their high recognition and regard. More importantly, a focus on humanism and intimacy were doubly attractive as they offered a stark contrast to the dominant view abroad of the Islamic Republic as a hotbed of hostility, violence, intolerance, and terrorism.

In her chapter, Nahid Siamdoust addresses the rise of pop music in Iran. The prominent narrative about the launch of state-sanctioned pop music is that the Islamic Republic, in a calculated move, launched young singers— often with voices and styles similar to popular Los Angeles stars—in order to draw Iranians' attentions away from what it regarded to be as cultural invasion by morally corrupt and wicked expatriates, and inward toward a state-controlled discourse compatible with local cultural traditions. The open climate of post-revolutionary Iran and a new generation keen on enabling independent pop music rather than centrally sanctioned production led to the emergence of pop music. Just as the heavy sadness of lyrics in some pre-revolutionary pop songs functioned as an oppositional idiom, the generous dissemination of themes of love in some post-revolutionary pop songs and concerts equally functions as an idiom that opposes the officially promoted culture of grief.

Political economy of social change

Although it is difficult to discern an emerging framework or pattern from Iran's evolving political economy, it is easy to pin down the key institutions and the role that they have played in Iran's modern economy. The clergy controls the major institutions of the state and has much leverage over the parliament, the Revolutionary Guard, and the Foundation for the Disinherited—also known as "Bonyads," that serve more or less as a kind of centrally managed corporate financial entity. It is unlikely that they will retreat from politics any time soon, even as there is growing evidence that the younger Iranians have begun to lose faith or interest in the Islamic regime. As with all authoritarian governments, the Islamic Republic has often played the nationalist card as part of its strategy to cling to power.[25]

Part Four examines the growing impact that the economic sector—Bonyads and corporate Iran in tandem with the apparatus of power—has had on the nation's economic development and social change. Acting independently of the powers of presidency and the supreme leader, "Bonyads continue to be an anomaly in Iran's complicated power structure. The recurring theme of this part is that as long as the Iranian government remains a key player in the economy, in large part because of its monopoly on oil and gas revenues, it is inconceivable to put in place a functioning liberal market economy and vibrant private sector." The nature of politicized decisions by rentier states like Iran renders such an eventuality highly unlikely.

A marked characteristic of Iran's economic structure in the aftermath of the 1979 Revolution, as Manochehr Dorraj argues in chapter eleven, "Bonyads operated as parallel institutions of power that enabled the clerical elite to bypass and keep in check the elected and representative institutions and the public organs of power such as the parliament, local governments, municipal councils, and even the presidency." This ensures that the real power resides in the unelected and ideologically loyal institutions that are free of the potentially challenging influences of civil society, and are committed to safeguarding the regime's survival as their top priority. The creation of these parallel centers of power, headed for the most part by the former military or paramilitary leaders, also militarizes the power structure, centralizing power in their hands, thus strengthening political authoritarianism. This does not bode well for the possibility of peaceful democratic transition in the near future.

The evolution of Bonyads also suggests that these institutions have emerged with a distinct interest and their own apparatus of power. By bypassing official governmental institutions and directly allocating money to their base, they buy loyalty for their distinct political agenda. This has led to the charge that they are a government within the government. Therefore, it is not clear how much power official political actors, including the president and the Supreme Leader, have over the operation of these organizations.

Similarly, as Bijan Khajepour in chapter twelve notes, the contemporary characteristics of the Iranian corporate landscape are heavily dependent on the country's political, economic, and social realities. Considering the major upheavals (revolution, war, reconstruction), as well as the internal and external uncertainties and the resultant transformations, one can argue that corporate Iran remains in a state of flux. If one can identify the trends of the past two decades, however, it should be possible to discern several future trajectories.

Privatization along with the consolidation of diverse, decentralized networks of power will create a new and more complex set of stakeholder relations for Iranian enterprises. While in the past an enterprise needed to develop a good working relationship with the government as the largest economic player, it will now need to understand the complexity of relations and competitions between networks around its business. This means that the country will witness the emergence of new formal and informal entities (guilds, industry associations, regional chambers of commerce, and cooperatives) that will represent the interests of corporate Iran. Eventually, a number of such entities will convert to political parties and potentially pave the way for a more democratic interaction between corporate Iran and the branches of power.

There is precedence for this phenomenon: the Islamic Motalefeh (Coalition) Party was originally an association of traditional merchants, but it gradually evolved into a political party that has participated in bargaining processes with the government. The Society of Industrial Producers (*Jamiayate Tolidgarayan*) is another example of a business interest group that has become a political entity. To project this form of enterprise into the future, Iran will witness a greater diversity of entities representing the interests of corporate Iran in political decision-making. Although the political engagement of these groups creates some positive glimmers of hope, it is uncertain whether this political representation will help the country's democratization, or whether it will set the stage for a dense set of informal relationships that would empower a tightly controlled interdependency between politics and business.

Along this line, the central government will gradually lose significance in operational business activities, focusing more on regulatory functions, with most large-scale enterprises being controlled by semi-state institutions. As such, the regulatory framework will become the central instrument for controlling any economic activity the government wields. In this process, the genuine private sector will most likely be overshadowed by the semi-governmental organizations and business networks. Finally, modern management concepts will have to become an integral part of enterprise development in Iran. This reality should materialize, thanks in part to a generational shift toward outwardness, which is partly due to increased domestic competition and a desire to participate in regional and international markets. There will be a greater emphasis on human resource management and skills development that could possibly distinguish between successful private companies and semi-state enterprises.

PART I

NATIONALISM, DEMOCRACY, THEOCRACY AND IDENTITY CONSTRUCTION

1

WHAT IS POWER IN IRAN?

THE SHIFTING FOUNDATIONS OF THE *VELAYAT-E FAQIH*

Arshin Adib-Moghaddam

In the revolutionary process that delivered the Islamic Republic, something rather novel happened in Iran.[1] For the first time in world history, a state endowed itself with both a republican mandate and a religious, clerically centered sovereignty. The leadership of the supreme jurisprudent (*Velayat-e faqih*), theorized by Khomeini in exile in Najaf in the 1970s, is at the heart of this institutional make-up of the Iranian state that has endured the vicissitudes of domestic revolts, invasion, sanctions, and threats of war for over three decades now. In this chapter, I will disentangle some of the foundations of power that underlie the system of the *Velayat-e faqih*. I will show how in the build-up of the post-revolutionary state, the nature of power of the *faqih* changed from a religious-theological ideal-type to a pragmatist-realist one. If Ayatollah Khomeini was a revolutionary cleric who brought about sudden and radical change in Iran and beyond, his successor Khamenei appears as a pragmatist "prefect" of Khomeini's contested political legacy, whose foundations of power are far more sober and formalized than those of the late leader of the Iranian revolution.

A (short) genealogy of the supreme jurisprudent

The history of the institutionalization of the role of the supreme jurisprudent has been thoroughly examined and well documented by many scholars.[2] According to the detailed study of Asghar Shirazi, for instance, the governmental system in Iran can be best described as a hierocracy that "has separated itself from the traditional religious foundations of legitimation which it had originally emphasized without finding new foundations which it can convincingly define and relate to the *Shari'a*, that is to say, to Islam."[3] Shirazi is right to argue that there has been a shift in the way power is legitimated in Iran, but he (and many others) adheres to a problematic dichotomy between religion (Islam) and modernity when he argues that the "only relationship the legalists have been able to create between their conception of Islam and the products of modern civilizations is reactive."[4]

At least since the emergence of the revivalist discourse of Islam in the late nineteenth century, pioneered by luminaries such as Muhammad Abduh and Jamal-ad din Afghani (Asadabadi), modernities and Islams have been engaged in an intense dialectic, which has not been resolved in favor of one or the other.[5] Muslim societies have modernized Islam and Islamicized modernity exemplified by the globalization—institutional and ideational—of Islamic symbols in contemporary metropolises such as Paris, London, Berlin, and New York. There has never been a single, Western modernity separate from other discourses, much as there has never been a monolithic, unitarian Islam unaffected by other events in global history, whether in Iran or elsewhere: Islams are as hybridized by global history as any other ideational system.[6]

If anything, the contemporary history of Iran is a very good example for overlapping temporalities or modernities that are constantly competing with each other—Islamic, Persian, Western, Shi'i and Zoroastrian, to name a few. The Shah tried to resolve this never-ending dialectic in favor of a Persianized temporal space. His decision to change the Islamic solar *hejra* calendar into an imperial one in 1976 is emblematic of the Persian-centric ideology that his state espoused. Suddenly, Iran was in the year 2535 based on the presumed date of the foundation of the Achaemenid dynasty, a brazen effort to create a new historical space and meaning for Iran that was not centered on the Islamic *hejra* calendar. After all, in the political imagination of the Shah, Iranians were meant to be first and foremost "Aryan" and racially different from the "Semitic" Arabs and "their" Islamic history.[7]

The Islamic Republic reversed these efforts and re-Islamicized the temporal space onto which their Iran was pasted. At the time of writing, Iran is in the year 1392, following the solar *hejra* calendar which begins on the vernal equinox in accordance with astronomical calculations. Consequently, the Iranian New Year (*Nowrouz*, literally "new day"), which is replete with Zoroastrian symbolism, always falls on the March equinox. At the same time the first year is fixed around the migration to Medina of the prophet Muhammad in 622 CE. The point of this foray into the way "Irans" have been dated is to show that the idea of the country and the corresponding invention of identities for Iranians are not processed in a vacuum.[8] The history of the country is as polluted and hybrid as that of any other.

This hybridity manifests itself in the institution of the supreme jurisprudent as well. The idea of the *faqih* as a central institution of the state was invented within the ideational fabric undergirding contemporary notions of the meaning of Iran and how the country should be governed. As such, the idea of the *Velayat-e faqih* is an expression of the historical vicissitudes that enveloped the historical consciousness of an influential segment of the clerical strata of society; it cannot be treated merely as an invention of Khomeini's politics, for he himself was the product of historical circumstances and educational influences that shaped his understanding of the realities in Iran and the world. Consequently, the concept of the *Velayat-e faqih* is replete with diverse residues of Iran's intellectual trajectories.

For instance, one finds strong affiliation with Platonic-Islamic philosophy in the idea of the supreme jurisprudent reflecting Khomeini's fascination with Ibn Arabi and classical Islamic philosophy in general. Terms such as reason, justice, wisdom, and oppression were central to the political discourse of Khomeini throughout his life. They are indicative of his education in *hekmat* (wisdom), and *irfan* (gnosis), taught to him by luminaries such as Mirza Mohammad Ali Shahabadi (d. 1950), a scholar of the classical Islamic philosophy of Ibn Sina (Avicenna), Ibn Arabi, and Nassir al-Din Tusi.[9] Accordingly, in *Kashf Al-Asrar*, his first major publication, Khomeini refers to the establishment of the "Virtuous City" that denotes an ideal and just polity. This concept entered political theory in Iran via the Platonic tradition in general and the classical Islamic philosophy of Farabi in particular. Such a utopian "ideal order," under the aegis of Islam, was exactly what Khomeini and his followers were striving for—hence the high costs that this "heavenly" project extracted from Iranian society.

Khomeini was an ardent student of philosophy, in particular the concept of *vahdat al-vojud* (unity of existence) and *tawheed* (unity of God) conceptualized by Ibn Sina and Ibn Arabi and, at a later stage, an enthusiastic lecturer on related themes in the seminaries of Qom.[10] The political aspects of this philosophical tradition that made the greatest impact on Khomeini, judging from the terms and methods permeating his discourse, are the quest for the ideal human being or *insane-e kamel* in Ibn Arabi's words. The development of this ideal human being must be the prime objective of governance of the community and the leadership of the supreme jurisprudent, whose "exalted" position is not entirely remote from the "philosopher-king" in the Platonic tradition.

So convinced was Khomeini of the superiority of classical Islamic philosophy that he urged the former leader of the Soviet Union, Mikhail Gorbachev, in a letter delivered to him in 1988, to study the Peripatetic philosophy of Farabi and Ibn Sina, the mysticism of Ibn Arabi, the transcendental philosophy of Mulla Sadra, and the Ishraqi theosophy of Sohrawardi.[11] Gorbachev politely declined, but according to one Russian scholar, the message was widely distributed in the Soviet Union in the period of its disintegration in 1989–90.[12]

It was not only his educational experience that shaped the idea of the *faqih* that Khomeini envisaged. Throughout his life he was determined to empower the clerical class in Iran. Especially after the death of Iran's main *marja-e taghlid* (source of emulation, the highest clerical rank amongst the Shi'i), Ayatollah Boroujerdi, in 1961, Khomeini increasingly agitated against the quietist tradition in Shi'i Islam, embarking on a systematic effort to politicize Iran's clerical establishment. This socialization of Khomeini into a senior cleric relatively independent from competing secular institutions was possible because of an institutional infrastructure that had abetted the clerical class in Iran at least since the Safavid dynasty (1502–1736), which established Shi'i Islam as the country's main national narrative.

Under the Safavids, and in particular during the rule of Shah Abbas I (1571–1629), the idea of Imamite jurisprudence in the Twelver-Shi'i tradition was institutionalized in the burgeoning *madrasas* and other educational and civic institutions sponsored by the state. These were increasingly populated by senior Shi'i scholars recruited from all over the Muslim world and in particular from Iraq, Syria, and Lebanon. Chief among them was Muhaqiq al-Karaki (also al-Thani, d. 1533), a pivotal clerical figure that readily carried the torch of the state-sponsored Shi'ism institutionalized during that period.

In his widely disseminated study, *Refuting the Criminal Invectives of Mysticism (Mata'in al Mufrimiya fi Radd al-Sufiya)*, Al-Karaki established one of the most powerful refutations of the Sufi tradition in Iran and set the jurisprudential guidelines for the predominant authority of the jurist based on the

Imamite succession.[13] As a consequence, the *usuli* (rationalist) school of Shi'i Islam increasingly dominated the seminaries and pushed back the followers of the traditionalist (*akhbari*) paradigm. Al-Karaki and other influential clerics emphasized the power of *ijtihad* or dialectical reasoning and made a strong case in favor of the leadership of *mujtahids* whose divine decrees would be emulated (*taqlid*) by their followers.[14] As such, Al-Karaki's reinvention of a Shi'i orthodoxy based on a religious hierarchy dominated by a supreme jurist can be seen as one of the main precursors to Khomeini's idea of the *Velayat-e faqih* or the rule of the supreme jurisprudent.[15]

Ultimately, in truly modern fashion, Khomeini the politician and revolutionary eclipsed the abstract, contemplative, and partially "non-Islamic" notions permeating the philosophy of the classical philosophers in favor of a highly utilitarian, theological, and interest-based interpretation. In the dialectic between philosophy and politics, Khomeini opted for the latter, especially in the 1960s when he focused his activities on combating the policies of the Shah. As such, it is not too far-fetched to argue that Ibn Arabi's emphasis on sainthood (*vilaya*) and his designation of the *vali* as a friend of God whose practices and devotion to knowledge of God enable him to claim succession to the Prophet, informed Khomeini's theory of *Velayat-e faqih*.

But at the same time Ibn Arabi and the Sufi tradition inspired by him would have rejected the positivistic (or ideological) certainty that Khomeini attached to the position of the *vali-e faqih* in favor of an individual path towards the "ideal human being."[16] Not unlike other Islamists of his generation—Muhammad Ala Mawdudi in the subcontinent, Hassan al-Banna and Sayyid Qutb in Egypt, Ayatollah Mohammad Baqir al-Sadr in Iraq, and others—Khomeini forged a particularly ideological interpretation of the role of Islam in politics and society. The abstract and contemplative ideas of the classical philosophers were not as easily applicable now, having been created during the heydays of Muslim empires, when Islam was not a contested ideational commodity. Ibn Sina, Farabi, and Ibn Arabi did not have to proclaim Islam as the solution to everything precisely because their Muslim identity, and the Islamic legitimation of the polity they lived in, was not threatened.[17]

The era of the post-colonial nation-state in the Muslim world changed all that. It turned Islam into a contested ideational system and a space of immense contestation. Islam is about identity, whether it is individual, religious, and imperial (or, since the break-up of the Ottoman Empire in the early twentieth century, national). As such, the organizational outfit of infant nation-states, as opposed to the organically "Islamic" confessional empires of yesterday, gave center stage to issues of governance and sovereignty in a way that was not apparent before. Enter the idea of a centralized state that would turn Islam at once into a source of legitimacy, sovereignty, and national ideology. In short, in the twentieth century a particular version of Islam extended its purview into uncharted territories exactly because it was pasted by Khomeini and others onto the fabric of the modern nation-state, a secular structure for which it has proven to be a loose fit.

In general, the political discourse of Khomeini was premised on two central themes: a particular emphasis on a strong state and a profound focus on independence from foreign influences. He was under the firm impression that in the quest for a stable state and independence, especially from "America," the role of Islam would be pivotal. Hence, at least in theory, the supreme jurisprudent resembles a Hobbesian Leviathan whose purpose it is to secure and stabilize the state and to ensure the Islamicity of the system. In order to entrench his political power, Khomeini equipped the state with a dual legitimacy: religious and popular. More specifically, he argued that in the absence of the leadership of the twelfth imam of the Shi'i, the so-called "occultation era," only the "just jurists" are entitled to the permanent guardianship and governance of Muslim societies. Indeed, from the perspective of Khomeini, no government can be deemed "reasonable" if it is not based on the "divine law of God" executed by a "just and wise governor" who would ensure the stability of the state in the absence of the superior leadership of the imams.[18] As he wrote in *Kashf Al-asrar*, undoubtedly with Reza Shah in mind:

> Reason can never accept that a man who is no different from others in outward or inward accomplishments, unless he is maybe inferior to them, should have his dictates considered proper and just and his government legitimate, merely because he has succeeded in gathering around himself a gang to plunder the country and murder its people.[19]

Given that absolute sovereignty and absolute legitimacy is attributed to God and his divine law (*Shari'a*) and given that only the *mujtahideen* and—*primus inter pares*—the supreme jurisprudent, have acquired superior knowledge of the political and religious criteria to establish an Islamic government, it is they who should be in charge of the guardianship of society.[20] In fact, they would lead the *umma* as representatives of the "infallible imams." As such any other form of governance is deemed "usurping" and an interference in the sovereignty of God.[21] The Iranian Leviathan did not merely wield a scepter, it was equipped by Khomeini with a distinctly other-worldly sovereignty that has given the office of the *faqih* disturbingly arbitrary powers that have been recurrently challenged both by other institutions of the state and the combatant Iranian civil society.

The faqih *and his discontents*

The clerical mandate to rule, which was inscribed so vehemently in the Iranian constitution by Khomeini and his followers, was never without its critics. At the beginning of the revolution, leading Shi'i authorities—in Iraq, Ayatollahs Khoi and Sistani, in Lebanon, Ayatollah Fadlallah, and in Iran itself Ayatollahs Shariatmadari and Qomi—were opposed to the direct clerical leadership of the state espoused by Khomeini and his followers. In a recent publication, Ali Rahnema meticulously demonstrates how at the beginning of the revolution there was no real consensus on the inclusion of the *faqih* between the various forces comprised in the provisional government and the Revolutionary Council which was mandated to draft the constitution.[22]

Yet, in the final analysis, Khomeini remained the point of fixation of the masses and most revolutionary parties—when he maneuvered, the nascent political system tilted in his direction. Whereas the liberal and leftist factions were increasingly paralyzed in their decision-making and harassed by their Islamist competitors, the elevated position of Khomeini provided him and his followers with the opportunity to inscribe the rule of the supreme jurisprudent into the political process and to put the *faqih*-centered constitution of a posited "Islamic Republic" to a referendum which was approved by 98.2 per cent of the electorate. Khomeini was actively positioned, and positioned himself, at the helm of the state until his death in 1989 and his formal and informal powers far outweighed that of any other institution of the Islamic Republic.

Despite the clear absence of a clerical consensus about the role of the *faqih*, at the beginning of the revolution Khomeini was flanked by leading sources of emulation (*marja-e taghlid*) such as Ayatollahs Golpayegani, Montazeri, Beheshti, Mar'ashiye-Najafi, Mousavi-Ardebili, Taleghani, and others. In contrast, the ranks of the major Ayatollahs surrounding the successor of Khomeini, Ali Khamenei, appear scattered, if not depleted. It is too farfetched to imply that "today, there is not a single grand ayatollah in power" as Olivier Roy does,[23] but it is true that Ali Khamenei does not possess the religious legitimacy originally associated with the position of the *faqih*. His power is religiously stunted; it does not reach into the labyrinthine spaces in Qom (and much less into the *howzas* of Najaf, Karbala, and Kazimiyah) which are guarded by senior Ayatollahs who operate largely independently from the politics of Tehran.

While in 1979 state power in Iran was infused with a distinctly utopian Islamic revolutionary fervor, personified by the charismatic and populist leadership of Ayatollah Khomeini, today power in Iran is professionalized, sober, and pragmatic. If Khomeini was the philosopher-imam with the aura of an uncompromising clerical revolutionary whose ideas were steeped in the metaphysics of the imamate tradition in Iran, Khamenei seems more like the technocratic CEO of a hyperactive multinational company. Whereas Khomeini took full advantage of his powerful position, both as a revolutionary and as a religious leader, Khamenei has relied far more on the political power that the office of supreme leader bestows upon him. If Khomeini could afford to move radically, Khamenei tends to tip-toe. The differences can be illustrated with a set of interrelated key words that characterize the sources of power exercised by the two leaders:

Khomeini ↔ revolution ↔ imam ↔ radical change;
Khamenei ↔ consolidation ↔ prefect ↔ conservatism.

Hence, the power of the state in Iran, devoid of its original revolutionary fervor, reveals itself in an increasingly secularized space where religious norms follow realist policies and where the interest of the system supersedes consensus building among the religious authorities of the country. In 1979, Iran produced a revolutionary-utopian Islam, whereas today it is producing a realist-technocratic one. Khomeini himself consciously contributed to this process shortly before his death when he favored Khamenei over Ayatollah Montazeri as his successor as *vali-e faqih* which necessitated a central constitutional amendment in 1989.

The constitution stipulates that the supreme jurisprudent must be "brave," "upright," "pious," and an expert of Islam with an excellent understanding of current affairs and the requirements of leading the Islamic state. Chapter 1 of the constitution clarifies the "fundamental principles" of that leadership further. In Article 2 it is emphasized that the Islamic system in Iran is based on the principle of "continued *ijtehad* by qualified jurists." Article 5 adds that the *faqih* (or a council of jurists, *fuqaha*) has the legitimate right to rule during the occultation of the 12th imam of the Shi'i (Imam Mahdi). Article 57 sets out that the *vali-e faqih* is responsible for the supervision of the three branches of the government and Article 110 specifies that this supervisory role includes appointing the jurists to the Guardian Council and the highest judicial authority, holding the position of commander-in-chief with wide ranging powers to appoint and dismiss the highest echelons of the military leadership, and confirming the presidency.

The power of the *vali-e faqih* to appoint six jurists of the twelve member Guardian Council is particularly central because the Council is mandated to veto bills by the legislature if they do not "comply" with Islamic tenets (as interpreted by the Council's members). The Guardian Council also vets the candidates for the presidency, the Parliament (*majlis*), and the Assembly of Experts, which is composed of *mojtaheds* and charged with supervising, electing, and removing the supreme leader, if he proves to be unfit for office.

More importantly, before the constitutional amendments of 1989, Article 109 of the constitution set out that the *faqih* had to hold the rank of *marja-e taghlid* or source of emulation, the highest clerical rank in the Shi'i hierarchy. At the time of his appointment as Khomeini's successor, Khamenei was a mid-ranking *hojatol-islam va muslimin*. As president of the Islamic Republic he had demonstrated political competency, the second pillar of the requirement for the *faqih*, but he was not a leading Ayatollah, his religious credentials did not match those of Ayatollah Montazeri, the designated successor to Khomeini. In order to pave the way for his ascendancy to the role of the supreme leader, the requirement of *marjaiyat* had to be dropped from the constitution. This was a main factor for the transformation of the discourse of power in Iran which, by necessity, tilted away from its original religious-revolutionary emphasis toward a rather more worldly and pragmatist syntax.

From the imam to the prefect

There is no suggestion here that the power exercised by Khomeini was inherently religious. True, the way it was legitimated was firmly rooted in an Islamicized discourse with distinctly Shi'i connotations, but that doesn't mean that power itself can ever be religious or metaphysical. Power is secular. It is physical, steeped in the dialectic between the ruler and the ruled. In power there is no mediating otherworldly figure exactly because power is exercised immediately, it is not remote; it is penetrative, real, and promiscuous.[24] So what shifted was not the secularity of power itself, but the religious claim according to which the sovereignty of the *faqih* was legitimated. This change was necessary, if not inevitable, because of the lack of the religious credentials of Khamenei at the time of his appointment as supreme leader in 1989.

In accordance with this circumscribed religious legitimacy and the constitutional amendments implemented, Khamenei has been forced to accept that the institution of the *marja* must retain its relative independence from the office of the *faqih*, at least in the domestic realm in Iran where it has to compete with the powerful clerics concentrated in Qom. Accordingly, Khamenei acknowledges on his official webpage the presence of enough *mojtaheds* in Iran who can delegate the religious affairs of pious Muslims in the country without impingement by him. "Therefore those who insist that I publish *risalah* [practical rulings] should pay attention," he emphasizes.[25] "This is why I refuse the responsibility of being *marj'a*. Thanks to Allah, there are others. Then, it is not needed."[26] At the same time, Khamenei claims *marjaiyat* in international affairs. According to him the situation outside Iran is different:

> What is the reason? It is because, if I do not burden myself with it, [the *marjaiyat*] will be lost. The day, on which I feel they—the mujtahids who are available in Qom... can afford its burden outside Iran as well, I [will] also go away. Today, I accept the request of Shias outside Iran, as there is no alternative. It is, like other cases, of necessity. However, regarding inside Iran, there is no need. The Holy Imam-e Asr [Twelfth Imam of the Shi'i believed to be in occultation] protects and witnesses hawzahs, supports great scholars and guides marjas and people here. I ask Allah to make this phase a blessed one for the Iranian nation as well.[27]

The emphasis on pragmatism is apparent here. Apart from the symbolic last sentence, Khamenei legitimates his *marjaiyat* in international affairs mainly through pragmatism: he "has to do it" because as the head of the state he has privileged access to the necessary resources. If he doesn't do it, Khamenei seems to claim, the leadership of the Shi'i will be lost to others outside of Iran because "there is no alternative." The decision had to be made by "necessity" in order to safeguard the interest (*maslahat*) of the *umma* in general and "the Iranian nation" in particular. Khamenei has seemed to be aware from the outset that he was appointed out of necessity, not out of preference—that he was the pragmatic option. As he declared upon his inauguration in 1989: 'I am an individual with many faults and shortcomings and really a minor seminarian. Yet, a responsibility has been placed on my shoulders and I will use all my capabilities and all my faith in the Almighty in order to be able to bear this heavy responsibility.'[28]

Of course, the state used its privileged access to the instruments of discipline and punishment, despite the seemingly humble declarations that Khamenei would respect the *marjaiyat* of the senior Ayatollahs. His stand-off with Grand Ayatollah Montazeri in 1997 is a good example. Montazeri repeatedly questioned the religious credentials of Khamenei and in 1997 published an open letter challenging his religious qualifications to rule as supreme leader. Subsequently he was put under house arrest until January 2003, when he was allowed to resume his classes on *fiqh* (Islamic theology) in Qom.

Yet at the same time, and despite occasional campaigns to project his authority, Khamenei has had to move cautiously around the clerical establishment in Iran; he could never really afford to provoke the higher echelons of the clerical hierarchy in the way Khomeini occasionally dared to. It is interesting, for instance, that Khamenei did not facilitate the house arrest of Ayatollahs Sa'anei and Dastgheib, even as they loudly supported the opposition during the heydays of the reformist "Green Movement" in 2009. When Khamenei went to Qom to a muted response by the clerical establishment, Dastgheib challenged his authority from Shiraz in a strikingly forthright manner. According to him, the power of supreme leadership had to be confined if the person is not a *marja-e taghlid*. Dasthgeib has been a member of the Assembly of Experts for two decades now. During the massive crackdown on protests after the re-election of President Ahmadinejad in 2009, he circulated an open letter amongst the assembly members criticizing the handling of the crisis by Khamenei. "It is not right," Dastgheib maintained in the letter, "for one person to be in charge of the country."[29]

In addition, he called an emergency meeting of the Assembly of Experts. Subsequently, his students in Shiraz were harassed, his website was shut down, and there were attacks on the Ghoba mosque where Dastgheib has led Friday Prayers for over four decades. Reassured by the support of most members in the Assembly of Experts, Khamenei dismissed calls for the expulsion of Dastgheib from the Assembly, deeming it—in truly managerial fashion—not "very appropriate" to do so.[30]

Khamenei has repeatedly acted as a "prefect" of Ayatollah Khomeini's legacy, rather than a leader in his own right. Exactly because he was not a *marja* when he was appointed supreme leader in 1989, his discourse of power has relied upon "managerial" themes. A quick perusal of the major speeches on his official webpage shows that apart from occasional references to Islamic imagery and symbols, usually slotted at the beginning and the end of the speeches, there is an overwhelming emphasis on functional issues of the state. Terms and themes such as leadership, management, reconstruction, security, and national development clearly dominate.

In an address to young army cadets at the Imam Ali military academy in December 2005, for instance, Khamenei reminded them that "military training, observing military discipline, boosting faith and determination" is their major duty.[31] In November 2005, on the occasion of the anniversary of Imam

Ali, the first imam of the Shi'i and the son-in-law of the Prophet Mohammad, Khamenei was equally adamant to stress raison d'état when he cautions that the officials should ensure that there "is no bribery, administrative corruption, enjoyment of undeserved privileges, waste of working time, disregard for the people, desire to make a fortune... and no embezzlement of public funds."[32] In a speech to the residents of Eastern Azerbaijan in February 2007, he addressed the "youngsters" who "have become aware of their inherent worth and merit and are looking for scientific knowledge and new discoveries."[33] In a clear reference to the recurrent theme of national development, Khamenei stressed that "they are seeking to tread the path to the high summits of progress."[34]

Adamant to remind his audience about the development that Iran has already accomplished, he reiterates in typical fashion that Iran "benefits from abundant talented human resources that are capable of making considerable progress in various areas of activities, and it is up to government officials to make proper use of these valuable resources."[35] Elsewhere, Khamenei appears more like a minister of education than a supreme leader when he "encourage[s] academics and the officials in charge of universities [to] promote self-confidence among university students. We should have confidence in our national resources and cultural heritage."[36] He adds:

> We should determine the country's needs and scientific priorities and base our educational plans on these two factors. Research and thorough investigation may reveal a number of priorities in the humanities, fundamental sciences, and various areas of experimental sciences. The results of these investigations must be taken into account when doing large-scale planning. Due to the limited amount of resources available and the large number of needs we currently have in the country, we should not spend our time on low-priority projects. Neither should we use our human and financial resources in these cases.[37]

When theological themes are touched upon, they are subordinated to the interest of the system in order to deal with the "complicated economic, financial, political and social problems" facing Muslims today: "Pundits who enjoy enormous capabilities in Islamic jurisprudence and who have a modern perspective on the current issues must rely on Islamic jurisprudence and its various aspects and double their attempts to clarify different issues and meet these new requirements."[38] In his emphasis on the interest (*maslahat*) of the system, Khamenei follows the lead of his mentor Ayatollah Khomeini, in particular toward the end of his life when Khomeini enshrined *maslahat* even more firmly as the principle of the state superseding religious ordinances including the first principles of Islam.[39] Indeed, Khomeini personally reprimanded

Khamenei in 1987 when the latter was president, reminding him that the state is the most important of God's ordinances and that it can suspend even central commandments of Islam such as prayer, fasting, or pilgrimage. Khomeini spoke with the full force of his religious and political authority in a way that Khamenei never really did as supreme leader. Addressing Khamenei, he said:

> From your comments during the Friday prayers it would appear that you do not believe it is correct [to characterize] the state as an absolute trusteeship which God conferred upon the noble Prophet, God bless him and his family and grant them salvation, and that the state is the most important of God's ordinances and has precedence over all other derived ordinances of God. Interpreting what I have said to mean that the state [only] has its powers within the framework of the ordinances of God contradicts my statements. If the powers of the state were [only] operational within the framework of the ordinances of God, the extent of God's sovereignty and the absolute trusteeship given to the prophet would be a meaningless phenomenon devoid of content.[40]

This discourse of power was emblematic of the era of Khomeini and never really returned in this form after his death. It was the particular historical juncture in Iran that allowed him to speak with such immense authority and lent itself to equating the power of the Iranian state with the holiest tenets of Islam. Aged eighty-five in 1987, and toward the end of the exhausting eight year war with Saddam Hussein's Iraq, challenged by domestic upheaval and international isolation, for Khomeini the politician, the stability of the Islamic Republic was paramount, hence his increasingly pragmatic discourse of power.[41]

Concluding reflections

When Khomeini was supreme leader, he was at the helm of a young state with nascent bureaucratic structures and a diffuse political system without much institutional depth. Today, by contrast, Khamenei is at the helm of a state that is far more professionalized, with a rather more differentiated and experienced underbelly and an inflated public sector that is financially tied to the bureaucracy sustaining the state.

Khamenei cannot afford to be arbitrary in the way Khomeini could. His movements have to be measured and strategic. His power is channeled through the diverse anchors scattered around the Iranian body politic from the nodal point of the *beit-e imam* in Tehran and from there to a whole cast of powerful loyalists: "representatives of the imam" at universities, ministries, and councils, the editors of the two major national newspapers, *Keyhan* and *Etelaat*, in addition to larger institutions that zigzag through Iran's political system, such as the heads of the economically powerful foundations, the director of the national radio and television network, the Baseej voluntary forces and the Islamic Revolutionary Guard Corps. The latter has become central to the economic and political power sustaining the Islamic Republic in general and the power of the *faqih* in particular.

At the same time, the office of the leader continues to be an institution in the competitive political market in Iran that has to be promoted with its own sophisticated public relations machinery like a commodity to be sold to a skeptical constituency who are exposed to the competing ideas of influential dissenters.[42] As a consequence of this pluralistic space that continuously impinges on his sovereignty and legitimacy, Khamenei seems to have chosen to rule as a "prefect" of an unrealized revolutionary dream.

2

POST-REVOLUTIONARY IRAN

DEMOCRACY OR THEOCRACY?

William O. Beeman

Many US citizens were given the impression by Washington politicians and the press during the George W. Bush administration that Iran is a "theocracy" with no democratic institutions. Moreover, it was often stated that Iran also opposed democratic institutions elsewhere. As the conflict in Iraq worsened, the Bush administration continually looked to blame Iran for US failures, citing Iran's anti-democratic ideology. A typical example of this position is Larry Diamond, a neo-conservative specializing in democratization at the Hoover Institution, who formerly advised the Coalition Provisional Authority in Iraq (CPA).

On 7 April 2004, Diamond told the Inter Press Service that "Sadr's Mahdi Army, and other Shi'a militias, were being armed and financed by Iran with the aim of imposing another Iranian-style theocracy." He continued:

> Iran is embarked on a concerned, clever, lavishly-resourced campaign to defeat any effort for any genuine pluralist democracy in Iraq," said Diamond. "The longer we

wait to confront the thug the more troops he'll have in his army, the more arms he'll have and financial support [sic]—virtually all coming from Iran—the more he will intimidate and kill sincere democratic actors in the country, and the more impossible our task at building democracy will become.[1]

Diamond's sentiments were echoed at the time by influential *New York Times* conservative columnists William Safire and David Brooks, among others, further compounding the banality of the misinformation. These allegations have over time proved false. No official body in Iran was supporting al-Sadr and the idea that al-Sadr could ever dream of imposing an "Iranian-style theocracy" was absurd. In fact, Shi'a clerical leaders in Iraq have consistently opposed the idea of clerics participating as officials in government, no Shi'a clerics have ever run for, or been elected to, high office in Iraq.

More to the point, the government of Iran in the post-revolutionary period may have religious leaders in central positions, but it is far from being a pure theocracy. Only 30 per cent of all Iranian officials today self-identify as clerics. Nevertheless, the impression that Iran has no democratic institutions has persisted, and is believed by many in the international community who know nothing of Iran and who are fearful of Islamic attacks on Western culture. Without begging the complicated question of what constitutes a "democratic institution," it is important to note that political structures in Iran have important features that any observer would classify as democratic, but also have features unique to Iran. Sayyid Hossein Mousavian, who was an "insider" counselor to three Iranian presidents has documented (with Shahir Shahidsaless) in great detail these governmental dealings. He shows first-hand that Iran's leaders not only came to office through lively electoral processes, but also were subject to lively internal political dynamics that were responsive to the public in a way that would not be unfamiliar to many Western nations.[2]

Foucault, governmentality, and social authority

I am pursuing this discussion in the spirit of Michel Foucault's widely explored notion of *governmentality*. Foucault's concept is broad, but generally covers the ways that government adopts a cultural ideology for carrying out its duties, a structural framework for implementing this ideology, and a rationality associated with that framework.[3] From an anthropological standpoint, it is expected that different forms of governmentality will be observed in different societies, with different cultural underpinnings resulting in unique institutions.

One of Foucault's emphases in his governmentality concept is the use of governmental structures to establish "the conduct of conduct." Although this has a somewhat totalitarian ring to it, Foucault has a broader palate for this concept. He defines governmentality as:

1. The ensemble formed by the institutions, procedures, analyses and reflections, the calculations and tactics that allow the exercise of this very specific albeit complex form of power, which has as its target population, as its principal form of knowledge political economy, and as its essential technical means apparatuses of security.
2. The tendency which, over a long period and throughout the West, has steadily led towards the pre-eminence over all other forms (sovereignty, discipline, etc) of this type of power which may be termed government, resulting, on the one hand, in formation of a whole series of specific governmental apparatuses, and, on the other, in the development of a whole complex of *saviors*.
3. The process, or rather the result of the process, through which the state of justice of the Middle Ages, transformed into the administrative state during the fifteenth and sixteenth centuries, gradually becomes 'governmentalized.'[4]

Certainly, Foucault's formulation implies power relations in the establishment of authority and the power any governmental structure has to enforce behavior in citizens living under its aegis. However, as a broad concept, the idea of governmentality is not limited to a specific kind of power relationship. Indeed, a cross-cultural comparison of governmentality shows a wide range of structures. Some governmentality structures rely on physical coercion. Others, especially in small-scale societies, rely on mutual social pressure. Moreover, governmentality cannot cover every aspect of human behavior. Some conduct is left to informal structures such as etiquette, while others are much more formalized. It is the specific quality and degree to which the conduct of those who are governed are subject that distinguishes one form of governmentality from another.

In this discussion, I hope to disentangle the complexity of these governmental structures in post-revolutionary Iran, and to argue that they are dominated by two important cultural structures. This is the contrast between legitimate esoteric and illegitimate exoteric roles, knowledge, processes, and structures. Concomitant to these two contrasting dimensions is the trope of martyrdom as the ultimate proof of legitimacy.

In demonstrating this, I will argue that the dominant question of legitimacy has many ramifications. As will be seen below, the post-revolutionary governmental structures, as outlined in the Constitution of the Islamic Republic, rely on the basic presumption that legitimacy confers infallibility of judgment. If the legitimacy of individuals or governmental structures is successfully challenged, then the infallibility of their decisions is nullified. Chief among these structures is the institution of the *Velayat-e Faqih* (the Regency of the *Faqih*). The *Faqih* does not have ultimate legitimacy; that resides with the "hidden Imam," the Mahdi. So the legitimacy and, concomitantly, the infallibility of the *Faqih* are relative, and he can theoretically be removed from office if he proves unworthy. Thus, legitimacy and infallibility are commutative structures.

The principle of relativity is filtered through a strong cultural presumption of hierarchy.[5] The highest hierarchical position confers the most legitimacy, and by extension the highest degree of infallibility. By extension, the institutions and officials that function in the governmental structure are infallible to the extent that they are well placed in the hierarchy of power, and legitimate within the government. It is through these structures that the government is able to exercise the power to legislate Foucault's notion of the "conduct of conduct" within the Iranian state. However, all of these institutions are mutable, even the office of the *Faqih*, as will be seen below.

I want to make a clear distinction between the framework of governmentality in Iran and the conduct of officials and political actors. Every governmental system has good and bad people in authority. Iran has been widely criticized for its government's poor track record on human rights. These criticisms are serious and important, but they stand apart from the structures of government. What is relevant to the perceived bad behavior of Iranian officials is the structural tolerance of the governmental system. Part of this tolerance, I would argue, is the invocation of legitimacy, which can be freely invoked to suppress dissent or public behavior deemed anti-social, whether justified or not.

The election of 2013

The presidential election of 2013 in which Hassan Rouhani (also transliterated as Rowhani in many press reports) was decisively elected is demonstrative of the inability of outside observers with no knowledge of Iranian culture to assess Iranian social and political processes. To be blunt, US, Israeli, and European commentators were flat wrong in predicting the election's outcome. Rouhani, seen as the most moderate of the six candidates, was not predicted to win by these pundits who, on a superficial ideological bias, predicted that the election would be rigged by ultra-conservative mullahs and the Iranian Revolutionary Guard Corps to favor the most conservative contender. As Iranians turned out in huge numbers, they gave the lie to this superficial

Western view. Refusing to accept their mistake, these same pundits claimed that Rouhani was obviously, in retrospect, the choice of Spiritual Leader Ayatollah Ali Khamenei, or else he could not have won. Former George W. Bush administration official Elliott Abrams, the deputy national security advisor for global democracy strategy from 2005 to 2009, reflected a typical opinion in Washington, stating that "Hassan Rouhani is Iran's new president, chosen in an undemocratic election."[6]

In fact, as analyst Nayereh Tohidi points out, another candidate, the hard-liner Saeed Jalili, was perceived to be the choice of the clerical establishment. The possibility of the election of another conservative may have prompted the outpouring of unanimous support for Rouhani. Tohidi notes:

> As in most previous presidential elections, the primary drive behind many people's reluctant participation in this election (after much initial hesitance) was the imme-diate goal of saving Iran from further troubles by preventing electoral victory of another Ahmadinejad-type of juggernaut, this time embodied in the most hardline candidate, Saeed Jalili. Many perceived Jalili to be the first choice of the establish-ment, namely the Leader and Islamic Revolutionary Guard Corps.[7]

As often happens in elections perceived as free, fair, and democratic, the Iranian presidential elections did not turn out as expected—happily for many Iranians, and not so happily for critics of Iranian society. Rouhani's election was won with adept diplomacy worthy of the finest Western political strate-gists. Indeed, Rouhani was somewhat of a dark horse, overturning expecta-tions even in Iran's short campaign period. Sharp, well-articulated political speeches, including criticism of the current government, garnered him imme-diate attention as a politician differentiated from the pack of conservatives favored by Iran's leaders. His endorsement by the former Presidents Khatami and Rafsanjani, both seen as relatively moderate, gave him a large boost. Finally, the strategic withdrawal of the other moderate candidate, Mohammad Reza Aref in favor of Rouhani, sealed the victory.

An employee working for Press TV, the Iranian international English lan-guage television news service, confirmed this dynamic: "After the withdrawal of Aref, the people saw that Rouhani had a chance of winning. Many who had planned to boycott the election then decided to vote." A last surge occurred in the two days before the election. As a result, the three conservative candi-dates split the conservative vote, and Rouhani, as the only moderate, surged in the polls and in the vote.

Rouhani's victory was decisive. He garnered three times the votes of his nearest rival for office, avoiding a runoff election. The results were met with delight in Iran. The BBC reported that the people were celebrating Rouhani's victory in the streets in huge numbers.[8] The social agenda presented by Rouhani had been taken up by the voters who were hungry for change. He vowed to increase freedom of expression, free political prisoners, establish greater roles for women, and encourage support of the arts, as well as to deal with the most important issue for Iranians, the economy, which was (and remains) decimated by US and European sanctions. These primary concerns over social and economic issues reflect the broader expectations of lively and functional democracies.

From the myopic perspective of Washington, London, and other Western capitals, however, the only issue worth talking about was Iran's nuclear program. From the perspective of the Iranian voter this was a minor issue, if it was mentioned at all. The nuclear question was largely seen as an unfair characterization by the US and its allies of a program in which Iranians take great pride, because of its demonstration of Iranian technological progress and knowledge. Bearing this in mind, it is perhaps not surprising that US sanctions designed to force Iran to stop enriching uranium were met with anger and defiance by the everyday voter.

Even with the Iranian public downplaying the nuclear issue, there is speculation that the election of Rouhani may open a new chapter in Western-Iranian relations. Rouhani was the Iranian nuclear negotiator from 2003–2005. In 2004, on his watch, Iran voluntarily suspended uranium enrichment as a confidence-building measure in approaching negotiations with the West. The United States and other Western powers pointedly ignored this gesture, and imposed further sanctions. After the election of President Ahmadinejad in 2005, uranium enrichment was resumed.

It is important to note that despite the obvious delight of Iranian voters at Rouhani's victory, his election is somewhat symbolic. His moderate views may be difficult to implement, given the weakness of the Iranian presidency relative to the nation's Spiritual Leader, Ayatollah Ali Khamenei, who occupies the principal seat of power in the Iranian government. Even the outgoing President Ahmadinejad, seen as a conservative, frequently ran afoul of Ayatollah Khamenei, which had a detrimental impact on his ability to lead.

Even so, this election has mitigated the public feeling that the last election, in 2009, had been rigged by the government to give President Ahmadinejad a second term, rather than allow the more moderate Mir-Hossein Mousavi to lead. This perception led to riots and demonstrations in Tehran that lasted for months.

As I hope to show, Rouhani's victory was a triumph of legitimate esoteric truth over illegitimate exoteric power. This is a constant theme in Iranian politics dating back to the Safavid Era (1502–1736) with roots that date even earlier—indeed, extending back to the origins of Shi'ism in the seventh century CE. In this formulation, legitimacy resides in the internal, the esoteric; whereas illegitimacy resides in the external, the exoteric. Virtue in Iranian symbolic life is the internal esoteric position. Illegitimacy must be resisted, even to the point of martyrdom—the ultimate proof of virtue.

Rouhani represented a pure, admirable, inner core of virtuous truth. The current power structure, despite its religious credentials, was increasingly seen by the Iranian public as illegitimate, and its leaders knew it. As many have observed, Rouhani's victory had to be tolerated by these officials, and their acquiescence to the public appetite for change may be seen as an attempt to realign themselves with the inner core of truth so valued by Iranians.

Theocracy vs. culture

Phenomena such as the Shi'a role in the Iraq invasion and the elections of 2009 and 2013 clearly confound non-Iranian observers. Those with a superficial understanding of Iranian culture are quick to make judgments based on stereotypes and half-understood notions of Iranian culture. However, Iranian society and politics are unique.[9] Understanding how and why the country works requires a deep knowledge of cultural patterns that are centuries old, as well as the ability to discern their modern manifestations. In this regard, it is important to see the difference between formal governmental and political structures and the hidden cultural patterns that govern day-to-day life. In order to explore this, it is important to first address the formal structures of Iranian politics and governance.

The very appellation "theocracy" used so pejoratively outside of Iran is in itself misleading, and shows a poor understanding of the governmental structure that was set up following the Iranian revolution of 1978–1979. Contrary to assumptions, the original government of the Islamic Republic of Iran was not "imposed" by anyone. It was established through an electoral process following the Iranian Revolution. Iranians may regret having ratified the constitution they did, but they follow its provisions assiduously. Every election in Iran in the last four decades, with the possible exception of the contested election of 2009, has been free, and has followed the prescribed electoral process to the letter. The problems that have arisen within the political system

stem from the fact that half the institutions in the Iranian government are unelected and have veto power over elected institutions. Furthermore, the army and the judiciary are both controlled by these unelected bodies. Members of these unelected bodies are typically the most conservative religionists in Iran. Therefore, problems with government in Iran stem not from the system of government, but rather from the political bent of those that occupy positions of power in the government. This is an important distinction, because it shows that much of what happens in Iranian political life is governed by informal cultural processes.

An accurate picture of Iranian electoral institutions helps in assessing both their strengths and weaknesses, and puts pay to the notion that Iran is a theocratic dictatorship. Consequently, I present here a sketch of the Iranian electoral procedure, the main governmental institutional bodies in Iran, and some of the underlying dynamics of political life in Iran today. But first, it is essential to understand some bedrock principles of Shi'a theology.

Shi'a symbolic structures, martyrdom, and ta'ziyeh

Shi'ism resulted from a controversy over the succession of leadership in early Islam. I will not rehearse this well-known history here, as it is easily found in innumerable sources on the history of the faith. Suffice it to note that all branches of Shi'ism—Alawites, Isma'ilis, Zayidis, and the dominant *Ithna-'Ashara* (Twelver)—acknowledge that leadership is traced through the daughter of the Prophet Mohammad, Fatima, and her husband and cousin, Ali.

For all Shi'a believers, the martyrdom of the second son of Fatima and Ali, Hossein, at Karbala in present day Iraq, is the central event in religious life, equivalent to the death and resurrection of Jesus for Christians. Hossein is a central symbolic figure, but his martyrdom is even more important as a model. It is proof of everything good, noble, and true in religion. It is also a demonstration of the most fundamental tenet of Islam—submission to God's will. Hossein, according to tradition, was fully aware of his impending martyrdom, and resisted every attempt at rescue. He submitted to his tragic fate, thus providing a model for all believers. No one following him could ever be as pure, as good, or as faithfully religious as Hossein.

Iranians and other Shi'ites commemorate Hossein's martyrdom and that of his followers incessantly. It is a central feature of everyday life. It is the implicit subject of every sermon. The story of Hossein's martyrdom is eulogized on a regular basis—there being professional reciters, *maddah*, who make their living by telling the story in mosques, Hosseiniehs, at funerals, in private homes and even in the streets.

It is particularly celebrated on the anniversary of Hossein's death—the 10th day of Muharram, the first month of the Islamic year. The celebrations consist of processions, ritual mourning, self-scourging, and, particularly in Iran, the passion drama, *ta'ziyeh*, an indigenous, elaborate dramatic form at least 200 years old, which dramatizes the death and martyrdom of Imam Hossein and his followers.

Ta'ziyeh is highly coded. The protagonists—Imam Hossein and his followers—are dressed in green and black. The antagonists—the Umayyid rulers of Damascus and their generals and soldiers—are dressed in red. The protagonists chant their lines; the antagonists declaim theirs. Those who are about to die wear a white funeral shroud into battle. There is no mistaking the clear structures of the story.[10]

With such a model, it not surprising that all of Hossein's successor imams were traditionally martyred themselves, with the exception of the Isma'ilis whose succession line continues today, the current leader being the Aga Khan. Martyrdom thus became the most powerful legitimization for revered religious figures. This is seen even in informal discourse today. The most common closing for a letter, and in informal discourse, is "*qorban-e shoma*" (I am your sacrifice).

Ta'ziyeh provides a symbolic legacy for Iranians. Adults do not wear red, the color of the Umayyids who killed Imam Hossein. As mentioned above, the color green is associated with Imam Hossein and his family (as well as for *sayyids*—descendants of the Prophet). White funeral shrouds show a willingness to be a martyr—a feature of the Iran-Iraq war, when young men, called *basij*, wore white shrouds before walking into mine fields, effectively committing suicide in order to clear them.

Ta'ziyeh also establishes the basic dynamic in Iranian theology between inside (*baten*) and outside (*zaher*). Iranian culture favors the inside, which is the direction of spirituality, esotericism, and purity, over the outside, which is the direction of secularism, exotericism, and corruption. Imam Hossein is clearly the most "inside" figure in Iranian culture, whereas those who would try to obtain power through illegitimate means, such as the Umayyids in the Moharram saga, are the most "outside."

This trope has been used again and again in Iranian political life. During the Revolution of 1978–79 the shah and the US government were equated with the killers of Imam Hossein. Iran was likened to the plains of Karbala, where the martyrdom took place, and the Iranian people were likened to the followers of Hossein—oppressed and pure. In 2009, the "Green Movement" supporting Mir-Hossein Mousavi against President Ahmadinejad tried to reverse this symbolism, painting the government as the outsiders and the supporters of Mousavi as pure insiders. The color green was enough to establish the symbolism.[11]

Esoteric knowledge and occultation

In the dominant "Twelver" Shi'ism, tradition states that knowledge of religion has an "outside" exoteric form and an "inside" esoteric form. The esoteric inner truth of religion was thought to have been passed from the Prophet to Fatima and Ali and in turn to their successors. Ali was thought to have had Qur'anic scriptures that were three times the size of today's canonical Qur'an, which was compiled and finalized under Caliph Uthman, the third Sunni leader of the faith.

The esoteric knowledge constituted the core truth of the Islamic faith passed from imam to imam, culminating in the 12th Imam, Mohammad al-Mahdi, who disappeared into occultation as an infant. Nevertheless, he is thought to be alive today and in possession of the true esoteric knowledge of the faith. The Mahdi, as he is known, will reappear at the Day of Judgment with Jesus to proclaim the true faith and rule over mankind.

The disappearance of the Mahdi creates a theological dilemma for Shi'ites. If the Mahdi is the only receptacle of the esoteric truth of Islam, then what is the community of believers supposed to do in his absence? This basic conundrum has dogged Shi'a theology for centuries. Even today it remains the subject of controversy, and it stands at the core of current theological and political discussion.

The role of the clergy

The Iranian form of government is unique. Although it is intrinsically bound up with Shi'a religious philosophy, as mentioned above, to label it a "theocracy" is to miss the characteristics that set it apart from other governmental institutions and make it unlikely to be adopted anywhere else in the world. In this, the role of the clergy is seen as protecting the "inside" core truth of religion from the "outside" forces of corruption. (Of course, critics of the clergy frequently reverse the formula, as seen in the Green Movement.)

In this formulation, anyone dying for the sake of religion is identified as a martyr, and receives the honorific *Shahid* (martyr) as a posthumous title when anyone refers to them. Many soldiers in the Iran-Iraq war are designated as *Shahid*. Wall murals showing their pictures are to be seen in every major Iranian city.

A number of assassinated clerics are written into the Iranian political hagiography. Monuments, schools, public buildings, and streets have been named for a number of them. One of the most prominent was Prime Minister Hojatoleslam Mohammad Javad Bahonar (1933–1981) who was assassinated by the terrorist opposition group Mujahedeen-e Khalq (MEK, or MKO) in a massive bomb blast. Also killed in an MEK bomb blast later in 1981 was Ayatollah Dr Seyyed Mohammad Hosseini Beheshti (1928–1981), an Iranian scholar, writer, jurist, and one of the main architects of the constitution of the Islamic Republic. He was the secretary-general of the Islamic Republic Party, and the head of Iran's judicial system.

The clergy, because of the particular doctrines in Shi'ism outlined above, have a more prominent role in religious life as identifiable individuals than in Sunni Islam. Shi'a Islam differs from Sunni Islam in a number of historical and philosophical ways. One important difference is that Sunni Islam is organized into legal "schools." Shi'ism is dependent on individual personalities—*Marja'* (Arabic and Persian: مرجع), also appearing as *Marja' Taqlid* (Arabic: التقليد مرجع,; Persian: مرجع تقليد), literally means "Source of Imitation," "Reference of Emulation," or "Source of Tradition," and refers to the second highest authority on religion and law in Twelver Shi'a Islam after Muhammad and Shi'a imams.

There is no formal clergy in Islam. Anyone (male or female) can study theology, and technically any Muslim can lead prayer or offer religious opinions. The Shi'a system is based on consensus. When a person is known for their knowledge and wisdom, they are a *Faqih* or "jurisprudent." A very prominent *Faqih* becomes known as a *Mujtahid*, or "practitioner of exegesis." Such people are trusted to interpret Islamic law. When such person due to his (or her) superior personal qualities and knowledge becomes a focal point for persons to follow and prominent religious persons endorse the views of that person, then the *Mujtahid* becomes a *Marja'-e-Taqlid*. Technically, a *Marja'-e Taqlid* is a grand ayatollah (in Persian, *Ayatollah al-'Ozma'*) in common parlance.[12]

*Marja'*s, as mentioned above, are accorded the title of grand ayatollah. This happens when the followers of one of the ayatollahs refer to him in many situations and ask him to publish a juristic book in which he answers the vast majority of daily Muslim affairs. The book is called a *Resaleh* (thesis) and contains their *fatwas* (opinions) on different topics, according to their knowledge of the most authentic Islamic sources and their application to current life. Where a difference in opinion exists between the *Marja*'s, each of them provide their own opinion and the adherent will follow their own *Marja*'s' opinion on that subject.

Several senior grand ayatollahs constitute the Howze Elmiye, a religious institution in Najaf, Iraq, and a separate one in Qom, Iran. These are preeminent seminary centers for the training of Shi'a clergymen, but also for the gestation of evolving political opinion. It is noteworthy in this context that President Rouhani completed his Ph.D. at the Caledonian University in Glasgow, Scotland, on the flexibility of Shari'a law. This is entirely in keeping with Shi'a religious theological practice, in which individual religious scholars are continually offering new personal opinions on Shari'a law. This discussion is continually framed by the two dominant themes I have identified above—the primacy of martyrdom and of esoteric knowledge.[13]

Solving the problem of the Mahdi

The problem of theological truth was debated extensively when Twelver Shi'ism became the state religion during the Safavid Period (1599–1750). Two schools emerged. The first felt that the leadership of the faithful should be invested in secular rulers with advice from the clergy. The second believed that only the wisest religious scholars could approach the esoteric knowledge invested in the Mahdi. The secularists warned that clerical rule was susceptible to corruption, endangering the purity of the faith. This controversy continued unabated, creating great stress in the early twentieth century with a constitutional revolution marking the decline of the Qajar Empire. The clergy were split on the question of secular and religious authority. Eventually, those in favor of secular rule prevailed, and Reza Khan, an army officer, was declared shah in 1926 over many clerical objections. Sheikh Fazlollah Nuri (1842–1909), who opposed secular rule, was executed. Mohammad Hossein Na'ini (1860–1936), who supported secular rule, was rewarded by the shah's government and died in his bed.

This did not end the controversy. Grand Ayatollah Ruhollah Khomeini, who at the time of the revolution was the *Marja'-e-Taqlid* with the largest number of followers in the Twelver Shi'a world, became gradually hostile to the Pahlavi regime. He leaned toward the idea of clerical rule and introduced a new doctrine: the *Velayat-e-Faqih* or "regency of the jurisprudent." according to this doctrine, the most prominent grand ayatollah would rule over the faithful in the absence of the twelfth imam, thus becoming the *Faqih*, often referred to as the leader, or the supreme leader. Lest anyone miss the connection with the long-running debate between secular and clerical rule, Ayatollah Khomeini declared Sheikh Nuri a martyr to the faithful and the forerunner of the Iranian Revolution of 1978–79. In this way, the defense of clerical rule became at once a continuation of the doctrine of the Mahdi, and a vehicle for declaring all who supported clerical rule as martyrs.

However, the controversy over legitimacy continues today. Ayatollah Khomeini's doctrine was rejected by every other grand ayatollah. Traditionally, Shi'a spiritual leaders had eschewed temporal power, and many felt that Khomeini's innovation was heretical. Nevertheless, his charisma and leadership skills were sufficient to convince the Iranian electorate to ratify a constitution granting the unelected *Faqih* power over all aspects of government.

Innovative structures

Once the *Faqih* was in place, other governmental institutions flowed from this office. Initially, the *Faqih* was intended to be a remote figure, intervening to resolve questions of government and national leadership only when other means failed. This was essentially the "secular" model of governance favored from the Safavid through to the Pahlavi dynasty. As the early years of the Islamic Republic devolved into factionalism between moderates and conservatives, Khomeini found himself having to intervene more and more, and began to practice a "clerical" model of governance. However, absolute rule by clerics was still greeted with suspicion.

The solution was to develop a hybrid system of government that would allow clerical authority to prevail, while introducing a number of features of secular rule, preserving the legitimacy derived from the doctrine of the *Velayat-e Faqih*. The result was the Constitution of the Islamic Republic, a highly complex document that tries to satisfy both sides of the theological argument with limited success. The concept of *Velayat-e Faqih* embraces clerical authority, while other governmental bodies simultaneously establish democratic mechanisms for public selection of officials.

The legitimacy of this innovation, though it has lasted more than forty years, is still being questioned. At present, the *Velayat-e Faqih* is not supported by either theologians or the public. The current *Faqih*, Ayatollah Ali Khamenei, has no clear successor, and may be replaced by a committee or by no one at all, effectively eliminating the position. This eventuality is greatly feared by the current power elite, and indeed by many theologians, because it will throw open the question of legitimate rule again, and will probably create more martyrs as well.

The governmental system—balancing exoteric and esoteric

In effect, this complicated mixture of clerical and non-clerical positions is an attempt to meld "inside" spiritual functions with "outside" secular functions. The institutions of the Iranian state, according to the Constitution, came after a few tweaks to the structure, to be distributed according to the schema indicated in Figure 1.

As shown in Figure 1, the *Faqih* controls, directly or indirectly, almost every aspect of government. However, the *Faqih* is himself chosen by an Assembly of Experts, who are elected by the people.

The electorate

Voting rates are typically high. In the parliamentary elections of 2000, 67.35 per cent of voters cast ballots. In the presidential election of 2001, voter par-

Figure 1: Iranian Government Structure

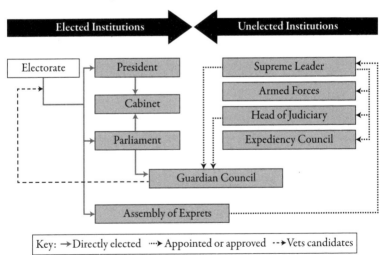

Source: BBC, "Iran, Who Holds the Power?", http://news.bbc.co.uk/1/shared/spl/hi/middle_east/03/iran_power/html/default.stm, last accessed 28 October 2015.

ticipation was 67.6 per cent. In the 2004 parliamentary elections, the rate remained above 50 per cent, despite a call from reformists to boycott. By contrast, the participation in Tehran was around 30 per cent, showing both the effect of the urban dwellers' disaffection, but also showing that rural voters continued to vote at high rates. In 2013, total voter turnout was approximately 70.7 per cent, reaching a new high, but also reflecting the public desire to see authority pass from clerical hands.[14]

Voters typically turn out in large numbers if they feel that the election is legitimate. Although it seems counter-productive from a Western standpoint, there are frequent calls to boycott elections when the voters feel there is not legitimate choice. This can change in the course of the election itself. President George W. Bush declared the Iranian elections of 2005 to be illegitimate, due in part to the large numbers of people who had planned to boycott. The Iranian government seized on President Bush's proclamation and broadcast it widely. The result was a surge of anger among the electorate who had not planned to vote, feeling that such a pronouncement by a foreign leader somehow legitimized the electoral process they had been protesting against. It created a public reaction in which people voted just to defy President Bush and the United States rather than because they wanted to support any particular candidate. The result of the election was the victory of President Mahmoud Ahmadinejad, who in some sense had President Bush to thank for his election victory.

In general, however, reformists and conservatives have traded victories in Iranian elections, and transitions have been smooth, with the exception of 2009. Conservative candidates made a comeback—aided by low voter turnout—in local council elections in March 2003 and the parliamentary elections in early 2004. Iranian voters today are concerned about personal freedoms, education, job opportunities, justice, economic and administrative reform and transparency, prosperity, and the rule of law.

In examining the Iranian governmental system, it is tempting to see it as an exercise of contrasts between exoteric and esoteric power. As will be seen below, there are a number of offices that are directly elected by the people, with open campaigning and clearly identified personalities. At the same time, these candidates are vetted by bodies that are semi-elected, or appointed, whose decisions are anything but transparent. Likewise, ultimate power resides with the *Faqih*, whose deliberative processes are, almost by definition, esoteric in the extreme. Indeed at its core, it is likely that no one, not even Iranians involved in the inner circles of government, know exactly how decisions of importance are reached.

Unelected bodies—esoteric governance

Faqih

The role of the *Faqih*, the spiritual leader or supreme leader, in the constitution is based on the ideas of Ayatollah Khomeini. The current *Faqih*, Ayatollah Ali Khamenei, appoints the head of the judiciary, six of the members of the powerful Guardian Council, the commanders of all the armed forces, Friday prayer leaders, and the head of radio and television. He also confirms the election of the president. The *Faqih* is chosen by the clerics who make up the Assembly of Experts and as mentioned above, who are directly elected by the voting public.

Tensions between the office of the *Faqih* and the office of the president have often been the source of political instability. These tensions have increased since the 1998 election of President Mohammed Khatami—a reflection of the underlying tensions between religious rule and the democratic aspirations of most Iranians.

Armed forces

The armed forces are made up of the Revolutionary Guard and the regular forces. The Revolutionary Guard was formed after the revolution to protect the new leaders and institutions and to fight those opposing the revolution. Today, it has a powerful presence in other institutions, and controls volunteer militias with branches in every town. While the two bodies were once separate, the army under the control of the president, and the Revolutionary Guard under the control of the *Faqih*, during the administration of President Hashemi Rafasanjani, both bodies were placed under a joint general command under the direction of the *Faqih*. Today, all leading army and Revolutionary Guard commanders are appointed by the *Faqih*, and are answerable only to him. Because members of the military alongside clerics are the most commonly identified martyrs in Iran, there is a special regard for them.

Following the war, the *basij* became self-appointed guardians of morality and political correctness. Operating as freebooters under the loose supervision of the Revolutionary Guard, they would attack people on the streets and occasionally murder people whom they believed to be undermining the Revolution. Their cachet as part of a corps of incipient martyrs gave them great individual power. They have been difficult to control, and are increasingly disliked by the general population, especially the youth who have no recollection of the Iran-Iraq War. The central government has tried to rein in their activities, but this has proved difficult because of their high symbolic status in the ideology of martyrdom.

Head of judiciary

The Iranian judiciary has never been independent of political influence. Until early in the twentieth century, the courts were headed by religious judges and were controlled by the clergy. During the Pahlavi dynasty, courts were secularized. Then, after the revolution, the Iranian Supreme Court revoked all previous laws that were deemed un-Islamic. New laws based on Shari'a law—derived from Islamic texts and teachings—were soon introduced.

The judiciary ensures that Islamic laws are enforced, and defines legal policy. It also nominates the six lay members of the Guardian Council (discussed in more detail in the next section). The head of the judiciary is appointed by, and reports to, the *Faqih*. As in the United States, different judges interpret the law according to their own judgments. In recent years, hardline conservative judges have used the judicial system to undermine reforms by imprisoning and occasionally ordering the execution of reformists and journalists, or by closing down reformist papers. Those imprisoned and executed become martyrs to those who see the clerical rule as illegitimate.

Expediency Council

The Expediency Council is an advisory body for the *Faqih* with ultimate adjudicative power in disputes over legislation between the parliament and the Guardian Council. The *Faqih* appoints its members, who are prominent religious, social, and political figures. Former President Ayatollah Ali Akbar Hashemi Rafsanjani turned this body into an influential strategic planning and policymaking body.

Elected bodies—exoteric government

Assembly of Experts

The responsibilities of the Assembly of Experts (*Majlis-e Khobregan* or *Majlis-e Khebregan-e Rahbari*) are to appoint the *Faqih*, monitor his performance, and remove him if he is deemed incapable of fulfilling his duties. They also appoint a new *Faqih* upon the death of the current leader. The assembly usually holds two sessions a year. The number of members has ranged from 82 to 88 (the number at this writing), last elected in 2006. Only clerics can join the assembly, and candidates for election are vetted by the Guardian Council. The assembly is dominated by conservatives, such as its former chairman, Ayatollah Ali Meshkini. For a long time the key role of the Assembly was played by Deputy Chairman Ayatollah Ali Akbar Hashemi Rafsanjani, a former president, who also heads the Expediency Council (discussed earlier).

Currently, the Chairman of the Assembly is Mohammad Reza Mahdavi Kani, elected in 2011. Kani is also the leader of the Combatant Clergy Association (Persian: *jāmeʾe-ye Rowhāniyyat-e Mobārez*), arguably the most influential political party in Iran today. Iran's current President, Hassan Rouhani, as well as former President Ayatollah Ali Akbar Hashemi Rafsanjani, and many other prominent political figures are members.

President

The president is elected by the voting public to serve for four years and for no more than two consecutive terms. Unlike most nations in the Middle East, where leaders have often been "elected for life," Iran has adhered strictly to presidential term limits. Nevertheless, former presidents have frequently been "recycled" into other leadership positions—the foremost being former President Ali Akbar Hashemi Rafsanjani, who served as deputy leader of the Assembly of Experts and head of the Expediency Council. The constitution describes the president as the second-highest ranking official in the country. He is head of the executive branch of power and is responsible for ensuring that the constitution is implemented. Presidential powers are limited by the members of unelected bodies in Iran's power structure, most of whom are clerics, and by the authority of the *Faqih*. Note that it is the *Faqih*, not the president, who controls the armed forces and makes decisions on security, defense, and major foreign policy issues.

Presidential candidates are vetted by the Council of Guardians for their "suitability" in terms of Islam and revolutionary ideology. This has led to much criticism, particularly in the West, that the presidential elections are illegitimate because candidates are not free to run unimpeded by the incumbent elite. However, since more than 400 people have presented themselves as candidates in past presidential elections (10–20 per cent of whom are women), it is problematic to hold an election without some kind of filtering mechanism, and this is the structure democratically ratified in the Constitution.

The last reformist President, Mohammad Khatami, was elected in May 1997 with nearly 70 per cent of the vote and re-elected in June 2001 with over 77 per cent. The Guardian Council, which is explained below, has frustrated most of his reforms, since they reserve a veto over all legislation. The principal areas in which Khatami's reforms have been frustrated are in the areas of presidential power and electoral supervision. His failure to carry out reforms largely resulted in disaffection on the part of the voters in the parliamentary elections of 2004.

President Mahmoud Ahmadinejad, elected in 2005 and controversially re-elected in 2009, ran afoul of both the reform-minded public and the conservative clergy. He appeared to try to establish a power base independent from Ayatollah Khamenei and the conservative members of Parliament who frequently refused to ratify his appointments and frustrated his legislation. The election of 2009 created consternation among those favoring clerical rule because it was thought that President Ahmadinejad's opponents might initiate measures that would try to eliminate the *Velayat-e Faqhi*. The current President, Hassan Rouhani will be discussed below.

Parliament

The 290 members of the *Majlis*, or parliament, are elected by popular vote every four years. The parliament has the power to introduce and pass laws, as well as to summon and impeach ministers or the president. However, all *Majlis* bills have to be approved by the conservative Guardian Council. In February 2000, the sixth *Majlis* was elected in free and fair elections. It was the first in which reformists gained a majority. However, the election of 2004 did result in a predominantly conservative parliament that carried forward through the entire term of President Ahmadinejad. It is too soon at this writing to assess the nature of the current parliament.

Cabinet

Members of the cabinet, or Council of Ministers, are chosen by the president and approved by parliament, which can also impeach them. The *Faqih* is closely involved in defense, security, and foreign policy, and holds influence in decision-making. Ministers responsible for cultural and social issues are heavily monitored by conservatives watching for any sign of deviation from Islamic law, resulting in a tug of war over contentious policies. During the past four years, for example, the judiciary would close newspapers, and the Ministry of Culture would re-license them under a new name. This game kept up for some time, to the frustration of the conservatives. The cabinet is chaired by the president or first vice-president, who is responsible for cabinet affairs.

Jointly appointed body—mediating the esoteric and the exoteric: Guardian Council

The most influential body in Iran is the Guardian Council. It is currently controlled by conservatives. It consists of six theologians appointed by the *Faqih* and six jurists nominated by the judiciary and approved by parliament, perpetuating a deep conservative bias under the present government structures. Members are elected for six years on a phased basis, so that half the membership changes every three years.

The Guardian Council has virtual veto power over every electoral candidate and every piece of legislation that passes parliament to make sure they conform to the constitution and Islamic law. It is this feature of government more than any other that has caused frustration throughout Iran. Reformists have tried to restrict the Council's veto power without success. When the Council disqualified nearly a third of all candidates who had presented themselves for parliamentary elections, they faced boycotts and resignations from sitting *Majlis* members. This did not faze them. Only when *Faqih* Khamenei personally intervened to relax their hard line did they allow a few hundred candidates back on the ballot. Even so, as a result of their disqualifications, the elections were virtually rigged in favor of the conservatives.

The elections: a unique Iranian exercise

The complexity of Iran's electoral system is revealed in the parliamentary election of 2004 and the presidential elections of 2005, 2009, and 2013. Over 6,000 people presented themselves for election to parliament in 2004. More than 200 candidates presented themselves for the presidential elections in 2005. They were affiliated with dozens of parties, large and small. Despite the many parties, they can be divided into conservative and reform camps.

In response to the elimination of most of their candidates by the Guardian Council, the Militant Clerics' Society, and the principal reform group, of which former President Khatami is a member, declared the election illegitimate, called for a boycott, and withdrew their own candidates. Seven smaller reform parties could not mount enough candidates to contest the election. Of the 290 seats, approximately 130 were completely uncontested, resulting in a conservative victory. In some cases, however, there were so many candidates that runoffs were authorized.

Despite the boycotts, a new parliament was elected in 2004. Many voters were already displeased with the reform candidates for failing to make good on their promise to change things for the better, and as a result were stoic about the takeover of the conservatives. Many Iranians simply wanted a better life for themselves and their families, and felt that perhaps with the parliament no longer expending its energy on internal political struggle, the focus would turn to the economy.

After vetting by the Guardian Council, seven candidates for president presented themselves in the summer of 2005. A run-off had to be held between the top two candidates, and Mahmoud Ahmadinejad was eventually elected president. In 2009, President Ahmadinejad was re-elected amid extensive demonstrations claiming that the election had been rigged. The election protests resulted in many deaths and injuries. Many who were killed were seen as martyrs by the public. In 2013, reformist candidate Hassan Rouhani was elected, partly, some observers believe, in order to placate the electorate, still angered over the 2009 election results.

Martyrdom and reform

Perhaps the most foolish idea in Washington in the past few years is the notion that the United States could somehow engineer the "overthrow" of the Iranian government and establish a "democracy" there. This idea has been promulgated incessantly in conservative think tanks, such as the American Enterprise Institute (AEI) and the Washington Institute for Near East Policy (WINEP). Although the government of the Islamic Republic has structural flaws that allow a dominant ideology to gain effective control over many areas of government, the system continues to function, albeit with considerable difficulty.

With the growing power of Iran's youth and women, the elderly clerics will undoubtedly be supplanted. Most of the citizenry has no personal knowledge of Ayatollah Khomeini or the revolution. Moreover, they are the best educated Iranian population in history. They have access to computers, satellite dishes, and every modern information technology. As a result, they are also exceptionally well-informed about their own lives and about international affairs. Very soon this new generation will come to political office. When they do, reforms that they are clamoring for will take place, and it will be sooner rather than later. The US neoconservative desire to depose the current government will not bring about reform; rather, it will set it back by unleashing social unrest. Iranians themselves have no desire for internal conflict. For the time being, they are able to continue with their functioning but flawed governmental structures, despite the undercurrent of social unrest that will bring reform in time.

One of the most interesting developments in modern political life surrounded the election of Mahmoud Ahmadinejad in 2005. He represented a challenge to the incumbent Iranian government, and increasingly a challenge to the doctrine of the *Velayat-e Faqih*. Not a cleric himself, he continually invoked the return of the Mahdi, undercutting the authority of Ayatollah Khamenei and his dwindling band of supporters. If the Mahdi was returning, then there was no need for a continued regency. Despite this, Ahmadinejad had no power over the military, foreign relations, or the nuclear program. His extreme pronouncements should have been discounted by the West, but the temptation to demonize Iran on the part of conservative elements in the United States, Israel, and other European nations caused them to overlook the Iranian president's weakness, and to claim his extreme remarks as indicative of Iranian government policy.

As mentioned above, the re-election of President Ahmadinejad in 2009 sparked a huge public backlash against the government, and generated a large number of martyrs. This was unexpected, since President Ahmadinejad had been as troublesome for Iran's power elite as for the public. Nevertheless, his "victory" was thought by the opposition to have been engineered by Ayatollah Khamenei or his supporters. The principal opposition candidate, Mir-Hossein Mousavi, was deemed to have won the election, though official tallies gave him 34 per cent of the vote. Despite a change in presidency, he remains under house arrest at the time of writing.

The Green Movement seized on the symbolic color green, associated with Imam Hossein and his martyred family. Public demonstrations against the results of the election lasted for weeks and were a tremendous embarrassment to the government. One innocent bystander, Neda Agha-Soltan, was shot during a demonstration. Her unusual situation as a female martyr gave her untimely death tremendous symbolic power for the movement. Her pictures were displayed in worldwide demonstrations protesting the election.

Sadly, verbal and economic assaults on Iran from the United States and its allies fit the Iranian trope of martyrdom perfectly. Economic sanctions against

Iran were implemented by the United States shortly after the revolution by President Ronald Reagan's administration, and were increased under the Clinton, Bush, and Obama administrations for a variety of non-comprehensive reasons. The United States, moreover, aided Iraq in the Iran-Iraq war. These and many other reasons have caused Iranians to view the United States as hostile to their interests.

Given the strong cultural tendency to viewing public affairs in terms of legitimacy, Iranians are easily able to see themselves as under siege from illegitimate external forces, like Imam Hossein at Karbala. This enormously symbolic metaphor is encouraged by Iran's political leaders. In terms of Iranian cultural logic, it rings completely true and few Iranians have the perspective that allows them to resist this formulation. This strong sentiment makes reform extremely problematic, as religious leaders accuse the reformers of being in league with the illegitimate outsiders—symbolically siding with the Umayyid murderers of the martyr Hossein and his followers.[15]

Who's afraid of Islamic government?

As mentioned at the beginning of this discussion, when the new Iraqi constitution was being drafted in 2005, there was dread in the West that the emerging state would be a de facto Islamic republic. This didn't happen, of course, largely because Shi'a leaders in Iraq were deeply opposed to clerical involvement in secular government (effectively rejecting the idea of the *Velayat-e Faqih*). Even so, the negative view of an Islamic Republic in the minds of Western observers remains worse than the reality.

The idea of Islamic governance is of critical symbolic importance for Muslims, since as a matter of faith, Islam is supposed to be the governing principle for all of human life. However, the simple truth is that even if a nation labels itself as an Islamic Republic, only the smallest part of specific governmental structures can actually be determined by *Shari'a* (sacred law) as a matter of theology. Even those aspects of governance that appear to be directly determined by *Shari'a* principles are subject to interpretation by religious officials, many of whom disagree on their application.

Though conservative theologians occasionally say that Islam is antithetical to democracy, this judgment is based on the highly remote possibility that a majority of voters could negate one or another principle of Islam. In fact, Islamic government cannot be effective in practice without democratic institutions. Islamic law says nothing specific about choosing leaders, conducting elections, determining citizenship rights, setting up legislatures, establishing bureaucracies, passing and codifying civil laws, taxation, establishing public order, governing the military, establishing systems of registration and transfer of property, creating systems of public education, running public utilities and services, and a myriad of other governmental functions that form the backbone and guts of any state system. Islam also provides for "consensus" as the ultimate form of arbitration in the case of any controversy over conduct, which seems to affirm the democratic process.

In short, Islamic governance is mostly just plain governance, with special attention to structures that do not controvert the small body of specific laws incumbent on Muslims. The Islamic Constitutions already in place make this "non-controvertability" clause prominent, and this small limited provision is frequently the most specifically Islamic part of the documents.

Beyond this, Islamic government incorporates a broad set of ethical principles that are shared with the West, namely that public resources should be used for the good of all, that honesty should be a hallmark of public life, and that the poor, sick, and disadvantaged should be provided for.

Most Americans conjure up a cartoon version of Iran, emphasizing clerical rule, mandatory head covering for women, and prohibitions on public behavior, as if that were all there was to governing. However, the Iranian government is an anomaly in the Muslim world, or even within the Shi'a sect, with few theologians agreeing with its bedrock principle of the *Velayat-e Faqih*, or rule of the chief jurisprudent. In the Sunni world, this doctrine is anathema. Given that, even in Iran, clerics are not dominant in the day-to-day workings of government, it is highly unlikely that any emerging Islamic state will ever be able to implement "clerical rule."

Iranian state structure, as I have tried to show, is a miracle of complexity with interlocking leadership positions, staggered election terms, and baroque combinations of direct and indirect election. Nowhere in *Shari'a* law has such a structure ever been contemplated. In fact, although Iran calls itself an Islamic Republic, the form of governmentality embodied both in the Iranian post-revolutionary constitution, and in the practice of government, has very little to do with Islam except in aspirational terms. However, it has a great deal to do with Iranian cultural sensibilities—dominated as they are by concerns with legitimacy, filtered through hierarchical social structures.

Moreover, even with clerical rule, Iran's application of Islamic law has evolved over time. Many punishments for crime specified in the *Qur'an*, such as stoning for adultery, have been modified. Iran's new penal code, announced in 2012–13, bans death by stoning and forbids the execution of minors.[16]

Other practices that Western observers attribute to Islamic rule, such as political imprisonment, have nothing to do with Islam at all. The illegitimate use of Islam as an excuse to violate basic human rights is simple garden-variety repression, common in many non-Islamic countries.

Of course, Islam does have a specific set of laws that pious Muslims want to see an Islamic state preserve and protect. These are principally family law (including custody of children), inheritance law, laws against charging interest, laws governing certain aspects of personal behavior (such as personal dress), and specific punishments for some crimes. These are frequently the battleground areas for those who want to protect the Islamic nature of the state, and those who want to approximate the secular laws of Europe and North America.

However, most people who object to *Shari'a* law have no idea how flexibly it is applied in the Islamic world. The laws are modified from country to country depending on who has religious authority. For example, the law that allows a man to have four wives is frequently modified by the equally important religious demand that he prove that he will be able to treat all of his wives equally. Devices such as requiring written permission from existing wives before a second, third, or fourth marriage can keep this practice in check, and preserve Islamic law. Many laws involving the rights of women are creatively modified in this way. *Shari'a* law makes no mention of the veil, for instance, only that both men and women dress modestly. The Islamic state is free to interpret this any way it wishes.

An Islamic government is also required to protect religious minorities. Jews, Christians, and Zoroastrians are all "people of the book," whose religious practices must be respected. This protection has been logically extended to Hindus, Buddhists, Jains, Sikhs, and Taoists in South and East Asia. In Iran, Jews, Christians, and Zoroastrians are allowed to manufacture, sell, and consume alcoholic beverages, even though alcohol is prohibited for Muslims.

Conclusion: semi-democratic institutions with religious underpinnings

I began this discussion citing the concept of governmentality as suggested by Michel Foucault, pointing out that this concept, seen in a comparative framework, would predictably lead to the realization of a variety of political and administrative forms in different cultures. Each different form would have a unique ideological base and a characteristic set of tropes to bring about the "conduct of conduct" in Foucault's terms. Nevertheless, it is possible to see that although the substance of governmental structures may vary from culture to culture, there may be similar structural principles in many systems of governmentality.

With this in mind, it is somewhat odd that Western commentators find it difficult to accept the desire to preserve a small number of characteristic religious structures in the laws of the Iranian state. Israeli law accommodates Orthodox Jewish religious practice. Several European nations, until recently, had prohibitions against divorce and abortion to uphold Catholic canonical law. The Queen of England is also the head of the Church of England—the official religion of Great Britain. Many religious-minded people in the United States would find the substance of Iranian laws welcome, and, in fact, regularly lobby for them. The opposition to same-sex marriage on religious grounds is a reality in US politics today, even though legal prohibition in the laws of the majority of states has been invalidated by the United States Supreme Court.

As I have tried to emphasize in this discussion, Iran's governmental system, in addition to its strong symbolic identification with Islam, has a strong ethic of legitimacy. Once again, I invoke Foucault's notion of governmentality. As I have tried to point out, legitimacy and its reinforcing structures is an important theme in Shi'a Islam, but it is hard to argue with this principle as a detrimental one for any system of governmentality. The particular form that this principle adopts in Iran and its centrality in political, social, and cultural thought is unique, and is a tribute to the imagination of the post-revolutionary constitution.

Despite its unique form, Iran's combination of appointed and elected officials is a feature of many democratic systems. In many nations, voters cast votes only for political parties. The parties choose their own leaders internally. Therefore the prime ministers, chancellors, and other political leaders in nations around the world are not directly elected by the public. Even in the United States, some of the most powerful political figures, such as supreme court justices, are appointed by the president and confirmed by the Senate with no direct public electoral input.

The United States in particular would do well not to obsess over the potential Islamic nature of the Iranian constitution (or the constitution of Iraq). Certainly there should be no imposition of an arbitrary set of secular Western values or institutions on any Middle Eastern nation. It is worth underscoring, to address the question posed by the title of this essay, that Iran is not a theocracy in any absolute sense. Moreover, its unique form has passed the ultimate functional test of governmentality; since the Revolution of 1978–79, it has proved robust, stable, and capable of sustaining itself. In fact, Iran's government is one of the most stable in the region, if not the world.

3

AFTER RELIGION

ASSESSING A LIBERAL SHIFT AMONG IRANIANS IN THE POST-KHOMEINI PERIOD

Mansoor Moaddel

Scholars of Iran's intellectual history have documented a major reorientation among intellectual leaders in the post-Khomeini period. This reorientation marks a departure from religion as a framework to guide sociopolitical behavior and toward an eclectic intellectual movement led by liberal nationalism. Two surveys carried out by Iranian researchers in 2000 and 2005 suggest that changes in values have also occurred among the Iranian public toward social individualism, democracy, gender equality, national identity and a decline in national pride and support for religion.[1]

This change may reflect a broader epistemic shift in Iranians' perception of the nature of their political community from religious nationalism-cum-fundamentalism, which has constituted the discursive framework of clerical absolutism since the 1979 Revolution, to liberal territorial nationalism that has emerged in opposition to it. These two modalities of nationalism represent two opposing perspectives on the basis of identity and the organizing principles of Iranian society, including religion, the state, gender, and outsiders, the West in particular. Religious nationalism considers Islam the basis of identity, rejects the secular state in favor of the unity of religion and politics, promotes male supremacy and gender inequality, and considers the West culturally decadent. Liberal territorial nationalism, by contrast, regards the nation as the basis of identity, defends secular democracy and the separation of religion and politics, promotes gender equality, and displays a favorable orientation toward the West.

To demonstrate this shift, this chapter will show the configuration of political values among Iranians in terms of these two modalities, arguing that the population can be divided between those who have liberal nationalist tendencies and those who lean toward religious nationalism. The test of this configuration is provided by varying relations of identity and national pride with a series of political values that ranges from religious nationalism, on one pole, and liberal nationalism, on the other. The analysis of the survey data shows that the change in basis of identity from the religion of Islam to the nation of Iran is associated, consistently, with significant changes in orientations that are favorable toward gender equality, Western culture, secular politics, democracy, and (except in 2005) immigrants, but less favorable toward religion. National pride, on the other hand, has an inverse relationship with these values; people with a higher national pride tend to be less in favor of gender equality, secular politics, Western culture, and immigrant labor, but more religious than people with lower national pride. The association of national pride with conservative values and hostility toward outsiders shows that this pride is linked to the regime's xenophobic and anti-Western rhetoric and international brinksmanship, which have served to galvanize support for its policies. National identity, on the other hand, is shaped by globalization, in opposition to the religious authoritarianism of the ruling regime.[2]

Insofar as the varying relations of national identity and national pride to political values are supported by the 2000 and 2005 survey data, the change in value orientations of Iranians toward liberal territorial nationalism between the two surveys may signify an epistemic shift in their perceptions of the features of their political community they consider more desirable—a shift from religious nationalism-cum-fundamentalism to liberal territorial nationalism.

Islamic regime and value change

For many scholars of Iran's intellectual history, the post-revolutionary period exhibits a dramatic decline of the religious extremism that was dominant in the 1977–79 Revolution, on the one hand, and the rise of secular and religious reformist oppositional discourses, on the other. The intellectual field is widely regarded to comprise secularist, religious reformist, and religious conservative factions.[3] Findings from the values surveys carried out in Iran in 2000 and 2005 suggest that broadly similar changes in value orientations have also transpired among the Iranian public. Over the five year period, Iranians expressed a more favorable attitude toward gender equality, considered religious institutions less trustworthy, attended mosque less often, became more supportive of social-individualistic values, and displayed a stronger support for democracy. Moreover, between the two surveys the number of Iranians who recognized the nation as the basis of their identity increased, while their feeling of national pride declined.[4]

This chapter assesses the extent to which variation in value orientations toward gender equality, secular politics, democracy, Western culture, hostility toward immigrants, and religiosity are configured as liberal territorial nationalism or religious nationalism by assessing their linkages with national identity and national pride.

Modalities of collective sovereignty

Liberal territorial nationalism and religious nationalism are examples of a wide variety of political ideologies and movements that have emerged on the world stage in the modern period.[5]

These ideologies define one or more human communities who reside in a specified territory as a people (or nation) based on certain characteristics shared by a significant section of the population living in those communities, bestow on this people the right to institutionalize a system of collective sovereignty, and advance an exclusive claim to represent this people. For some this nationalism is a continuation of the primordial essence of group formations, including extended family, kinship, and ethnicity. For others, it is a perennial phenomenon that comes and goes throughout human history. Scholars, however, widely agree that nationalism is a *modern* movement and ideology. It represents, in Smith's description, "a single red line" that "traverses the history of the modern world from the fall of the Bastille to the fall of the Berlin Wall."[6] Nonetheless, the modernist paradigm or the alternative primordial and perennial perspectives provide few guidelines for handling historical and cross-national variations of nationalism. It is not clear, for example, how these perspectives explain such diverse movements as the pan-Arab nationalism of

Jamal Abdul Nassir in Egypt, the liberal (economic) nationalism of Mohammad Mossadeq in Iran, the monarchy-centered nationalism of different kingships in the Middle East, and the religious nationalism-cum-fundamentalism of Ayatollah Khomeini or the Taliban above and beyond the premise that the movements they represented have been the outcomes of contemporaneous social conditions.

Commonly recognized as instances of nationalism, these movements have vastly differed in their sociopolitical and cultural orientations and the type of regime they constructed. Lumping all together under the umbrella of nationalism may lead one to gloss over serious differences among these and other varieties of nationalism that coexist even in the same society. The concept of modality of collective sovereignty may thus be useful in order to capture such variations.

Modalities define the identity of political systems. They specify the governing principles of politics and shape the hierarchical structure of power relations—they define the basis of legitimacy and national sovereignty, demarcate the norms governing in-group and out-group relationships, and project their own distinctive political maps and territories. They dictate the way history is officially remembered, constructed, or invented. Modalities are constrained by the existing sociopolitical conditions and the structure of economic, class, or group relations. The governing principles, however, cannot be derived logically from these socioeconomic conditions or social structures. Similar social structures may sustain different modalities or different structures the same modality. Rather, modalities are produced as intellectual leaders attempt to resolve historically significant issues facing their communities. Because modalities are the outcomes of the conscious efforts of human agency to shape politics, modalities thus represent public, discursive components of the process of regime formation.

Modalities rest on different conceptions of identity. In territorial nationalism, collective sovereignty belongs to the nation. Connections to territory, rather than religious or ethnic affiliations, determine membership in the political community and construct an identity like Egyptian, Iranian, or Iraqi. This is exemplified in the discourse of Egyptian nationalist Mustafa Kamil (1874–1908), who claimed that "nationalism is the noblest tie for men and the solid foundation upon which great and mighty kingdoms are built... Life is merely transitory and it has no honor without nationalism and without work for the welfare of the fatherland and its children... Fatherland, O fatherland: To you my love and my heart. To you my life and my existence. To you my blood and my soul. To you my mind and my speech... You, you, O Egypt are life itself, and there is no life but in you."[7]

In pan-Arab-nationalism, the nation consists of those born into the Arab-speaking communities living in Arab territories. Attachments to Arabic language and culture, rather than to a territory or religion, thus define the criteria for membership in the political community. The ideology of pan-Arab nationalism revolves around Arab identity and the belief that Arabs, despite living in diverse countries (called provinces in the Arab-nationalist lexicon), constitute one people, and therefore hold the right to establish a unified Arab state. In a clear contrast to the nationalist view of Mustafa Kamil, Sati' al-Husri (1880–1968) rejects territorial nationalism. "Is it possible for us," he asks rhetorically, "to consider, for example, the people of Syria as forming a true nation, different from the people of Iraq and Lebanon? Never, gentlemen. All that I have explained indicates clearly that the differences we now see between the people of these states are temporary and superficial... We must always assert that the Syrians, Iraqis, Lebanese, Jordanians, Hejazis, and Yemenis all belong to one nation, the Arab nation."[8]

The Islamic-nationalist modality considers Islam the basis of legitimacy and the source of legislation, negates secular politics and instead upholds the unity of religion and politics in Islamic government, promotes religious centrism and intolerance of other faiths, endorses male supremacy and restricts women's involvements in the public sphere, and rejects Western culture as decadent. For Sayyid Qutb, "the homeland (*watan*) a Muslim should cherish and defend is not a mere piece of land... His jihad is solely geared to protect the religion of Allah and His Shari'a and to save the Abode of Islam and no other territory... Any land that combats the Faith, hampers Muslims from practicing their religion, or does not apply the Shari'a, becomes ipso facto part of the Abode of War (*Dar al-Harb*). It should be combated even if one's own kith and kin, national group, capital and commerce are to be found there... A Muslim's homeland is any land governed by the laws of Islam. Islam is the only identity worthy of man."[9] Likewise, Shi'a fundamentalist Ayatollah Ruhollah Khomeini proclaimed that the "slogan of the separation of religion and politics and the demand that Islamic scholars not intervene in social and political affairs have been formulated and propagated by the Imperialists; it is only the irreligious who repeats them."[10]

Identity is the cognitive aspect of nationalism. Feelings of national solidarity and pride constitute its affective side. These feelings, however, do not form a coherent set of emotions. According to Viroli, "love of country can be generous, compassionate, and intelligent, but it can also be exclusive, deaf, and blind."[11] The similar concepts of nationalism and patriotism capture these contradictory feelings: whereas the former taps into the perception of superiority and xenophobia, patriotism relates only to love of country, its cultural heritage, and historical achievements.[12] Nationalism is relational and synchronic in that it is expressed in relation to a presumed superiority of one's nation over other nations. It is reproduced in simultaneous interaction with real or imagined belligerents. Patriotism, by contrast, is historical or diachronic. In a patriotic sense, the feeling of attachment to one's nation has no relevance to outsiders but to what the nation represents to the individual citizen: its natural beauty, culture, and achievements in philosophy, science, and technology.

In the same way that the basis of identity varies between modalities, varied categories of national solidarity are tied to different modalities. Religious nationalism, for example, is often associated with nationalistic solidarity and feelings of national pride. The modality of liberal territorial nationalism, by contrast, tends to be associated with patriotism. Liberal territorial nationalism promotes freedom and intellectual debate, which may uncover deficiencies in the existing social order or in institutional practices, promoting egalitarian social relationships. It thus encourages self-criticism and critical evaluation of the existing order. Such practices naturally tend to lower national pride.

Because there was no measure of survey respondents' patriotic attachments to Iran's contributions to human civilization, science, and philosophy, this chapter cannot assess the relationship between patriotism and other sociopolitical values. This chapter, however, proposes that the measure of national pride used in the survey is positively linked to conservative values.

Using these theoretical propositions, this chapter argues that people who consider Iran, rather than Islam, the basis of their identity tend to display stronger attitudes in favor of gender equality, secular politics, democracy, and Western culture, but lower religiosity and weaker hostility toward immigrants. People who express a stronger feeling of national pride have the opposite orientations toward these values. These varying relationships may thus indicate the configuration of liberal nationalism and religious nationalism-cum-fundamentalism in Iran.

Religious nationalism versus liberal nationalism in the post-Khomeini era

The formation of the Islamic-nationalist regime was an outcome of the revolutionary movement that toppled the monarchy in 1979. After the revolution,

Ayatollah Khomeini repressed rival power contenders, established a system of clerical absolutism, and launched a program of forced Islamization of society. It would be inadequate, however, to define the regime simply as a religious government, whose interest is to defend the cause of Shia Islam and promote religious virtue, and in doing so to associate its decline with the weakening of its value system among ordinary Iranians. The appropriation of religion by the ruling clerics has certainly undermined the norms and social functions of organized religion and weakened its social standing among Iranians. In fact, decades of religious authoritarianism did not create an Islamic order in the country. Iranians appear to be less religious and less trusting of religious authorities than those in other Muslim-majority countries, and the trend in their value orientations is toward individualism, gender equality, democracy, and national identity.[13] Nonetheless, Iranians have remained faithful to their core religious beliefs without necessarily adopting the state religion promoted by their government.

Rather, the current clerical government is best conceived as an embodiment of religious nationalism, whose primary interest is to maintain itself in power, even where the preservation of this power necessitates "temporary" suspensions of religious codes.[14] While it purportedly ordinates society according to religion, promotes religious identity, turns politics towards Islamic obligations, and performs power rituals in Shia trappings,[15] the nationalism of the regime organizes society in terms of the principles of other social institutions, which are not necessarily religious, but help entrench its power in society and maintain cultural hegemony. Thus, the revival of the monarchical power structure under clerical absolutism, rigorous promotion of the institution of patriarchy and male supremacy, the enforcement of a certain style of dress, a strict insider-outsider duality, and a projection of majestic power in the region epitomized by anti-American rhetoric—which may provoke the feeling of national superiority and serve as a reminder of the country's ancient glories and grandeur—all function to transcend the regime's immanent religious fundamentalism. As a result, many are long-accustomed to a centralized system of absolutist power, attached to the institution of patriarchy and the conservative lifestyle, have strong feelings of in-group solidarity and an ideology of national supremacy, and are ardent supporters of state socialism. For these citizens, the regime displays familiar and appropriate features, the undesirability of its fundamentalism notwithstanding.

While it is hard to advance causal arguments based on cross-sectional data, the proposed linkages between national pride and conservative values may lead one to speculate on a vicious cycle: first, national pride as a result of anti-Americanism and international brinkmanship; second, national pride reinforcing conservative values; third, these values contributing to the strengthening of religious nationalism, which in turn emboldens the ruling clerics to further hostilities against outsiders. One may also speculate that people who have access to alternative sources of information, such as the Internet, or have a higher level of education develop more comprehensive awareness of alternative perspectives on collective sovereignty, including liberal nationalism, and are thus more likely to break out of this vicious cycle. In the present context, those who change their perspective by abandoning Islamic identity in favor of Iranian identity are more likely to change attitudes in favor of gender equality, secular politics, immigrant labor, and religiosity.

The proposed varying relationships of national identity and national pride with these values may highlight not only the presence of religious nationalism-cum-fundamentalism and liberal territorial nationalism as two opposing modalities of collective sovereignty in the country but also the significance of these modalities as conceptual vehicles for a better understanding the process of change in post-Khomeini Iran.

Globalization, national identity, and national pride

National identity and national pride are linked to both domestic and global processes. It has been argued that individual identity is formed in opposition to the identity of the ruling authoritarian regime. A secular authoritarian regime that has appointed itself the sole representative of the nation tends to provoke religious identity among opposition groups. In the same way, a religious authoritarian regime may give rise to secular identity those who oppose such a regime. Foreign occupation may also produce a similar effect, tending to provoke nationalist or patriotic feelings among the members of a subjugated nation. Territorial nationalism in Algeria and Egypt, for example, emerged in opposition to the French and British occupations. Findings from Iraqi surveys conducted between 2004 and 2011 also support this thesis. The percentage of Iraqis who defined themselves as "Iraqis above all" (as opposed to Muslims, Arabs, or Kurds) rose from 23 per cent in 2004 to 63 per cent in 2008, and then dropped to 57 per cent in 2011. The rise of religious extremism also contributed to the desirability of secular politics. Iraqis who agreed that Iraq would be a better place if religion and politics were separated increased from 50 per cent in 2004 to 70 per cent in 2011.[16] The feeling of national pride has also been linked to attitudes against foreign presence and to conservative values.[17]

Furthermore, national identity and national pride may also be affected by manifestations of globalization, such as the Internet. The pluralist perspectives of the Internet tend to attenuate ethnocentrism and contribute to a decline in the feeling of national pride among Internet users. Furthermore, given that national pride tends to be higher under a singe dominant culture imposed from above by authoritarian regimes, the Internet by providing access to alternative sources of information and to a plurality of ideas may also contribute to a decline in support for conservative values. Under the conditions of authoritarianism where religion is vigorously promoted as the basis of collective identity, access to the Internet may be associated with a change in identity from religious to national. Thus, Iranians who have access to personal computers (PCs) or the Internet are more likely to identify with the nation than with religion and have a weaker feeling of national pride.

Hypotheses on contrasting effects of national identity and national pride

This chapter proposes that globalization contributes to liberal nationalism. To assess this proposition, it assesses the linkages between access to the Internet and the use of PCs, on the one hand, and national pride and national identity, on the other. The main purpose of this chapter, however, is to show how liberal values relate to (1) a shift in identity from religion to the nation and changes in orientations toward liberal values, and (2) the feeling of national pride. It proposes that:

Hypothesis 1. The shift from religious to national identity entails:

(a) a more favorable attitude toward gender equality;
(b) a more favorable attitude toward Western Culture;
(c) a more favorable attitude toward democracy and secular politics;
(d) a weaker religious orientation; and
(e) a weaker hostility toward out-groups, such as immigrants.

Hypothesis 2. The feeling of national pride is associated with:

(a) a less favorable attitude toward gender equality;
(b) a less favorable attitude toward Western Culture;
(c) a less favorable attitude toward democracy and secular politics
(d) a stronger religious orientation; and
(e) a stronger hostility toward out-groups, such as immigrants.

Hypothesis 3. Modernity thesis: a higher socioeconomic status is linked to:

(a) a more favorable attitude toward gender equality;
(b) a more favorable attitude toward Western Culture;
(c) a more favorable attitude toward democracy and secular politics;
(d) a weaker religious orientation; and
(e) a weaker hostility toward out-groups, such as immigrants.

Independent variables

National versus religious identity is proposed as the key difference between people supporting liberal nationalism and those supporting Islamic fundamentalism. Respondents were asked, "Which of the following best describes you: (1) above all, I am an Iranian, (2) above all, I am a Muslim, (3) above all, I am a Turk, a Kurd, or other, specify____?"

Differences in national identity are measured as a dummy variable (0 = Muslim, above all, 1 = Iranian, Kurd, Turk, etc., above all). However, if the analysis focuses on only Iranians versus Muslims, the results are not significantly different from the results presented in this chapter. This variable is intended to measure whether the respondents' primary allegiance is to the territorial national or to religious modality of collective sovereignty. In the Iranian context, it is proposed that national identity is more closely tied to patriotic feeling than is religious identity. National pride, on the other hand, is proposed to be associated with the norms and values of the current Islamic regime. A single item measure of national pride is used in this study: "How proud are you to be Iranian: (1) very proud, (2) quite proud, (3) not very proud, or (4) not at all proud?"

Dependent variables

The following one or more indicators are used to measure the dependent variables of the study. These are:

1. Gender equality. Three indicators are used to measure this construct: (1) "How important is it that a woman wears the veil in public places (1 = very important, 6 = not at all important [unfavorable to veil])?" (2) "Men make better political leaders than women (1 = strongly agree, 4 = strongly disagree)?" Finally, (3) "A wife must always obey her husband (1 = strongly agree, 4 = strongly disagree)?" Higher values on these measures indicate

less favorable attitudes toward the veil, toward men as better political leaders, and toward wife obedience—hence a stronger support for gender equality and a weaker orientation toward the teachings of the regime.

2. Religious orientation. The Islamic Republic is a religious state and the cornerstone of its policy has been to promote religiosity among the public. This study uses four indicators to measure orientation toward religion. Two of these measures focus on religiosity; one is mosque attendance, and the other is the importance of religion in one's life. The third indicator focuses on trust in the religious institutions. Finally, the fourth indicator measures people's attitude toward the *Shari'a* as the guiding principle of a good government. Survey respondents were asked: (1) "How important is religion in your life (1 = not very important..., 4 = very important [religion important])?" (2) "How often do you participate in mosque services (1 = don't go to a mosques... 7 = more than once a week [mosque attendance])?" (3) "How much trust do you have in mosques (1 = none at all..., 6 = a great deal [trust in mosque])?" (4) "How important is it for a good government to implement only the laws of the *Shari'a* (1 = not very important..., 4 = very important [*Shari'a*])?" Higher values on these measures reflect a stronger religious orientation and thus a stronger support for the ideology of the Islamic Republic.

3. Western Culture. Religious fundamentalism rests on the notion that the Western culture is decadent and that Islamic culture must be protected against Western cultural invasion. One question is used in order to measure attitudes toward Western culture: "In your view, how important is Western cultural invasion (1 = very important..., 6 = not important at all)?" Lower values on this measure indicate stronger attitudes against the Western culture.

4. Hostility toward out-group. Orientations toward immigrants have featured prominently in the study of national pride and in the nationalism-patriotism debate.[18] A sizable Afghani population lives in Iran. These Afghanis have been migrating in search of work and better living conditions since the late 1970s.[19] The presence of these immigrants has generated widespread debate among Iranians on how to deal with foreign workers. To assess the extent to which followers of the two modalities differ in their attitudes toward immigrant workers, a question that taps into hostility toward immigrants is included in the model: "How about people from other countries coming here to work. Which one of the following do you think the government should do (1 = let anyone come who wants to...,

4 = Prohibit people coming here from other countries [Hostility toward immigrants])?" Higher values indicate a stronger hostility toward immigrant workers.

5. Form of government. The form that government should take has been hotly debated among intellectual leaders and the public at large throughout the twentieth century in Iran. To measure people's orientation toward this issue, two measures are used. The first measures attitudes toward democracy and the other measures secularism. (1) "Democracy may have problems but it is a better system of government (1 = strongly agree.... 4 = strongly disagree)." (2) "Iran would be a better place if religion and politics were separated (1 = strongly agree..., 4 = strongly disagree)?" Both variables are recoded such that a lower value indicates a stronger support for democracy and secular politics.

Control variables

The control variables include socioeconomic status and gender.

1. Socioeconomic status. This construct is measured by three indicators: Education, income, and self-reported social class. (1) Education: "What is the highest educational level that you have attained (1 = no formal education, 2 = incomplete primary school, 3 = complete primary school, 4 = incomplete secondary school: technical/vocational type, 5 = complete secondary school: technical/vocational type, 6 = incomplete secondary: university-preparatory type, 7 = complete secondary: university-preparatory type, 8 = some university-level education, without degree, and 9 = university-level education, with degree)?" (2) Social class: self-reported class identification is measured by asking respondents to describe their class background: "People sometimes describe themselves as belonging to the working class, the middle class, the upper or the lower class. Would you describe yourself as belonging to the 1 = upper class, 2 = upper middle class, 3 = lower middle class, 4 = working class, or 5 = lower class?" (3) Income: This variable is measured in terms of the respondents' placement of their household income on a scale of income: "On this card is a scale of incomes on which 1 indicates the lowest income decile and 10 the highest income decile in your country. We would like to know in what group your household is. Please specify the appropriate number, counting all wages, salaries, pensions, and other incomes that come in." (4) Gender: a dummy variable on gender is constructed (1 = male and 0 = female).

Structural equation models

Structural equation models are used to estimate the effect of national identity and national pride on gender equality, Western culture, hostility toward immigrants, secular politics, democracy, and religious orientation, controlling for socioeconomic status and gender. They show the influence of measurement errors (labeled 'e') on the endogenous variables; the arrows indicate the proposed directions of causal influence between variables. The 2000 survey does not include data on all the specified measures. As a result, two structural equation models are used and estimated. One is for the 2000 survey (Figure 2) and the other for the 2005 survey (Figure 3). In the second model, secular politics is used as a more appropriate indicator of form of government than democracy. The former gives a clearer definition between those who favor liberal nationalism and those supporting religious fundamentalism, since the concept of democracy has also been appropriated by the ruling regime.

The data are from the two national values surveys conducted by Iranian researchers referred to at the beginning of this chapter. The first used a nationally representative sample of 2,532 adults and was carried out in 2000, and the second used a nationally representative sample of 2,903 adults and was carried out in summer 2005. Both surveys used multistage random sampling procedures in different provinces, broken down into urban and rural areas of the country in proportion to their size, with roughly equal male and female respondents. The response rate in both surveys was calculated at 90 per cent.

The interviews, which required approximately one hour on average to complete, were conducted face-to-face in respondents' residences. Importantly, they were conducted by Iranian personnel. The 2000 sample includes all provinces in Iran except Sistan-Baluchistan and Kurdistan; the 2005 sample covers all provinces of the country. In this case, it oversampled the Kurdish population by about 300 cases.

Analysis and findings

Table 1 shows the means and standard deviations of the variables used in the analysis for the 2000 and 2005 data. In comparing the variables from the two datasets, two caveats should be considered. First, the 2000 data does not include information on all the variables of interest, including questions on "*Shari'a*," "secular politics," and "globalized network." Second, the response categories of some of the variables were not identical in the 2000 and 2005 surveys. For example, questions on "unfavorable to veil," "men are not better leaders," "mosque attendance," "trust in mosque" and "Western culture" had

Figure 2: Structural Equation Model: Iranian Social Values (2000 Survey)

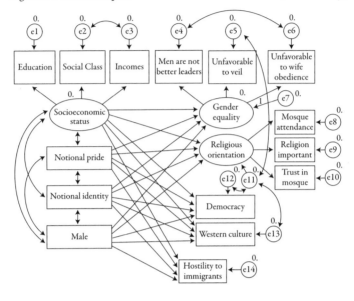

Figure 3: Structural Equation Model: Iranian Social Values (2005 Survey)

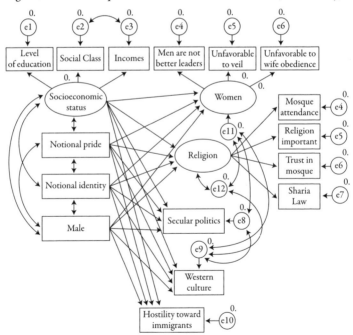

5, 4, 7, 4, and 5 response categories, respectively, in the 2000 survey. In the 2005 survey, they had 6, 5, 6, 6, and 6 categories, respectively. Therefore, it would be hard to directly compare the responses to these questions across the two surveys. To make the two survey data comparable, the 2005 response categories are first recoded to correspond to the response categories of the 2000 survey. Then, the means and standard deviations for all the variables are computed and the results are reported in Table 1.

According to this table, significant changes in value orientations have occurred among Iranians between the two surveys. The percentage identifying with the nation/ethnicity went up from 38 per cent in 2000 to 50 per cent in 2005, while the feeling of national pride on average declined from 3.86 to 3.55. On average, unfavorable attitudes toward the veil increased, from 1.49 to 2.27, as did unfavorable attitudes toward wife obedience, from 2.65 to 2.76. The table shows that more Iranians on average agreed that "men make better political leaders" in 2005 than they did in 2000 (from 2.14 to 2.07). This finding, however, must be interpreted with caution. The 2005 data included five response categories and about 20% of the respondents chose "neither agree nor disagree" option. This option was not available to the respondents in the 2000 survey. Out of those who agreed or strongly agreed, the figure dropped from 66 per cent in 2000 to 59 per cent in 2005.

On religious orientation, while those who mentioned that religion was important in their life did not change significantly, mosque attendance and confidence in mosque on average declined between the two surveys from 4.61 to 3.97, and from 3.46 to 3.4, respectively. Likewise, fewer Iranians were concerned with Western cultural invasion in 2000 than in 2005 (the mean dropped from 1.80 to 1.61). Between the two surveys, Iranians developed a more hostile attitude toward immigrants, with the mean increasing from 2.81 to 3. However, they adopted more favorable attitudes toward democracy or secular government (increasing from 2.89 in 2000 to 3.15 in 2005).

Table 2 and Table 3 show the correlation matrices between the variables for the 2000 and 2005 data that were used in the structural equation model 1 and model 2, respectively. According to Table 2, national identity and national pride are negatively linked ($r = -0.082$) and have opposing relationships with almost all the dependent variables: 0.234 and -0.234 with unfavorable to veil, 0.108 and -0.011 [not significant] with unfavorable to wife obedience, 0.126 and -0.005 [not significant] with men are not better leaders, -0.242 and 0.246 with religion is important, -0.255 and 0.180 with mosque attendance, -0.237 and 0.217 with trust in mosque, 0.025 [not significant] and -0.028 [not significant] with Western culture, -0.079 and 0.127 hostility toward immigrants, and 0.073 and −0.038 [not significant] with democracy, respectively. This table also shows that education and socioeconomic status are positively connected to national identity (0.104 and 0.114, respectively), and that education is negatively and socioeconomic status positively linked to national pride (−0.091 and 0.066, respectively). Gender has no significant relationship with national identity or national pride.

Table 1: Descriptive Statistics for Variable Indicators Used in Social Values Analysis

	2000 Mean (S.D.)		2005 Mean (S.D.)	
National identity/national pride				
National identity (1 = Else, 0 = Muslim)	0.38	(0.484)	0.50	(0.500)
National pride (4 = Very proud)	3.86	(0.536)	30.55	(0.679)
Gender equality				
Unfavourable to veil (5 = Not at all important)	1.49	(0.869)	2.27	(1.290)
Unfavourable to wife obedience (5 = Strongly disagree)	2.65	(1.337)	2.76	(1.262)
Men no better leaders (4 = Strongly disagree)	2.14	(0.974)	2.07	(0.863)
Religion				
Religion important in life (4 = Very important)	3.75	(0.573)	3.73	(0.591)
Mosque attendance (7 = More than once a week)	4.61	(1.449)	3.97	(2.184)
Trust in mosque (4 = A great deal)	3.46	(0.795)	3.40	(0.718)
Shari'a (6 = Very important)			4.46	(1.312)
Western culture				
Western cultural invasion not serious (5 = Not serious)	1.80	(1.199)	1.61	(0.895)
Attitudes toward outsiders				
Hostility toward immigrants (4 = prohibit people)	2.81	(0.842)	3.00	(0.799)
Forms of government				
Democracy best form of govnt (4 = Strongly agree)	2.89	(1.011)	3.15	(0.637)
Better if religion and politics separated (4 = Strongly agree)	–	–	2.44	(0.954)
Sources of information	–	–		
Internet/email usage (1 = used last week)	–	–	0.19	(0.396)
PC (3 = use frequently)	–	–	1.57	(0.831)

Table 2: Correlation Coefficients between National Pride, National Identity, and Dependent and Control Variables for 2000 Social Values Survey

	Identity	Pride	Veil	Obey	Men	Relig.	Mosque	Trust	West.	Immig.	Democ.	Edu.	Income	Class
National pride	−0.082[a]													
Unfavorable to veil	0.234[c]	−0.234[c]												
Unfavorable to wife obedience	0.108[b]	−0.011	0.168[c]											
Men no better leaders	0.126[c]	−0.005	0.050	0.323[c]										
Religion important in life	−0.242[c]	0.246[c]	−0.509[c]	−0.110[b]	−0.041									
Mosque attendance	−0.255[c]	0.180[b]	−0.254[c]	−0.108[b]	−0.097[b]	0.272[c]								
Trust in mosque	−0.237[c]	0.217[c]	−0.404[c]	−0.143[c]	−0.135[c]	0.382[c]	0.332[c]							
Western culture	0.025	−0.028	0.003	−0.008	0.026	0.023	0.004	−0.001						
Hostility toward immigrants	−0.079[a]	0.127[c]	−0.035	−0.037	−0.030	0.079[a]	0.016	0.014	−0.029					
Democracy	0.073[a]	−0.038	−0.009	−0.192[c]	−0.122[c]	0.103[b]	−0.114[c]	−0.034	0.156[c]	0.011				
Education	0.104[c]	−0.091[b]	0.159[c]	0.165[c]	0.024	−0.089[b]	−0.166[c]	−0.145[c]	−0.029	−0.010	0.018			
Income	−0.115[c]	0.083[b]	0.015	0.111[c]	0.150[c]	−0.069[a]	−0.039	−0.029	−0.036	−0.019	−0.117[c]	0.190[c]		
Social class	−0.092[b]	0.040	0.057	0.110[b]	0.070[a]	−0.074[a]	−0.100[c]	−0.074[a]	−0.032	−0.031	−0.006	0.294[c]	0.594[c]	
Male	−0.035	−0.044	−0.033	−0.281[c]	−0.192[c]	−0.023	0.042	−0.007	−0.046	−0.086[b]	0.007	0.121[c]	−0.025[c]	−0.033[c]

Listwise N=970.

[a] p < .05, [b] p < .01, [c] p < .001.

Table 3: Correlation Coefficients between National Pride, National Identity, and Dependent and Control Variables for 2005 Social Values Survey

	Identity	Pride	Veil	Obey	Men	Relg.	Mosq.	Trust	Sharia	Secular	West	Immig	Edu.	Incom	Class	Male	PC
National pride	-0.160c																
Unfavorable to veil	0.207c	-0.195c															
Unfavorable to wife obedience	0.089c	-0.152c	0.416c														
Men are no better leaders	0.066c	-0.132c	0.243c	0.287c													
Religion important	-0.275c	0.373c	-0.315c	-0.189c	-0.078c												
Mosque attendance	-0.215c	0.263c	-0.398c	-0.258c	-0.161c												
Trust in mosque	-0.247c	0.243c	-0.419c	-0.229c	-0.116c	0.324c											
Sharia	-0.192c	0.135c	-0.386c	-0.244c	-0.106c	0.411c	0.352c										
Secular politics	0.221c	-0.255c	0.293c	0.162c	0.125c	0.269c	0.302c	0.325c									
Western culture	0.174c	-0.345c	0.194c	0.151c	0.076c	-0.273c	-0.267c	-0.290c	-0.272c								
Hostility toward immigrants	-0.020	0.076b	-0.056b	-0.028	-0.001	-0.339c	-0.228c	-0.229c	-0.230c	0.243c							
Education	0.069c	-0.054b	0.369c	0.272c	0.150c	0.044a	0.041a	0.049a	0.025	-0.057b	-0.047a						
Income	0.034	-0.048a	0.136c	0.156c	0.086c	-0.145c	-0.180c	-0.221c	-0.216c	0.068c	0.047a	-0.012					
Social class	0.026	-0.03	0.164c	0.171c	0.094c	-0.066c	-0.081c	-0.021	-0.066c	0.046a	0.079c	-0.019	0.243c				
Male	-0.106c	0.025	0.057c	0.183c	0.229c	-0.035	-0.085c	-0.053b	-0.071c	0.03	0.078c	-0.008	0.303c	0.647c			
Computer use	0.072c	-0.110c	0.336c	0.216c	0.091c	0.102c	-0.058b	0.092c	0.060b	-0.037	-0.065c	0.005	-0.045a	0.065a	0.067c		
The Internet and E-mail	0.111c	-0.156c	0.257c	0.154c	0.071c	-0.183c	-0.141c	-0.220c	-0.203c	0.134c	0.088c	-0.026	0.538c	0.256c	0.255c	-0.121c	
						-0.222c	-0.129c	-0.181c	-0.176c	0.151c	0.120c	0.002	0.362c	0.170c	0.172c	-0.116c	0.557c

Listwise N = 2473.

[a] p < .05; [b] p < .01; [c] p < .001.

Likewise, in Table 3, national identity and national pride are negatively linked (r = –0.160). They have opposing relationships with all the dependent variables (except for men are not better leaders and democracy). The correlation coefficients of national identity and national pride are: 0.207 and –0.195 with unfavorable to veil, 0.089 and –0.152 with unfavorable to wife obedience, 0.066 and –0.132 with men are not better leaders, –0.275 and 0.373 with religion is important, –0.215 and 0.263 with mosque attendance, –0.247 and 0.243 with trust in mosque, –0.192 and 0.135 with *Shari'a*, 0.221 and –0.255 with secular politics, 0.174 and –0.345 with Western culture, and –0.020 [not significant] and 0.076 with hostility toward immigrants. Furthermore, national identity is higher among people with higher education (0.069), lower among male (–0.106), and positively linked to PC (0.072) and the Internet (0.111). National pride is lower among people with higher education (–0.054) and income (–0.048) and negatively linked to PC and the Internet (–0.110 and –0.156, respectively).

That national identity is positively linked to almost all the variables measuring attitudes toward gender equality, negatively with variables measuring religious orientation, positively with secular politics, and negatively with hostility toward immigrants supports the view that territorial nationalism and liberal values are linked. That national pride has just the opposite relationship with all these variables—negatively with liberal values of gender equality and secular politics and positively with indicators of religious orientation, and positively with hostility toward immigrants—shows the affinity of national pride with conservative values. The link between national pride and conservative values, however, is understandable; people express a higher feeling of national pride when they are more satisfied with or benefit from the ruling regime. Those who, on the other hand, are more egalitarian in terms of their orientation toward women, less religious, and more supportive of secular politics, may find fewer policies in their country to be proud of. Therefore, they express a weaker feeling of national pride.

However, the structural equation models advanced in this chapter evaluate the extent to which the specified relationships among these all these variables altogether fit the 2000 and 2005 data and thus lend credence to the presence of two opposing models of political sovereignty: liberal nationalism versus Islamic fundamentalism.

Table 4: Estimates of the Effects of Feelings of National Identity and Pride on Social Attitudes in 2000

Independent Variables				
National identity	*Dependent variables*	*B*	*S.E.*	*Critical Ratios*
	Gender equality	0.222	0.029	7.754[c]
	Religious orientation	−0.272	0.019	−14.226[c]
	Democracy	0.119	0.056	2.121[a]
	Western culture	0.027	0.054	0.506
	Hostility toward immigrants	−0.072	0.037	−1.945[a]
National pride	Gender equality	−0.211	0.025	−8.346[c]
	Religious orientation	0.182	0.017	10.912[c]
	Democracy	0.000	0.050	0.004
	Western culture	−0.100	0.048	−2.067[a]
	Hostility toward immigrants	0.151	0.033	4.595[c]
Control Variables				
Socioeconomic status	Gender equality	0.135	0.015	9.11[c]
	Religious orientation	−0.062	0.008	−7.622[c]
	Democracy	−0.018	0.02	−0.913
	Western culture	−0.028	0.02	−1.424
	Hostility toward immigrants	−0.042	0.014	−3.099[b]
Male	Gender equality	−0.296	0.027	−10.891[c]
	Religious orientation	0.046	0.017	2.687[b]
	Democracy	0.057	0.052	1.093
	Western culture	−0.091	0.05	−1.819
	Hostility toward immigrants	−0.044	0.034	−1.286
Measurement				
Socioeconomic status	Education	1.000		
	Social class	0.279	0.026	10.693[c]
	Income	0.283	0.034	8.216[c]
Gender equality	Men no better leaders	0.721	0.074	9.724[c]
	unfavorable to wife obedience	1.342	0.107	12.515[c]
	Unfavorable to veil	1.000		
Religious orientation	Religion important	1.000		
	Trust in mosque	1.314	0.053	24.643[c]
	Mosque attendance	1.592	0.09	17.688[c]

χ^2 = 509.19, degree of freedom = 65, α < 0.001, CFI = 0.90, RMSEA = 0.05[a] p < 0.05,[b] p < 0.01,[c] p < 0.001.
'B' represents standardized estimates of the structural coefficient of the effect of the independent, control and measurement variables on the dependent variables. 'SE' represents the standard error of the estimate.

Globalization and value change

This chapter proposed the Internet and use of PCs as a key mechanism through which the globalized flow of information and knowledge shapes the value orientations of its users. Among Iranians, as shown by the data from the 2005 survey, access to this globalized network appears to have a liberalizing impact on their value orientations. According to Table 3, the use of PCs and the Internet are positively linked to national identity (0.072 and 0.111, respectively) and negatively to national pride (–0.110 and –0.156, respectively). At the same time, they are both positively connected to unfavorable attitudes to the veil (0.336 and 0.257, respectively), unfavorable attitudes toward wife obedience (0.216 and 0.154, respectively), and men no better leaders (0.091 and 0.071, respectively). Both are negatively linked to all religion variables: religion is important (–0.183 and –0.222, respectively), mosque attendance (–0.141 and –0.220, respectively), trust in mosque (–0.194 and –0.181, respectively), and the *Shari'a* (–0.203 and –0.176, respectively). These variables are positively linked to attitudes toward secular politics (0.134 and 0.151) and Western culture (0.088 and 0.120, respectively).[20]

Considering these relationships, it is plausible to conclude that globalization has positively contributed to the popularity of liberal nationalist values and the weakening of religious values among Iranians, hence the rise of the liberal nationalist modality of political sovereignty.

Estimates of structural equation models

Table 4 reports the estimates of the structural equation model on the relations of national identity and national pride with the dependent variables, controlling for socioeconomic status and gender for the 2000 survey. The goodness-of-fit indices (χ^2 = 509.19, degree of freedom = 65, α < 0.001, CFI = 0.90, RMSEA = 0.05) show a somewhat good fit.[21] As are indicated by critical ratios shown on this table, many of the structural coefficients are significant in the predicted direction. National identity is positively linked to gender equality (b = 0.222), negatively to religious orientation (–0.272), positively to democracy (0.119), and negatively to hostility toward immigrants. Notably, there is no significant connection with attitudes toward Western culture. National pride, on the other hand, is negatively linked to gender equality (–0.211), positively to religious orientation (0.182), no connection with democracy, negatively linked to Western culture (–1.00), and positively linked to hostility toward immigrants (0.151).

The results of the estimates of the structural equation for the 2005 data are reported in Table 5. The fit of this model is slightly better than the first model as indicated by the goodness-of-fit indices (χ^2 = 632.35, degree of freedom = 77, α < 0.001, CFI = 0.933, RMSEA = 0.05). As this table shows, all the structural coefficients of the effects of national identity and national pride on the dependent variables are significant in the expected direction. The only exception is that national identity has no significant effects on hostility toward immigrants. As was predicted, national identity is positively linked to gender equality (0.359), secular politics (0.347), Western culture (0.196), and negatively linked to religious orientation (−0.266). National pride, on the other hand, has an inverse relationship with all these variables. That is, national pride is negatively linked to gender equality (−0.270), secular politics (−0.273), and Western culture (−0.327), but is positively linked to religious orientation (0.198) and hostility toward immigrants (0.177).

Thus, both sets of estimates support the proposition that a shift in the basis of identity among Iranians from religion to territorial nation entails a significant increase in their attitudes toward gender equality, secular politics, and democracy, but a weakening in religious orientation. Conversely, national pride is linked negatively to gender equality, secular politics, and democracy, and positively to religious orientation and hostility toward immigrants. In other words, while national identity is linked to liberal values, national pride reinforces conservative values. The 2005 data also showed that Internet and PC use, as measures of connectivity to the globalized flow of information and knowledge, have positive linkages with national identity and liberal values and negative linkages with national pride and indicators of religious orientation. It appears that access to the Internet is positively linked to the development of a liberal-nationalist modality of political sovereignty.

Discussion

Historical analysis of intellectual change and findings from the values surveys carried out among Iranians in 2000 and 2005 suggest that significant changes in cultural orientations have occurred in post-Khomeini Iran. An important dimension of this change is a departure from religious fundamentalism and an orientation toward liberal territorial nationalism. It would be hard to establish a trend in values based on only two observations in time, particularly given that the time of the second survey—summer of 2005—coincides with a shift in the power block in the Islamic Republic toward religious fundamentalism, extremist

Table 5: Estimates of the Effects of Feelings of National Identity and Pride on Social Attitudes in 2005

Independent Variables				
National identity	*Dependent variables*	*B*	*S.E.*	*Critical ratios*
	Gender equality	0.359	0.042	8.527[c]
	Religious orientation	−0.266	0.018	−14.886[c]
	Secular politics	.347	0.036	9.741[c]
	Western culture	0.196	0.029	6.844[c]
	Hostility toward immigrants	−0.028	0.073	−0.381
National pride	Gender equality	−0.270	0.026	−10.516[c]
	Religious orientation	0.198	0.011	17.668[c]
	Secular politics	−0.273	0.022	−12.604[c]
	Western culture	−0.328	0.017	−18.831[c]
	Hostility toward immigrants	0.177	0.044	4.009[c]
Control Variables				
Socioeconomic status	Gender equality	0.269	0.024	11.025[c]
	Religious orientation	−0.063	0.007	−9.185[c]
	Secular politics	0.028	0.010	2.917[c]
	Western culture	0.008	0.008	1.054
	Hostility toward immigrants	−0.019	0.019	−1.021
Male	Gender equality	−0.468	0.041	−11.297[c]
	Religious orientation	−0.030	0.017	−1.802
	Secular politics	0.027	0.035	0.777
	Western culture	0.054	0.028	1.917
	Hostility toward immigrants	−0.006	0.072	−0.081
Measurement				
Socioeconomic status	Education	1		
	Social class	0.164	0.015	10.763[c]
	Income	0.266	0.027	9.789[c]
Gender equality	Men no better leaders	0.438	0.025	17.259[c]
	unfavorable to wife obedience	0.708	0.028	24.945[c]
	Unfavorable to veil	1.000	–	–
Religious orientation	Religion important	1.000	–	–
	Trust in mosque	1.293	0.051	25.543[c]
	Mosque attendance	2.953	0.128	23.038[c]
	Sharia	1.388	0.064	21.593[c]

$\chi^2 = 632.35$, degree of freedom = 77, $\alpha < 0.001$, CFI = 0.933, RMSEA = 0.05[a] $p < 0.05$,[b] $p < 0.01$,[c] $p < 0.001$.

politics, and international brinksmanship under the presidency of Mahmoud Ahmadinejad. It is thus unclear how this political reorientation affected the values of Iranians since the 2005 survey or whether it may have contributed to a new upsurge in conservatism. The aim of this chapter, however, was to assess the connection between identity and value orientations among Iranians, or more specifically, how territorial nationalism is tied to orientations toward liberal values and tolerance of outsiders. The chapter has also evaluated the connection between national pride and conservative values.

The association between changes in identity from religious to national and changes in values from conservatism to liberalism, and between increases in the feeling of national pride and changes in values toward conservatism, were interpreted as a reflection of the presence of two modalities of political sovereignty: Islamic nationalism-cum-fundamentalism and liberal territorial nationalism. This presence does not mean that the Iranian society is polarized between those who are religious nationalists and those who are liberal nationalists. While the polarization of values among Iranians may not be farfetched, the data supports only tendencies; one toward religious nationalism and the other toward liberal nationalism. The two modalities are, however, driven by two opposing sets of sociological variables. On the national level, liberal nationalism and anti-clerical secularism have developed an oppositional relationship to the religious authoritarianism of the Islamic Republic. On the international level, liberal nationalist values are reinforced by global connectivity through access to the Internet and PC use.

The feeling of national pride, on the other hand, appears to be a driver of the conservative values among Iranians. This finding lends credence to the notion that the provocation of national pride has been a keystone of the regime's attempt to mobilize popular support for its policies. It may be speculated that since the overthrow of the monarchy in 1979 and the establishment of Islamic theocracy, the leadership has pursued policies that incited national pride in order to legitimize itself and its Islamization program, as well as to silence its political rivals. National pride was mobilized in the seizure of the US embassy in Tehran in November 1979 and the slogan of "death to America;" in the regime's orientation toward Iraq, leading to the outbreak of Iran-Iraq war; in condemning Salmon Rushdie to death for allegedly insulting the faith; in supporting religious extremism in the Middle East; and in mobilizing support for its nuclear program. At the same time, Islamization and religious authoritarianism appear to have provoked an awareness among the opposition that they are tied to the land, with a history and civilizational accomplishments that go far beyond the Islamic period.

Insofar as national identity is linked to egalitarian values of gender equality, secular politics, and tolerance of outsiders, the modality of liberal nationalism has an affinity with the patriotic feelings (or national identity) of Iranians. On the other hand, given the linkages of national pride with conservative values and intolerance of outsiders, this feeling may correspond to nationalistic and authoritarian tendencies among the Iranian public.

PART II

WOMEN, FAMILIES, HUMAN RIGHTS AND IMMIGRANTS

4

WOMEN AND CRIMINAL LAW
IN POST-KHOMEINI IRAN

Arzoo Osanloo

In the summer of 2010, international human rights organizations unleashed a worldwide campaign to bring attention to the death sentence by stoning of Sakineh Mohammadi Ashtianti, a forty-three year old mother of two charged with the crime of adultery and as an accessory to the murder of her husband.[1] The sentence was all the more disturbing given that the former Head of the Judiciary, Ayatollah Shahroudi, had issued a decree banning the use of stoning as punishment.[2]

This campaign was particularly strong in France. When the sentence appeared to be imminent, the French press, human rights activists, politicians, and public intellectuals, most notably Bernard Henri Levy, dispatched letters, statements, and calls to action. The campaign was in part aided by the advocacy of Iranians in the diaspora, and key human rights lawyers in Iran, especially Mohammad Mostafaei, Ashtiani's lawyer until July 2010, when he fled the country out of concern for his own safety. Mostafaei, like other human rights lawyers working inside Iran, was instrumental because he sent details of his cases to human rights organizations and individuals outside of Iran for public circulation. His legal know-how also gave important procedural depth to the legal issues and process.

The French press publicized a web campaign to save Ashtiani. Entitled, *Pour* [For] *Sakineh*, the site released appeals by a number of well-known French politicians, actors, and activists, including then First Lady Carla Bruni-Sarkozy. Other personalities included former Presidents Jacques Chirac and Giscard D'Estaing, French Socialist Leader Ségolène Royal, Minister of Culture, Frederic Mitterrand, actress Isabelle Adjani, and activist Bernard Henri Levy, who spearheaded the initiative. Appeals ranged from calling for consideration of Persian culture to appeals to love and human dignity.

Whatever their motivations, Iranian government officials halted the stoning; some said it was because it was the month of Ramadan, while others claimed that the weighty sentence was being given its due legal consideration. Officials suspended the sentence, but not before state-run television and conservative newspaper, *Kayhan*, ran a story blasting the French women supporting Ashtiani. In a story with the headline, "French prostitutes enter the human rights uproar," the article described Bruni as "this woman with a bad history," who "supports an Iranian woman who has committed adultery during marriage and is an accomplice to the murder of her husband who is sentenced to death, and in fact she also deserves death."[3] Iran's Senior Deputy Foreign Minister at the time, Ramin Mehmanparast, attempted to distance the government from the paper's commentary by stating that "insulting the authorities in other countries and using inappropriate words is not approved by the Islamic Republic."[4]

Name-calling aside, the provocative exchange placed in sharper relief the Islamic Republic's renewed emphasis on Islamic principles that began when Mahmoud Ahmadinejad first came to office in 2005. In other words, the public pronouncement of the immorality of the French president's wife underscored a revitalization of the discourse of moral rehabilitation reminiscent of the years just after the revolution. The response was not only intended for foreign actors or the pro-monarchical diaspora, but a growing population of dissenters born of the post-revolutionary government's own edification and tutelage.

For the condemned Ashtiani, death by stoning or by other means was not carried out. In 2006, judicial authorities in her province of East Azerbaijan had also tried Ashtiani for complicity in the murder of her husband, through a charge of disrupting public order. For this, they handed her a ten year prison sentence.[5] After serving some eight years in prison, in the spring of 2014,

Ashtiani was released. The head of the Iranian Judiciary's Human Rights Council, Mohammad Javad Larijani, stated that Ashtiani received a pardon for the remainder of her sentence on grounds of her good behavior in prison.[6] While the Islamic Republic often appears to ignore or criticize international pleas, and frequently disputes outside assessments of its human rights record, such worldwide attention does seem to have some influence,[7] although recent debates question just how far that influence extends.[8]

Iranian criminal sanctioning laws are notoriously severe, and in some categories, carry disproportionate penalties for women. As I will argue, women's moral virtue plays a crucial role in the utopian vision of Islamic society envisioned by the religious leaders of the Islamic Republic. In the mindset of these lawmakers, the harsh criminal sanctions serve a deterrent purpose in the broader project of regulating morality and rehabilitating social values, first corrupted by the previous regime, and second undermined by the reformists.[9] From the start, this rehabilitation was to be borne by women, who were called upon to serve as the representatives of the moral order—at once new and yet part of reclaiming an Islamic utopian cosmology—as they saw it.

Women, of course, were the focus of the post-revolutionary social rehabilitation project when, immediately after the revolution, Khomeini moved to suspend the Family Protection Act of 1967 (rev. 1975). The 1982 enactment of the first of a series of revisions to the penal code, the Law concerning *Hudud* and *Qisas* (Limits and Retribution, respectively) further aimed to reintroduce the element of religious moral sanctioning. Not long after, women were to embody morality physically under the legal authority of the Mandatory Veiling Act (1983). They were, however, to bear this role through broad social reforms, and laws were only one channel for transmitting them to the public.

Constant refinements and debates around what comprises virtue notwithstanding, in the Islamic Republic, women continue to serve as vehicles of social virtue.[10] Alongside an unflagging emphasis on women's morality and societal rehabilitation, Mahmoud Ahmadinejad's government (2005–13) introduced important changes to the Civil Codes on Marriage and Family and to the Islamic Penal Codes, which were widely debated, from the floor of the *Majlis* to the World Wide Web.[11] In this chapter, I will examine the latest changes to the criminal codes as they affect women.[12]

Women as agents of social rehabilitation

As I have argued elsewhere, since the revolution, state officials' steadfast attention to women's legal status has served to reinforce particular and often competing views on how women best serve the aims of the post-revolutionary state.[13] Exploring how those views have changed with the various different administrations in existence since 1979 allows for a better understanding of changes to the laws as well. An investigation into legal reforms will also allow for reflection on the persistent debates about Islam, the Republic, and how, for the religious leadership, women's roles were to serve in the wider project of producing a utopian Islamic society, despite their discordant views. In the debates about women and their legal status in the post-revolutionary society, moreover, state officials concerned themselves with addressing women's contemporary problems and concerns, while at the same time attempting to emulate an idealized vision of the community of believers during the time of the Prophet.

While Khomeini suspended the pre-revolutionary Family Protection Act upon his return to Iran in February 1979, his discourse about women claimed to elevate women's status to one that was in greater conformity with women's important roles as mothers and wives, according to Islamic principles and traditions. For this discursive shift, Khomeini invoked the image of the Prophet's cherished daughter and Ali's wife, Fatimeh, an important symbol for the revolutionary struggle for justice. For Khomeini and his retinue, women's roles were best served by affording greater attention to the figure of Fatimeh. Law would serve as a vehicle to reshape the conditions in society toward this end.

Many were troubled by the critical changes to the laws affecting women and families, but some secular nationalists and leftists who had rallied alongside the *ulama* (religious leaders) to topple the monarchy were not immediately concerned by the leadership's restrictions on women's legal status. While some saw themselves struggling for the greater good—overthrowing a monarch—others saw themselves simultaneously challenging the bourgeois commoditization driven by Western capitalism that was overtaking their social and cultural values, and, at the same time, participating in the global anti-colonial and nationalist movements of the 1960s and 1970s. Thus, the turn to Islamic principles to reframe social life, including gender roles, appealed to some as a forthright embrace of local values.

Thus it was that many looked the other way when tens of thousands protested the immediate changes to the laws affecting the rights women had recently won by way of the Family Protection Act (1967), which allowed them to petition the courts for marriage dissolution and custody of children. Many of the protestors likely had benefited from these and other Pahlavi-era modernization programs.[14] The counter-protestors who referred to female dissidents as *gharbzadeh* ("Western-struck") and attacked them also advanced the narrative of cultural deterioration that Khomeini had mobilized, and conferred it more firmly on the bodies of urban Iranian women.

As a foil to the *gharbzadeh* woman, revolutionary leaders appealed to the person of Fatimeh as the ideal woman for the revolutionary state. Fatimeh's qualities were earlier recorded by Ali Shariati, an inspiration both to religious and secular revolutionaries. Shariati, a sociologist educated in the West, worried that Western cultural imperialism was threatening native mores. Shariati's writings on oppression may have been the crucial ingredients that brought leftist and religious groups together. One of the key subjects on which Shariati wrote of oppression was women's issues. In his important text, *Fatimeh Fatimeh-ast* (Fatimeh is Fatimeh), Shariati employed the image of Fatimeh to emphasize the transcendent qualities of Muslim women. For Shariati, Fatimeh replaced the Western woman as the model modern woman for Iranians and offered an indigenous exemplary of womanhood for Muslim Iranian women.[15]

Khomeini described Fatimeh as the ideal figure of femininity. Her birthday replaced 8 March, International Women's Day, as Iran's official women's day. In numerous addresses, Khomeini sanctified Fatimeh as the perfect Islamic woman, whose qualities of justice-seeker, educator of children, and pious Muslim, others should strive to emulate.

> Strive to purify your character and to make your friends do likewise. Strive so that you react to the outrages committed against you. In your attempts to uphold all the qualities that make up the great character of woman, be as that unique woman, Hazrat Fatima Zahra, upon whom be peace, was. All of us should take our exemplar from Islam by looking at her and her children, and being as she was. Strive to acquire learning and godliness, for learning is not the preserve of any one person, learning is for all, godliness is for all, and striving to acquire learning and achieve godliness is the duty of us all.[16]

In annual speeches on Iranian Women's Day, Khomeini aimed to demonstrate how Fatimeh speaks to the concerns of the Iranian state. This was especially true during the Iran-Iraq war when the state asked women to send their husbands and sons to the front. As a national trope, Fatimeh displaces and supersedes concerns for gender equality. With Fatimeh's image, state leaders attempt to move from a discussion of equality before the law to the promotion of the exemplary figure of *Shi'i* female devotion—to family, nation, and ultimately, to God.

According to the Iranian Constitution, family is "the fundamental unit of society."[17] The ultimate success of the family, and thus the nation, depends on women's moral virtue. For this reason, women's honor is a matter of public concern, subject to surveillance and discipline. By recognizing women's roles in nurturing the nation and its citizens, however, the state also acknowledges the potential for women to play more explicit roles in the politics of the nation.

The revolutionary aim of improving society through the rehabilitation of women gave women unexpected social and political power, as improvements in the conditions of women's lives were indicative of the success and legitimacy of the new state. The significant attention Khomeini and other state officials gave to women's issues—as the basis of a healthy society—served to keep a steady focus on women's concerns and the need to improve society through attention to women's status.

The revolutionary leaders' use of women's status as a primary locus of the revolution, literally, the site of the nation's rehabilitation, made women's issues markers of the state's very legitimacy. Discourses about women's objectification stressed the need to focus on women's intellectual development. This, in turn, intensified the focus on women's education and productive social and political participation. The increased attention to women's status led to gains in women's health, literacy, education, and labor force participation. Additionally, women's groups have used the focus on their actions, roles, and comportment to make specific demands for legal redress, especially in the context of family laws, criminal sanctioning, and in broader calls for an end to gender discrimination.

After the revolution, Iran's penal codes along with family laws, which together were considered by Khomeini to fall under the authority of Islamic leaders, were revised in several stages. At first, the leaders introduced these measures as a temporary efforts to introduce the principles of Islamic jurisprudence to law-making on a trial basis. These temporary changes were at long last finalized in June 2013, with debates on the fate of defendants such as Sakineh Ashtianti still looming large. The laws, albeit modified to better accommodate principles of *Shi'i* Islam as interpreted by the leaders of the revolution, remain codified. As we will see, codification has implications for the meaning and procedural administration of laws, even in the context where the laws are derived from Islamic principles.

Iran's hybrid legal system

In early 2012, both the Iranian parliament and its oversight body, the Council of Guardians, passed and approved the revised penal code. In October 2012, however, in an unusual move, the Council of Guardians retracted their earlier approval and set out to further amend the new penal code. The Council of Guardians modified the code in significant ways, then again sent the new penal code to parliament for approval on 1 May 2013. After parliament ratified the penal code a second time, it was sent to the president for signature. Upon the president's authorization, the new penal code was published in the official legal gazette and came into force on 12 June 2013.[18] These events were notable because when the penal codes had been revised soon after the 1979 Revolution, ostensibly to conform to the *Shari'a*, they were considered temporary and extended every five years. With the passage of the 2013 law, the judiciary attempted to finalize the Islamic penal code for the first time since the revolution.

The codification of Islamic principles into law is an important component of legal modernization in many Muslim-majority societies, and the debates around the Islamicized codes expose the difficulties of integrating scriptural texts into a centralized legal system. In Iran, a study of the historical foundations and present-day effects of codified *Shari'a* allows for a more nuanced understanding of how civil (tortious) and criminal proceedings are blended and how this blended form serves certain logics surrounding punishment and gender disparities, especially pertaining to *diya* (compensation).

After the Constitutional Revolution of 1906–11, the new Iranian parliament drafted the country's first Constitution. To construct a centralized body of law, the government imported civil and penal codes primarily from France and Belgium while also asserting the laws' conformity with *Shi'i* Islamic principles.[19] Between the constitutional period and the 1979 Revolution, Iranian criminal codes went through a series of secularizing reforms that systematized offenses and punishments while establishing a hierarchy of courts to adjudicate allegedly criminal behavior and to arbitrate over disputes. By 1939, the Iranian civil and criminal codes no longer contained references to *Shari'a*.[20]

In 1979, when the popular revolution removed the monarchy, a coalition of leaders, including religious and secular nationalists, established a new system of governance: an Islamic Republic. A referendum vested the *'ulama* with great political authority through the power of the *Velayat-e Faqih* (Guardianship of the Jurisprudent).[21] In this newly envisioned branch of government, the religious leadership consolidated state power by supervising all judicial, military, and other matters deemed important to the political organization of the state. When Ayatollah Khomeini was elected as the country's highest authority, as the *Vali-ye Faqih* (Ruling Jurist), he moved quickly to dissolve the bases for the existing judicial apparatus and renewed his call to integrate *Shari'a* into state law. In an apparent revitalization of *Shari'a* principles, Khomeini and the supporting *'ulama* called for conformity of state laws to Islamic principles.[22] This was a substantive shift from the previous era in which laws were not to conflict with the *Shari'a*.[23]

Many of the post-revolutionary revisions to the laws arose from the leadership's goal of grounding the institutions of government in *Shi'i* Islamic traditions. Thus, after the revolution, much of the systematization of the previous era was dismantled. For instance, municipal courts that handled a wide range of disputes were initially replaced by revolutionary *shariat* (Islamic) courts that gave judges broad jurisdiction over the kinds of cases they heard, with marked attention to crimes against the state and the aims of the revolution.[24]

Between 1982 and 1983, the Council of Guardians reintroduced the penal codes through four laws: (1) the Law Concerning *Hudud* and *Qisas* and Other Relevant Provisions; (2) the Law Concerning *Diyat* (plural of *diya*); (3) the Law Concerning Islamic Punishments; and (4) the Law Concerning Provisions on the Strength of *Ta'zir*.[25] *Ta'zir* are discretionary punishments that serve a deterrent purpose in criminal sanctioning. They include public offenses of immoral behavior or threats to security and order, for which no punishment is specified in sacred texts. In 1991, the first three laws were brought under one common penal code, followed in 1996 by the introduction of a revised chapter on *Ta'zir*.

By the early 1990s, an Islamic criminal justice system was organized through a reintroduction of the criminal procedures.[26] An amendment to the penal code in 1991 created a category of public injury for what were regarded, up until then, as private crimes, including murder. This provision made homicide both a public matter, for prosecution, and at the same time, a private tort, with a plaintiff. Thus, in murder cases, tort and criminal liability are assessed by the same court. First, under a theory of tort, the private plaintiff or family of the victim can make an appeal under the Islamic penal code for *qisas* (retributive sanctioning). Then, the state uses its discretion under the *Ta'zir* provisions to assess the nature of the public harm.[27] There are at least two plaintiffs: the next of kin and the public. In such cases, only the former possesses the right to retributive punishment. The state's prosecutor, on behalf of the public, makes a case for punishment based on public interest and deterrence with sentencing ranging from a minimum of three years up to a maximum of ten years imprisonment.

The criminal codes codify evidentiary requirements drawn from *Shi'i fiqh* (jurisprudence) to prove criminal cases. These include *eqrar* (confession) by the accused, *shahadat* (witness testimony), *qassameh* (sworn oath), and finally, *elm-e qazi* (judge's knowledge). With regard to the last method, *Shi'i fiqh* permits a judge in certain "fixed punishments and death sentences by-way-of-retaliation to sentence on the basis of his own knowledge."[28] Article 211 of the penal code attempts to define judge's knowledge as "certainty resulting from evidence brought before him," and requires judges to state the evidence that serves as their source of knowledge in the decision.[29]

The criminal codes of 1982 and 1983 reintroduced the provisions to the laws that, according to some, aim to bring the Iranian laws in line with classical *Shi'i fiqh*. The laws divide crimes into three categories of punishment: *hudud* (crimes against God), *qisas* (retribution), and *diyat* (compensation). As we shall see, with their introduction into the Iranian legal system in the early revolutionary period, these laws made for extreme, sometimes frightening, changes to the degree to which malfeasance was now sanctioned over the previous period.

Changes to *zina* *punishments*

The crime of *zina*, or extra-marital intercourse (including adultery and fornication), is categorized under the *hudud* (singular *hadd*) punishments, deemed to be "crimes against God." With the introduction of *hudud* crimes into state law, leaders were attempting to reinscribe a particular moral order onto post-revolutionary society, in line with their discourse of cleansing the moral depravity characterized by the previous rulers.[30] By their nature, *hudud*, which literally mean 'limit', suggest specificity with reference to the punishment and the conduct being penalized. They are thus regarded as crimes having fixed punishments. Therefore, with a *hadd* crime, there is, ostensibly, no possible reduction in sentencing, although Iranian law permits appeal. Iran's penal code lists eight crimes subject to *hudud*: sodomy, imbibing (of alcoholic beverages), adultery, false accusation of adultery, lesbianism, pandering, special cases of theft, and crimes against the state such as unlawful rebellion.

In general, the crime of *zina* divides punishments into two categories: death for (separately) married parties and flogging for unmarried parties caught in sexual intercourse. In the latter case, *zina* is not under the *hudud* penalties, but rather is codified in the discretionary deterrent laws, *Ta'zir*. Thus, the 1982 laws re-introduced a penalty of death for *zina*, which had been prohibited in the 1928 revisions to Article 207 of the General Penal Codes (of 1926). The

1928 amendment carried a prison sentence of six months to three years and gave standing only to the injured spouse.

Until the 1982 laws were introduced, courts seemed to have discretion to rule either with reference to Islamic principles, under Article 167 of the Constitution of the Islamic Republic (1979),[31] or the pre-revolutionary penal code that had prohibited execution for adultery and other *hudud* crimes.[32] The 1982 law not only reinstated the sanction of death, but introduced the penalty of lapidation or stoning (*rajm*) for adulterers.[33] The legal requirements for proving adultery include the concurrent oral testimony of four just (*adel*) mature male eyewitnesses to the act of penetration.[34]

According to some interpretations of the sacred sources, stoning is the sanction for adultery, but there is hardly a consensus among the *'ulama* on this matter. While some jurisprudential debate on the topic exists, many contemporary scholars have argued that this form of punishment, which is not stated in the Qur'an, is not permissible at all, and that the Iranian penal code is at odds with Islamic jurisprudence on this matter.[35] On the other hand, some scholars believe that this punishment is noted in some of the secondary scriptural sources, *ahadith*, and entered into Islamic jurisprudence by way of Talmudic law.[36] Others believe that it nevertheless comes from weak or unreliable *ahadith* and thus, is neither fixed nor unalterable.[37]

Although the *zina* proscription is meant to penalize both men and women, and thus is neutral on its face, there is a discriminatory effect on women adulterers because men can legally have more than one wife, permanent and temporary, while women cannot have more than one husband at any one time. Only in cases where both parties are married would the sanction apply equally. In cases where one partner is unmarried, he or she would instead face the possible sanction of flogging, while the married adulterer could be punished with stoning. Moreover, when a married man is committing adultery with an unmarried woman, he could still marry her to avoid *zina* punishment, while the same is not the case for married women. Flogging is also the sanction when both parties are unmarried, although a general exception to this rule, when it is enforced, is to convince the parties to marry.

It should be noted, however, that the enforcement of stoning is quite rare in Iran, especially since 2002 when then-Judiciary Head, Ayatollah Shahroudi, circulated a memorandum imposing a ban on it. The ban was unenforceable and thus some local judges did in fact issue the sanction, as evidenced by the Ashtiani case.[38]

In the revised penal codes, the punishment of stoning had initially been deleted. This deletion allowed for the insinuation that the sanction has been removed from the penal codes altogether. Analysts reviewing the new code, however, noted that although it was deleted as a sanction for adultery under *hudud* crimes, later provisions reference stoning, and thus suggest it is still one of the sanctions available to judges.[39] Both Article 132, dealing with multiple offenses of *hudud* crimes, and Article 173, addressing confession, mention stoning, and thus appear to preserve it as a penalty.[40] Moreover, Article 220 of the new penal code refers the punishment of *hudud* crimes not specified in the penal code to Article 167 of the Constitution, which states that in the absence of code law, judges must base their decisions on Islamic sources or legal opinions.[41] Indeed, Article 167 of the Constitution of the Islamic Republic provides the judiciary with powerful recourse to Islamic principles in almost any context.

After the second revisions to the penal code in May 2013, the Iranian government's legal oversight body, the Council of Guardians, clearly reinstated stoning as a penalty for *zina* as Article 225. The penal code defines *zina* in Article 221 as an act of intercourse between a man and woman who are not married to each other, and who have no doubt as to the nature of the relationship.[42] This broad definition includes intercourse such as rape within its purview. Given this far-reaching definition, it appears that adultery can now be punished through three different methods: as *hadd*, in which depending on the type of adulterous relationship, the penalty can be either the death penalty or, when it is *ta'zir*, flogging.[43] Article 225 provides that the punishment for adultery is stoning, but then permits an alternative where it is "impossible" to carry out the execution by stoning.[44] Thus, although Article 225 reinstates stoning as a punishment for *zina*, it seems to leave the punishment up to the judge's discretion, with the permission of the head of the judiciary, to determine a manner of execution other than stoning, or even 100 lashes. In light of the diverging viewpoints among judges and the *'ulama* on the validity of stoning as a punishment in the jurisprudential sources, Article 225 appears to leave the field open to diverse interpretations. The broad latitude left to judges may also lead to vastly different sentences across the country—from 100 lashes (still the penalty for unmarried persons convicted of *zina*) to execution by hanging or even stoning.

The earlier ambiguity in the first version of the new penal code (January 2012) may have been suggestive of the broader debates between legislators who might have been seeking a compromise and a face-saving way to prohibit stoning without overtly (over)reaching into the domain of Islamic jurists—jurisprudential interpretation of the sacred sources, especially in light of the international attention Iran received through Ashtiani's case. Now, however, the amended final version of the penal code (June 2013) clearly restores the sanction of stoning for adultery committed by married persons.

In the next section, I investigate another crucial set of amendments to the Iranian penal codes involving juvenile sentencing, which also have significant gendered consequences.

Qisas *and girls: gender disparities in sanctioning under-age defendants*

The harsh sentences also apply to youth under the age of eighteen. For criminal liability, the new penal codes set out to establish a determined age for maturity and thus criminal responsibility, which in the laws of the Islamic Republic, vary in different socio-legal contexts. According to the Iranian penal codes, the determination of culpability of an accused depends, in part, on the consideration of the age at which the youth reaches maturity (*sen-e buluq*), which is to be distinguished from the age of majority, considered eighteen under international law. Age, however, is taken alongside of the gender of the accused. Considerations of age, moreover, do not simply evaluate physical age, but mental age, as determined by a judge's knowledge (*elm-e qazi*). The new penal codes break the age of maturity into a complex set of assignments according to the youth's age and gender. Age is given the further consideration of the youth's mental and physical make-up in order to determine whether he or she possessed the necessary element of intent at the time the criminal act was committed.

Perhaps in a partial bid to conform to its international obligations under the Convention on the Rights of the Child (CRC), which Iran ratified in 1994, the new penal codes appear to allow those who were under the age of eighteen when they committed a crime the chance to avoid the death penalty. The pre-2013 penal code stated that youth under eighteen were exempted from criminal responsibility.[45] The penal code defined a youth as one "who had not reached the age of maturity under Islamic *Shari'a*."[46] The previous code, however, did not construe the meaning of the clause, "age of maturity under Islamic *Shari'a*."[47]

Given the criticisms, both at home and abroad, of the Islamic Republic's practice of executing juveniles under the age of eighteen, the judiciary took some measures to curb the negative attention. First, the judiciary initiated a mechanism whereby the head of the judiciary was required to sign an order granting permission (*estizan*) for execution to take place anywhere in the country. Using this mechanism, the judiciary often held off signing the order until the defendant had reached the age of eighteen, thus postponing the death sentence. Since the CRC considers the defendant's age at the time of the crime, rather than the time of execution, this was still a violation of international law.

The new penal code excludes from criminal responsibility youth whom it deems immature. Article 146 states that "immature youth have no criminal responsibility." Article 148 provides correctional and security measures for immature offenders. In a significant revision from the old penal code, the new code stipulates the age of maturity for criminal responsibility. Article 147 of the new penal code provides that the age of maturity is nine lunar years (eight years and nine months) for girls and fifteen lunar years (fourteen years and seven months) for boys.[48] Thus, the new penal code appears to define the age of maturity clause drawing from *Shari'a* sources. This age of maturity conforms to the *Shari'a*. By stating the age explicitly, the new code appears to eliminate the possibility of using other sacred sources that propose older ages for criminal responsibility. Calendar years, however, are not the only measure of maturity. Physical signs may permit the age to be reached earlier if a girl has begun menstruating or a boy has begun producing sperm.

Regardless of the new problems presented by specifying the age for criminal responsibility, some important clarifications to the old penal code do appear. Article 88 of the new law spares youth offenders from the death penalty under the discretionary *Ta'zir* laws. That is, girls under the age of nine or boys under the age of fifteen when the crime was committed will not be executed. The new penal code creates additional age groupings for consideration in criminal responsibility, also disparate between male and female offenders. The new code creates four categories of criminal responsibility based on age. These categories, stipulated in Articles 88 and 89, subject youth offenders to different rules in association with the different categories of punishment: *ta'zir*, *hudud* and *qisas* (*qisas* also includes *diya*). The following discussion of Articles 88 and 89 will divide the crimes by gender, age, and category of crime. The burden of proof rests solely with the youth, who, having been deemed to have reached the age of maturity, must now argue that s/he does not possess the requisite mental capacity for criminal responsibility.

1. Under nine years old, gender matters only in cases of *hudud* or *qisas*:
   a. *Ta'zir* offense: Neither boy nor girl will be held criminally responsible. On a discretionary basis, judges may sentence youths to correctional measures, which include surrendering him/her to his/her parents with

the pledge of reform, sending the youth to a social worker or psychologist, or prohibiting him/her from going to certain sites or seeing specific persons.

  b. *Hudud* and *Qisas* offenses: Article 88 states that boys who are deemed not to have reached the age of majority could be subject to correctional measures, as discussed above. Girls could be held criminally responsible, but only through a very strict reading of the provision as it refers to lunar years. Girls who committed a *hudud* or *qisas* crime under the age of eight (solar) years and nine months will be treated the same as the boys. Girls over eight years and nine months could be found criminally responsible if they are deemed to possess the requisite age of maturity, both physical and mental.

2. Between nine and twelve years old, gender matters only in the cases of *hudud* or *qisas*:

  a. *Ta'zir* offense: Neither boy nor girl will be held criminally responsible. As above, they may be subject to correctional measures, based on the judge's discretion.

  b. *Hudud* and *Qisas* offenses: As noted above, there is a stark difference between boy and girl offenders in this category. Again, based on Article 88, a boy who has not reached the age of maturity will be subject to correctional measures. A girl in this age range, however, is said to have reached the age of maturity. She may be subject to the punishments prescribed in the penal codes, unless she can prove that she does not possess the maturity to be held responsible.

3. For children and juveniles between twelve and fifteen years old, gender matters only in cases of *hudud* and *qisas*:

  a. *Ta'zir* offense: There is little difference between boys and girls. Generally, youth will be sentenced to correctional measures, as stated above. In severe cases only, a judge may sentence the youth to be held in a Correctional and Rehabilitation Center from between three months to one year.

  b. *Hudud* and *Qisas* offenses: In such cases, a boy who has not reached the prescribed age of maturity, fifteen lunar years or fourteen (solar) years and eight months will be subject only to correctional measures or, for severe offenses, up to one year in a youth correctional facility. Boys and girls who are deemed to have reached the age of maturity will be subject to adult criminal responsibility.

4. Juveniles between fifteen and eighteen years old, gender matters only in cases of *hudud* and *qisas*:

a. *Ta'zir* offense: There is little difference between boys and girls, but the severity of the crime is important for sentencing. Generally, youth convicted of minor crimes will be sentenced to no more than two years in a Correction and Rehabilitation Center. The possibility of additional fines and public service sentences exists. For severe crimes, the youth could be sentenced to up to five years in a youth correctional facility.

b. *Hudud* and *Qisas* offenses: In this context, it is important to note that boys and girls between fifteen and eighteen, who are deemed to have reached the age of maturity, will bear adult criminal responsibility for their offenses.

To the above categorizations, however, an important qualification is attached by way of Article 91 of the new penal code. Article 91 provides the presiding judge in such cases the opportunity to consider maturity in both physical and mental terms, and states:

> With regard to crimes punishable by *hudud* or *qisas*, where the accused have reached physical maturity and are under eighteen years old, if they do not understand the essence of the crime committed or its inviolability, or if there is a doubt as to their complete mental growth, then the appropriate measure of punishment shall be accorded with attention to their age, based upon the punishments provided in this chapter.[49]

Thus, Article 91 of the new penal code creates a provision stipulating that under certain circumstances, offenders younger than eighteen may be exempted from *hudud* and *qisas* punishments and sentenced instead to correctional measures, based on the judge's discernment. This is an important application of the judge's knowledge (*elm-e qazi)*. In a note to this provision, the penal code requires the court to consult experts or other means necessary to determine mental maturity.

From my fieldwork interviews in the summer of 2012, I learned that judges and some juvenile defenders appreciated this provision in that it allows lawyers to present evidence of a youth's immaturity and thus lack of legal responsibility. A lawyer who worked at the Society for the Support of the Rights of the Child told me, "[i]t opens the hand of the judge to make decisions based on evidence we present."[50] One judge also mentioned that this could allow for diminishing the gender disparities that exist in the law. The result is a mixed bag. On the one hand, the law allows for judicial discretion, providing judges, as in the context of *zina*, with wide latitude to tailor sentencing to the nuances of a case. On the other hand, this discretion affords judges a great deal of autonomy, opening the door to wildly uneven and disproportionate sentencing, even in light of Article 211 stipulating acceptable sources of judge's knowledge.

Another children's rights attorney living outside Iran, Mohammad Mostafaei, is a critic of this law, not only because it diverges from Iran's responsibilities under the CRC, but because it is dependent on each judge. "Instead of having a law strictly based on the age of majority in accordance with the international human rights system and the Convention on the Rights of the Child, this law still leaves too much power in the hands of judges and will lend itself to disparate outcomes in the provinces of Iran."[51] As if responding to this critique, another lawyer working in Iran told me that although this new law is not perfect, "at least this leaves the judges some leeway in making decisions, whereas the previous law did not. And this, in turn, allows us [advocates] to try to persuade the judges."[52]

In Iran, therefore, the system both codifies laws that are to be implemented by judges serving as functionaries and, at the same time, provides a legal framework for judges to act as Islamic jurists in certain kinds of cases and in some categories of crime. The system of codification, derived from Western law, presides over an ossification of the more fluid jurists' system, where Islamic scholars make decisions based on vast amounts of study and knowledge of the jurisprudential logics of the *Shari'a*. If this system is to work, however, it places a burden on the state to train jurisprudents at the bench. On the other hand, the codification provides a basis for transparency and predictability, both of which are important indicators of the just legal system.

In the final section, I examine the jurisprudential and legal debates over the amount of *diya* (compensation) remitted to men and women in case of accident or death.

Disproportionate diya[53]

Crimes of homicide and bodily harm against individuals are further separated according to appropriate punishments, those subject to retributive punishments (*qisas*) and those corresponding to financial compensation (*diya*). Such crimes include battery, assault, murder, and manslaughter.

In addition, in crimes subject to the punishment of *qisas*, *Shi'i fiqh* and the corresponding Iranian legal code affirm retributive death for homicide in intentional murder, and *diya* in unintentional homicides. The Iranian penal code stipulates that the surviving heirs of a murder victim (*awliya-ye dam*) may decide whether to demand punishment in-kind or forgo it. In cases where the victim's *awliya-ye dam* accepts *diya*, the charge is effectively pled down to an unintentional murder. The earlier version of the penal code provided that where a man murders a woman and the victim's next of kin demand retribution, the next of kin would also pay one half of the *diya* to the offender's family because the *diya* of a male is twice that of a female.[54] This is still the case, although it appears that through Article 551 of the new penal code, gender equal *diya*, in some limited contexts, has been introduced. Thus far, this provision does not apply to homicides.[55]

Forbearance (*Gozasht*) is possible in multiple kinds of sanctioning. Sometimes the plaintiff's offer of *gozasht* will dismiss the charge, but other times it will reduce it and thus lessen the punishment. In cases where the victim's next of kin permits the offender to save his or her life, thus offering *gozasht*, the offender is not automatically freed. The offender is subject to a criminal sentence as a sanction in conjunction with the public prosecution. In the 1991 revisions to the Iranian penal code, a section was added to recognize the dual nature of the harm created by murder (both private and public). In addition to the private harm, for which *qisas* or *diya* may be appropriate, there is also a public harm that the state may prosecute on behalf of society as a whole.

The involvement of the family of the victim in Iranian criminal sanctioning confirms the state's concerns with victims' interests in the enforcement of retributive punishments.[56] In cases where *diya* is at issue, it is effectively monetary payment to compensate the family for injuries "arising from a specific type of tort."[57] In this context, *diya* is no longer only a criminal sanction, but constitutes a bridge between criminal and civil tort liability. *Diya* is paid by the offending party and, as such, represents compensation for physical injuries analogous to those found in European civil code and British and American common law traditions. When the family of the victim opts for retribution, technically there is no *diya*. Sometimes, however, families negotiate extralegal arrangements that allow the defendant to exchange a sum of money or property for forbearance.

Thus, although *gozasht* is a form of private forbearance and is available for some crimes, *diya* may or may not be included. In addition, *diya* operates as both a form of punishment and a type of compensation for damages. In a contemporary context, *gozasht* and *diya* are among the components used in alternative dispute resolution practices. Some legal scholars argue that by encouraging the payment of *diya*, countries with *Shari'a*-based judicial systems may avoid extralegal acts of revenge, and even lawful in-kind retribution, while encouraging forbearance.[58]

One of the primary *Qur'anic* sources to which *diya* is linked is a verse interpreted to encourage Muslims to forego their right of lethal retribution: "In the law of retaliation there is life for you—O you who are endowed with intelligence so you may restrain yourselves."[59] Jurists and scholars, moreover, have identified a number of other *Qur'anic* verses that counsel and praise the act of individual forgiveness by the family of the victim. According to Baderin, at least one *ahadith* reports that whenever a case of *qisas* was brought before the Prophet Muhammad, he counseled forgiveness.[60] However, the *Qur'an* does not specify the rate of *diya*, nor any discrimination based on gender. Only in the *hadith* does one find a basis for the claim that *diya* for a woman should be half that of a man. Further, interpretations of the *hadith* have, over time, continued to express the value of the *diya* for a woman as one-half that for a man. Some scholars suggest that this discrepancy emerged after the death of the Prophet Muhammad and after the evolution of *diya* as a mechanism for securing or paying for forbearance in retributive sanctioning. In this context, the gender disparity in *diya* likely grew out of the tribal feudalism that emerged after the Prophet's death.[61]

The gender disparity in *diya* may be based on Islamic principles of property and inheritance. The eleventh century jurist, Mohammad al-Sarakhsi, found that the discrepancy emerged from the varying capacities of men and women to own property. In property ownership, a female was considered "half of that of a male person" because while a woman could be the proprietor of land, "the male person combines the capacity to be a proprietor of marriage and of property."[62] Ayatollah Azari-Qomi, a contemporary cleric in the Qom seminary, expressed a similar logic for the gendered disparity in inheritance laws. He asserted that Islamic principles emerged to grant women economic autonomy after a time when patriarchy was the rule throughout most of the world.[63] In a shift from a time when a woman was chattel, *Qur'anic* dictates prescribed that women and men would own the property of their respective labor. By the same token, men became and remain duty-bound to provide for the material needs of their womenfolk.

Based on the above reasoning, Ayatollah Azari-Qomi further inferred that a woman's *diya* is half that of a man's because of the difference in inheritance among men and women. Because *diya* is the rightful property of the heirs, the imbalance in *diya* arises from the fact that as a result of death, there will be a loss of income. In such a case, "heirs need resources for securing their maintenance, and, because if a man is killed, his heirs will lose all their resources. Therefore they need higher blood money than for a woman. But if a mother is killed, usually heirs need fewer resources."[64] Women have no legal or religious duty to provide for anyone—not even themselves.

In Iran today, the gender disparity in *diya* continues to be debated among the *'ulama*, legal scholars, and the public.[65] For instance, *Bohran*, an Iranian television program, aired a similar response to the question of unequal *diya* posed to a member of the *'ulama*. He explained that since a man is the breadwinner and a woman is the "help-spender" (*komak kharj*), their *diya* cannot be one and the same. Because men have economic responsibilities that women do not, he explained, their *diya* cannot be equal.[66] Taking a different tack, a conservative member of the *'ulama*, Ayatollah Javadi-Amoli, said in an interview with the Iranian Students' News Agency (ISNA) that *diya* "is a criterion of the physical body... [it] is not operative in determination of worth and is only an economic tool, not a criterion for determining [the] value [of a person]."[67] Then, just a few days later, ISNA reported that the rule of equal *diya* in compensation for bodily harm would be implemented.[68]

Lawyers I have spoken with over the years have suggested that discrepancies in the codified laws persist in accordance with long-held cultural practices and are not necessarily based on religious views. Assigning *diya* as half the amount of that of men rests on the idea that if a woman were to die, it would be less of a financial burden on the family than if a man were to die. This jurisprudential reasoning follows current legal logic, since the victim's *awliya-ye dam* decides whether to accept *diya*. As we have seen, the *awliya-ye dam*, once presumed to be only males, are now in many cases females.

This jurisprudential debate entered the public space when Iran's first and only women's daily newspaper, *Zan* (Woman), addressed this issue in 1999 through a series of articles about Islam, gender, and the discriminatory laws in Iran. The newspaper's legal expert, Reza Ansari-Rad, trained in Islamic jurisprudence, offered careful readings of the relevant verses of the *Qur'an*[69] to argue against gender discrimination.[70] Some reform-minded *'ulama* have also called for gender parity in *diya*. Grand Ayatollah Yusef Saanei, who is among the few *marja-ye taqlid* (sources of emulation), the highest ranked *'ulama*, has stated, "Blood money is the price of a human life, [d]eath occurs when the soul departs the body. As men and women have an equal soul, so should they have equal *diya*."[71] In a 2007 interview, Saanei reiterated his justification for equal *diya*, and based it on his knowledge of the *Qur'an*: "How can we say that women are equal to men, as the *Qur'an* has decreed, then say that the women's *diya* is half the sum of the compensation received for killing a man?"[72]

Similarly, former president Hashemi Rafsanjani told a group of women in 2007 that the compensation for men and women should be equal because of the changes in society where women are now equal contributors.[73] A conservative member of the *'ulama*, Ayatollah Mohsen Gheravaian, likewise agreed that the laws should be modified to make *diya* equal for men and women.[74]

In compensation for an injury, much like in personal injury laws, the amount of *diya* is determined by worth or value. Two factors are crucial to making this determination: (1) the utility or purpose of the body part damaged and (2) the cost of the loss or harm to the victim. For instance, if an individual loses a finger, the *diya* for that finger would be determined by the value of the finger to the individual. The *diya* for an eye, however, would be higher, as one's eye is defined as more valuable than a finger. In cases of homicide, the victim's family suffers a loss of income as well as affection. While the amount of *diya* is decided based on the family's needs, in Iran, this evaluation is determined and set annually by the judiciary.[75]

In the summer of 2008, Iran's Insurance Ministry closed the gender gap for compensation in car accidents, as *diya* is also built into compulsory vehicle insurance. The ministry suggested that in automobile accidents, the role *diya* plays is to compensate victims, and that compensation should not be related to the victim's gender. Explaining this decision, judiciary spokesman, Alireza Jamshidi, stated that because an individual's agreement with an insurance company has a "contractual basis and both sexes pay equal premiums, the compensation should also be equal and the law is not in contravention of the *Shari'a*."[76]

Closing the disparate rate of *diya* in this context is framed in pure economic terms, based on the relationship between a driver and the insurance company. Since the same money is paid into insurance premiums, the logic in these cases suggests that *diya* should be the same. This logic, however, is incompatible with the reasons offered by some *'ulama* regarding the financial responsibility borne by men. Should a man die in a car accident or otherwise, the economic void experienced by his family would be the same as if he were to die as a result of murder.

Debates over the topic of *diya* continue today. The dissemination of ecclesiastical debates in the press, along with activism around the issue of the gender disparity, likely contributed to the changes to the insurance laws. Varied opinions in the jurisprudential sources provide the competing rationales through which *diya* takes shape in Iranian legal codes. The classic *Shi'i* texts afforded higher compensation for males than for females, in accordance with the gendered divisions in social roles at that time. Scholars, intellectuals, and journalists today cite current trends as the basis for closing the gender gap in *diya*.

While some of the hardline *'ulama* argue that a woman's *diya* should be fixed at half that of a man's in order to balance a system in which men and women receive wealth and property differently, in practice, this logic does not work. Rarely is it the case that a widow has recourse to her paternal family's funds for survival, and even less frequently does the tribal logic of housing the deceased's wife among the family members of the deceased take place. Moreover, women are seldom completely provided for by men, and increasingly women are the primary earners for their families. If the issue is more broadly defined as one about family survival, then the gendered disparity in *diya* could be reconsidered in accordance with the exigencies of life in increasingly urbanized, modernized, and individuated Iran. Since *diya* often involves negotiation, any dispute-settling sum could attempt to tailor it to the needs of the family, compensating for the economic and affective loss of a deceased family member.

In any case, the language of Article 551 seems to provide for at least the possibility of equal diya: "In all cases of crime (*jenayat*) where the victim is not a man, the difference between the amount of *diya* and the *diya* for a man shall be paid by the state's Compensation Fund for Bodily Harm." This provision comes immediately after a provision affirming that a woman's *diya* in murder is half that of a man's (Article 550). While Article 551 does not appear to apply in private murder cases, the state has provided proportionate compensation in a recent case involving girls in a classroom in which the gas heater exploded, killing two students and badly injuring twenty-seven others.[77]

Conclusion

In the current period where rights activists in Iran are facing a tremendous backlash, their ability to raise awareness both inside and outside of the country, as in the case of Sakineh Ashtiani, is notable. While the leaders of the Islamic Republic appear to ignore international pressure on its laws, the debates that are sparked inside the country, and even among members of the religious leadership, are important because changes to the law must pass through them. Another important consideration is that Iran's hybrid legality has some impact on the procedural format of the cases, such that they can be compared and contrasted with legal systems in other parts of the world. The Islamico-civil legal system, as I have elsewhere called it, is thus not altogether exotic and beyond the reach of Western analysts for scrutiny, precisely because it borrows its framework and indeed some of its laws from Western legal systems, notably the French.[78] Hybrid legality also sets the stage for advocacy and change.

In codifying the laws that are said to be derived from Islamic principles, Iranians give a sort of intelligibility to these principles, but also fix and solidify the very jurisprudential doctrines that were intended to be fluid and accommodating. Before codification, the Islamic principles were historically flexible, constantly debated, and thus contingent and ever changing. The notion that a law cannot be changed because of the *Shari'a* is based on a rather short-sighted, politicized understanding of Islamic principles.

Legal scholars and activists on behalf of women are voicing their opinions through scholarship and public awareness campaigns, not only because of their increasing education and understanding of gender issues in the law, but also because of the role that the post-revolutionary state has assigned to women as signifiers of morality.

Iranian lawmakers have attempted to connect the gender discrimination in the legal system to Islamic principles, while noting the significant moral position Iranian women occupy in the post-revolutionary nation. The emphasis on women, however, also affords them agency to react to unfair treatment and unjust laws. This chapter may not have been uplifting, but the incremental changes (and even the challenges) discussed herein have materialized in large part due to gender activism and social movements that are deeply connected to the dramatic expansion in the negotiating power of Iranian women over the past three decades, and the direction of change is unlikely to shift.

5

A REVOLUTION WITHIN TWO REVOLUTIONS

WOMEN AND LITERATURE IN CONTEMPORARY IRAN

Farzaneh Milani

In a sermon in 2010, the supreme leader of Iran cautioned his audience not to provoke the regime and its moral codes. Ayatollah Khamenei singled out the iconic and iconoclastic poet, Forugh Farrokhzad (1934–1967), as an exemplar and a warning. "Her early death," he proclaimed, "was her saving grace."[1] At a time when the drumbeats of a military attack on Iran were loud, international sanctions were getting more stringent, the nuclear negotiations were practically stalled, the economy was severely ailing, and people's discontent had reached a record high, what, we might ask, was so menacing about a poet, who had died well over four decades ago at the age of thirty-two? What could Farrokhzad do—beyond the grave—to fight a whole arsenal of the regime's weaponry?

Not long before this puzzling sermon addressed to a group of writers, the Islamic Republic, in its ever-widening anti-dissident net, confiscated another iconic poet's passport on 8 March 2010. Simin Behbahani (1927–2014) was leaving Tehran airport for a poetry reading on International Woman's Day in Paris. Prevented from leaving the country, the eighty-two-year-old poet was

113

interrogated all night, sent home without her valid passport, told to report to the revolutionary court, and put under country-arrest until 2012. Again, we might ask what was so dangerous about an ailing poet, who had serious heart problems and suffered from the near loss of her vision due to macular degeneration. What was so threatening about a woman who had never belonged to a political party, and who had consistently believed in the futility of fighting violence with violence?

The ayatollah might be happy that Farrokhzad died young, and that Behbahani was a virtual prisoner in her own country. But he knows their message cannot be handcuffed, arrested, jailed, or simply wished away. He knows that politicians come and go, and that governments are voted into office and chased out of it, but the magical, mystical power of words remains. Indeed, as Farrokhzad announced triumphantly, "It is only the voice that remains,"[2] and as Behbahani reminded her avid readers, "To stay alive/you must slay silence."[3]

The Iranian literary scene can serve as an indicator—a barometer—of the post-revolutionary political theater. During the last three decades, book publishing blossomed during times of political tolerance. It suffered when reaction collided with reform, only to resurface again with baffling speed and intensified commitment to freedom of expression. The gratuitous violence perpetrated against literary figures and the strategies implemented to deal with real or perceived threats reached a pinnacle after the contested 2009 election. Writers and the 7,000 national publishing firms confronted unparalleled state censorship. Vast numbers of books awaited publication permits. Even books previously licensed had to be granted reprint permission.[4]

The regime, it seems, refuses to accept that art cannot be murdered, and that poets and writers can be censored, but their aspiration for democracy cannot be put behind bars. They can be denied the right to move about freely, or to travel abroad, but their message cannot be detained. They can be wished dead, but their words are undying. Iranian history confirms the long-term effectiveness of literature.

Although social and literary movements, unlike pregnancies, cannot be traced back to a precise date or a single event, despite the fact that it may require years, even decades, to see a large-scale shift in literary production, an unprecedented flourishing of women's literature is one of the unexpected benefits of the 1979 Revolution. Although the Islamic Republic in its early years banned some prominent women writers and poets, and succeeded in driving others into exile, it failed to silence them in the long run. In spite of all the problems—sex re-segregation, social and economic hardships, the eight-year war with Iraq, censorship, and conformity to the Islamic Republic's interpretation of morality—women poets and writers have attained a stature previously reserved for men. The pantheon of Persian literature is finally integrated in terms of the gender of its producers, consumers, and objects of representation.[5]

It is the aim of this chapter to study the desegregation of a predominantly all-male tradition and the remarkable emergence of women writers as a transformative socio-political force in post-revolutionary Iran.[6] Living in a sex-segregated society, consigned to absence or immobility, women writers had to defy the age-old patterns of gender apartheid implemented in the name of beauty, religion, chastity, class distinction, or safety. Denied the privilege to enjoy free movement without incurring penalties, women writers knew they had to gain access to the public arena and the public discourse. To break the spell of their textual quasi-invisibility, they knew they had to make the circulation of their bodies and their voices central to their artistic universe. That is why, thematically speaking, the literary universe of contemporary Iranian women writers is built on spatial tropes of movement and containment. This is not only a novel literary landscape. It is a radical socio-political upheaval. Women writers' subversive challenge to established familial and political hierarchies as well as the religious underpinnings, sexual overtones, long-term social consequences, and literary corollary of desegregation have been their major preoccupation and are this chapter's object of inquiry.

Literary renaissance: a collateral benefit of the 1979 Revolution

After a temporary lull the first decade after the revolution, women emerged with renewed energy on the literary scene. The literary trajectory of Goli Taraghi (1939–), one of Iran's most critically acclaimed and talented novelists and autobiographers today, is an eloquent case in point. Her tale of temporary silence and suffering followed by great literary success parallels the trajectory of women's post-revolutionary writing.

Taraghi migrated to France soon after the revolution. In her own words, "I left Iran in 1979, the year of the Islamic Revolution, and settled in Paris with my two small children. I was naïve enough to think that the chaotic upheaval of the beginning eventually would settle into normal life, and I could return. The increased hostility of the government toward the intellectuals and the war with Iraq, which lasted eight years, forced me to stay longer than I had imagined." Taraghi's life in France was fraught with difficulties and landed her in a mental institution. "Fear of an uncertain future, financial worries, being lost and homesick and many other problems, conscious and unconscious, all contributed to my nervous breakdown. I believed I could fight back personally. I underestimated the destructive force of the enemy. After a year of suffering, I was finally hospitalized in a psychiatric clinic."[7]

Taraghi's description of her depression and hospitalization, unique in its candor and precision, also bears witness to the healing power of words and her refusal to give in. "Taking the right medication restored my mental stability and helped me to overcome my dreadful anxieties," she explains, "but what came to my rescue and pulled me out of the dark well of depression was the magical force of literature." In an autobiographical short story entitled "The First Day," she writes, "I make a rope of words and slowly pull myself up from the depth of darkness, from the bottom of the well."[8] After regaining her health and her command of words, she is now publishing in France and in Iran, producing increasingly more complex work with both local and global content and appeal.

The involvement of women writers in various literary genres, the unprecedented popularity of their works, and their varied themes, concerns, and backgrounds are beyond comparison with any earlier period of Iranian literature. Publishing a record number of books—fiction, non-fiction, and poetry—women are creating a strong and vital literature. For the first time in Iranian history, a woman—Simin Behbahani—became the most prominent poet alive. Unofficially, she became the national poet of Iran. Despite her physical fragility, and in spite of all the obstacles—of which there were many, from the monetary to the political, from street harassment to court summons and interrogations, from anonymous slander to official denunciation, and from anxiety and anguish to fear for her life—the "lioness of Iran" continued to write, knowing but not fearing consequences. "We write our books not with ink but with our blood," she famously said, and her pen, like her words, continues to bear witness and speak truth to power.[9] Through all the injustices and hurdles, Behbahani remained sure and confident, charming and challenging. "I am the tall, unyielding pine tree/In me is the essence of resistance/Even if I am cut into pieces.../Let the willow tremble/Let the wind billow/The shame of the wind and the willow is not for me/I'm the tall unyielding pine tree."[10]

Women's contribution to Iran's rich treasure trove of poetry is, of course, nothing new. It can be traced to more than a thousand years ago, to Rabe'e

Qozdari, a tenth century female poet, writing at the very beginning of Persian literature. For a variety of reasons, poetry has proved to be more female-friendly than other public forms of art such as prose fiction, music, painting, sculpture, photography, or cinematography. Ali Akbar Moshir-Salimi, for instance, includes 294 women in his three-volume anthology, *Women Writers from a Thousand Years Ago until Today*, and all are poets.[11] Moreover, neither access to education and leisure, nor the two essential conditions for creativity that Virginia Woolf insisted on—mainly a room of one's own and financial independence—were within the purview of most women until recently. Out of the 107 poets anthologized by Keshavarz Sadr in his book, *From Rabe'e to Parvin*, forty-three are members of the royal court, and the rest belong almost exclusively to the aristocracy.[12]

For centuries, the power and privilege of the written word belonged mainly to men. In a society concerned with keeping the worlds of men and women apart, with an ideal of femininity as enclosed, silent, and invisible, women writers could not easily flourish. They had to subvert a powerful system of control and confinement. They had to negotiate rules of modesty that not only minimized physical contact between the sexes, but also forbade free circulation of female bodies and voices in public spaces. It is only in the mid-nineteenth century that women appeared in public places, and demanded expansion of their citizenship.[13] Women writers, always at the forefront of socio-political movements in Iran, broke the spell of their textual quasi-invisibility by entering public and discursive spaces. They were no longer isolated exceptions. There was finally a considerable number of authors and texts and an uninterrupted chain of literary foremothers.

While poetry has been their preferred medium for centuries, women are now also publishing some of the most interesting and well-liked works of prose fiction. Even an established poet like Behbahani published, in the post-revolutionary era, four books of prose—two collections of short stories and two life narratives. Although more archival research needs to be done on the genealogy of novels written by Iranian women inside and outside the country, their first attempts don't seem to go back any further than 1930, when Irandokht Teymurtash published *Dokhtar-e Tireh Bakht va Javan Bolhavas* (The Ill-Fated Girl and the Unfaithful Boy). Three years later, Zahra Kiya brought out *Parvin-o-Parviz* (Parvin and Parviz). The prolific novelist and biographer, Emineh Pakravan, published *Le Prince Sans Histoire*, in France in 1945. The novel was highly acclaimed and won the Prix Rivarol. Prior to the publication of her prize-winning novel, Pakravan used the pseudonym

Irandokht (Daughter of Iran) and published *Destinees Persanes* in installments in Cairo, in Huda Sha'rawi's journal *L'Egyptienne*.[14]

From the 1930s to the 1960s, only about a dozen women, compared to 270 men, published works of fiction. The prominent novelist and translator, Simin Daneshvar (1921–2012), reached widespread acclaim during this period. She published *Atash-e Khamoush* (Fire Quenched), the first major collection of short stories by a woman, in 1954. Fifteen years later, she produced her masterpiece, *Savushun*, a bestseller in pre-revolutionary Iran.

According to Hassan Mirabedini, the number of female novelists now is 370—thirteen times as many as ten years earlier and about equal to the number of male novelists.[15] Noteworthy, too, is the welcome diversification of women writers' social, political, and cultural backgrounds. Religious and secular, Westernized and traditional, highly educated and holders of high school diplomas, upper-, middle-, and lower-class, and young and old women, such as Mahshid Amir Shahi, Shiva Arastoui, Farideh Golbu, Fataneh Haj Seyed Javadi, Moniru Ravanipur, Shahrnush Parsipur, Zoya Pirzad, Nazanin Safavi, Parinoush Saniee, and Fariba Vafi write from a variety of perspectives and enrich the literary discourse.[16] Unlike several influential women writers of an earlier generation—Parvin E'tessami, Zahra Kiya, Simin Daneshvar, Simin Behbahani, Forugh Farrokhzad, Lo'bat Vala, and Goli Taraghi—younger women writers today are not necessarily related to or connected with prominent male writers.

Women dominate the fiction bestseller lists and often outsell men. While the average Iranian novel has a print run of about 5,000 copies, several books by women have enjoyed printings of well over 100,000 copies. Although not enough work has been done on literary reception in general, and women's writing in particular, the statistics available indicate a substantial increase in the popularity of books by women. Fataneh Haj Seyed Javadi's novel, *Bamdad-e Khomar* (The Morning After), Nazanin Safavi's *Dalan-e Behesht* (Passage to Paradise), and Parinoush Saniee's *Sahm-e Man* (The Book of Fate), engaging and detailed portraits of love and loss, strength and vulnerability, published in 1995, 1999, and 2002 respectively, have gone through numerous printings.

Although the literary merit of these books varies widely, the stories they tell resonate with an ever-increasing readership. They explore taboo topics such as family and gender relations, domestic violence, the difficulties of reconciling family commitments with artistic aspirations, mental illness, depression, attempted suicide, the tyranny of older brothers, drug addiction, child custody, sexual relationships, the right to choose one's partner or lover, and the desire to be free and unfettered.

The same phenomenal growth can be seen in the number of women working as literary translators. Whereas in 1997 Iran had 214 women translators, the number soared to 708 six years later. According to a recent report released by the United Nations' Commission on the Status of Women, women working in the Iranian publishing industry, as a whole, numbered more than 2,000 in 2003, as compared with 700 in 1997. The number of women publishers almost doubled in that six-year period, rising from sixty-six to 103.

There is also an exciting new development outside the country. Iranian women are producing highly acclaimed bestsellers and attracting remarkable attention from mainstream Western media. Gina Nahai, the celebrated author of four novels, captures this phenomenal emergence of writing by women of the Iranian Diaspora. "Once upon a time (in the early 1990s)," she states, "I was one of two Iranian women authors writing and publishing in the West. I know this is hard to believe, given the current wave of novels and memoirs by Iranian women authors about Iran, or by American authors about Iranian women, or any other variation thereof... That was then. Nowadays, hardly a week goes by when I don't meet or hear about another Iranian woman writing a book. I find them everywhere—at readings and lectures around the country, at the hair salon and the grocery store."[17]

Some of these books, written in English and addressed to a Western audience, have migrated back to Iran and found a propitious market inside the country. For example, Homa Sarshar's biography of Sha'ban Ja'afari sold only 7,000 copies in the United States. Its publication inside Iran, however, was a great success.[18] As a bestseller, it went through seventeen printings soon after it was translated and published. Likewise, the translated version of Firoozeh Dumas' *Funny in Farsi: A Memoir of Growing up Iranian in America* went through six printings in its first year of publication in Iran.[19]

Whether inside or outside the country, gender issues are no longer the concern only of elite, highly educated, and urban women. Nor are they considered class-specific, personal, private, or unavoidable. To the contrary, they are presented as gendered iniquities, endemic to an entire social structure that can and ought to be changed. Fervent objection to discriminatory laws, advocacy for a structural reorganization of physical and discursive spaces, and the struggle for human rights and human dignity are common themes in women's literature.

Competing narratives: mobility and entrapment

Women have offered a complex and multilayered portrait of their nation from the street level up. They have captured the reality of the Iranian experience during one of the most challenging times in its history. This is the kind of history that is often unavailable in books. It describes the chaos and vibrancy of a culture in transition and of a country defining, un-defining, and redefining itself. It is the voice of a nation in search of itself. It is a history of hopes betrayed and renewed, of disillusionment and dissent, and of compliance and resistance. It is a quest for beauty and elegance, and for clarity and moderation in the midst of turbulence, war, and revolution.[20]

Underneath this vast thematic diversity, however, the twin topics of flight and captivity constitute the very basis upon which this body of work is built. The complex network comprising space, power, and literary productivity is the key to a better understanding of women writers, who have suffered the constraints of gender apartheid on their bodies and voices. Metaphors of control—walls, veils, imposed silences, fences, cages, blind windows, closed doors, and iron bars—coexist in their works side by side with the desire to sprout wings, to fly, flee, run, dance, and sing.

For centuries, stringent codes of sex segregation separated the worlds of men and women who were unrelated to each other by marriage or blood. In other words, in addition to divides defined by class, religion, and ethnicity, there exists another partition of the social order that is based strictly on anatomy.[21] Men belonged to the outside world (*mard-e meydan*) and the outside world belonged to them. Implicitly if not explicitly, the option to be outdoors without permission or chaperone, without fear, and without penalty, was a masculine prerogative. The ideal woman was locked out of all that was considered "public." She was *aftab-o-mahtab nadideh*—that is, "one who has not been glimpsed by the sun or the moon." Gender politics was intertwined with theology, notions of beauty, and manly honor, and a long-lasting apartheid was put in place.

Regardless of how it is justified, sex segregation, like racial apartheid, revolves around power through the control of space. It is not about faith, chastity, or safety. It is about social domination. It is about political exclusion and economic exploitation. Power is closely interconnected to the control of space. Who controls what space and to what effect determines socio-political authority and autonomy. Restrictions placed on mobility subordinate the segregated group in multiple ways. It excludes them from certain crucial political activities. It confronts them with difficulties in fully exercising their economic rights. It prevents them from pursuing a variety of careers in the public sector. It denies them admission to public educational institutions and seminaries. It hampers their artistic potential and does not allow them to fully develop their talents in public forms of art.

Pages of Persian literature are filled with tales of men who have been seekers after truth, after knowledge, or enlightenment. It is replete with male travelers, male pilgrims, male explorers, adventurers, and trailblazers. It is packed with Sufi masters who provide their readers and disciples with a roadmap for spiritual illumination. Physical mobility, it seems, is a prerequisite of ideal masculinity. It is hard to imagine Rustam without his horse, Raksh. It is hard to imagine Shams of Tabriz or the traveling Dervishes as confined to one place. It is hard to envision Sa'di without his unending travels. The liberty to roam at will has not only been a masculine privilege, it has also been a cultural imperative. A stay-at-home man is considered un-virile. He is depicted as childlike and effeminate. Like Hassan Kachal in the popular folktale of that name (Hassan the Baldy), he is worthy of ridicule and social scorn. On the contrary, rare are the women who claim the road in more than a thousand years of Persian literature. There is no female equivalent of the wandering Shams of Tabriz. There is no female version of the traveling Sa'di. Even the birds, which are sent on a journey to attain spiritual perfection and eternal beauty, are gender-marked and male. As Attar proclaims in his exquisite masterpiece, *The Conference of the Birds*, "Completion of this road needs a man."[22]

Like the many birds that wing through their works—phoenixes, eagles, doves, crows, and finches—women writers have never relinquished the desire to fly and soar into the many pleasures of the sky. Shahrnush Parsipur, who bemoans the fact that women "have never passed through the seven cities of love," and, unlike Attar's birds, "have not climbed to the Ghaf mountaintop in order to see themselves in eternal mirrors," rejects this caged life.[23] She devotes her masterpiece, *Touba and the Meaning of Night*, to a female wandering Dervish, and turns *Women without Men* into a journey novel. The latter, for the writing of which Parsipur was incarcerated twice by the Islamic Republic, is the story of five female protagonists who feel constrained by their roles and their spaces. They desire to be on the road, to be free, and to come and go as they please.

Although they are told time and again, "home is for women, the outside world for men," they refuse confinement within the four walls of domesticity. "I can't stay home any longer,"[24] they admit with candor and conviction. Eventually, they manage to escape their confinement and transform their lives by trespassing into masculine territories and disturbing the age-old boundary lines dividing masculinity from femininity. Discarding exemplary paradigms of ideal womanhood, they venture out and leave home and their normal narratives. They become the architects of their own destiny.

Women writers translated the desire to fly into words and action. Prompted by forces of modernity, exasperated by gender inequities, they used their ingenuity to slip across traditional lines, overstep limits, and stride onto forbidden grounds. Beginning with religious activism in the mid-nineteenth century and expanding into politics during the Constitutional Revolution of 1905–11, they increasingly inserted their bodies and voices in the public arena. They rose above their spatial and literary ghettos and produced layered narratives of frontier crossings.

It is no exaggeration to claim that contemporary women writers and poets have been consistently concerned with the issue of space and movement. In one of her most anthologized poems, Tahereh Quorratol'Ayn leaps into the arms of the wind to reach the wider world. She escapes from the narrow confines of the *andaroun*, the inner sanctum, and passes from one house to the next and from one alley to another. Uninhibited by obstacles, using the wind as her freedom machine, she moves from place to place, running away from the space socially prescribed to her.[25] "I would explain all my grief dot by dot, point by point/If heart to heart we talk and face to face we meet/To catch a glimpse of you, I am wandering like the wind/From house to house, from door to door/From place to place, from street to street."[26]

Fear of immobilized stagnation was a pressing concern for Tahereh then and remains the preoccupation of women to this day. Farrokhzad's body of work, which epitomizes a relentless search for the open road, and for mobility and speed, is a case in point. It is the tale of an Iranian Icarus, who refuses to live a life disciplined by delineated spaces. In one of her most memorable poems, "It is only the voice that remains," she asks six times in sixty verses why she should stop. "Why should I stop? Why?/The birds have gone off to find the gateless blue/The horizon is vertical/And movement gushing."[27] And Shiva Arastui (1962–), who has garnered prestigious literary awards, announces that the narrator of her stories "has been involved in a revolution; she has been a student, has attended the university, has been present in the streets with boys her own age at every step of the way." Such a woman can no longer live a segregated life, confined and controlled "inside the house."[28]

Ending the patriarchal bargain or the tale of a dying patriarch

If defying the age-old patterns of gender apartheid is the central trope of women's artistic universe, advocating and mirroring the shifting lines of power within the family is its most consequential outcome. No longer playing into their subordination in order to reap the allocated benefits of what Deniz Kandiyoti calls the "patriarchal bargain," women have reassessed traditional codes and conventions regulating gender relations within the family unit and, by extension, in the society at large. Rearranging priorities, they have rejected established hierarchies whereby men, as breadwinners and heads of the household, exercise control over women as their helpmeets.[29]

For centuries, masculinity, as epitomized by the figure of the Father, was glorified in Iran. Traditionally, marriages established a relationship of status between husbands and wives, whereby male sovereignty was considered divinely ordained or consolidated through laws and conventions. While in the Iranian monarchical tradition, kings were the crowned fathers of the nation (*pedar-e taj dar*), in the Iranian patriarchal family, fathers were the undisputed kings in their little castles. It is no coincidence that grooms are called *shah-damad* (king-groom) at their wedding ceremonies, and a Persian proverb, "The nuptial night is not unlike the dawn of royal reign," makes it clear that a man's matrimony is the beginning of his sovereignty. Iranian life narratives abound in comparisons of fathers to kings. "In the rush of my memories," writes Sattareh Farman Farmaian in her memoir, "my father has the most presence." Identifying him as "a courageous lion from an extant dynasty," she acknowledges that "for us, he was the ultimate sultan."[30] The authors of the graphic novel, *Zahra's Paradise*, are also convinced that "when it comes to idolizing almighty fathers, Iran's worse than the Catholic Church."[31] The Persian word for "shrew," meaning a disobedient wife or female citizen, *saliteh*, comes from the same root as *salteh* and *saltanat*: dominance and kingship, confirming the relationship between political sovereignty and domestic absolutist power.

A democratic society cannot be achieved without a democratic family. Structural inequities at the political level find their reflection in and are based upon inequities implemented within the family unit. Refusal to accept injustice or the display of superior force within the household not only establishes domestic harmony, it also serves as an instrument for the establishment of collective justice and the validation of non-violence on a national (even international) scale. Without an egalitarian family, where gender equity and mutual respect govern, enduring democracy and genuine advancement of social justice is impossible. Tyranny at home prepares the grounds for accepting and perpetuating political tyranny.

Beginning in the mid-nineteenth century, women writers increasingly created a new breed of female and male characters who defied traditional definitions of femininity and masculinity and posed a challenge to the authority and sovereignty of the old patriarch. Indeed, the rupture of tradition has been most visible not only in the new generation of women who are interested in gender diversification, but also in men who want a more egalitarian society. Women's abandonment of their "divine" duties within the family unit is blamed as the cause of many of society's ills. These gallivanting women came to personify a more general loss of cultural identity. Hard to control, always on the move, they were the emblem of threatening changes in the spatial organization of gender relations. They disturbed "natural" or "divinely ordained" gender categories and challenged the very integrity of the privileged term, "masculinity," defined traditionally in its opposition to femininity.

Men who believed in desegregation and gender equity also were ridiculed and criticized. Personifying the painful loss of Iranian cultural identity, they, like their female counterparts, were considered the emblem of threatening changes amid a quickly changing world. Although the study of Iranian masculinities is lagging far behind and is a serious gap in the field of Iranian Studies, there has been, for decades, concern with the emergence of a diminished form of manhood. In fact, a new term, *zan zalil*, has gained currency and widespread usage in Iran these days. Shortened to ZZ, it means a "hen-pecked man," an effeminate "girly man," or a diminished man dominated by a woman.

At least three new books with *zan zalil* in their titles study this crisis of a particular kind of masculinity, the kind that was glorified for centuries in Iran. These are haunting obituaries, describing, with much chagrin, the death of the old patriarch. They portray men who suffer at the hands of disobedient, sharp-tongued, and obdurate wives. They deride unmanly men who help around the house, participate in child rearing, and bend to their wives' will. They depict pitifully emasculated husbands, who are tamed and dominated by women. Basing the nature and construction of masculine and feminine identity on rather simplistic binary opposites, these books glorify traditional, provider/protector manhood and lament the emergence—on a massive scale—of "aggressive women" who do not stay in their "proper" place. They consider recent changes in longstanding gender roles stifling, and predict the woeful birth of a dangerous matriarchy.[32]

Motherhood by choice

One of the major contributions of women to modern Persian literature is their redefinition of the family unit. For instance, their portrayal of motherhood is far different from the tales of consummate motherly love, especially that between mothers and sons that has dominated both classical and modern Iranian literature.[33] Instead, they have written of divided maternal loyalties, of relations between mothers and daughters, and of mothers at war with themselves. They have portrayed women who do not take naturally to homemaking and mothering, and have written about those who fail to reconcile life as a wife-mother with that of a poet-writer. They have depicted mothers who bemoan the sacrifices extracted by literature, dubbed, at times, a "bloodthirsty Goddess."[34] In short, they have refused to uphold the master narrative of motherhood, a narrative that has demanded self-sacrifice, singularity of commitment, and undivided loyalty.

Although biological motherhood is an incontrovertible fact, "motherhood" is not a right in Iran. It is a privilege. It has to be earned. Even though it is in giving birth that a woman becomes a "mother," to remain one she has to follow a stringent code of conduct and consider motherhood her sole calling in life. If a divorced mother remarries, or should a woman be considered an "unfit mother," she can lose even her minimal custodial rights. Forugh Farrokhzad is a case in point. Considered unfit, she became an ex-mother, and was denied even sporadic visitation rights with her biological son, Kamyar Shapour. The pain of this merciless punishment and the corollary emotional and psychological anguish of this forced separation from her biological child is a central trope of Farrokhzad's body of work—poetry, film, travel narrative, essay, and short stories.

It is only in post-revolutionary writing by women that one witnesses a hard-won reconciliation of motherhood and intense commitment to art. Consider *My Bird* by Fariba Vafi. Published in 2003, this first novel of a previously unknown author took the Iranian literary scene by surprise. It won a number of prestigious literary awards and was chosen as Iran's best novel of the year. Containing fifty-three short, relatively self-contained chapters, it reads like poetry. It is minimalist, dazzling in its candor and courage, and attentive to details. It offers competing visions of truth and avoids absolutist pronouncements. Set in post-revolutionary Tehran, and all the more poignant for its condensed brevity (141 pages in Persian), it delineates the coming-of-age story of a woman writer.

My Bird is the first-person narrative of a nameless, thirty-five-year-old woman who lives with her husband and two children in Tehran. Feeling alienated and isolated, she begins to examine her place in society. Although a devoted wife and mother, she awakens gradually to the truth that she does not want to be restricted by traditional definitions of femininity. "I was sick and tired of my assigned role," she writes.[35] "I am not a mother, not a daughter, and not a wife... I cannot perform any of the roles that have been assigned to me," she laments.[36] She feels bored, "bored of constantly having to take care of the kids, of the peeling walls, the broken water heater, the cockroaches that do not die with any kind of bug killers." She is "tired of the long days turning to night, and of long nights that are filled with tears."[37] And, so it is that she promises to define herself on her own terms and never again "to be dependent," never again to be captive of a role foisted upon her.[38]

Seeking and finding salvation in the act of writing, the narrator takes up the pen, confronts the truth of her life head on, and throws away "such nonsense like a shared life, the warm family unit, and other rubbish."[39] All the silence, all the secrecy, and fear she has carried on her tired shoulders for years, all the compromises she has painfully consented to and cannot forget, and all the feelings she has buried unceremoniously in the fabric of her soul come unglued over the course of the novel. She vows to explore her life, her feelings, and her surroundings more carefully, and to describe them as accurately as she can. From now on, she will make up her "own definitions," re-imagine her relationships and hence rebuild them.

And she succeeds in incrementally changing her consciousness. Although originally she resented being the sole care-taker of her two children, eventually she comes to view motherhood neither as stifling nor as her sole mission in life. She neither begrudges her maternal responsibilities nor does she romanticize motherhood as woman's sole commitment in life. And refusing to be sucked in by traditional roles, she breaks out of the cage of her former self, freed from the finitude of her circumstances. No longer harangued by a nagging sense of entrapment, she defines for herself a new life as a woman—daughter, sister, wife, mother—and no less vitally important, a writer. The constraints of motherhood as obligation are transformed to the joy of motherhood by choice.

Freeing motherhood from the cage of its restrictive definition, women also have offered an expanded definition of family possibilities and alternatives. For instance, they have questioned the primacy of biology in Iranian kinship, the premium placed on biological parenthood, and the attitudinal stigma attached to adoption. While biological fatherhood and motherhood take central stage in Persian literature, non-biological parenthood has been covered up with perplexing resolve. Women have resisted this narrow definition and have dealt with taboo topics such as adoption.

In 1962, Farrokhzad adopted a son during her trip to Bababaghi Leprosarium to direct her documentary, "The House Is Black." From all available accounts, the decision to adopt Hossein Mansouri was spontaneous. Farrokhzad was shooting a scene when she noticed the young boy, who eerily resembled her biological son, and was about his age. Bonding was just a glance away. That night the divorced director decided to adopt Hossein. She is the first Iranian woman on record to become a single parent. By adopting Hossein, Farrokhzad announced the birth of a transformed sense of motherhood.

Legalized adoption is, strictly speaking, forbidden in Iran. Although caring for abandoned or orphaned children is highly encouraged and considered a meritorious act, the lineal identity of the child has to be kept unaltered and paternity needs be established without doubt or ambiguity.[40] There is no exact equivalent for the word "adoption" in the Persian language. Phrases such as *farzand khandeh*, which literally translates as "a so-called child," or "a child only by name," and *bacheh-ye sar-e rahi*, which means "a child picked up or left by the side of the road," an abandoned child, are used to refer to adopted children. Intra-family exchanges of children have been practiced, of course, as have culturally sanctioned forms of foster-parenting, but adoption has been avoided or shrouded in secrecy. Persian literature is mainly silent on this taboo topic. There is, however, the story of Zal, father of Rustam, the warrior-hero of the national epic, *Shahnameh* (The Book of Kings). Abandoned in the foothills of the Alborz Mountains because he was born with hair white as snow, Zal is picked by none other than the legendary Iranian Phoenix, who looks after him. But as soon as Zal's biological father reclaims him years later, Simorgh returns Zal to him.

Tales of adoption by human parents find public expression in exceptionally few books. One such aberration is Daneshvar's "The Man and the Snake," included in a collection of short stories, *Be Qui Salam Konam?* (Whom Should I Salute?), published in 1980.[41] This is the tale of a young woman named Nasrin, who, like her creator, is, without proof, deemed to be sterile and whose desire to adopt a child is resisted and ultimately thwarted by her husband. Nasrin's parents, in-laws, well-meaning friends, neighbors, and relatives want to know why she has not started a family. Tormented by her own desires, beleaguered by people's insensitive remarks and cruelties, she subjects herself to ordinary and out of the ordinary "cures." When all fertility treatments fail, she considers adopting the baby of an unwed, but pregnant royal princess. Delighted with the prospect of creating a legal fiction in which, she, the putative mother, "gives birth" to her adopted child while the princess quietly slips back into her virginal maidenhood, the mother-to-be finds her hopes quickly dashed. "After all the papers were in order and everything taken care of, Anvar (the husband) reneged. He said he did not wish to see the illegitimate child of a princess at his table."

As a last resort, a frustrated Nasrin goes on pilgrimage to the shrine city of Mashhad. On the way, she meets a gypsy who presents herself as a high priestess of fecundity. She hands her a small ball with the instruction to insert it in her vagina. Following the gypsy's prescription, Nasrin becomes pregnant. Amidst great jubilation, she carries the baby to full term, unaware that the much-awaited "biological child" will not deliver the expected joy. An unexpected tragedy is in the making. Months later, Nasrin gives birth to a snake, which is promptly put in a cage. Fantastical though Nasrin's story might be in some of its twists and turns, its thematic heart is autobiographical.

Daneshvar was married to one of Iran's celebrated authors, Jalal Al-e Ahmad, and her readers have the benefit of hearing her husband's version of the same ordeal in *A Tombstone on a Tomb*, which by all accounts is an unconventional autobiography. Considering the ability to procreate central to his definitions of masculinity and sexuality, even virility, Al-e Ahmad sees the failure to produce a child, preferably a son, as a real tragedy. Lest his name and memory not be carried into the future, like a tombstone on a tomb, he resolves to father a child of "his own." He makes his wife go through long ordeals of diagnostic testing, consultations with experts, and emotionally draining medical procedures. He even begins an affair with a European woman while traveling abroad, presumably to end his childlessness. All his efforts end in failure. Blame and frustration thicken into marital strife, while resolution turns into obsession.

Meanwhile, writes Al-e Ahmad, an opportunity for adoption presents itself. A princess, desperate to find a caring family for her unborn love child, is willing to fully relinquish her parental rights with a guarantee of full anonymity. The informal transaction would not have involved intrusive screenings, bureaucratic red tape, reams of paperwork, or exorbitant fees. It would be simple and easy. Reluctantly, the father-to-be contemplates what he had rejected earlier. After some emotional wrangling and preliminary negotiations, however, he calls off the secret adoption. Driven by a genealogical passion, he concludes that,

> In reality, a swaddled child left on the side of the road, behind a police station, or in an orphanage has made the permanence of the parent-child bond impossible. Either the parents are poor or the child is an obstacle to their future. Otherwise, he is congenitally defective. What place, then, could such a child—unwanted in his

own mother's lap, like a corpse rejected by the tomb or a bud unable to germinate out of its seed—have in my life?"[42]

A bloodless revolution

Women have played a pioneering role in redesigning and re-imagining the family unit. And unsurprisingly, more than their transgression of a range of literary taboos—fervent objection to discriminatory laws, advocacy for a structural reorganization of physical and discursive spaces, and refusal to have their bodies, their voices, and their desires kept under lock and key—it is their resolve to fight tyrants in bedrooms and kitchens that has proven to be most alarming and intolerable to conservatives.

Although the implications and ramifications of this challenge to traditional authority on a most intimate level remain to be fully analyzed and understood, history proves that one of the Islamic Republic's top priorities was to reinstitute the patriarchal family. The reigning clerics lamented the decline in cherished ideals of masculinity and femininity, and proceeded to accentuate the differences between the sexes, insisting on their separation. No wonder, then, that the very first decree of the Islamic Republic, before the compulsory veiling act, even before the ratification of the constitution, was the repeal of the 1967 Family Law. Convinced that the rebirth of Islamic society would be possible only through the recasting of the nuclear family, it suspended previous modifications and liberalizations in personal status laws.[43]

While searching for justice and harmony in the family unit, women have advocated a structural and systemic change in their society. They have, in effect, depicted a bloodless revolution raging privately within the country. Even though this revolution does not coincide with traditional definitions of revolutions, it has nonetheless shaken one of the ideological underpinnings of Iranian society. In fact, it is accomplishing what the other two revolutions—the 1905 and 1979 revolutions—did not and could not carry out. This is a revolution within the other two revolutions, a bloodless revolution, and one with words more powerful than explosives.

Acknowledging the regenerative power of words and commemorating the storyteller Scheherazade and her literary daughters as role models, Shirin Ebadi, the human rights activist and Nobel Peace laureate, writes in her autobiography *Iran Awakening: A Memoir of Revolution and Hope*:

> Propped up on my desk in Tehran is a clipping of a political cartoon I like to keep in sight while I work. The sketch is of a woman wearing a space-age battle helmet,

bent over a blank page with a pen in her hand. It reminds me of a truth that I have learned in my lifetime, one that is echoed in the history of Iranian women across the ages: that the written word is the most powerful tool we have to protect ourselves, both from the tyrants of the day and from our own traditions. Whether it is the storyteller of legend Scheherazade, staving off beheading by spinning a thousand and one tales, feminist poets of the last century who challenged the culture's perception of women through verse, or lawyers like me, who defend the powerless in courts, Iranian women have for centuries relied on words to transform reality.[44]

Even when women writers tell a harrowing tale—and there have been many—and even when their works bleed with sorrow and grief, an inspiring sense of courage and resistance shines through them. These women have created an alternate reality, spun with words. Theirs are luminous tales of audacious survival, non-violent resistance, and a declaration of victory.

Women writers leading the "caravan of women"

In the turbulent history of contemporary Iran, doubts about modernity, about relations with the West, about the place of religion in politics, and proper codes of morality have been projected upon the emerging patterns of masculinity and femininity. The Islamic Revolution is the epitome of this anxiety over the collapse of tradition and the breakdown of the moral fiber of society. In fact, as early as the 1940s, Ayatollah Khomeini warned against a stolen and dying patriarchy. "In your European hats," he bewailed in his book, *The Unveiling of Secrets*, "you strolled the boulevards, ogling the naked girls, and thought yourselves fine fellows, unaware that foreigners were carting off the country's patrimony and resources."[45] The Ayatollah was in the company of many writers, who ridiculed this mutant character, this bad imitation of the West, and this perversion of traditional Iranian masculinity or femininity.[46]

Denying women agency, refusing to see their longstanding struggle for desegregation, social critics and writers blamed unmanly men for making "way for the arrival of the women's caravan." One such example is a disgruntled Jalal Al-e Ahmad who asked in desperation, "What have we really done?" His response to his own emblematic question boggles the mind. "We have simply given women permission to display themselves in society. Just a display. That is exhibitionism. We have placed women, who are the protectors of tradition, the family, the bloodlines, and the generations in a position of irresponsibility. We have brought them into the streets, to exhibit themselves, to be without duties, to make up their faces, to wear new styles every day and to hang around."[47]

Hang around? Is this what pioneering women, like Al-e Ahmad's own wife, Simin Daneshvar, have accomplished? These circulating women—visible, vocal and mobile—along with their anonymous sisters, and an increasing number of men have advocated the reform of the family unit from within, and pushed against the boundaries of gender apartheid from without. While searching for justice and enduring harmony, they have advocated structural and systemic change in their society. Refusing to be silenced and kept out of sight, they have transgressed religious, philosophical, political, as well as spatial boundaries.

Defying sex-segregation, they have reconfigured the very definitions of masculinity and femininity. The path to full and lasting gender-integration has been long and paved with difficulties. Further backlashes are inevitable. Still, traditional gender relations have broken down and the conventional distribution of space, visibility, and power has been modified. A woman's presence, voice, and vision have been inserted in the public square and the public discourse. The genie is out of the bottle and the caravan of women, led by women writers, has re-drawn the cultural geography of Iran and reorganized its political landscape without shedding a drop of blood.[48]

6

THE IRANIAN FAMILY IN TRANSITION

Djavad Salehi-Isfahani

The last three decades have seen a complete transformation of the Iranian family. To appreciate the extent of this transformation, consider these changes in the living condition of the average family: at the time of the Islamic Revolution in 1979, the average family lived in a home in a rural area with no running water (60 per cent of homes had electricity) and no access to a nearby school beyond primary. It was headed by a couple who could not read or write, of whom the woman would give birth to seven children. Her main role in the family was to cook, clean, and struggle to keep her children alive past the age of five (only one in eight would survive to that age). About one-third of Iranians lived in an extended family.

Three decades on, the average family is urban with access to most household amenities, including a washing machine. The average couple has basic education (eight years of schooling) and, most importantly, has only two children, focusing on the education rather than mere survival of their children. More than 85 per cent of Iranians live in nuclear families composed of parents and children. The new family is not only more modern in its outlook, being less paternalistic and granting women and children a greater voice in its affairs, but also contributes more to economic growth because of its reorientation from large, struggling families to fewer, better educated children.

This transformation, in terms of government policies as well as ideas, had been in the making for decades before the revolution. Family planning, mass education, and progressive family laws were initiated under the Pahlavis. Women writers, professionals, and activists fought for greater gender equality, and paved the way for the modernization of the family before and after the revolution. What is interesting about the post-revolution period is the transmission of social change that, before the revolution, was mostly confined to urban families and to the upper income strata of the population rather than to the average family. The practices of smaller families and better education for women that characterized the lifestyles of rich urban families of Tehran in the 1960s became the norm for lower income families in the 1990s.

Ascribing cause and effect to social change is always hazardous and not always useful, but it is impossible to discuss positive social change in post-revolutionary Iran without raising questions about what would have happened without a revolution. To lay this issue to rest, let me note at the outset that most of the changes that I discuss in this chapter are not caused by the revolution in a meaningful way because they are part of the same socioeconomic transformation that has taken place in most countries as they have developed. However, I do credit the revolution with accelerating the pace of transmission of social change to the lower segments of the Iranian society.

The rapid diffusion of modern infrastructure and amenities—paved roads, piped water, electricity, and television—to the disadvantaged rural population, then a majority, was a direct result of a popular revolution that mobilized resources for the poor. The heightened government concern with the welfare of the poor after the revolution was critical in persuading poor people to participate in modernization from above. Family planning and girls' education succeeded in poorer rural areas where similar programs had either failed or been slow to penetrate before the revolution. To the extent that socioeconomic modernization is measured by the transformation of the average family rather than the elite, the revolution played a role in promoting social change.

My focus in this chapter is the changing role of the family in Iran's economic development and modernization. I use the term modernization rather loosely to mean orientation toward economic growth as reflected in fertility and education behavior of the family. In many ways it corresponds to the common understanding of a modern family, as families that switch from high fertility to low fertility and from low investment to high investment in child education also change their behavior in other ways, for example, by shifting the emphasis from extended to nuclear family and towards more equal gender roles within the family. The latter is particularly relevant from the viewpoint of economic growth. In Iran, changing gender roles brought about by lower fertility have contributed to the widely known phenomenon of women in public universities now outnumbering men. It has also led to less visible improvements in the balance of power within the family that favor women, which in turn favors child education, in particular that of girls. This chapter emphasizes these significant but less visible changes in family life in Iran.

Family behavior responds to government policy. I discuss the extent to which public policy has promoted the kind of change I consider pro-growth and modern, and the extent to which it has hindered it. In particular, in a section on marriage, I discuss how marriage laws are out of sync with the behavior of modern families. I end the chapter with a discussion of the conservative backlash against the modernization of the average family, which has eroded conservatism in the rural and poorer sections of Iranian society, and represents a much more subdued form of modernization than the loud display of Westernization that upper class Iranians represent.[1] The more subtle type of modernization of the lower income families is perhaps more threatening to conservatives in Iran than the lifestyle of the rich. I would argue that the conservative backlash against the women's movement in Iran, demonstrated by attempts to limit their presence in public universities, or limit women's access to birth control, has more to do with this type of quiet modernization than the most strident kind visible in the affluent districts of northern Tehran.

I begin with a discussion of the role of the family in economic development from the point of view of recent theories of economic development. Section two provides a description of access to basic services, such as electricity, water, schools, and health services, which I believe were the foundation of other improvements in living standards. Section three describes changes in fertility and mortality that helped transform family life. Section four discusses education and section five the evolution of marriage and family laws.

The family in theories of economic development

To understand the significance of change in family behavior in Iran and its contribution to economic growth, it is important to review the new theories of economic-demographic change that put family behavior at the center of modern economic growth. Economic development is often synonymous with modernization. The essential characteristics of a modern family may not be the same for a development economist, a sociologist, or a political scientist. Malthus was the first classical economist to put family behavior at the center of his model of economic development. In his view, families, except for those belonging to the nobility, played a destructive role, pulling back progress caused by economic growth. At the center of his dismal theory was a theory of family behavior in which higher incomes raised fertility and lowered mortality. This caused population growth and thus dissipated the benefits of technical advances into a larger population rather than a higher standard of living.

The advent of economic growth in England in the eighteenth century, known as the Industrial Revolution, which was already underway when Malthus was born and later spread to the rest of the Western world, clearly disproved his dismal predictions. Demographic transition, which has occurred worldwide and describes the decline of fertility following a sustained decrease in mortality, is now seen as an integral part of economic development. In particular, economic theories of fertility behavior, developed mainly by Gary Becker, and the voluminous empirical literature that developed following Becker's work, argue that rising education, especially of women, was the reason why fertility declined and families began to look and behave in a modern way.[2]

But more recent theories go much further in connecting demographic transition to economic development. They point out that fertility decline, and change in family behavior, is an essential contributor to economic development because it enables societies to increase their investments in human capital. Building on the work of Becker, Robert Lucas has advanced a theory of the Industrial Revolution that places family behavior at the center of the development process.[3] Lucas proposes a theory that argues why certain technological advances lead to a sustained increase in per capita income while others do not.[4] Ancient Iran and Mesopotamia are important examples of periods in human history when significant advances in technology took place, mainly in agriculture, that did not bring about the kind of economic growth experienced in Europe after the eighteenth century. These advances, as Lucas has noted for ancient China, dissipated in population growth rather than raising per capita incomes, confirming Malthus' dire predictions. He proposes that the technological advances identified with the Industrial Revolution, which were backed by scientific progress, raised the returns to human capital, encouraging families to change their behavior from procreators to producers of human capital.

This transformation brings about a change in the direction of intergenerational transfer, which is also considered a marker of economic development. John Caldwell considers underdeveloped countries to be those in which the direction of intergenerational transfer is from children to parents—children help with farm work and provide for old-age security—and developed countries to be those in which the transfer runs in the opposite direction—parents invest in their children's education and leave them financial assets and property as bequest.[5] Clearly, this type of change in the direction of intergenerational transfer is necessary if sustained economic growth, in the sense of one generation being better off than the one before, is to take place.

This typology of family behavior, based on the direction of intergenerational transfer, is closely bound up with modernization, which is too often associated with superficial aspects of modern life, such as material possessions, clothing, and personal manners. Limiting modernization to these aspects that have little impact on the contribution of families to economic development leads to confusion when we discuss Islam, economic development and modernization. This confusion is the reason why in discussions of women's status after the revolution the Islamic dress code has received much more attention than the fact that a large proportion of the same women use modern birth control technology. This broader view of modernization as involving change in family behavior is important in interpreting social change after the Islamic Revolution, in particular in assessing whether it reversed the modernization that was underway under the Shah.

Confusion about the course of economic development before and after the revolution is demonstrated by the widespread belief that Iran before the revolution was ahead of South Korea in terms of economic development. Indeed, during the 1960s, Iran, like Korea, was experiencing a "miracle" growth phase, with an average growth rate in GDP per capita of 9 per cent annually, and per capita income in Iran was higher than in South Korea and remained so until 1984.[6] As late as 1980, Iran's per capita GDP (measured in constant 2005 international dollars) exceeded that of Korea by as much as 30 per cent. But this comparison in incomes is flawed because it ignores the fact that Iran's living standard was sustained by oil exports while Korea's was sustained by human capital.

A more relevant comparison would stress differences in the level of education in the two countries and by implication the behavior of the average family with respect to fertility and investment in child education. When viewed from this perspective a different picture emerges: in 1979, the average woman in

Korea had 2.9 births, compared to 6.4 in Iran, and the gap increased by one full birth in the years that followed. In 1970, only four in five children made it to age five in Iran; in Korea child mortality was four times lower. In 1980, women aged fifteen and higher had 2.4 years of schooling in Iran, compared to 7.3 years in Korea.[7] Only in 1990 did Iranian women reach the level of education that Korean women had three decades earlier. This comparison should dispel a common misunderstanding of economic development that ignores the role of the family, the unit that is most responsible for the education of the next generation. In Iran, the predominant modes of thought about economic development emphasize the role of the government, and oil in particular. While governments no doubt influence the rate of economic growth, modern development theory emphasizes family behavior.

Demography

At the core of the transformation of the Iranian family in the last three decades is their demographic transition, which began in the mid-1980s, later than most countries of the Middle East, such as Lebanon, Tunisia, or Turkey, but was completed very quickly, by about 2000. Demographic transition is the change in mortality and fertility period. Figure 4 compares demographic transition in Iran and Turkey to highlight a major peculiarity of Iran's transition. Turkey began its demographic transition about two decades before Iran, even though child mortality started to fall in both countries at the same time (right axis). The latter indicates that the most important precondition of fertility decline—child health improvements that reduce the urgency of high fertility—existed in Iran but fertility remained high, and even increased in the early 1980s. Iran's fertility transition was more steep, a record by world standards, having reduced fertility by three to five children per couple in urban and rural areas in about fifteen years. By 2000, it had caught up with Turkey at replacement level fertility.

The reasons for delayed fertility transitions are important for understanding the origin of the transformation of the Iranian family. Two competing explanations can be offered. One explanation is that in critical respects, such as female education, the country was less developed than its per capita income indicated, so fertility transition, which is more closely connected to female education than income, was delayed. The second explanation blames the lack of access to family planning technology. Iran had started family planning as early as the 1960s, but rural fertility had proven highly resistant to government policy.[8]

After the end of the war with Iraq, in 1988, having rejected the pre-revolution family planning program as a Western ploy, in a famous policy reversal the government restarted family planning. The reversal came as a result of the realization that the Islamic government's pro-natal policies had accelerated the rate of population growth. The 1986 census showed that Iran's population had grown at an average rate of 3.9 per cent since the last census in 1976. Record cohorts of first graders were showing up for classes, forcing schools to teach in two or three shifts.[9] With Ali Akbar Hashemi Rafsanjani in power, a moderate president interested in promoting economic growth, the government passed the family planning law through its extensive network of rural health clinics, providing free birth control to rural families.[10]

It is commonly believed that the new program was more effective, especially in rural areas, and was therefore responsible for the fertility transition starting in the late 1980s. But evidence does not support this view. As Abbasi-Shavazi et al have shown, fertility decline began before the start of the program's implementation, in the mid-1980s.[11] Evidence from a causal analysis of the impact of rural family planning clinics on fertility suggests that while the program was effective, it explains less than 20 per cent of the decline in fertility.[12]

Education and fertility

In the economic-demographic transition model discussed above, fertility transition is closely related to investment in children. It is not clear as to whether families that acquire birth control technology and are able to have fewer children decide to invest more in their children, or whether increased returns to investing in children prompts families to seek family planning and have fewer children. Either way, we expect that economic development is closely correlated with change in family behavior, from high fertility and low investment in children to low fertility and high investment. This is relatively easy to check using cross-country data on fertility, schooling, and GDP per capita. Guriev and Salehi-Isfahani use a two-dimensional graph to show that for a sample of developing countries fertility and schooling are negatively correlated and, furthermore, that countries with high fertility and low education tend to be poor and those with low fertility and high education rich.[13] According to their classification, countries with a fertility rate above 3 and on average 5 years of schooling are underdeveloped and those with fertility rates less than 3 and years of schooling above 5 are developed or are about to enter that stage.

Figure 4: Demographic Transition in Iran and Turkey

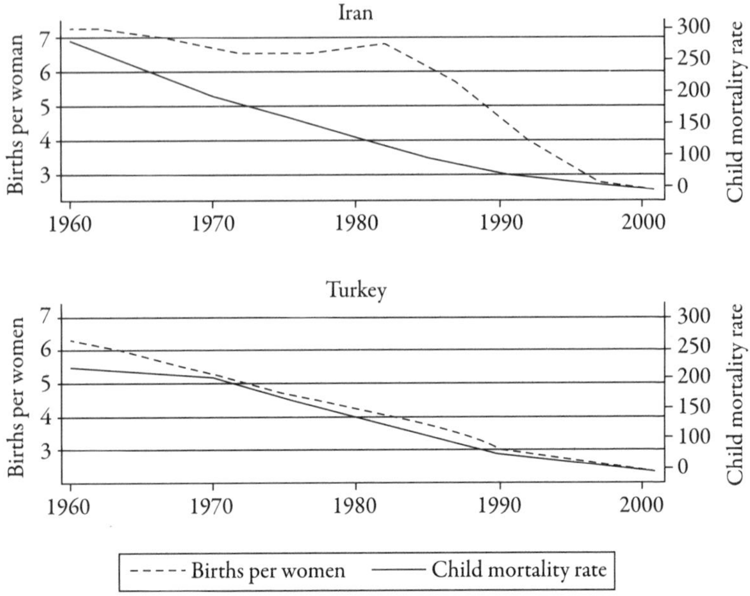

Source: Author's calculation; data from World Bank, World Development Indicators database, http://data.worldbank.org/products/wdi, last accessed 2 Feb. 2012.

According to these criteria, as early as 1980, South Korea was in the developed group while Iran and Turkey were in the underdeveloped group, and remained there until 1990. Iran's position changed dramatically after 1990, when, along with Turkey, it was able to reduce fertility and increase education.

An important feature of the economic-demographic transition described by Lucas is the extent to which it involves the average family or ordinary citizens rather than the elite. In most countries, as in Iran, elite and upper class families started a process of modernization long before ordinary families did because they were focused on the upbringing of their children and considered them as objects of intergenerational transfer rather than as sources of labor or old-age security. Often they did this without a decline in fertility because of their superior means.

However, as Lucas notes, it is the transformation of the average family that is the key to economic-demographic transition, not just the upper classes. In Iran, this has meant in particular changing the behavior of the majority rural population, which accounted for two-thirds of the population in the 1980s. In this respect, the transition of the Iranian family, which began in the 1980s, has been broadly based. The gap in fertility between rural and urban families and, more broadly, between the rich and the poor, has declined. Rural fertility is now only slightly above urban fertility. The prevalence rate of modern contraceptive methods is in fact higher among rural women than urban women: 60.6 per cent compared to 55.5 per cent.[14]

Differences in fertility based on socioeconomic development still remain high. In Sistan and Baluchestan, which is the least developed province of Iran and has the lowest prevalence rate for modern contraceptives (47 per cent), the fertility rate has remained quite high. In 2006, it registered a total fertility rate of 3.7, which is 80 per cent above the national average and three times that of the Gilan province, which had the lowest fertility.[15]

Figure 5 shows the narrowing gap in education between urban and rural residents and between men and women by birth cohort. The most striking part of Figure 5 is the narrowing gender gap. A generation ago, women had less than half the education of men. Today, urban women are on average more educated than urban men and in rural areas women have about the same level of education as men. Equality in education, coupled with the lower burden of fertility, has improved women's status within the family, helping channel family resources in the direction of child education.

Figure 5: Average Years of Schooling by Year of Birth

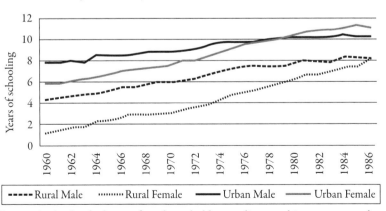

Source: Author's calculations from household expenditure and income survey data files, Statistical Center of Iran, various years.

The greater balance in power between wives and husbands is also evident in the changing age and education gaps of married couples. Figure 6 shows that in both rural and urban areas the age gap of married couples has been declining, beginning with the cohort of men born in the 1940s. But the education gap has behaved differently. It was constant in urban areas and actually increasing in rural areas until the cohorts of men who were born in the 1960s and reached marriage age in the 1980s. The rising education gap of rural cou-

Figure 6: Age Gaps of Married Couples by Birth Year of Husband

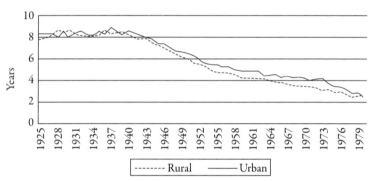

Source: Author's calculations from household expenditure and income survey data files, Statistical Center of Iran, various years.

Figure 7: Schooling Differences of Married Couples by Birth Year of Husband

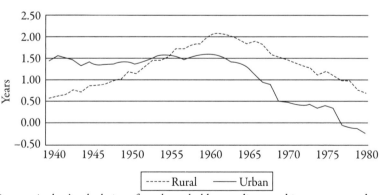

Source: Author's calculations from household expenditure and income survey data files, Statistical Center of Iran, various years.

ples is consistent with the point I have stressed that before the revolution rural families had not yet started on the path to modernization.

International evidence suggests that more balanced families in which women have greater bargaining power are more likely to invest in child health and education.[16] When women are more like their husbands in age and education, they are more likely to participate in decisions about the allocation of family resources. Evidence from a number of countries shows that when women have greater control over family resources, expenditures on child health and education increase.[17] This is the reason why, in the widely quoted words by the former World Bank Vice President Larry Summers, "Investment in girls' education may well be the highest return investment available in the developing world."[18]

Marriage

While new families are more balanced than those in the past, the marriage market itself has been less favorable to family formation, prompting many to speak of a marriage crisis in Iran. The outward signs of this crisis are the inability of youth to get married and a high divorce rate among those who do marry. Rising age of first marriage, rising education and greater opportunities for women to work outside the home are normal consequences of lower desired fertility, and are all associated with modernization. But a marriage crisis is when marriage is delayed involuntarily and later than these factors warrant.

It is instructive to note that since the revolution, the legal minimum age of marriage has always been much lower than the age at which the vast majority of Iranian men and women get married. After the revolution, with the return of the *Shari'a* law as the basis for marriage, the age of marriage for women was lowered from eighteen to nine, though in 2002 it was raised to thirteen for girls and fifteen for boys. But, as the 1984 round of the Household Expenditure and Income Survey (HEIS) records, less than 1 per cent of married women under the age of forty-five in that year were under the age of fifteen. This percentage had decreased by 0.33 per cent in 2011 (census figure). According to the 2010 Demographic and Health Survey of Iran, in 2009 the proportion of women aged fifteen to twenty-four who had married before the age of fifteen was 2.7 per cent.[19] The low proportion of early marriages suggests that when family laws do not restrict individual choice, as in the case of the minimum age for marriage, Iranian families exhibit much more modern behavior than the legal system.

Conservative forces see the rising age of marriage as a source of sexual promiscuity, which has become an odd feature of life in the Islamic Republic. To save youth from what the government considers moral corruption, it has adopted various policies to promote marriage, from loans to pay for marriage ceremonies to low-cost housing (*Maskan Mehr*, literally "housing for love"), to government staged mass marriage ceremonies, but to no avail. The age at first marriage has been rising and Iranian youth are having a hard time forming families.[20]

There are three causes of the marriage crisis, namely demographic, economic, and legal. The demographic factor is a consequence of the high fertility of the early 1980s, as shown in Figure 4, when Iran experienced a baby boom. The children of that baby boom reached marriage age by the late 1990s, but the larger cohort of women of that generation did so about five years ahead of their male counterparts. This is because the age gap that still prevailed in the 1990s matched the larger cohort of women with an older but smaller pre-boom cohort of men.

To show the extent of the marriage crisis over time, Figure 8 takes this age gap as fixed and depicts the age-imbalance in the marriage market as the ratio of men aged twenty-five to twenty-nine to women aged twenty to twenty-four. According to this figure, during the past several decades there has been a "male shortage," with roughly four men of marriage-age for every five women. This ratio reached a low of 0.76 in 2005, at which time it began to increase. The 1390 (2011) census registered an imbalance of only 5 per cent in favor of men. The force of this imbalance has been lessened by the adjustments in the marriage market that, as shown above in Figure 6, reduced the age-gap of the more recently formed couples. Interestingly, the future looks very different from the past. Starting about 2013, the imbalance in the marriage market has turned in favor of women; a female shortage is forming as men of marriage age begin to outnumber women. The consequences of this change are difficult to predict, but it is likely to lower the age at marriage while improving the bargaining position of women in marriage.

The economic factors stem from the inability of young people to start independent families. Young men are increasingly unemployed, in part because of their cohort size, which makes it hard for them to find jobs and get married.[21] They are also unable to secure housing (to rent or own) because of the high cost of housing relative to income, a phenomenon that is common to oil-rich countries where oil incomes raise the price of real estate. The legal factor is the result of changes in family law that were hastily introduced after the revolution. The 1967 Family Protection Law was suspended and replaced with the

Figure 8: Imbalance in the Marriage Market: Ratio of Men (25–29) to Women (20–24)

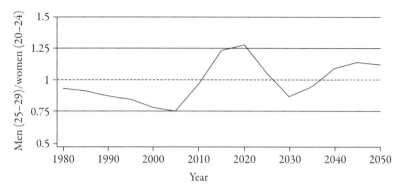

Source: Author's calculations using data from United Nations, "World Population Prospects", 2012.

Shari'a, which was not uniformly interpreted, leaving young people, women in particular, unsure about what they faced in marriage and in case of divorce. The 1967 Family Protection Law and its 1975 revisions had given women rights in marriage and in divorce that they had been denied under the *Shari'a* laws and the interpretation of those laws then in force. For example, it took away men's right to unilateral divorce and replaced it with a more equal treatment. Equality was also extended to child custody in case of divorce. Because these rights were replaced with religious decrees that declared the *Shari'a* the basis of family laws, rather than with new laws, women became much less certain of what to expect from marriage.[22]

As a result of this legal uncertainty, women chose to either postpone marriage or demand hefty bonds in the form of *mahrieh* (an option for the property, a sum of money, or an amount of gold that the woman could claim at any time).[23] The rising size of the *mahrieh* is a direct result of this uncertainty. One of the ways in which the government has tried to lower the cost of marriage has been to put caps on the *mahreih*, again to no avail. Instead, the government recently declared that it will no longer prosecute men for claims for *mahrieh* of over a certain amount (about 100 gold coins worth approximately ten years of a teacher's salary).

In February 2013, after six years of wrangling between the government, the parliament, and the Guardian Council, and objections from many women activists, the Family Protection Law of 1391 (2013) was passed. Although it has settled some of the uncertainty regarding marriage and divorce, in some respects, women activists see it as a step backward. In particular, they object to its controversial articles that recognize and permit polygamy, though, as under the 1975 law, it makes obtaining a second wife conditional on the first wife's approval. In 2010, only 2.9 per cent of married women were in a polygamous relationship.[24]

Youth

The tribulations of Iranian youth, as with youth in the Arab world, have become a hallmark of the social and economic failures of these societies.[25] Unusually high rates of unemployment and long periods of waiting between leaving school and finding their first job have been identified as the root causes of social malaise in these societies. Youth live in families and their unhappiness quickly spreads to the rest of the family. In fact, the proportion of Iranian youth who live with their parents has doubled in the last two decades.[26] The size of the youth population has been growing at a very rapid rate, thanks to the baby boom of the early 1980s, as noted earlier. Between the censuses of 2006 and 2011 the population of the age group twenty-five to thirty-four grew by 4 per cent per year, three times the growth rate of the total population.

The ratio of youth to adults has been exceptionally high in Iran.[27] Figure 9 shows that Iran's youth (fifteen to twenty-nine) have outnumbered the adults

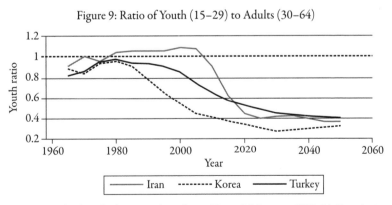

Figure 9: Ratio of Youth (15–29) to Adults (30–64)

Source: Author's calculations; data from United Nations, "World Population Prospects," 2012.

(aged thirty to sixty-four) in the last decade, something that did not happen in South Korea or neighboring Turkey, which are included in the graph for comparison. All three countries had similar ratios in the 1970s, but diverged afterwards. Korea experienced the most rapid decline in this ratio after 1980 followed by Turkey a decade later, while in Iran the ratio increased and stayed above 1:1 until well into the twenty-first century. Looking forward to the next decade, Iran is expected to experience an even faster decline than Korea in the ratio of youth to adults, to around 0.4:1 by 2020.

The high ratio of youth to adult population implies that in recent years Iran's youth have faced a very unfavorable labor market condition. Figure 10 shows the ratio of those who enter the labor market in a given year (proxied by the age group twenty to twenty-four) and those who retire (proxied by the age group sixty to sixty-four). This ratio recently peaked at 6:1, a number that is so high that it is very rarely observed, as the comparison with the South Korea in this graph shows. The same ratio in Korea peaked at 4:1 and at a time that its economy was growing very fast and was able to absorb increasing number of workers. Iran's economy has been anemic in terms of job growth for the past decade, causing high rates of youth unemployment.[28]

Figure 10: Imbalance in the Labour Market: the Relative Size of the Entering to Exiting Labour Cohorts in Iran and South Korea

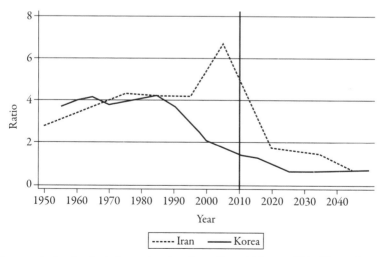

Source: Author's calculations using data from United Nations, "World Population Prospects," 2012.

Figure 11: Imbalance in the Labour Market: the Relative Size of the Entering to Exiting Labour Cohorts in Jordan and Turkey

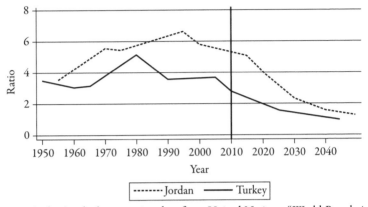

Source: Author's calculations using data from United Nations, "World Population Prospects", 2012.

The challenges youth face in the labor market are directly transmitted to their families. Iranian families have become the unwilling social protection system for the losers of the country's ill functioning education and labor markets. A majority of youth now lives at home, a nearly 50 per cent increase from a generation ago. Figure 12 shows the proportion of men and women in their twenties who live with their parents, which for men has increased from 47 per cent to 73 per cent and for women from 20 per cent to 48 per cent. The inability of youth to find a job and live independently puts pressure on the older cohorts of parents and transmits the pain of unemployment to their extended families.

Concluding Remarks

The Iranian family has gone through a fundamental transformation, which is best characterized by change in the lives of the average woman. The average woman today has one-third as many children as her mother and is more than three times as educated. The family is more balanced in terms of the bargaining power of the husband and wife, and, as a result, spends more of its resources on investing in its children than ever before. The development economics literature considers these changes as pre-conditions for sustained economic growth. In underdeveloped countries, the average parents have

Figure 12. Young People (20–29) Living with their Parents (percentage)

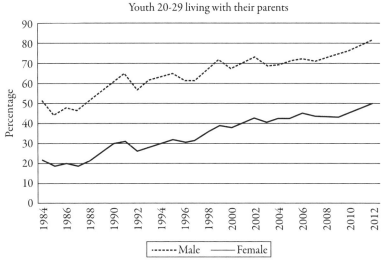

Youth 20-29 living with their parents

Source: Author's calculations from household expenditure and income survey data files, Statistical Center of Iran, various years.

many children and expect to benefit from their children as extra hands in home production or as a source of old-age security. In developed countries parents have few children, invest heavily in them, and leave them with more physical and human capital than they themselves enjoyed. In this chapter, I have argued that this reversal in the direction of intergenerational transfer has already occurred in Iran, boding well for Iran's future.

There are a few caveats, however. Although lower fertility and higher education have resulted in more balanced families, women are still largely cut off from opportunities to earn an income on parity with men. Women account for only one-fourth of the income-earning labor force, and their rate of unemployment is twice that of men. One out of two college educated women who seek jobs is unemployed. Since earned income is correlated with bargaining power, the low participation of Iranian women in market work means that the average family still has a distance to go in its path to modernization. Barriers to women's employment are in part related to the lack of appropriate jobs for women, but there is also a strong ideological barrier. In recent years, after winning some ground on the legal side—for example, the amended family law requiring men to seek their wife's permission before taking a second wife—

women now have to contend with a conservative push-back on a wide front. There has been discussion in the parliament of limiting women's access to public universities; some universities have decided on their own to block women's access to certain fields and subjects.

The strongest challenge to women's status is now the decision in 2014 to suspend the family planning program, which not only provided women from poorer families with free access to reproductive rights, health and contraception, it also offered many women who live in conservative communities the necessary moral support to use birth control. While it is not yet clear how far the government will go to prevent women from limiting the number of pregnancies, the government has begun offering financial incentives to women who go for a third or fourth child.

Can government policies turn back the clock on the transformation and modernization of the Iranian family? It is hard to believe decisions regarding the size of the family that have deep implications on the relationship between husbands and wives and between parents and their children will be susceptible to transient financial benefits. To the extent that the economic-demographic theory of growth discussed in this chapter, which places the family at the center of the economic growth process, is valid, policies to increase fertility are anti-growth. While increasing the size of the population may seem to raise Iran's stature in the region, it reduces the country's ability to grow economically, thus undermining its ambition to become a key regional power in the Middle East.

7

THE STATE OF HUMAN RIGHTS IN IRAN

Mahmood Monshipouri and *Mehdi Zakerian*

Post-Khomeini Iran has been marked by pragmatic impulses and practical considerations, displaying shifting conditions conducive to the development of human rights. Driven by top-down forces of economic and political liberalization during the administrations of Rafsanjani and Khatami, reform-minded Iranians experienced a sense of empowerment amid the expansion of a vibrant civil society sensitive to human rights, an unprecedented development in their contemporary history. The contested 2009 presidential elections, however, have dampened that spirit by starkly revealing the formation of a new power structure, namely an alliance between the Revolutionary Guard and the ruling clerics, aimed at controlling the main levers of power and marginalizing reformist agendas.[1] As economic and security-oriented realities have taken center stage, the hopes of Iranian reformers for progress on human rights have been waylaid.

For much of their contemporary history, Iranians have borne witness to the ebb and flow of human rights.[2] The struggle for reform and modernization at the turn of the twentieth century in Iran, dubbed the "constitutional revolution" (1905–1911), included all social strata and classes, and signaled the national aspirations of the vast majority of Iranians for democratic reform. But the collective hopes for democracy were dashed by the British- and US-engineered coup in 1953 that deposed Iran's popularly elected Prime Minister Mohammad Mossadeq.

In the ensuing years, the Pahlavi regime ushered in a new era of repressive rule and politics, with the Shah acting above the law, and his monarchical regime sweeping away institutionalized democratic processes. The 1979 Iranian Revolution, while seeking such egalitarian goals as social justice, income equality, and human rights, did not fulfill its promise.

Much has been said about the political and international aspects of the revolution, with a view toward explaining the root causes of a nationwide revolt that toppled the Pahlavi dynasty. Several key factors—including systematic repression, widespread corruption, and disruptively fast-paced modernization—led to the momentous downfall of the Shah's regime. The post-revolutionary transformation has spurred a rigorous debate among the region's scholars over what interpretation of democratic reform and cultural politics will shape Iran's human rights in the future. In recent years, the country's moral and political divide has further deepened, with the ruling elite facing both normative and institutional challenges.

The revolutionary fervor of the late 1970s, however, encountered wide-ranging challenges, as new social, economic, and political problems compounded the Islamic Republic's attempt to advance its ideological goals. A population explosion, the Iran-Iraq War (1980–1988), and the emigration of some three million Iranians created a host of problems that undermined the ruling elites' revolutionary vision.[3]

While the First Republic (1979–1989) following the revolution became engulfed in revenge, purges, and the war with Iraq, the second Republic (1989–1997) under President Akbar Hashemi Rafsanjani initiated reconstruction and economic liberalization, a period marked largely by pragmatism and economic advancement. The third Republic (1997–2005) under President Mohammad Khatami pitted theocracy against democracy in a move toward political liberalization from the top. By 1999, Iran began to actively comply with the International Covenant on Civil and Political Rights as well as the International Covenant on Economic, Social and Cultural Rights, both of which were ratified by the Shah's regime. Moreover, under the Khatami administration, Iran ratified the UN Convention on the Rights of the Child and the International Convention on the Elimination of All Forms of Racial Discrimination; the Convention Relating to the Status of Refugees, as well as the allied Protocol Relating to the Status of Refugees.

The reform process under Khatami met with considerable resistance from conservative actors, factions, and foundations, giving rise to the emergence of neoconservatives such as President Mahmoud Ahmadinejad. The result was that the steady political evolution toward the emergence of a liberal, democratic republic was effectively blocked. Ahmadinejad's return to populist and revolutionary ideologies, policies, and programs upended the reformist agenda, putting it on the backburner for some time to come.

The aftermath of the 2009 re-election of Ahmadinejad shook the foundation of the Islamic Republic, as a new wave of street protests, known as the "Green Movement," posed a homegrown and popular threat to the country's power structure. The reach of social networks and digital communication had dramatically undermined the legitimacy of the "external enemy" argument as a means of sidestepping intractable internal problems. The ensuing crackdown on journalists, rights activists, and lawyers in a bid to stifle dissent led to a pervasive climate of fear, and lingering tensions and factions within the regime.

This chapter seeks to examine the root causes of human rights violations and progress in Iran since 1989. Although it is difficult to distinguish all causes, the interrelatedness of factors makes the study of human rights an intriguing yet daunting task. Identifying one category of human rights violations as the key source of human rights abuses is woefully inadequate. Rather, we argue that protecting and promoting human rights in Iran involves a multipronged strategy aimed at simultaneously overcoming domestic, individual, and systemic barriers. In addition to teasing out these factors, we contextualize three periods of social change in post-Khomeini Iran—namely, reconstruction and pragmatism under Rafsanjani, political reform under Khatami, and populism and the return to revolutionary principles under Ahmadinejad—in an attempt to demonstrate the key factors that have influenced the state of human rights.

To set the stage for analyzing human rights conditions in Iran, we first turn to Islamic perspectives on human rights with a view toward evaluating Iran's theocratic orientation. In doing so, we may understand the governing elites' interests and whether such leaders use their political power to advance human rights or, instead, act solely in the interest of the regime. We will examine the policies and practices of the three administrations of post-Khomeini Iran to determine whether they have positively or adversely affected the state of human rights. Finally, we argue the need to fight for human rights in Iran, underscoring the importance of education, international organizations such as the United Nations, and local and regional non-governmental organizations (NGOs) in fostering the interaction between internal and external political dynamics.

Human rights and Islamic views

The issue of whether human rights should remain independent of conservative religious influences, such as scriptural revelations and literal interpretations of the *Qu'ran*, lies at the heart of the ongoing disagreement between Islamic and Western scholars.[4] While some observers call for synergy between religion and human rights, others insist that secularism, premised solely on reason and natural law, provides the most defensible platform for promoting human rights.[5] The debate over the metaphysical grounds of human rights, however, remains unresolved. The issue is further complicated by the politicization of the human rights agenda.[6] Still others have underlined the need to legitimate the culture of human rights in the historical context of the Muslim world, while accommodating a range of different reasons for belief in universal human rights.[7]

The discourse over modernity and Islamic feminism and how they relate to human rights sheds light on the broader analysis of the Muslim world's dynamic sociocultural and political contexts. The most noteworthy facet of social change in the Muslim world has been the political and legal struggle over who controls modernity, rationality, and culture, and whose interests are being served in that struggle.

Some experts have advocated a major epistemic shift—from a juridical to a theological-ontological status of human personhood—as a key condition for the development of human rights discourse in the Muslim world. A point of departure for these experts is their espousal of a foundational theory of human rights based on pluralistic features of Islam, as manifested in its juridical-ethical discourses. Abdulaziz Sachedina, for example, argues that Islamic religious thought is based on the human ability to know right from wrong. Through God's endowment for all of humanity, each and every individual possesses a nature (*fitra*)—that is, the receptacle for intuitive reason—as well as human dignity (*karam*), which enables humans to perform obligations as God's creatures and relate to one another as members of the universal human community. These intrinsic and universal properties together with divine revelation guide human beings to a spiritual and moral wellbeing.[8]

Increasingly, however, debates around human rights have been embedded within broader political, economic, and social debates in the transnational

Muslim world.[9] While describing the top-down control of culture as the main impediment to free expression, some have argued that the dogmatic and exclusive stance that the official interpreters of Islam claim poses a great threat to political rights. Using political power to reinforce their religious authority, these so-called "guardians" use religion as an instrument for obtaining broader political and material goals. "Marrying religious and political power is dangerous," writes Anthony Tirado Chase, "because it necessarily militates against pluralism and democracy by virtue of monopolizing religious-political power in the hands of a small group who claim access to 'truth' as a basis of their rule."[10] The three administrations of post-Khomeini Iran have grappled with reconciling Islamic traditions, principles, and practices with modern standards of human rights, each in its own unique way while facing multiple challenges.

A pragmatic republic: Rafsanjani, 1989–1997

In the aftermath of Khomeini's death, factional infighting and competition flourished. Through a national referendum in 1989, the post of prime minister was abolished and was replaced with a popularly elected president as head of the government who did not need to be approved by the *Majlis* (parliament). At the time, this was taken to mean that the *velayate-e faqih* (guardianship of the jurist) would no longer dominate the political sphere. Consequently, the president emerged as the most potent figure in the state. This transformation appeared to mark the transition from the consolidation phase to the reconstruction phase of the regime. The radical leadership of the revolution lost their majority in the fourth *Majlis* in the April and May 1992 elections. With their defeat, the country's revolutionary ideals became a much lower priority. Rafsanjani's most visible impact on the economy came in 1992 when he removed virtually all barriers to foreign investment in Iran, including regulations that limited foreign ownership of industries and firms to 49 per cent of shares and capital investments.

Iran remained officially neutral in the first Persian Gulf War of 1991. The Islamic Republic's relations with most Arab states remained poor, and the prospects of improving ties with the United States and the West more broadly were dim. Then, in September 1992, four Kurdish opposition leaders were assassinated at the Mikonos Café in Berlin. The German media published legal findings demonstrating the involvement of Iranian Minister of Intelligence Ali Fallahian in these terrorist acts. In March 1996, a German court issued an arrest warrant for Ali Fallahian for his role in the Mikonos

Café assassinations. In April 1997, the court asserted that the government of Iran had pursued a deliberate policy of eliminating the regime's opponents living outside Iran, including the opposition Kurdish Democratic Party of Iran (KDPI). The judge also implicated other senior officials of the Iranian government in the Mikonos Café murders.

On the domestic front, President Rafsanjani broadened women's activities in public arenas. In fact, Faezeh Hashemi Rafsanjani, daughter of the president, played an important role in bringing women into sport. Subsequently, Iranian women's participation in major sporting events, such as soccer, tennis, skiing, and volleyball, opened up a new opportunity for women with broad and lasting impact on other Islamic nations in the region. Since 1995, professional women's sports in Iran have developed at a rapidly accelerating rate. Rallying for Iran to be represented at international sporting competitions for women, Faezeh Hashemi Rafsanjani has persistently pushed for broadening women's participation in all sports.[11]

On the local level, however, the real challenge facing the Islamic Republic in the mid-1990s was its ailing economy. Reform of foreign trade and correction of the exchange rate were crucial elements of Rafsanjani's liberalization program. During Rafsanjani's presidency, real GDP grew by an average annual rate of 7 per cent. Investment increased from 11 per cent of GDP in 1989/90 to 14 per cent in 1992/93. But corruption and the mismanagement of resources complicated and inhibited the state's liberalization programs. The rentier nature of the Iranian economy, which resisted sociopolitical pressure from below, strongly discouraged democratization.

The expansion of political liberalization in Iran had been forcibly stunted up to this time. Vigilante attacks and vilification served as a prelude to the prosecution of several magazines and newspaper editors and staff. The press law, passed in 1985, allowed the Ministry of Culture and Islamic Guidance to ban any publication that insulted religious elites. Subsequently, the courts shut down many periodicals. The government repeatedly used the press law to charge journalists with espionage when many had been carrying out routine journalistic practices. Ali Akbar Saidi-Sirjani, a prominent writer and social critic, died in detention under mysterious circumstances in November 1994. The works of the best-known Iranian film directors, including Bahram Beizai and Mohsen Makhmalbaf, were frequently censored.

In 1994, public discontent over economic and political conditions resulted in riots in several Iranian cities. Violent confrontations between demonstrators and security forces were reported in Tehran, Tabriz, Zahedan, Qazvin, and Najafabad. Officially sponsored vigilantism became widespread in 1995 as the militant organization Ansar-e Hizbollah directed attacks against critics of state corruption, such as Abdol-Karim Soroush. Domestic human rights organizations—including the Parliamentary Human Rights Committee, the Organization for Defending Victims of Violence, and the Human Rights Commission—were not allowed to operate openly.

In the March 1996 parliamentary elections, the Council of Guardians, a twelve member council that vets presidential candidates, excluded nearly half of the more than 5,000 candidates for parliament on the basis of discriminatory and arbitrary criteria. This practice obstructed access to the political process and citizens' freedom of choice. In the same month, Maurice Copithorne, the UN human rights rapporteur, painted a bleak picture of the human rights situation in Iran, arguing that the social climate in Iran had become less tolerant.[12] The UN report pointed to the fact that the regime harassed and violated the rights of Baha'is as a religious minority and continued to assassinate dissidents living abroad.

Toward achieving political reforms: Khatami, 1997–2005

In recent times, it can be argued that one of the most encouraging administrations for human rights was that of President Mohammad Khatami (1997–2005). By using an Islamic civil society paradigm, President Khatami provided a progressive view of Islam and its rich traditions. He drew a bridge between the civilized societies of the West and the great achievements of Islamic societies. Khatami brought greater freedom and tolerance not just to the political scene, but to Iranian society as a whole.

Khatami's landslide victory (winning almost 70 per cent of the vote) was a firm rebuke to the hardline clerics who had dominated Iranian politics since the 1979 Revolution. Perhaps the most striking facet of the 1997 election was Khatami's overwhelming support from both youth and women. In gaining the youth vote, Khatami succeeded in winning the trust of a generation that had not been born at the time of the revolution. Moreover, although no general consensus on the meaning and feasibility of civil society emerged, there appeared to be a broad agreement that civil society could solve many of the country's social and political problems.[13] This expansion of modern Islamic civil society, including the growth of professional associations and trade organizations, posed new challenges to the hardliners who had alienated large segments of Iranian society.[14]

Khatami underplayed the distinction between Muslims and non-Muslims, reinforcing the religious minorities' sense of solidarity and their interest in their religion and ethnic heritage. Khatami frequently welcomed delegates from the Assyrian community, among other religious minority groups, into the *Majlis*. He emphasized how Iran and its cultural and geopolitical interests have equally affected all of its nationals, irrespective of their religion, while at the same time underscoring the need to prepare proper and humane living conditions for the followers of all religions.

Khatami's views were in keeping with those experts of religious minorities in Iran who have strongly advocated a society in which citizens are identified not on the basis of religion, but rather one that is predicated on pluralism.[15] Others have noted, however, that despite his conciliatory words, the plight of religious minorities under Khatami failed to improve in any meaningful way. This may have been a result of Khatami's inability to rein in conservative clerics, who largely controlled the *Majlis* in his second term. The fact remains that he had pledged certain legislative initiatives that, if they had been enacted, might have been helpful to Iran's religious minorities.[16]

Threatened by reform, pluralism, and the expansion of civil society, the radicals who served as enforcers for conservative clerics changed track, expanding their strategy of defamation in dealing with internal reformers to include "disappearance" and murder—a violent approach reminiscent of the killings of Iranian dissidents abroad. These tactics included calculated attacks on major political and religious figures. Such attacks took the forms of verbal and physical assaults on media members, frequent and violent disruptions, the cancellation of public lectures (such as by philosopher Abdol-Karim Soroush), vandalizing the offices of opposition media and organizations, and beating up their leaders.[17]

President Mohammad Khatami's record was often overshadowed by the intense power struggle between those who demanded change and those who defended the status quo—that is, the struggle between reformers and hardline conservatives. Nowhere were such power struggles more evident than in the debate over whose vision of an Islamic society would prevail. Another tension that characterized Khatami's years was the perceived incompatibility between global and local paradigms. Prominent Iranian intellectuals and journalists began to challenge the underlying concepts of Islamic governance. Many newspapers emerged and were subsequently closed down, and many journalists and editors were imprisoned or called before what became known as the Press Court.[18]

During Khatami's reign, the judiciary, which was accountable to Supreme Leader Ali Khamenei rather than the elected president, was at the center of many human rights violations. Many abuses were carried out by the so-called "parallel institutions" (*nahad-e movazi*)—that is, the undercover intelligence agents and paramilitary groups who violently attacked peaceful protesters, students, writers and reformist politicians, and operated illegal and secret prisons and interrogation centers. Groups such as Ansar-e Hizbollah and the Basij are examples of such organizations.[19]

The operation of these parallel institutions alongside formal government institutions demonstrated the lack of real control in the executive branch. The serial murder case of secular dissidents after President Khatami's election in 1997 illustrated the extent of the struggle between moderates and hardliners in Iran. Security agents assassinated five prominent dissidents, beginning on 22 November 1998, with the stabbing of Dariush Forouhar and his wife Parvaneh, who ran a small opposition party. In the following weeks, outspoken secular writers Majid Sharif, Mohammad Jafar Pouyandeh, and Mohammad Mokhtari disappeared; their bodies were later found dumped on the outskirts of Tehran. Their killers were captured, but the closed trials of these serial murderers led to vague verdicts since there was no admission that they were sent on these missions by more powerful superiors. On 27 January 2001, a judge handed down the sentences: several "rogue" agents from the intelligence ministry were sentenced to death or to life imprisonment.

From his election in 1997, President Khatami was successful in creating political and cultural environments highly conducive to women's participation. During his two-term presidency, women were empowered in both the media and government-approved NGOs and civil society networks. Before this time, only women who were known to be ideologically loyal to the Islamic Republic, strictly religious and thus faithful to the principle of *velayat-e faqih* (which underpinned the supreme jurisprudent's right to rule Iran) could create an organizational structure for the promotion of women's rights. Khatami's policies allowed women who sought equality with men under the law to organize and make their dream of running non-profit organizations to enhance women's rights a reality.[20]

Acutely aware of women's role in his election as the country's president, Khatami appointed a woman, Masumeh Ebtekar, as his vice president for environmental protection and appointed Zahra Shojai as his women's affairs adviser. In his second administration, he chose Zahra Rahnavard as his senior adviser on cultural affairs. Khatami also appointed Jameileh Kadivar, the wife of Minister of Culture and Islamic Guidance Attaollah Mohajerani, as his special adviser on press affairs. Ms. Rahnavard was later appointed as chancellor of Al-Zahra University, a women's institution; she became the first woman in the Islamic Republic to head a university.[21] Rahnavard noted that the moral guidance of Islam can be presented through democratic methods. As an Islamic reformer, she emphasized a more dynamic interpretation of *Shari'a* known as *fiqh-e pouya* (dynamic jurisprudence).

Struggles for women's rights

In its early years, the Islamic Republic attempted to reinforce women's domesticity by confining their space—and hence their role—to home. Since the reform era, 1997–2005, Iranian women have fought to reconstruct their gender role by building their social capital in both private and public spheres. In 2006, according to Nayereh Tohidi, the "One Million Signatures" campaign, which was designed to help repeal discriminatory laws against women in Iran, propelled the women's rights movement to the public consciousness. This mission of the campaign was neither overthrowing the government, nor seizing state power. Rather, its activists aimed to transform the dominant cultural, socioeconomic, and political relations of Iran to achieve greater equality. "Women's struggle in today's Iran," Tohidi writes, "is primarily a cultural and legal one, which is fought in a historical context rather than a battlefield."[22]

Women's participation in sports became a dramatic area of success, involving more women and girls than in the pre-revolutionary period. Barred from being spectators at men's soccer matches, women broke into a stadium in a politically significant 1997 event. In 2003, one soccer club announced it would admit female spectators. Women embraced and were encouraged by such social openings. By 1996, women's share of the total economically active population had reached 12.7 per cent; as well as 11.7 per cent of the urban economically active population; 11.2 per cent of the urban employed population; and 16.4 per cent of total public-sector wage earners. Of the 271,565 unemployed women, 53 per cent were urban and 47 per cent rural.[23]

By 2003, females made up 44 per cent of professionals in the field of education. Women's share of health services workers was 39.3 per cent across the country, though it was higher in urban areas (40.4 per cent) than in the rural areas (33 per cent). Ministries with relatively low female participation included Culture and Higher Education (perhaps surprisingly only 20 per cent female, given women's access to education), Labor and Social Security

(11.3 per cent), Agriculture (7.2 per cent), Development and Housing (13.7 per cent), and Culture and Islamic Guidance (17.8 per cent).[24]

In the first two years of Khatami's presidency, the *Majlis* enacted several laws significant to women, including a provision for readjusting the value of the *mahr* (monetary sum the husband pledges to his wife in the marriage contract, which is payable whenever his wife claims it) in keeping with inflation. A law was also passed that permitted female civil servants to retire after twenty years of service. Between 1956 and 1966, the female literacy rate in Iran had increased from 8 per cent to 17.9 per cent. In 1971, some 25.5 per cent of women were literate. Just before the revolution, 35 per cent were literate, and, by the late twentieth century, the rate had reached 74 per cent.[25] Today, Iranian women are among the most educated and accomplished in the Muslim world.

In the same period, junior secondary-level enrollment increased from 36 per cent to 43.5 per cent female, and senior secondary-level soared from 39.6 per cent to 45.4 per cent female. UN data suggests, however, that educational enrollments, particularly at secondary and tertiary levels, continue to favor males, and that the illiteracy rate is considerably higher among females than males.[26]

The rise of feminism

Islamic and secular women alike began to reject their traditional confinement to the home, and moved toward participation in the public sphere and socioeconomic activities. In doing so, they significantly contributed to the development of a broader civil society in Iran. Many NGOs have actively promoted women's rights in both rural and urban areas. The Iranian Islamic Women's Institute of Iran, established in 1992 and headed by Azam Taleghani, is one such NGO. Its aim is to improve women's status by providing literacy classes, educating women on their rights, offering them free legal advice, and bolstering their financial independence with training in commercial activities such as carpet weaving, pottery works, and sewing.[27]

Secular women have also created solidarity networks for mutual assistance. Lawyers and jurists provide legal advice. Through informal groups, they organize debates on such topics as *hijab*, motherhood, employment, feminism, and activism. Women's press organizations, including *Zanan, Farzaneh, Payam-e-Hajar, Zan-e Ruz, Huquq-e Zanan, Zan* and *Zan-e Emruz*, to which secular women have regularly contributed, have provided a valuable forum for social and political protest.

The increasing number of third-generation feminists—who emphasize rationality and dynamic jurisprudence over textual reinterpretations—is bound to expand the ranks of opposition reformers. There is always tension when the new and old collide, and disagreements among feminists (first, second, and third generation) will naturally continue, but the potential costs for expressing themselves and organizing for their demands have become less severe.

The more open social climate of the Khatami years, along with the strengthening of civil society and the expansion of freedom of expression, allowed secular feminists to participate in addressing women's issues and concerns. Shirin Ebadi, the 2003 Nobel Peace Prize winner, operated in a far less restrictive environment than women in the earlier years of the movement. Some observers reject the argument that the Islamic Republic faces serious gender problems and that drastic action must be taken to avoid a gender crisis. Others maintain that Iranian society faces severe gender problems that, if not addressed properly, will adversely affect the vitality of civil society.

Violent opposition to social change

The student protests of 8–14 July 1999, motivated mainly by the closure of the daily *Salaam*—a reformist and left-leaning Islamic newspaper that had begun to release vitally important information regarding the fall 1998 serial killings of secular reformists, including writers and journalists—made clear that students were willing to voice their dissent over the suppression of the media. Controlled by the conservatives, the Press Court had banned several pro-reform dailies, including *Tous*, *Jame'h*, *Salaam*, *Khordad*, and *Norouz*.

In one issue (September 1999), *Neshat* called for an end to the death penalty, while questioning Iran's law of retribution (*qasas*). The daily suggested that Iranian law replace "using violence" against criminals with the "modern" approach of reforming rather than punishing criminals. It also published an open letter to the supreme leader from Yadollah Sahabi, an opposition leader and one of the founders of the Freedom Movement of Iran, to refrain from showing any favoritism toward conservatives, and to dissociate himself from the so-called pressure groups—a euphemism for the bands of street thugs who terrorized their opponents. The subsequent closure of *Neshat* set off a new battle between the reformers and the conservatives, with the former arguing that the closure lacked a legal basis.

In the absence of legitimate political parties, and given the myriad obstacles it faced, the press became not only a symbol of the struggle against the conservatives but also a driving force behind the country's political development. In many respects, the press—especially those supporting reform—took the place of political parties in Iran, a development that alarmed the right-wing clergy and their supporters.

The students' demands—transparency, accountability, integrity, and fairness in the government—reflected broader societal demands. Many experts held that they signified the cumulative resentment of the public, not just against the suppression of the press, but more broadly against the restriction of other fundamental civil liberties and rights—and, as such, were not restricted to the views of university students alone. Others argued that Iranian politics, highly complex and evolving, had to come to terms with the country's new political realities. The religio-political establishment characterized the demonstrations as foreign-inspired and, to avoid imminent political chaos, stopped the rallies, successfully sabotaging the trend toward political liberalization and social reform.

Another perspective held that the student protests, which revolved around the curbs on press freedoms, were hijacked by hardliners determined to provoke violence in order to prove that President Khatami was incapable of maintaining order. Perhaps the most obvious message to emerge from these protests was the existence of a crisis of legitimacy and confidence in the ruling conservative establishment. The ensuing pro-regime demonstration, organized by the conservative establishment to counter student protests, failed to restore the public confidence.

The return to Islamic principles and populism: Ahmadinejad, 2005–2013

By 2005, the reformist camp had all but disappeared from the Iranian political scene. The regime's power base had shifted in favor of the militaristic, conservative, and revolutionary camp, which included clerics such as Ayatollah Mohammad Taqi Mesbahe Yazdi and members of the security and intelligence organizations, especially the Revolutionary Guard and the Basij. Today, these groups still have enormous influence over the *Majlis* and the office of the president.

The victory of Mahmood Ahmadinejad as the new president of the Islamic Republic meant the return of Islamic populism to the forefront of Iranian politics. Despite their flaws, the final results of the Iranian elections demonstrated that reformists had essentially failed to come to grips with broader popular realities. During the Khatami era, a new generation of activists, intellectuals, journalists, writers, and lawyers had emerged, who were non-violent and organized, and who had operational strategy and style. They tended to support the buildup of "social" or "soft" power that relied heavily on popular consensus and peaceful methods of power struggle and political mobilization.

But economic difficulties gave rise to the return of populism in Iran. Those Iranians who participated in the elections sent a strong signal to Iranian politicians that there were serious cultural and economic gaps in society and that the principles of civil and political rights were secondary to economic security. This is no different from the way in which voters have traditionally acted in Europe and the United States—"voting with their pocketbooks." As in the rest of the world, economic issues proved to be a deciding factor in the Iranian elections.

The cultural gap between reformers and the broader popular perspective stems from the fact that Islamic cultural traditions have always placed social justice above civil or political rights, hence Ahmadinejad's key slogan: "Islam without justice is not Islam." It is important to bear in mind that the focus of religion is not on human rights, but on ethical teachings, duties, and social justice. In the case of Iran, where nearly 29 per cent of the population lived below the poverty line and where in 2006, some 70 per cent of the economy was state controlled, liberal democracy failed to resonate deeply with the Iranian masses.[28]

Human Rights Watch has argued that Iran's judiciary, which has been implicated in many cases of human rights abuses, is demonstrably unable to conduct an impartial investigation into serious violations.[29] The organization, along with other human rights organizations such as Amnesty International, expressed grave concern at the persistent crisis of accountability at the highest levels of the Ahmadinejad administration, which called into question the legitimacy and credibility of the government. Human Rights Watch asserted that it is imperative to establish a serious independent inquiry to determine if these new ministers were among the perpetrators of human rights violations.

Some experts offer a more balanced perspective on the progress of human rights during this time. Iranians, especially in rural areas, saw some improvements in their basic socioeconomic rights, including access to water, healthcare, and education. Evidence points to the fact that access to water and electricity has improved in rural areas and that improving access to medical services in Iran has resulted in a decline in child mortality rates.[30] The government also increased access to birth control. In the 1980s, the government developed a policy called the National Birth Control Policy, which provided free contraceptives to married couples via the primary healthcare system.[31]

Iranian women have also benefited from the government's efforts in education. By 2006, the literacy rates for girls ten years and older was 80 per cent.[32]

It should be noted, however, that one of the biggest socioeconomic problems Iran faces is demographic. Iran's population increased from 37 million in 1979 to 78 million in 2012. Population growth has placed a heavy burden on public services, while creating a large pool of surplus labor and a poverty rate of around 18 per cent.[33] Young people continue to present a major social challenge to Iran's governing elites. Almost 60 per cent of today's population is under the age of thirty. High levels of youth unemployment, despite the fact that the majority of this population is well educated, have contributed to frequent social unrest.[34]

The Green Movement

The Green Movement emerged in opposition to the 2009 presidential elections, when massive crowds took to the streets to contest the results. Ahmadinejad was swiftly announced as the winner. Reformist candidates Mir Hossein Mousavi and Mehdi Karroubi were unceremoniously placed under house arrest. In the following months, security forces cracked down on bloggers and human rights activists, journalists, and lawyers. Leading reformers were placed either under house arrest, in jail, or sent into exile. The ongoing crackdown and climate of fear marginalized reform leaders and movements. The increasing parallel power of the Revolutionary Guard and politicization of their functions led to the militarization of the regime and concurrent widespread human rights abuses. The election of Hassan Rouhani as Iran's president in 2013 has raised hopes that human rights conditions will improve (more on this later).

Meanwhile, this increased militarization has ironically exposed internal feuds that were once kept behind the scenes, bringing to the surface major tensions and rifts among Iran's ruling elites. Further confounding any progress on human rights is the lack of a resilient political and constitutional structure necessary for carrying out reform from within. There can be no denying that the Islamic Republic, which came to power in 1979 with the goal of restoring the mantle of moral leadership by combating tyranny and decadence, has increasingly found itself subjected to those same charges.[35]

Ahmed Shaheed, the UN special rapporteur on human rights in Iran, has characterized Iran's human rights situation as one of systematic violations, punctuated with frequent reports of forced confessions, inadequate opportunities for legal defense, and widespread disregard for legal safeguards: "[Iranians] continue to be subjected to harassment, arrest, interrogation and torture, and are frequently charged with vaguely defined national security crimes, which is seemingly meant to erode the front line of human rights defense in the country."[36] Shaheed has also highlighted a "culture of impunity" within the Iranian judiciary. These accounts corroborate the fate of Sattar Beheshti, an Iranian blogger who died on 3 November 2012, several days after being arrested by the Iranian Cyber Police for criticizing the government on Facebook. Reports show that it is highly probable that Beheshti died of injuries sustained due to torture under interrogation.[37]

Moderates' turn: Hassan Rouhani (2013–)

Hassan Rouhani marshaled a stunning victory in Iran's presidential election of 14 June 2013, in which nearly 36.7 million Iranians—roughly 72 per cent of eligible voters—participated. Rouhani managed to gain 18 million votes, approximately 51 per cent of votes cast. Rouhani's victory was a clear protest vote against the Ahmadinejad administration's mismanagement of the economy and, no less important, the deterioration of Iran's relations with the Western world, particularly the escalation of tensions over its nuclear program. Rouhani won overwhelmingly because of the votes of reformists and the moderate electorate. Although the last minute endorsement by former Presidents Rafsanjani and Khatami, respectively known for their centrist and reformist agendas, proved crucial to Rouhani's victory, this was, by all measures, a victory for the pragmatist agenda and mobilizational politics of his supporters in Iran.[38]

Rouhani's support for broader social freedoms, his criticism of the presence of security forces in and wide-ranging social restrictions placed on Iranian society, and more importantly, his strong advocacy for women's rights, gave him a clear advantage as a candidate. In a politically important symbolic gesture, Rouhani pardoned eighty political prisoners on his accession—including a prominent human rights lawyer and activist, Nasrin Sotoudeh, who had been imprisoned following the disputed 2009 presidential elections—prior to his visit to the 2013 UN meetings in New York. This appeared to usher in a climate of relative liberalization under his presidency.[39] Significantly, however, economic insecurity and decay—largely caused by the imposition of economic sanctions by the Western world in reaction to Iran's nuclear program—was a key factor in his victory. Rouhani built his campaign around a moderate and pragmatic course, with an underlying message of regional *détente* and constructive dialogue with the West.

Many international observers have criticized the persistent human rights violations in Iran. Christoph Strässer, Germany's human rights commissioner, has noted that the human rights situation in Iran has not improved under Hassan Rouhani despite his promises. Strässer has called for more pressure on the Iranian regime to observe international standards, given that the Rouhani administration has failed to allow greater freedom of expression and there has been a sharp surge in executions since his election.[40] Similar sentiments were echoed by a report to the UN Human Rights Council, in which Ban Ki-Moon, the general secretary of the United Nations, criticized the frequent use of capital punishment in Iran, while calling for the release of activists, lawyers, journalists and political prisoners, who have been in custody for exercising their rights to free speech and assembly.[41]

"Both offline and online [news] outlets," Ban points out, "continue to face restrictions including closure."[42] Ban goes on to assert that "the new government has not changed its approach regarding the application of the death penalty and seems to have followed the practice of previous administrations, which relied heavily on the death penalty to combat crime."[43]

The extra-judicial house arrest of the 2009 presidential candidates—Mir Hossein Mousavi and Mehdi Karroubi—has continued with no signs of ending it in sight. One critic has argued that Rouhani's mantra that "we want change and transformation" has fallen on the wayside due to his lack of leadership.[44] Rouhani may claim, notes Hadi Ghaemi, the director of the International Campaign for Human Rights in Iran, that "as President he has limited authority, but he has not yet exhausted all his powers... He has put all his eggs in the foreign policy basket, but that has also made him vulnerable. Opponents of his foreign policy are emboldened by their ability to perpetuate domestic repression and will sooner or later undermine his foreign policy too."[45]

With the nuclear deal successfully completed, many observers have noted that Rouhani faces even more significant challenges at home. Rouhani may soon discover that negotiating a nuclear deal was the easier task, given that he will most likely face pressure from both his supporters and opponents in the near future. Not only must he demonstrate that the nuclear deal does indeed improve the economy, he will also have to fulfill his campaign promises of loosening of social restrictions on the population and building a new relationship with the United States in coming years. His hardline opponents, however, will almost certainly be unwilling to allow for progress on either issue in the name of the country's national security.[46] By late 2015, the Islamic Revolutionary Guards Corps (IRGC) had started rounding up journalists, human rights activists and public intellectuals. State security agents, in a nation-wide crackdown on the reformists, had arrested several prominent figures, including Isa Saharkhiz, a well-known journalist, and reformists like Ehsan Mazandarani, the managing editor of the newspaper *Farhikhtegan*, who was arrested on 2 November, 2015 by intelligence agents of the Revolutionary Guards and taken to an unknown location, and Afarin Chitsaz, an actress and newspaper columnist.[47] What this suggests is that the hard-liners, using the intelligence unit of the IRGC, are sending a strong signal that the post-nuclear deal period cannot lead to further relaxation of the political climate.[48] President Rouhani has subsequently criticized these arrests, as his website's report said he had called on the intelligence authorities to stop "toying with terminology" used by the Supreme Leader Ayatollah Khamenei, who had warned of the "enemy's plot to infiltrate the country."[49]

The role of the systemic factors

Human rights in Iran have always been impacted by external actors. Close ties with foreign states have always increased the confidence of Iran's abusive regimes. After the 1979 Revolution, Iran's foreign allies—especially those that had liberated themselves from the yoke of colonialism, such as India, Libya, Syria, and Indonesia, as well as other countries that solely pursued their national interests, like China and Russia—supported Iranian rulers in their attempts to suppress liberal opponents.

Western countries have also proven unreliable friends of human rights advocates in Iran, owing in large part to their inconsistent policies. While human rights are frequently being abused by the Bahraini or Saudi regimes, Western countries, which have avoided criticizing such regimes harshly and directly, have regularly condemned the Syrian government for its human rights violations. Such hypocrisy has not escaped Iranians' notice. Even as the Iranian president travels to New York to attend UN annual meetings, Iranian citizens cannot obtain US visas to visit their own relatives. Moreover, the West's economic sanctions on Iran, some of the toughest economic sanctions ever imposed on a country, have done enormous harm to ordinary Iranians, causing tremendous pain and hardship for the vast majority of the people whose human rights have already been trampled upon.

The threat of regime change via military intervention has proven counter-productive given the country's nationalistic sentiments. An airstrike, such as the one on the Osiraq Iraqi nuclear reactor carried out by the Israeli Air Force in 1981, stands little chance of success in a huge country like Iran that has dispersed its nuclear power plants across its territory. An attempt would also undermine any confidence in an eventual compromise. More notably, in the years following 9/11, the threat of regime change from the Bush administration, which ordered the invasion of two of Iran's neighbors—Afghanistan and Iraq—was employed as a blunt instrument by many of the region's governments seeking to stifle dissent and avert international scrutiny by closing their borders to human rights NGOs and UN monitoring agencies such as the International Atomic Energy Agency.[50]

The Bush administration conducted a propaganda campaign aimed at vilifying Iran on the assumption that Iran was trying to become a nuclear power. The economic sanctions on Iran persuaded Rouhani come to the negotiating table, even as the threat of invasion proved ineffective in holding back a nuclear assembly line. Iranian officials have repeatedly questioned why other nuclear capable countries are not subject to such sanction threats. Iran's leadership has said that they would withdraw from the Non-Proliferation Treaty (NPT) if faced with further military and economic threats. Withdrawal from the NPT is, however, unlikely, since it would prove detrimental to a country where industrial infrastructure has traditionally been heavily dependent on production of machinery and industrial components imported from EU countries.

The nuclear issue will undoubtedly hinder progress on human rights. The international community's focus on preventing the Islamic Republic from becoming a nuclear power has shifted the spotlight away from human rights. Economic sanctions are seen not only as a punishment of those in power but also an existential threat to their political survival. Real or perceived threats account for some of the human rights violations in Iran. Hence, as one expert notes, removing threats—both internal and external—will be essential to improving human rights protection in the future.[51]

The EU started the so-called "critical dialogue" with Iran in December 1992 with the aim of softening Iran's policies on the Middle East peace process, global terrorism, the production of weapons of mass destruction, and human rights. The dialogue was suspended in April 1997 after the Mykonos Café assassinations. The EU resumed talks with Iran in March 1998 after the diplomatic haggling over the Berlin court ended. The EU and Iran re-launched their negotiations as a "constructive dialogue" in July 1998, following President Mohammad Khatami's new policy of *détente* in 1997. The "constructive dialogue" covered such areas of bilateral cooperation as energy, transportation, commerce and investment, narcotics, refugees, and the environment.

The EU has since increased both economic and diplomatic relations with Iran, pledging to tie human rights standards to this process. But ongoing human rights abuses in Iran have clouded Iran-EU relations. In a June 2004 statement, the EU warned Iran that if it failed to rectify the human rights conditions of its citizens, it would be denied the opportunity to sign the Trade and Cooperation Agreement. In December 2002, under pressure from the EU, the Iranian government officially banned stoning to death as a method of punishment for adultery. Australia and Switzerland have now also initiated "human rights dialogue" with Iran, but with no benchmarks made public, it appears unlikely that these initiatives will have any more impact than the dialogue conducted by the EU.[52]

Despite the fact that the UN special rapporteurs on torture and on extrajudicial executions were allowed to visit the country, relations with the United States remained poor, especially after Iran was labeled by President Bush as part of an "axis of evil." The Bush administration, according to Human Rights Watch reports, consistently opposed loans to Iran from international financial institutions such as the IMF. Subsequently, the Obama administration has ratcheted up economic sanctions on Iran. The resumption of several rounds of talks, known as the five-plus-one, have thus far produced no tangible impact on human rights conditions in Iran.

Sanctions have resulted in severe inflation and restricted international banking capabilities, and have also halved its overseas sales of oil—the country's chief export. As a result, the value of Iran's national currency has fallen over the past few years.[53] Even more critical has been the impact of sanctions on the import of agricultural and medical goods, making it impossible to finance such transactions because banks will not extend credit for the sale of any item into Iran.[54]

The role of universities and the press

Universities continue to play a key role in human rights.[55] Activities initiated and organized by Iranian universities, including conducting research and promoting instruction, have been laudable.[56] Their achievements are clearly manifested in the emergence of a new generation of graduates who are motivated to seek a better understanding of democracy, human dignity, fundamental rights, and human rights more generally. Although universities have faced a multitude of barriers—and at times their performance has been stagnant—they and their students nevertheless played a salient role in the human rights agenda throughout the country, especially after the victory of the Islamic Revolution.

The student movement played a central role in the 1999 protests over press censorship as well as the Green Movement, even as it has faced harsh reactions and stagnation since then. Historically, students and the press in Iran have been critical in laying the foundations of democracy. Perhaps the most obvious message to emerge from these protests was the existence of a crisis of legitimacy and a crisis of confidence in the ruling conservative establishment.

The recent increase in the number of self-serving academics has caused further stagnation of human rights research agendas at Iranian universities. A number of university professors, who once were among the staunch supporters of President Khatami, later shifted to a fundamentalist ideology, creating doubts and inconsistencies in academic leadership. Some students came to believe that their teachers were unreliable, since many professors who spoke to the media rehashed—or even justified—government positions on student protests. This discouraged many people from the view of universities as vibrant generators of the ideas, activities, and knowledge necessary for social change.

In time, those professors became part of the regime's propaganda machine, ending the role of universities at the vanguard of progress. Given that universities are meant to serve as a place for free and open public discourse to take shape, this shift illustrated the allure of power and position over national interests and the pursuit of broader human rights. That said, the role of universities more generally in promoting international standards on human rights is crucial, because these institutions play a key role in informing society as well as setting new standards. Although there are very few universities whose focus on the introduction and advancement of human rights is thorough and direct, there is no doubt that their activities in working with the community and other organizations to foster democratic change and promote human rights is essential.

IGOs and NGOs

Undoubtedly, Western pressure on governments in support of NGOs has produced human rights gains. At the same time, the Middle East's engagement with the concepts of human rights is increasingly being shaped by local actors and their lived experience of injustice and repression.[57] That said, a great many international organizations—governmental as well as non-governmental—have a significant influence on the human rights conditions in Iran. Their reporting and supervisory role in protecting and promoting the human rights of Iranian citizens, especially the protection of human rights activists, is extremely important. Periodic and annual reports of NGOs and intergovernmental organizations (IGOs) shine a light on the conditions within states, rendering authorities accountable for indigenous human rights violations. These organizations not only monitor states' conduct, but they also boost people's understanding of human rights by offering technical assistance and instruction. The United Nations has introduced many major projects to Iran's foreign ministry, Tehran University, and the judicial system.

These projects inform Iranian civil society about the critical importance of human rights, but it is also pertinent to note that international organizations' operations inside Iran encounter many obstacles, and are not allowed to work in certain areas.[58] A case in point is the prohibition of regular visits from UN special rapporteurs on human rights. In some areas the technical, legal, and educational assistance of the United Nations has been eliminated altogether over the years. Some NGOs have no office or representatives in Iran, and are not even allowed to visit the country. So, even though their lack of access is a statement in itself, they have limited insight and knowledge of internal conditions in Iran.

Information and communication technologies and social media

Social networks, satellite communication, email, smartphones, and visual and audio media all serve the cause of human rights. Modern information and communication technologies (ICTs) have made it possible to share ideas, experiences, and viewpoints with individuals across the globe. These tools, coupled with social media, such as Facebook and Twitter, have increased the speed, volume, and intensity of the distribution of information and news around the world. The information monopoly of governments has been broken, and human rights violations can no longer remain hidden. Fortunately, and despite some limitations, Iran continues to have the highest Internet penetration of any country in the Middle Eastern region.

Young Iranians, and especially those under the age of eighteen, who make up virtually 70 per cent of the population, are tech-savvy, adept in using modern information and communication technologies, and tend to be avid watchers of satellite television. In those virtual and real spaces, the youth have begun to claim their public role in politics, while at the same time laying informal claims on the government. Although the government has imposed restrictions on Internet use, youth movements continue to utilize such technologies to publicly blame the government for not protecting the interests of its citizens.

It should be noted that developments during the so-called reconstruction period (1989–1997) under President Rafsanjani, as well as the reform period (1997–2005) under President Khatami, paved the way for a slow transition from mass society to a segmented civil society. The emergence of civil society associations, independent student organizations, writer and journalist associations, the independent press, and the increasing independence of arts and culture from state control were all signs of this transition.[59] Although the broadly-based mass mobilization of the 2009 Green Movement was not strong enough to sustain a full-blown opposition movement, no one can deny the role that ICTs and, to a lesser extent, social media have played in organizing public opposition. Social media allowed the protestors to present their message to the nation as well as to the global community, even as the Green Movement failed to achieve its goals.

Both the Iranian Green Movement and the democratic uprisings in the Middle East and North Africa have dispelled any notion that human rights are irrelevant to the Muslim world. These movements have demonstrated the diversity and breadth of their political, social, and economic aspirations. The so-called "Arab Spring," according to one expert, raises the hope that, whatever the backlash in the short and medium term, "space has been created for more fluid and engaged forms of grassroots politics."[60]

Yet at the same time, internal factors, including gender bias, traditionalism, religious dogmatism, illiteracy, and ignorance have contributed to the abuse of human rights in the Muslim world generally and Iran specifically. At both individual and societal levels, some acts are unbelievably cruel. The incarceration of young girls, early marriage of children, family revenge acts, ethnic and tribal revenge acts, patriarchy, and localism perpetuate abusive behaviors.

Some obsolete and archaic Iranian legal traditions have also allowed abusive human rights conditions. "Blood money," or *diyah*, is the payment by a murderer to the victim's family in return for waiving the right to insist on the death penalty; *diyah* for women is only half of that for men. Likewise, civil law regards the witness of two females as being equal to that of one male. These criminal and judicial rules manifestly contradict modern standards of gender equality and human rights.

Freedom of movement is another issue in Iran. Married women cannot leave the country without their husband's written consent. Unless mentioned as a marriage condition, women's freedom to choose the place of their residence is limited. The actions of some agents of the state, such as attorney generals, judges, security forces and law enforcement agents, have led to blatant human rights violations. Building democracies and institutionalizing the rule of law requires public support in order to take root in the long term. The unfolding experiences of many developing countries, such as Egypt, Myanmar, and Malawi, highlight the importance, and difficulty, of getting the right mix of political system, ideas, and public commitment. If these democratic uprisings have faltered in the Arab world's most populous country—Egypt—it may well be because of insufficient public support.[61]

Conclusion

In post-Khomeini Iran, social change has come through pragmatism and political reform, rooted in a popular struggle to achieve higher standards of internationally recognized human rights. Yet violent opposition to social change has also assumed the form of political populism, ideological conservatism, and Islamic militancy. Disparate factors such as Islamic tradition on the one hand and ideological relativism on the other, tough economic sanctions, and ruling elites preoccupied with profit-driven motives while operating under the pretext of protecting Islam and *Velayat* (homeland), have rendered the protection and promotion of human rights complicated and difficult.

Although the Islamic Republic has given education far greater attention in post-Khomeini Iran, it is important to note that the Green Movement—as an opposition to the conservatives and subsequently as a resistance movement—was an unintended outcome of those higher educational standards, and has proven challenging to the regime's legitimacy. Many human rights violations—in the form of crackdowns and repressive policies—have arisen as a result of perceived threats to the regime's stability and, more significantly, to those who control the levers of power.[62] While the improvements in basic rights, such as access to water, healthcare, and education, have been significant and visible, the regime's use of violence against its own people has increased, regardless of which administration—reformist or conservative—has been in power.

Although many Iranians under Khatami's presidency (1997–2005) enjoyed a period of enhanced civil society activities and public expression, Iranians today are living in far more desperate times. Increasingly, however, Iranians have developed a sense of citizenship, not only of Iran, but of the rest of the globe, and a commitment to the reform and participatory politics of democracy and the rule of law. To protect and promote human rights conditions in Iran, a stable economy and improved living conditions are necessary. But, it is also important to have an educational system that teaches inclusiveness and a government that allows UN technical support, as well as steady supervision by the UN and NGOs. Progress also relies on Iran being treated with true empathy from foreign countries across the globe that have been successful in advocating human rights, and on progressive views of religion and tradition.[63]

8

US-IRAN TENSIONS IN POST-KHOMEINI IRAN AND IRANIAN IMMIGRANTS IN THE UNITED STATES

Mohsen M. Mobasher

As indicated by many social scientists, the Iranian Revolution of 1979 was one of the most powerful historic events in the twentieth century with considerable demographic, economic, political, and cultural consequences for Iran and the Middle East. The economic and political roots and outcomes of the Iranian revolution have generated a vast amount of outstanding interdisciplinary debate, research, and scholarship. However, the consequent demographic changes, particularly involving international migration, have received much less attention. This chapter focuses on the experience and community of Iranian immigrants to the United States, most of whom left Iran during and after the revolution and settled in America indeterminately. With the exception of a mass exodus of Iranians to India in the seventh century, this is the greatest emigration of Iranian nationals from various socio-economic, political, and ethno-religious backgrounds in history. The revolution and its social changes were a pivotal point in the creation of a contemporary Iranian diaspora, with major social, economic, and political consequences for Iran and Iranian migrants. The effects included a "brain drain" and loss of human capital; the exile of thousands of intellectuals, political activists, artists, entertainers, reporters and political commentators; the departure of a significant number of religious minorities; the admission of a large number of political asylum-seekers and refugees to Western countries; the loss of national identity and veiling of religious identity among Iranian immigrants in the West; the establishment of large Iranian communities in major cities in Europe and North America with extended major political, cultural, and social ties to Iran; the creation of transnational Iranians who maintained a simultaneous connection to Iran and their host societies; and the creation of a new cumulative culture of migration, with hundreds of formal and informal networks and institutions, helping millions of Iranian nationals to leave the country and settle abroad. No migration study can adequately capture the experience of immigrant groups, nor understand the complex forces that shape their journey, without taking account of both home and host, as well as the historic, economic, and political links between the two. For this reason, this chapter is divided into two parts, corresponding to Iran and to emigrants' destination country.

Following a brief overview of the impact of the Iranian Revolution on the emigration of Iranians, the first part of this chapter describes political, economic, and social forces that have pushed many Iranians to leave Iran and migrate to the United States since the overthrow of the nationalist government of Mossaddeq and the return of the Shah to power in 1953. This section ends with the most current demographic profile of Iranians in the United States provided by the 2010 census. The second part of this chapter discusses the ongoing social and political challenges confronting Iranian immigrants in the United States since 1979. The primary aim of this section is to examine the growing political tensions in the US-Iran relationship, exacerbated further by the Iranian hostage crisis in 1979, and their subsequent impacts on discrimination and integration in Iranians' host society. This chapter concludes by examining the impact of the 9/11 attacks on political mobilization among second-generation Iranian-Americans and their significant accomplishments in the last ten years.

In keeping with this chapter's focus, one crucial point needs to be stated at the outset. The fundamental element that has linked home and host for Iranian migrants and has shaped their overall experience has been the drastic political shift in US-Iran relations from allies during the pre-revolutionary era to political antagonists since the revolution. By focusing on US-Iran relations over half a century, this chapter highlights two major theoretical underpinnings, both of which have been ignored by most scholars of Iranian migration.

First, unlike many migration scholars who emphasize the role of human capital, cultural beliefs, and practices of migrants in the host society, this chapter reiterates the political nature of migration. It underscores the powerful impact that political ties between emigrant and immigrant countries has on the integration of immigrants. As research has shown, the mode of entry and the political relations between the migrant-sending and receiving states as well as the social, political, and economic conditions of the host society at the time of migrants' arrival are the key factors that shape the experience of immigrants in the United States.[1] The degree of stability or social change in a migrant's home society also has a profound impact on an immigrant's community structure, political orientation, and lifestyle in the host society.

The second theoretical underpinning of the chapter examines the extent and impact of exclusionary and discriminatory US immigration policies on Iranian immigrants since the revolution. The impact of the political schism between the United States and Iran after the revolution, and its impact on the integration of Iranian immigrants in the United States, have yet to be properly scrutinized. Despite the increased interest in the Iranian diaspora by social scientists in recent years, there is a lack of theoretical work on both political ends of the migration process for Iranian immigrants. This chapter turns our attention to these much-needed dimensions.

The Iranian Revolution and the emigration of Iranians: an historical overview

The Iranian Revolution of 1978–79 has been one of only two instances in Iranian history that has catalysed mass emigration.[2] The revolution not only intensified the emigration of Iranians in terms of their number, but also had an impact on the demography of emigrants in terms of their gender, age, class status, political orientation, religious background and family composition.

In addition to significant demographic changes, the revolution had enduring psychological and cultural consequences for Iranian migrants to the United States, particularly among those who left Iran involuntarily.[3] Due to the extensive demographic, psychological, social, and cultural consequences for Iranians in diaspora, the 1978–79 Revolution is perceived as a turning point in the migration history of Iranians and divides it into pre-revolutionary and post-revolutionary periods.

The exact number of Iranians who left Iran after the 1979 Revolution is unknown. Neither the Iranian government nor the host countries where Iranian nationals reside provide a precise figure of Iranian immigrants, though estimates range from two to four million.[4] The most reliable data on the number of Iranian nationals in the diaspora comes from government sources in Europe, Canada, the United States, and Australia, where a majority of Iranian immigrants live. For example, the data collected by Federal Statistical Office of Germany, Sweden Statistics, and Statistics Canada between 1980 and 2005 suggest accurate figures for Germany (97,177), Sweden (61,057), and Canada (87,379). Similarly the UK Home Office reports that, between 1991 and 2005, 21,305 Iranian immigrants were admitted to the United Kingdom.[5] A report by the Australian Bureau of Statistics reveals that by 2005 the number of individuals with Iranian ancestry in Australia had reached 24,588.[6] However, these numbers are limited to immigrants or permanent residents only and do not include Iranian refugees and asylum seekers.

A distinctive characteristic of the post-revolutionary Iranian diaspora is the large number who fled for political or religious reasons and applied for refugee status or political asylum.[7] In 2004, Iranians ranked tenth highest out of all nationalities seeking asylum in Europe. More than half of the applications filed by Iranians were submitted in Western European countries including the United Kingdom, Germany, Belgium, Austria, and the Netherlands. According to data compiled by the United Nations High Commissioner for Refugees, between 1995 and 2004, countries that received large numbers of asylum applications from Iranians included Germany (34,828), Turkey (22,708), the United Kingdom (22,290), the Netherlands (19,230), Austria (11,315), and Canada (6,919).[8]

The immigration of Iranians to the United States before the revolution

Much like in the case of Europe, Canada, and Australia the immigration of a large number of Iranians to the United States was the consequence of the revolution. All available published annual reports and statistical yearbooks published by the former US Immigration and Naturalization Service (INS) and the Department of Homeland Security indicate that Iranian immigration to the United States before 1950 was negligible. As indicated in Table 6, between 1921 and 1929, around 208 Iranians immigrated to the United States. The number of Iranians who entered the United States during 1930–1939 declined to 198, and increased to 1,144 during 1940–49. Other reports suggest that a few hundred Iranian nationals had been admitted long before 1921. It is believed that the total number of Iranians in the United States had reached 130 between 1842 and 1903 and 780 between 1925 and 1932.[9] Despite the inconsistency regarding the early migration history of Iranians, all available data for the last seventy years suggests that the significant migration of Iranians to the United States began after the return of the Shah to power in 1953, increased during the 1960s and early 1970s, reached its peak shortly before and during the revolutionary turmoil in 1977–78, and continued to grow after the 1979 Revolution until today. Between 1953 and the outbreak of opposition to the Shah in 1977, approximately 29,840 Iranian immigrants and 238,291 non-immigrants entered the United States.[10] A sizable proportion of non-immigrant Iranians who entered the US during this time were students who later became residents and eventually obtained citizenship. Most Iranians who migrated were urban middle-class men, who left mainly because of a series of economic and political reforms in Iran that had begun more or less with the 1953 coup. After the coup, the Shah's determination to secure strong political, financial, military, and economic ties between the Iranian and American governments made the United States a dominant foreign power in Iran.[11]

Moreover, Iran's dependence on loans and direct financial aid from the United States expedited economic development along Western lines in Iran during the 1960s and 70s. These economic developments, combined with the Shah's investment in industrialization, modern technology, and the military increased the demand for skilled workers significantly and motivated thousands of young middle and upper-middle class Iranians to migrate to the United States to advance their education. Consequently, the number of Iranian students in the United States increased sharply.

Likewise, the increased economic and political ties between Iran and the American government facilitated an exchange of government officials, and inspired thousands of affluent Iranians to visit the United States temporarily for business, pleasure, or both. Between 1960 and 1970, nearly 11,410 government officials and 28,489 visitors from Iran arrived in the US for pleasure or business. The comparable numbers between 1971 and 1977 were 25,984 and 140,539 respectively, indicating an annual average of 3,712 government officials, and 20,219 visitors. In addition to those who visited temporarily each year, thousands of Iranians entered permanently as spouses, children, and parents of Iranians who were US citizens.[12]

Between 1970 and 1976, a little less than one-third (6,240) of all Iranian immigrants (19,664) admitted to the United States were spouses, children, and parents of naturalized US citizens from Iran.[13]

Overall, during the 1960s, an average of 5,116 government officials, temporary visitors for business and pleasure, students, international representatives, exchange visitors, intracompany transferees, along with their spouses and children, visited the United States annually. This number increased eightfold to 43,310 between 1970 and when the Shah was deposed from power in 1978.[14]

The most notable non-immigrant group in the 1960s and the 1970s was students. Between 1960 and 1977 around 82,288 students travelled to the US to study.[15] A salient characteristic of Iranian students in the US and other Western countries in the 1960s and 1970s was their political activism against the Shah's government led by the Confederation of Iranian Students, National Union (CISNU).[16] The intense political activism of Iranian students abroad was in reaction to the Shah's repressive dictatorship and his suppression of open political activism and opposition in Iran after the overthrow of the nationalistic government of Mossaddeq.[17]

Between the outbreak of open opposition to the Shah's government in 1977 and the establishment of the provisional Islamic government in 1979, thousands of Iranians were uprooted and forced to live in exile. Never before, in the history of Iran, were so many young Iranians admitted to the US as immigrants and non-immigrants in such a short time period. As in the pre-revolutionary period, a significant number of these were students: approximately 46,000 (or 24 per cent) of the 190,000 non-immigrant visas issued to Iranians between 1978 and 1979. After students, the great majority of Iranians who migrated were members of the former ruling class, high-ranking officials, bankers, investors, members of parliament, ministers and members of the former political classes holding managerial positions, and members of religious minorities, particularly Jews and Baha'is.[18]

Some left the country legally while others first crossed the border into neighboring countries illegally, before travelling to the United States as refugees after a few years of residence in another country. Most expected to return home soon. However, as the revolution and its aftermath unfolded, the hope for return gave way to indefinite exile. Thus, many changed their visa statuses and obtained permanent residency or green cards through kinship ties, marriage with US citizens, or their occupation after their arrival. As in the previous period, male Iranian immigrants outnumbered their female counterparts. Almost 57 per cent of all immigrants who entered the United States during the revolutionary period were men.[19]

Table 6: Iranians Obtaining Permanent Residence: 1921–2010

1921–1929	208
1930–1939	198
1940–1949	1,144
1950–1959	3,195
1960–1969	8,895
1970–1979	36,955
1980–1989	140,290
1990–1999	104,078
2000–2010	115,595
Total	410,558

Sources: Office of Immigration Statistics, 2002–2008 Yearbook of Immigration Statistics, *Washington, DC: US Department of Homeland Security; Immigration and Naturalization Service*, 1970–1977 Annual Reports, *Washington, DC: US Department of Justice; Immigration and Naturalization Service*, 1978–2001 Statistical Yearbook, *Washington, DC: US Department of Justice*.

Immigration of Iranians to the United States after the revolution

After the 1979 Revolution and the establishment of the Islamic Republic of Iran, the pattern and the nature of Iranian emigration to the United States changed drastically. Compared to the pre-revolutionary and the revolutionary periods, the post-revolutionary emigration of Iranians has been more complex in nature and involved a more demographically, culturally, politically, economically, and religiously diverse group. Unlike the previous periods, the post-revolutionary period has been more gradual (albeit often erratic) and has consisted of several distinct phases of exodus.

The first phase began soon after the establishment of the new government and the *Paksazi*, or cleansing process, as part of the "Cultural Revolution," which forced a large number of religious minorities, political opponents of the new regime, professors, students, leftist political activists, and intellectuals to leave Iran. In addition to the disenchanted and alienated intellectuals, political activists, scholars and scientists, a large number of entrepreneurs, artists, musicians, entertainers, journalists, and self-employed professionals left the country as well, preferring exile to a socially and politically deteriorated life in post-revolutionary Iran.

Soon after the Cultural Revolution, Iraq's invasion of Iran on 22 September 1980 marked the beginning of the second phase of mass departure for many

Iranians. During the eight-year Iran-Iraq war, thousands of educated middle class professionals and many young Iranians eligible for military conscription left Iran.

The third phase of post-revolutionary migration, which began between 1986 and 1988, was initiated by a combination of powerful political changes in Iran and the United States, including the US Immigration Reform and Control Act (IRCA) of 1986, the end of the Iran-Iraq war, and a series of economic and political reforms initiated by the pragmatist leader of the Iranian government after Khomeini's death in June 1989.

The combined effect of these legal forces altered the demography of Iranian immigrants and impacted the Iranian family in exile in two important ways. First, the IRCA provided a legal opportunity to thousands of Iranians who had lived in the America illegally to become legal permanent residents and eventually naturalized US citizens. Second, changes in the military draft policies of the Iranian government after the end of Iran-Iraq war, and an amendment that enabled Iranian immigrant men to obtain temporary exemption from military service for a fee, provided an opportunity to many young Iranian men to return to Iran and visit their families.[20]

Figure 13: Iranian Born Individuals Obtaining Permanent Residency, 1960–2010

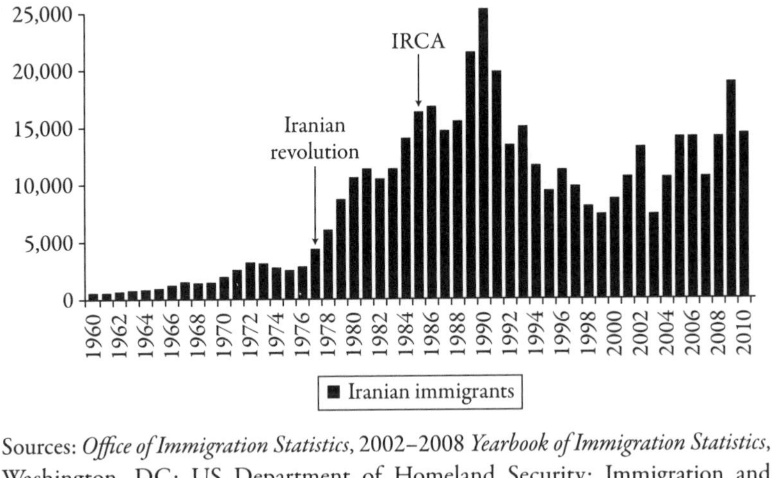

Sources: *Office of Immigration Statistics*, 2002–2008 *Yearbook of Immigration Statistics*, Washington, DC: US Department of Homeland Security; Immigration and Naturalization Service, 1970–1977 *Annual Reports*, Washington, DC: US Department of Homeland Security; Immigration and Naturalization Service, 1978–2001 *Statistical Yearbook*, Washington, DC: US Department of Homeland Security.

The attainment of permanent residency through the IRCA of 1986 and the removal of barriers such as Iranian military conscription not only made it possible for thousands of young Iranian men to go home more often; but also facilitated a new migration wave of Iranians, particularly women, to the United States, and significantly altered the demographic structure of Iranian communities in two consequential ways. First, the legalization of thousands of Iranians after the IRCA subsequently increased the number of Iranians who became naturalized citizens of the United States.[21] Second, an increase in the naturalization trend in turn increased the number of new migrants joining their family in the United States. This has been especially the case for many Iranian women who entered the United States as wives of any naturalized Iranian. As indicated in Figure 14, due to the migration of thousands of Iranian women as wives of naturalized Iranians, a new trend emerged and, for the first time in 1992, more than 50 per cent of all Iranian US immigrants were women.[22] This trend has continued until today and each year nearly 55 per cent of Iranians admitted to the United States are women.

Another important demographic consequence of the political and legal reforms in Iran and the United States for Iranian immigrants, as demonstrated in Figure 15, was a significant growth in the immigration of older Iranians.

Figure 14: Immigration of Iranians to the US by Gender, 1960–2001

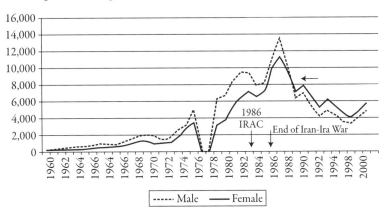

Sources: *Office of Immigration Statistics*, 2002–2008 *Yearbook of the Immigration Statistics*, Washington, DC: US Department of Homeland Security; Immigration and Naturalization Service, 1970–1977 *Annual Reports*, Washington, DC: US Department of Justice; Immigration and Naturalization Service, 1978–2001 *Statistical Yearbook*, Washington, DC: US Department of Justice.

Figure 15: Immigration of Iranians over the Age of Fifty to the US, 1960–2001

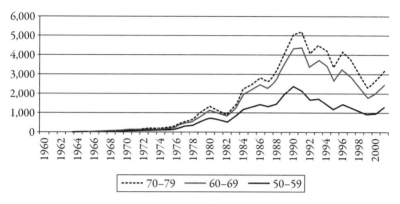

Sources: *Office of Immigration Statistics*, 2002–2008 *Yearbook of the Immigration Statistics*, Washington, DC: US Department of Homeland Security; Immigration and Naturalization Service, 1970–1977 *Annual Reports*, Washington, DC: US Department of Justice; Immigration and Naturalization Service, 1978–2001 *Statistical Yearbook*, Washington, DC: US Department of Justice.

As shown in Figure 13, between 1980 and 2010, approximately 359,963 Iranian immigrants entered the United States for a variety of reasons. Despite the significant decline shortly after the revolution, since 1980 an average of 11,611 immigrant and 22,635 non-immigrants from Iran have entered the United States annually.[23] The most distinctive feature of Iranian immigration during the post-revolutionary period has been a sharp increase in the number of individuals granted refugee or asylum status. The number of Iranian refugees and asylum seekers increased from 13 in 1979 to 6,051 in 1989. In 2006, 2007, and 2008, with an estimated refugee population of 2,792, 5,481, and 5,270, respectively, Iran was among the top four source countries of refugees arriving in the United States.[24]

Socioeconomic and demographic characteristics of Iranian immigrants

By 2011, as indicated in the American Community Survey (ACS) report produced by the US Census Bureau, there were 470,341 individuals of Iranian heritage living in the United States.[25] Geographically, Iranians in the United States are concentrated in a few states and metropolitan areas. As was the case in the 2000 Census report, close to half reside in California. After California, the other largest concentrations of Iranians are in New York, Texas, Virginia, Maryland, Florida, Illinois, New Jersey, Massachusetts, and Washington. The Iranian population in the United States is extremely diverse, dynamic, complex, and stratified, with a significant number of foreign born educated professionals, entrepreneurs, and self-employed business owners. Contrary to expectation, it does not consist of a single ethnic or religious group. Ethnically, those with Iranian heritage include Turks and Persians as well smaller numbers of Lors, Kurds, and Ghashgha'is. Religiously, the Iranian immigrant population is composed of Muslims, Christians, Baha'is, Jews, Zoroastrians, and many with no religious orientation.

As indicated before, differences among Iranian immigrants also appear with regard to the time of and purpose for entrance. Half the current Iranian immigrant population entered the United States before 1990 and close to 65 per cent (303,234) are foreign born and could be classified as first-generation. A majority (71 per cent) of foreign born Iranians (216,760) are naturalized US citizens. The number of Iranians who have become US citizens has accelerated in the last fifteen years. This is in part related to the Immigration Reform and Control Act of 1986 which made thousands of Iranian immigrants eligible for permanent residency.

Unlike many other immigrant groups who have migrated in search of menial jobs, a small number of Iranians left Iran as economic migrants for purely economic reasons. A substantial number of foreign-born Iranians left Iran to further their education The majority of Iranians in the United States are Muslims. Members of the other religious faiths such as Baha'is, Jews, Zoroastrians, and Christians, although small, also migrated from Iran. While Iranians in the United States remain diverse in character ethnically and religiously, a shared language, history, and cultural heritage binds members together. Despite these distinctions within the diaspora, the feeling of Iranian identity is stronger than any sub-ethno-religious differences.[26]

A remarkable characteristic of Iranian immigrants in the United States is their high rate of economic activity and labor force participation. Of the total population of Iranians over sixteen years old (261,779) 64.9 per cent (169,873) are in the labor force. Of this number, only 2.9 per cent are unemployed and the remaining 62 per cent are employed. More than half of Iranians who are in the labor force work in management, business, or science occupations.

After management, the largest concentrations of employment are in sales and office work, followed by the service industry, with 26 per cent and 11 per cent respectively. The high concentration of Iranians in professional occupations is consistent with their remarkable educational training. In 2011, close to 58 per cent of Iranians over 25 years of age had a bachelor's degree or higher, and another 21 per cent had either an associate's degree or some college education but no degree. This exceptionally high level of education is mainly due to the heavy influx of Iranian students to the United States in the late 1970s and early 1980s.

Another remarkable characteristic of Iranian immigrants in the United States is their high level of English proficiency, which is linked to their high level of education. Although 76 per cent of Iranians spoke a language other than English at home, only 30 per cent of Iranians over the age of five assess that they speak English less than "very well." Iranians' income is as impressive as their level of education and English fluency. According to the 2011 ACS, the median household income for Iranians in 2010 had reached $57,097. The family incomes of Iranians in 2010 were even more impressive. With a median family income of $75,827 in 2010, Iranian families ranked among the most affluent groups in the United States. The high family and household incomes have affected Iranians' settlement patterns in the United States and have led to high value home ownership in predominantly middle and upper-middle class neighborhoods of major US cities. As indicated in the 2011 ACS reports, the number of Iranian homeowners in 2010 had reached 55 per cent. The median value of houses occupied by Iranians in the same year was $415,800.[27]

A majority of first-generation Iranian immigrants stay in contact with family members, relatives, and friends in Iran. Contact with Iran is primarily retained through frequent reciprocal visits between Iranian immigrants and their family members. In the last ten years, there has been an increase in the number of expatriates who have returned to Iran. These tend to be visits rather than permanent returns. Although the myth of return to Iran is very alive among Iranian immigrants, most first generation Iranians have established roots in the US and may never return to Iran permanently.

The increase in reciprocal contact between Iran and its expatriates has had varying repercussions. Since second generation Iranians arrived at a very young age or were born, raised and schooled in the United States, their knowledge of Iranian culture is very limited. Thus, the contact between Iran and Iranian emigrants has helped to maintain Iranian culture and reinforced the attachment in the second generation. It has also made many of the first generation realize how far they differ from those who have remained in Iran since the revolution. This realization has been a major motive for the formation of numerous ethnic institutions and online ethnic associations for Iranian communities across the

United States, through which they can express their cultural identity and ethnic roots. Today, the Internet contains more than 1,000 blog sites, chat rooms, news groups, and other electronic sites devoted to cultural, professional, ethnic, religious, political, academic, and business activities of Iranians throughout the world. Through the Internet, Iranians have been able to create a virtual Persian community where cultural, economic, and political news about Iran and Iranian migrants are exchanged and discussed.

Other institutions such as the Iranian media, informal and professional associations, Persian concerts, plays, lectures, poetry readings, Persian feasts and celebrations such as *Noruz* (the Iranian new year festival), film festivals, and religious organizations constitute important means for facilitating social interaction among the dispersed Iranian immigrants in the United States. Moreover, these ethnic institutions and events help Iranian immigrants to express their ethnic identity and preserve their culture.

One of the most ubiquitous ethnic institutions is Iranian ethnic television. Most programs are produced in Los Angeles. As indicated by Naficy, most of these are syndicated, have secular orientation, oppose the Islamic Republic of Iran, and promote an Iranian ethnic identity by using images, icons of pre-Islamic Iran in television titles, logos, and programming.[28] Furthermore, by focusing on cultural authenticity, Iranian nationalism, secularism, and monarchy, Iranian television programs in exile disavow the revolution and the modern state. The predominance of male producers and hosts, Naficy notes, reflects the traditional Iranian patriarchy. Moreover, by breaking for commercials, Iranian television programs in exile not only promote a consumerist ideology, but also sustain an ethnic economy.

US–Iranian political tensions and the rise of discrimination against Iranian immigrants

Prior to the revolution, the US government and informed American citizens viewed Iran as an ancient civilization with a rich cultural heritage. Iranian immigrants were respected as professionals who had made great educational and entrepreneurial contributions to the United States. In a 1976 Gallup poll, conducted two years prior to the revolution, the number of Americans who gave Iran a low rating of respect and esteem was only 37 per cent.[29] In a speech given in 1978, President Carter recognized Iran as an "island of stability in one of the more troubled areas of the world."[30] As indicated above, this relatively positive image before the revolution was a result of strong economic, political, and cultural ties with Iran, which was one of the greatest allies of the US in the Middle East. The 1979 hostage crisis and the subsequent diplomatic breakup between Iran and the United States, replaced this benign image with an unprecedented prejudice and discrimination against Iranian immigrants that continues today.

After the Iranian revolution and the hostage crisis, the image of Iran as "an island of stability" was demoted by President Carter to an "extremist," "terrorist," and "fanatical" regime dominated by a "crazy group"[31] of mullahs. Such assertions by an American president, and the subsequent representation of Iranians in the American media, created a wave of backlash protests across the country and prompted a series of recriminations.

Immediately after the hostages were taken, hundreds of American demonstrators in major American cities burned an Iranian flag and carried placards reading "Have a Happy Thanksgiving—hold an Iranian hostage," "Roast an Iranian for Thanksgiving," "Deport Iranians," "Send in Marines," "Death to Khomeini," "Eat your oil," "Bomb Iran," "Nuke Iran," "War with Iran," "We won't take this anymore," "Support Iran's revolution, send an Iranian home," and "Go home dumb Iranians." In Texas, for two days a group of 1,000 vocal anti-Iranian demonstrators gathered at the Dresser Tower in downtown Houston, the site of the Iranian consulate, carrying placards saying "Give American Liberty or give Iranians death," "Kill Khomeini," and "10 Iranians equal a worm." Other posters read "60 Americans for 10,000 Iranians," suggesting that the United States should trade the Iranians living in the United States for the hostages being held in Iran.

In another demonstration in Houston, a crowd of 100 anti-Iranian demonstrators appeared outside the Grand Hotel and protested the hiring of Iranian students.[32] On another occasion, a biplane dropped leaflets signed by the John Wayne Society urging Americans to boycott stores where Iranians work, fire Iranian employees, deny housing to Iranians and take other discriminatory action.[33] In addition to these demonstrations, hate crimes and discriminatory policies directed against Iranians increased across the United States.[34] A man was arrested after police said he pointed a loaded shotgun at a telephone operator at St Louis University and demanded the names of Iranian students.[35] Meanwhile, campus police at the University of Wyoming were also called to protect Iranian students who had received death threats.[36]

The same day, an Independent School District trustee in Houston refused admittance of Iranian youngsters to school.[37] The board of Greenville, a two-year college in South Carolina, voted to bar Iranian students from classes during the quarter after the hostage crisis if the American hostages were not released. State universities in Louisiana and New Mexico stopped enrolling Iranian students. The Mississippi legislature passed a bill doubling the tuition for Iranian students attending public universities in that state. Local radio and television programs encouraged callers to boycott Iranian-owned businesses and to carry anti-Iranian bumper stickers.

In addition to the implementation of discriminatory policies at American universities and colleges, Iranian diplomats and military trainees were expelled and Iranian immigrants in the United States were given one month to report their location and visa status to the closest Immigration and Naturalization Service (INS) office. Furthermore, all Iranian assets in the United States were frozen, tighter restrictions on visas for Iranians were implemented, all visas issued to Iranians in the US were revoked, and as many as 6,906 students were subject to deportation.[38]

These widespread discriminatory practices stigmatized and devalued Iranians and established a level of social distance between Iranian immigrants and Americans that continues today. In a poll taken about one year after the revolution, 60 per cent of Americans viewed Iran as an enemy of the United States and a further 34 per cent as an unfriendly country. In another poll conducted in 1989, a decade after the revolution, the number of Americans who held an unfavorable opinion toward Iran had increased to 91 per cent.[39] Seven years after the hostages were released, 60 percent of Americans still believed that Iran was the only "enemy" of the state, compared to 39 per cent who considered the Soviet Union an enemy.[40] In another poll, over half of the respondents cited "hostages," "Khomeini," "oil," "the Shah," "anger," "hatred," "trouble," and "troublesome country" as coming to mind when Iran was mentioned. Moreover, close to half of the respondents described "all" or "most" Muslims as "warlike," "bloodthirsty," "treacherous," "cunning," "barbaric," and "cruel."[41] As Edward Said's critical evaluation of "the Iran story" indicates, after the hostage crisis, night after night television programs such as America Held Hostage and Nightline represented the Iranian people, culture, and religion as "militant, dangerous, and anti-American."[42] The same Orientalist images and discourse were evident in *Time* and *Newsweek*.[43] Similarly, as pointed out by Jane Campbell, all films portraying Iranians released between 1978 and 1991 in the United States, whether comedic or action-adventure, depicted them as "terrifying, alien, irrational, cruel, barbaric people who threaten our national economy and our very safety in the United States."[44] Without offering any background or contextual understanding of Iranian society and culture, these movies and television programs ignored diversity within Iran and the Iranian community in exile and constructed a distorted, homogeneous image of Iran in the minds of millions of Americans.

Between 1985 and 1993, the percentage of Americans who believed that the presence of Iranians in the United States created problems for the country increased from 40 to 60 per cent. Only 20 per cent of Americans interviewed in 1993 held a positive view of Iranians and perceived their presence to be beneficial to the country.[45] Sparrow and Chretien's research among 415 college students at the University of Chicago gives a clear indication of the low degree of affinity and social interaction Americans desired with Iranians.[46] Applying the seven-item Social Distance Scale developed by Emory Bogardus in 1926, Sparrow and Chretien found that most college students would prefer to have intimate social interactions with any group rather than Iranians.[47] Whereas most minority groups were accepted as personal friends, members of clubs or as neighbors, Iranians were consistently kept at the greatest social distance, tolerated no closer than as citizens. Ranking all thirty-one groups in the study, Sparrow and Chretien found that Iranians acquired the lowest score on the Social Distance Scale.[48] This disturbing finding clearly demonstrates the extent to which negative stereotypes perpetuated by the media barred Americans from accepting Iranians as a group, marginalized them in the United States, and increased inter-group conflict.

Negative images of Iran and Iranians were revived in 2001 after the 9/11 attacks on America. In official pronouncements echoing those made during the hostage crisis, Iran was again labeled by George W. Bush as a state that sponsored terrorism, with apparent ties to the "axis of evil," and Iranian immigrants were subject to new forms of discrimination, prejudice, and civil rights violation by government and private entities. Immediately after 9/11, the US government ordered males between the ages of sixteen and sixty-five from twenty five Middle Eastern countries including Iran, who had entered the United States by 10 September 2001, to register with the INS, comply with the new federal alien registration program, and to submit to being fingerprinted, photographed, and interrogated by federal agents or face deportation.

This process was called the National Security Entry Exit Registration System (NSEERS). Iran was among the first five countries whose nationals were subjected to special registration. Hundreds of Iranians in Los Angeles were among the 1,000 registrants who were arrested and detained when they arrived to register with the Immigration and Naturalization Service in California.

The full extent of the prejudice and discrimination against Iranian immigrants after the hostage crisis and 9/11 is still not known. However, in an online sample study of 3,880 young educated, first-generation Iranian immigrants conducted by an Iranian Studies Group at MIT in 2005,[49] 32 per cent of respondents indicated that they "sometimes" experienced discrimination. Another 8 per cent responded they "often" experienced discrimination.

In a telephone survey of 800 Iranians in California conducted by the Institute of Government Studies at the University of California-Berkeley (2007), 25 per cent of the respondents indicated that they had experienced discrimination by being singled out for special search or questioning at airports since 9/11.[50] Another 43 per cent reported denial of visa for family members or friends who had intended to visit the US after 9/11. Moreover, 5 per cent of the respondents stated that they had been turned down for a job and 12 per cent reported general hostility from members of their local community since 9/11. Finally, in a multi-lingual study of 1,000 ethnic Californians conducted by Bendixen & Associates in 2002, nearly 60 per cent of Iranians in the sample stated that they had been the victim of racial or ethnic discrimination more often after the events of 9/11.[51] Moreover, 50 per cent of Arab, Iranian, Pakistani, Afghani, and Asian Indian participants in the same survey indicated they had both experienced racial or ethnic discrimination, and suffered depression, after 9/11.

Iranians are not the only immigrant group in the United States whose members have been discriminated against by the United States government because of the political actions of their home country's government. In fact, the case of Iranians bears comparison to the treatment of Japanese and Cuban migrants in some respect. Nearly forty years before the revolution, over 70,000 American citizens of Japanese ancestry and another 40,000 legal permanent resident Japanese in the West Coast were evacuated, relocated to camps, and imprisoned without charge, trial, or conviction because of hostilities between the US and Japan.[52] Analogously, Iranian immigrants in the United States have never been proven to have been involved in 9/11 or any other terrorist act, before or after 9/11.

The migration experience of Iranians in the United States also bears a strong resemblance to that of Cubans. Both groups came to the United States because of a revolution and associated political turbulence in their home country. Just like the Iranian revolution, the Cuban revolution threatened the economic and political interests of the US government and led to open hostility between the two governments that has continued until a tentative softening of relations in 2015. Nevertheless, unlike Cuban exiles, who benefited from the federally funded billion dollar Cuban Refugee Program for resettlement, employment, health services, food, and educational training programs,[53] Iranians were subject to various forms of individual and collective prejudice and discrimination.

Despite broad similarities to the immigrant experiences of Japanese and Cubans, there is a fundamental difference that makes the case of Iranians more complex, and sets it apart from other immigrant groups. Whereas Japanese nationals in the Unites States could turn to their government for assistance, and often did, when they experienced discrimination before the aerial attacks on Pearl Harbor,[54] Iranian immigrants have been deprived of any support from the government, legal or otherwise, since widespread discrimination began in 1979.

Moreover, whereas the financial aid provided by the Eisenhower and Kennedy administrations was a major asset in helping Cuban exiles to build and sustain their community and economic infrastructure, the cancellation of visas issued to Iranians and the freezing of assets by President Carter decimated Iranian communities and punished many Iranians who had fled the common "enemy" a few years earlier. Therefore, it can be argued that no other recent refugee group in the US has experienced the same sense of double loss or exile as Iranians.

Coping with prejudice and the stigma of being Iranian

To minimize the extent of prejudice and to cope with the social and psychological effects of stigmatization, first- and second-generation Iranian immigrants have adopted multiple strategies. Some Iranians have opted to modify their physical appearance. Others have hidden their cultural and national identity, avoided any public display of Iranian culture, maintained very low ethnic and national profiles, limited their association with other Iranians, minimized their collective visibility as a group, and avoided participation in and public support of community events.

Ansari's field observations during his research indicate that because of anti-Iranian attitudes and negative images, many school-aged Iranians asked their parents to buy them green contact lenses so they would look more like white non-Iranians.[55] In another more recent study among Iranians in Southern California, Mostofi describes how Iranians alter their bodies through plastic surgery, contact lenses, diet, and various other cosmetic changes to "whiten" their bodies and construct a new identity to facilitate their assimilation and economic success.[56]

Adopting Americanized names has been another stigma management strategy for many Iranians. Blair's study of *Personal Name Changes among Iranian Immigrants in the United States* illustrates that, despite Iranians seldom changing their names elsewhere, many in Los Angeles, especially women, have adopted an unofficial American name.[57] A significant factor is competition against Americans in the mainstream job market.

In addition to changing their physical appearance and adopting American names, many Iranians either concealed their national identity or began to identify as "Persians" or "Persian Americans."[58] Many also presented themselves in terms of their sub-national and sub-religious heritage, such as Armenian or Baha'i, rather than their national origin.

Although these strategies were effective for many individual Iranians in coping with causes of anti-Iranian prejudice and discrimination, they were far from enough for Iranians as a collective in coping with the damaging social consequences of the prevailing anti-Iranian stereotypes in their interactions with Americans. The anti-Iranian images perpetuated by the mainstream American media not only destroyed Iranians' confidence in the American government and people and pushed many naturalized Iranians to be less invested in social or political, it also fostered a reactive prejudice against Americans among many first-generation Iranian immigrants. Some Iranians began to denounce the American way of life, resisting assimilation into US society. Negative portrayals also heightened naturalized Iranians' social distance from other Americans and motivated many second-generation Iranians toward less self-identification as American.[59]

Iranians' detachment from American society and culture, caused by the hostage crisis and the subsequent stigmatization of Iranians, created a major crisis for Iranian immigrants, whose social life was characterized by double exile, double loss, and double trauma. Unable to find effective coping mechanisms, there were a considerable number of institutional crises within the Iranian community in diaspora.[60]

9/11 attacks and shift in political orientation of Iranian immigrants in the United States

It was not until the 9/11 attacks and the beginning of a new wave of anti-Iranian discrimination that Iranian immigrants were politically awakened and began to mobilize to protect their civil rights and liberties. Although the extent and consequences of discriminatory practices against Iranians after the

9/11 attacks were as significant as the legal immigration restrictions imposed on Iranians during the hostage crisis, the political reaction of Iranians after 9/11 was radically different and more constructive.

Despite their terrible consequences, the new post-9/11 immigration policies and the substantial rise in the level of discrimination against Iranian nationals forced many first-generation Iranians to unite and participate in the political processes of their host society, encouraged many second-generation youths to become more interested in understanding their ethnic background, and motivated many to become politically empowered and condemn the new immigration regulations. 9/11 also provided the impetus for Iranians to learn more about the American political system and to realize the power of their vote. This improved understanding propelled the Iranian community to find effective vehicles for political action and political mobilization across America, to engage in political processes in their communities, and even run for office.

The political concerns and orientation of first-generation immigrants seem to be guided by a complex set of factors in the home country and host society, according to a study by Portes and Rumbaut.[61] In addition to specific social and political events in both countries, the past socialization of immigrants, the desire to return, and the national situation left behind all affect an immigrant's political perspective. Depending on the characteristics of the sending countries and the contexts of reception, Portes and Rambaut argue that immigrants may choose between several sets of political activities.

First, they may passionately commit themselves to political causes in the home society, either to support or to oppose the existing government. Second, they can act as overseas representatives of their government. Finally, immigrants may turn away from everything at home and concentrate on establishing a new socio-political life in their new home. Ever since the mass immigration of the late 1970s, most first-generation Iranians, both opponents and supporters of the new Islamic government, have been primarily concerned with the post-revolutionary political conditions in Iran. Even when sanctions were imposed by the US government after the hostage crisis in 1979, despite their large number and financial resources, Iranian immigrants refrained from any political action that would challenge or oppose this discrimination. Except for the lawsuit filed by Iranian students against Carter's immigration restrictions, no other major legal challenge on behalf of Iranians emerged.

The passive reaction of Iranian immigrants during the hostage crisis was due to several factors including: political division and lack of a unified voice in the

Iranian immigrant community; lack of political power and awareness of legal rights as US citizens; an already stressful cultural adjustment for the majority of newly arrived Iranians; preoccupation with the revolution and its socio-political consequences for them and their family and friends.

In the decade since the 9/11 attacks, Iranian immigrants as a group have matured politically and gained a different perspective toward political processes in the United States. This has been particularly the case with the second-generation Iranian-Americans who were born and socialized in the United States. Unlike their parents, the second generation are gradually socializing into political institutions and are actively trying to enter mainstream politics and promote the welfare of Iranians in diaspora and in Iran. This gradual political socialization, coupled with an inherent attachment to both American society and Iranian culture, deeper understanding of American culture, society, and language, and the availability of professional, legal, and human capital resources inspire many second-generation Iranian-Americans to be more politically active locally and nationally.

In addition, civil rights violations and the political vulnerability of Iranians after 9/11 have prompted many to become more vocal in challenging immigration sanctions and discriminatory practices. Their primary political aim is to gain greater political power and visibility so they can protect the civil rights of naturalized Iranians in the US, and to reclaim, retain, and redefine the Iranian ethnic identity that has been under attack since the revolution. To that end, unlike their first-generation parents who passively submitted to the sanctions and discriminatory practices during the hostage crisis, the second-generation Iranian-Americans have actively challenged sanctions that targeted Iranians and other Muslim groups through multiple channels.

Many reached out to their local congressional offices for legal assistance on immigration issues for their parents and community members. Others formed public relations groups and national organizations in Washington DC and California, contacted members of Congress and lobbied for the protection of their civil liberties. These actions at the local and national levels have been a major step in challenging arbitrary racial and ethnic profiling, and the isolation of Iranians as a suspicious group by the US authorities, creating a crucial avenue for the empowerment of Iranian immigrants in the United States.

In addition to these collective actions, second-generation Iranian-Americans have formed political advocacy and action committees, designed informational websites, and established student organizations. After the 9/11 attacks, Iranian-American activists established a number of non-profit, non-political organizations, such as the National Iranian American Council (NIAC), Persian Watch Center, Iranian American Political Action Committee (IAPAC), Iranian American Bar Association (IABA), and National Legal Sanctuary for Community Advancement (NLSCA). Through these legal establishments, Iranians organized various meetings with government officials and civil rights experts to discuss their concerns regarding the post-9/11 backlash and discrimination against Iranian-Americans.

Most of these grassroots advocacy organizations were founded by second-generation Iranian-Americans primarily for combating anti-Iranian legislation and immigration policies initiated after 9/11, protecting Iranian immigrants against discrimination and galvanizing their personal and social identity. They also educate members of the Iranian community and provide them with information about their legal rights in the event they are approached by the FBI or singled out at the airport or a national border. Through public immigration forums, these organizations bring members of US Citizenship and Immigration Offices together with leading Iranian American legal advocates to discuss the general concerns of Iranians regarding the post-9/11 immigration policies, FBI background checks, delays in the processing of immigration cases, deportation and removal proceedings.

Furthermore, they aim to selectively reconstruct a new depoliticized Iranian-American ethnic identity that binds together a Persian pride rooted in Iranian cultural heritage and an American civic identity based on notions of democracy, freedom, and liberty. Finally, these organizations encourage Iranians to take advantage of their citizenship rights and be more active and visible in the American political scene. In recent years, these organizations have strongly encouraged Iranians to take a more active role in American politics and have acted to help prevent potential military conflict between Iran and the United States.

Despite the significant political accomplishments of Iranian-Americans since 9/11, first-generation Iranian immigrants remain politically divided and oriented toward Iran. They are still predominantly guided by political processes and trends in their home country. With the exception of a few political offices held by first-generation Iranians in California, where the largest Iranian community in exile exists, first-generation Iranians have remained marginal in American politics and refrain from engaging in political activities beyond US foreign policy toward Iran.

PART III

CINEMA AND POP MUSIC

9

THE POLITICS AND POETICS
OF IRANIAN ART-HOUSE CINEMA

Hamid Naficy

Of all the different types of cinema produced in the Islamic Republic of Iran, the one that stands out in terms of its global reach and impact is art-house cinema. This constitutes only a small percentage of the total output of the country's feature film industry, which produces about sixty to seventy movies a year.[1] Yet, because of their global impact, art-house films have come to erroneously represent the "national cinema" of Iran for most film spectators, programmers, scholars, critics, and students abroad. This chapter briefly discusses the reasons for the global impact of Iran's art-house cinema, and examines at length its politics and aesthetics.

The Iranian art cinema, or art-house cinema, has deeply impressed Western critics and audiences for many reasons. The reorientation of cinema from a morally corrupting and imperialist enterprise to an indigenous and self-empowering industry was a major one. The reorganization and modernization of industry infrastructure; the de facto banning of film imports, particularly those from Hollywood, which could overpower domestic productions; government financing, production, and wide-ranging censorship; the rehabilitation of veteran Pahlavi-era new-wave directors; and the emergence of a new cadre of post-revolutionary filmmakers, including women and ethnic minority directors were other reasons for the high quality of the films. The state's involvement intensified for a time after the revolution to the point of de facto monopoly on film production and distribution, but privatization muscled in, as did independent directors and, later, underground filmmakers. The modest, humanist topics and the often deceptively simple but innovative styles with which these were treated, offered additional reasons for the high quality of, and enthusiastic reactions to, art-house films. These were characteristics of their production.

There were certain characteristics of their global reception that further contributed to their high recognition and regard. Their simple, quiet stories, told without the gloss and glamour of stars, special effects, violence or car chases—their smallness—offered a refreshing contrast to the blockbusters and high-octane movies that dominated the world markets. These qualities were doubly attractive as they seemed to offer a total contrast to the dominant view abroad of the Islamic Republic as a hotbed of hostility, violence, intolerance, and terrorism.

These multiple contrasts made the art-house films innovative stylistically, ethnographically exotic, and challenging to the political hegemony. Arbiters of film culture and taste—influential film critics at major periodicals and broadcast stations, curators and programmers at film festivals, museums, art galleries, repertory cinemas, university professors, students, and bloggers—showcased these films, critiqued them, programmed them, analyzed them, wrote about them, taught them, and organized conferences about them, paving the way for their wider distribution and deeper penetration by sale, exhibition, transmission, web presence, and spectator reception.

The Islamic Republic's severe censoring and its periodic banning and imprisonment of the filmmakers, as well as the way its politics and policies were continually in the news for over three decades, further whetted the curiosity and appetite for these films. Finally, the large media-savvy Iranian diaspora (sometimes estimated to number as many as 3 million), residing in major metropolitan centers of the world with large film and media industries, provided an enthusiastic and loyal secondary market which helped give these films additional success.

THE POLITICS AND POETICS OF IRANIAN ART-HOUSE CINEMA

A "postal" cinema

The art-house cinema is one of the ten types of films emerging in Iran after the revolution, in what may be called "postal" cinema.[2] Art-house films produced since the late 1980s are postal because they surfaced after the iconoclastic destructions of nearly a third of the nation's movie-houses and the subsequent re-institutionalization of cinema. They also emerged after the imposition of the veil on women, after the eight-year war with Iraq (1980–88), and after Ayatollah Ruhollah Khomeini's death (1989). In their humanism, they may be regarded, if not as a secular cinema, at least as a post-Islamic, but nevertheless spiritual and ethical cinema.

The prefix "post" denotes not a complete break but a movement out of a closed Islamist doctrinal milieu or from the dictates of popular and other narrative film genres toward deeper and more expansive thematic and stylistic horizons. The art-house cinema is also "postal" in the way some films reject the exclusionary high culture, authoritarian certainties, and politicized aesthetics of modernism and realism for the more nuanced, open, ambiguous, self-reflexive, intertextual, pluralist, playful, and humanist ethics and aesthetics of postmodernism. Finally, the art-house films are post-national and post-cinema, in that they exist both outside the originating nation and traditional movie houses: they live in transnational, international, and global mediascapes—film festivals, commercial movie houses, art-house venues, galleries, museums, television, video distribution, and the Internet.

Art-house cinema's emergence was facilitated by both veteran new-wave filmmakers of the Pahlavi period who were "rehabilitated" in the mid-1980s, such as Abbas Kiarostami, Amir Naderi, Bahram Baizai, Masud Kimiai, Naser Taqvai, Parviz Kimiavi, Dariush Mehrjui, Khosrow Sinai, Ali Hatami, and Bahman Farmanara, and by newly-minted post-revolutionary cinéastes, such as Mohsen Makhmalbaf, Rakhshan Banietemad, Tahmineh Milani, Majid Majidi, Samira Makhmalbaf, Marziyeh Meshkini, and Ebrahim Hatamikia, and by a coterie of young filmmakers schooled in Kiarostami's cinema, such as Ebrahim Foruzesh, Jafar Panahi, Bahman Ghobadi, and Alireza Raisian. While the first group of veteran filmmakers was entirely male, the second was a mixture of female and male as well as of Persian and ethnic minority directors.

In these ways, the art-house cinema was also postal—post-masculine and post-Persian national. Because of their roots in secular cinema, even though in the Pahlavi era new-wave movement, the Islamic regime initially considered the veteran directors, in the parlance of the *hijab*, as "unrelated" (*namahram*) and "outsiders" (*gharibeh*) to the revolution, and viewed them with suspicion.

On the other hand, the emerging post-revolution talent was generally considered to be "related" (*mahram*) and "insider" (*khodi*), and thus trustworthy.

"Rehabilitation" took several years and it was limited, for the veteran new-wave directors were not trusted to cover the "sacred defense" war with Iraq, and the filmmakers themselves may not have wished to make such films. Those new-wave directors who made films directly or indirectly about the war, such as Baizai (*Bashu, the Little Stranger*, or *Bashu, Gharibeh-ye Kuchak*, 1985) and Naderi (*Second Search*, or *Jostoju- ye Do*, 1981, *The Runner*, or *Davandeh*, 1985, and *Water, Wind, Dust*, or *Ab, Bad, Khak*, 1987), had their films banned as pacifist. It was left to the new cadre of post-revolutionary Islamist directors to make war movies. In time, some of these insider directors, such as Makhmalbaf, Panahi, Ghobadi, and even Hatamikia were rejected as outsiders due to their own evolution into critical or oppositional filmmakers. The postal art cinema is nothing if not evolving.

The family production mode

A new author-reinforcing development was that many art-house directors engaged in what I am calling the "family production mode." Many prominent directors hired their family members as cast and crew, among them Baizai, Kiarostami, Mehrjui, Makhmalbaf, Banietemad, Milani, and Kumars Purahmad.[3] Some of these were professionally qualified, while others were perhaps just trustworthy and quick learners. While the film industry moved toward industrialized production, involving division of labor, specialization, and the mass production of an increasing output of movies, the family production mode offered a counter-industrializing practice, which protected auteur filmmakers against the ravages of industrialization, the insecurity of market capitalism, the dearth of reliable personnel, and political and artistic censorship, while allowing them to take advantage of artisanal and collective capabilities.

This was a peculiarly Iranian collective production mode, which was different from the kind of repertory production practiced by Ingmar Bergman and the early Atom Egoyan, whereby a director works with a specific cast and crew over several films as a way of ensuring artistic and stylistic continuity. Artistic continuity may have been a factor for Iranian directors, but other reasons were more important in a society and time in which social, political, financial, and technological uncertainties were rampant. This production mode worked for a transitional society in which pre-modern social structures like kinship and nepotism were still meaningful and had not fully given way to autonomous identities and professional social relations. The family production mode made sense for a society in which descent relations (based on blood) still prevailed over consent relations (based on contract).

In addition, like all cinematic production modes, this too somewhat paralleled the production mode of the society at large. Under the Islamic Republic, rich and powerful families, many of them religious or clerical, became highly influential by creating networks and occupying key positions within the country's businesses, industries, governing institutions, and politics. Some families were so large and powerful that they could rightly be regarded as political parties.[4]

A hothouse cinema

Although the art-house cinema was initially state-financed and state-supported, like the Pahlavi-era new-wave cinema, an increasing number of directors began to make their movies for the private sector, which grew in strength. This turn to private sector financing was an important component of capitalist postmodernity and globalization. Art-house directors set their sights not only on the domestic audience but also on international spectators and box-office earnings. Many wrote their own screenplays (Abbas Kiarostami, Dariush Mehrjui, Baizai, Naderi, Majidi, Rakhshan Banietemad, Tahmineh Milani, and Mohsen Makhmalbaf), several collaborated with writers on screenplays (Mehrjui, Banietemad), and a few edited their own films (Baizai, Makhmalbaf, Kiarostami), consolidating their authorial control.

Some critics dismissively characterized the art-house cinema as a "hothouse cinema" or a "festival cinema" (*sinema-ye golkhanehi*).[5] The films nurtured in this atmosphere, so went the theory, were shielded from domestic market vagaries and presented as pretty bouquets at international film festivals. To the extent that government funding was instrumental in sustaining this cinema early on, this was true. However, to suggest that the films became ideologically compromised is erroneous, for many art cinema filmmakers, like their prerevolutionary predecessors, managed to bite the hands that fed them in various manifest and latent ways. They retained a critical distance both from society and government and from the mainstream cinema. This critical edge, encoded in the films' realism, surrealism, and metarealism, constitutes an important characteristic of art cinema.

Government funding and censorship were important factors both of auteur filmmaking and of art-house cinema, for they both enabled and shackled these filmmakers and their films. As Andrew Sarris noted in his classic definition of auteur filmmaking, the interior meaning, which he called the "glory of cinema," results from the tension between a director's personality and her material, and the impediments to its expression.[6] Some of the "glory" of Iranian art-house films must be sought in this tension between individual originality and sociopolitical impediments, as we will discuss below.

The art-house authorial style: neorealism and its deconstruction

Art-house film directors are auteurs because their vision and personality dominates the work from conception to completion, and because of certain shared practices and stylistic features. These included a neorealist sort of "realism," affirming a profilmic Iranian reality; a religiously inflected "surrealism," offering a spiritual reality and a sacred subjectivity, particularly in Morteza Avini's multipart television series, *Chronicle of Victory* (*Ravayat-e Fath*, 1985– 1992), which highlighted the religious subjectivity both of the Iranian fighters willingly sacrificing and martyring themselves in the war with Iraq and of the cameramen who selflessly covered the war; and a self-reflexive "metarealism," offering a fresh postmodernist vision of cinema. The latter two features problematized cinematic realism and modernist aesthetics in the service of rendering a truer, a more nuanced, more contingent take on reality. As a result, if the Pahlavi-era new-wave cinema was about realistically rendered subject matter, the Islamic Republic-era art-house cinema is about its subject matter and cinema itself, rendered metarealistically.

Much has been made of Abbas Kiarostami's (and, more generally, of Iranian art-house cinema's) debts to Italian neorealism, but this is a complex matter.[7] Kiarostami's career and cinema embody only some neorealist characteristics; over the years, they have accrued other attributes leading to a post-neorealist postmodernist cinema. Because of the dominant impact of Kiarostami's personality, films, and style on domestic art cinema and its globalization, I will present a case study of his style and, later, of one of his most important films, *Close-up*, which embodies many of the characteristics and "glories" of postmodernist art-house cinema. Art cinema under the Islamic Republic, like the Pahlavi-era new-wave cinema before it, both of which Kiarostami participated in, is heterogeneous, dynamic, and multifaceted. Neither Kiarostami nor his films fully embody or exhaust its attributes. Other art cinema filmmakers thus are discussed throughout.

We can consider Kiarostami's neorealist features briefly by invoking Georges Sadoul, one of the first to call neorealism a "school," who identified several of its characteristics.[8] He contended that neorealist films were geographically and temporally bounded, that they functioned based on a master and disciple arrangement, and that they employed certain specific cinematic and aesthetic rules, including location filming, long takes, an unobtrusive style of filming and editing, the predominance of medium and long shots, use of contemporary true-to-life subjects, open-ended plots, working class protagonists, non-professional casts, vernacular dialogue, and implied social criticism.[9]

Applying these criteria, both the similarities and differences between Iranian neorealism and its Italian progenitor become clear. In addition, as noted elsewhere, Iranian neorealism has not been homogenous, exhibiting itself in two different styles under two different political systems, and that it has been neither a fully formed film "school" nor a "movement," but a "moment of convergence" in the social history of Iranian cinema.[10]

The stories of Kiarostami's films are socially, historically, and geographically bounded: they spring from contemporary middle- and lower-class milieus within Iran and, in the 2000s, abroad. However, with success, Kiarostami's works began to exceed these bounds, as he began receiving coproduction funding from Europe and started working abroad, with such films as *A.B.C. Africa* (2001), *Tickets* (2005), *Certified Copy* (*Copie Conformé*, 2010), and *Like Someone in Love* (2012).

Classic neorealism, as a school, operated within a master-disciple structure. Kiarostami has been a sort of master whose works have influenced disciples, either indirectly by emulation, or directly by assisting him or using his ideas and screenplays for their own films. Ebrahim Foruzesh, Jafar Panahi, Alireza Raisian, Mohammad Ali Talebi, Iraj Karimi, and Niki Karimi all made films that were inspired by specific film ideas of Kiarostami, or used his screenplays. Others who worked for him as assistants but did not use his screenplays, such as Bahman Ghobadi, were nevertheless influenced by his style. Even actors working with Kiarostami made films in a style inspired by him, such as Mania Akbari who made her daring debut directorial film, *Twenty Fingers* (*Bist Angosht*, 2004) and later works, *Ten Plus Four* (*Dah Beh Alaveh-ye Char*, 2007) and *One Two One* (*Yek Do Yek*, 2011), in his shadow.

However, the public dispute between Kiarostami and Ghobadi over the latter's film about the vibrant underground music scene in Iran, *Nobody Knows About Persian Cats* (*Kasi az Gorbehha-ye Irani Khabar Nadareh*, 2009), showed that the master-disciple dyad is not a lasting configuration in the creative arts. The government banned the film inside Iran, partly because it was filmed without official permission, causing Ghobadi to leave the country in protest (he now generally lives and works in Kurdistan, Iraq). When Kiarostami publicly criticized his former protégé on his filming and departure, Ghobadi responded in an emotional public letter: "On what basis do you give yourself permission to ridicule the efforts of filmmakers who stand with the oppressed people using unacceptable words and, worse than that, speak with the same voice as religious dictators?"[11]

Finally, through his films, Kiarostami developed a set of "rules," which both paid homage to the aesthetics of the Italian neorealism and evolved a new Iranian and Kiarostamian definition, which was, ironically, a deconstructed version of the original. The spirit and style of neorealism is strongly present in Kiarostami's early short films, such as *Bread and Alley* (*Nan va Kucheh*, 1970) and *Traveler* (*Mosafer*, 1974), in which his actors are untrained ordinary people. The protagonists are usually male children on dogged true-to-life quests or journeys to get something, to redress a wrong, or to prove something. He shows himself to be an artist of the everyday, but not of "everydayness," for he does not seek the tediousness, repetitiveness, and degradation of the everyday, but instead searches and discovers the moments of rupture, tension, and glory hidden in the quotidian.

These early Pahlavi-era films placed him within the new wave category.[12] Inspired by the neorealist style and ethos, almost all of Kiarostami's films are shot on location in cityscapes and in the countryside—not in the studio—and in available light, using a small crew and simple equipment—and now digital cameras—and vernacular dialogue that is often devised on the spot. The filming style generally consists of long shots and long takes.

However, while his films treat these ordinary social worlds and encounters with the ethos and aesthetics of neorealism, they embody certain deconstructive metarealist practices that counter neorealism, resulting in formally rigorous works that are quietly operatic in their humanism and in their celebration of life's small victories, as well as filmmaking itself. The mixing of fiction and non-fiction elements has a long history in Iranian cinema that dates back to Ovanes Ohanians's *Mr. Haji the Movie Actor* (*Haji Aqa, Aktor-e Sinema*, 1933), Kimiavi's *The Stone Garden* (*Bagh-e Sangi*, 1976), and Kamran Shirdel's *The Night it Rained... or, the Epic of a Gorgani Peasant* (*Unshab keh Barun Umad... Ya Hamaseh-ye Rustazadeh-ye Gorgani*, 1967), but this factional mode came to the fore only in the 1990s, not only breaking into new territory, but also making it harder to verify either the authenticity of documentary or the fictitiousness of fiction.[13]

Kiarostami's deconstructive and counterrealistic practices include self-referentiality, self-inscription, and self-reflexivity as well as the ironic blending of reality and fiction, forms of distancing, indirection, and sly humor. By these means, the best-known practitioner of neorealism is also the best violator of what Kamran Shirdel aptly called "the dictatorship of neorealism."[14] Other art-house cinema directors employed some of these neorealist and counter-realist strategies; however, in Kiarostami's films, the veracity is never revealed to spectators, who must constantly parse the truth of fiction from the fiction of realism.

A younger generation of filmmakers introduced even more radical hybridization of the documentary and the fictional to break down what had become known as the "genre" of Iranian art-house cinema. For example, in his award-winning debut feature, *Be Calm and Count to Seven* (*Aram Bash va ta Haft Beshomar*, 2008), Ramtin Lavafipour deftly grafted the slow-paced neorealist tempo of Iranian art-house "village films"—emphasizing integrity of character, place, and time and engagement in quotidian activities—with the turbo-charged pacing of the new "global films"—emphasizing nervous hand-held camerawork, sonic bursts, and dynamic editing which violated the viewer's sense of place and border. The result is a technically audacious film that seamlessly weaves these seemingly contradictory aesthetics—as well as fictional and documentary elements—to tell the story of destitute fishermen and their women trafficking people to and from the Qeshm Island, in the Persian Gulf.

The ambiguity in Iranian art-house films is in part driven by the filmmakers' personalities and styles, partly by the authoritarian systems under which they have lived, and to some degree by the Iranian hermeneutics and psychological orientations of veiling, dissimulation, accismus (*ta'arof*), cleverness, inner purity (*safa-ye baten*), lyricism, and indirection—in short, by strategies that demonstrate distrust in the manifest and, instead, valorize latent meaning. These endow authorial cinema and arts in Iran with idealism over realism and with what Bahram Baizai calls "visual duplicity," reveling in duality, ambiguity, complexity, evasiveness, playfulness, relativity, deferment, and hedging. These hermeneutics continually favor idealism and defer as well as problematize realism.

Instead of practicing clarity and frankness, which can cause problems in a highly collective, dual, and hierarchical and authoritarian society, according to Baizai, Iranians have learned to engage in "saying things without appearing to have said them [...], but in such a way that those who should, understand that you have said it. Many Iranian filmmakers live this visual duplicity, as they have to follow unerringly the various written and unwritten supervisory [censorship] regulations without believing in a single one of them. And the supervisory office knows this."[15] This is another dimension of Iranian art and its style of improvisation, which permeates all the arts. The "glory" of Iranian art-house films lies in the manner in which these sociopolitical and authorial tensions are negotiated.

Even when Kiarostami uses the continuity filming and editing schemes of classic realist (and neorealist) cinema, such as shot reverse-shot, he undermines them. Many of his films, particularly his later road movies such as *Taste of Cherry* (*Ta'm-e Gilas*, 1997), in which a driver and a passenger are filmed in a moving car talking for long periods, contain not only long takes, but also shot reverse-shots. However, while using shot reverse-shot exchanges between the two characters in the car, there is no over-the-shoulder shot placing both in the same visual space. This is because, as he told me in an interview, these shots are all filmed without the driver and the passenger ever being present together in the car. Each time that one person is on camera, Kiarostami occupies the other front seat.[16] In a sly subversion of codes of realism and neorealism, the protagonists are forced to react not to each other, as is customary in those styles, but to the director next to them, a presence that insinuates Kiarostami's authorial control into each profilmic scene, as he coaches the cast and feeds them lines of dialogue. His apparent casualness and improvisation, which consolidate his connection both to Italian neorealism and to the French new-wave films, is illusory.

Nevertheless, the film is to a large extent improvisational, as Kiarostami did not use a traditional screenplay or written dialogue for the actors. Instead, the dialogue was improvised during filming. As a result, these are manufactured impressions of casualness and realism that he has strived hard to provoke, not innocent recordings of unfolding reality, as many believe. They conceal his considerable planning and tinkering with locations, prop arrangements, acting, dialogue coaching, and filming.

Regarded as the engine of classical realism, shot reverse-shot filming and editing, often involving over-the-shoulder shots, creates audience identification with characters by suturing them into the diegesis. The classical realist style is highly psychological and fictional; Kiarostami's sparing use of these strategies, and their undermining when he does use them, render his films more social and realistic, even didactic. In this manner, his techniques may work against cinema's mechanism of individualized subjectivity, a hallmark of modernity. Instead, they favor postmodernist distancing and collective identity.

His early and mid-career works tend to be didactic because their understated characters do not appear to discover much in their quests, or seem unaware of any discovery. They are determined, but are not often transformed by their own discoveries, as characters in modernist novels and films are. We get this impression because the films make little use of subjective point-of-view filming and shot reverse-shot editing.[17] Instead, Kiarostami's primary filming style, involving long shots and long takes, tells us more about his own subjectivity. This strengthens his authorial grip. It is the audience that discovers something universal, by which it is potentially transformed. Hence the gripping power of his films on spectators, particularly non-Iranians. In addition, because Kiarostami breaks the fourth wall and self-reflexively inserts the process of filmmaking into his stories, the focus of inquiry is shifted from the characters to the camera, the cinema, the director, and ultimately the spectators, who become aware of their own act of watching.

A metarealist cinema

Among the stylistic features that turn art-house films into a metarealist cinema, in addition to the deconstructive strategies problematizing neorealism already noted, are self-reflexivity, self-referentiality, self-inscription, and intertextuality. Self-reflexivity in Iranian cinema, and in Kiarostami's films in particular, takes several forms. One is self-inscription, by which filmmakers insert themselves into their films diegetically, sometimes as themselves, as Kiarostami does in *Taste of Cherry* and *A. B. C. Africa*, and sometimes by proxy, as he does in *Life and Nothing More...* (aka *And Life Goes On*, or *Zendehgi va Digar Hich*, 1991) and *The Wind Will Carry Us* (*Bad Ma Ra Khahad Bord*, 1999).

Kiarostami is a diegetic character in *Close-Up*, appearing as himself, investigating Sabzian's story, instigating certain scenes, and in general directing the film. Only glimpses of him are shown from the back, but we hear his voice frequently as the investigative filmmaker just outside the frame researches the magazine story, visits locations, interviews players, and recreates and directs scenes. In their home, he interviews the Ahankhah family members who attempt to save face by pretending not to have been fooled by Sabzian's impersonation.

In Qasr prison, he interviews Sabzian who confesses to having impersonated Makhmalbaf, an act that, he admits, appears to be fraudulent, but deep down is very sincere, since it was motivated by his love for cinema and by his respect and admiration for the director. Kiarostami also interviews the judge in his chamber to obtain permission to film Sabzian's trial, whose crime he regards as not worth filming. In addition, he recreates many scenes, including Sabzian's bus encounter with Mrs. Ahankhah, and the scene of his arrest. The latter is reenacted twice, once from outside the Ahankhah home and a second time from the inside, once again playing into the Iranian opposition of inside and outside.

This investigative structure, a feature of Kiarostami's research film methodology, inscribes the director as both author and actor who simultaneously records the film and invents it as he goes along, mixing documentary footage with fictional accounts. Such self-inscription simultaneously heightens filmic realism and undermines it in order to investigate both reality and cinema.

Earlier Kiarostami films beget later films and later films refer to earlier films; his characters, locations, and stories migrate from one film to another, making his films self-referential and intertextual. His so-called "Koker trilogy," consisting of *Where is the Friend's Home?* (*Khaneh Dust Kojast?*, 1987), *Life and Nothing More*, and *Through the Olive Trees* (*Zir-e Derakhtan-e Zaitun*, 1994), are intertextual in that they take place in the same area, Koker, and characters and stories migrate from one film to another. By referring to, quoting, or provoking one another, the films create an intertextual nexus that requires a knowing audience to decipher. Director Rakhshan Banietemad, too, employs a dense and creative intertextuality in her oeuvre, where characters in earlier films live on and evolve in later films.

Self-reflexivity, incorporating the process of creation into the film's story by showing filmmakers at work, breaks the spectatorial illusion of witnessing a seamless and authorless "real world." Self-reflexive structures are usually considered to be modernist devices and Western avant-garde tropes. In the case of Kiarostami and some of the art-house auteurs, though, they originate in what they have absorbed from traditional Iranian theatrical performances, particularly the *taziyeh*, the Shi'ite passion play. The tragic, grief-ridden, and justice-seeking contents of *taziyeh's* Karbala paradigm are less relevant to Kiarostami than its self-reflexive distancing.[18] In *taziyeh*, the stage apparatus is made visible, the artificiality of acting and the separation of actor from part are acknowledged, the actors perform stereotypes which do not evolve, and the fourth wall is broken and spectators are addressed directly, as Kiarostami does. He said, when asked about Brechtian distancing:

> Yes, but I haven't taken it from the theory of Brecht only. I came to that through experience. We are never able to construct truth as it is in the reality of our daily lives, and we are always witnessing things from far away while we are trying to depict them as close as we can to reality. So if we distance the audience from the film and even film from itself, it helps to understand the subject matter better. I found distantiation in Taazieh [sic]....
>
> Many of the audiences believe my films are documentaries, as if it just happened that there was a camera there to record them. I think if the audience knows they are

watching a performance, something which has been constructed, they will understand it more than they would in a documentary film. [...] This year I went to a village near Teheran to watch a Taazieh. In the scene of the Yazid's and Imam Hossein's battle, Imam Hossein's sword suddenly became bent because it was made of very cheap, soft metal. Yazid went to him and took his sword and put it on a big stone and straightened it with another stone and gave it back to him and then they continued fighting. [...]

This is exactly the opposite to what at the moment Hollywood is doing, which is brainwashing the audience to such an extent that it strips them of any imagination, decision-making or intellectual capacity, in order to captivate them for two whole hours. In my films, there are always some breaks—such as when a prop assistant brings a bowl of water, and hands it to an actor in the film. This gives the audience time to breathe a little and stops them from becoming emotionally involved, and reminds them that, "Yes, I'm watching a film." In *Through the Olive Trees* always keep this distance between the reality of the scene and the reality of the subject matter.[19]

In *Close-Up*, the imposter Sabzian, the Ahankhah family members, the judge, the journalist, and the film directors Makhmalbaf and Kiarostami are both themselves and actors self-consciously playing parts. They recreate certain scenes (Sabzian impersonating Makhmalbaf in the Ahankhah home or on the bus), act in new scenes (Sabzian and Makhmalbaf meeting for the first time), and sometimes directly address the camera either in interview situations (Sabzian, judge, and Ahankhah family members) or in what amounts to an internal monologue (Sabzian speaking to the close-up camera).

In the process, the real, the recreated, and the fictional are juxtaposed. The status of the film is complicated and thrown into doubt; it is neither a documentary faithfully reproducing a profilmic reality nor a fiction film producing a new fictive reality. In his own words, it represents an attempt to "reach fiction through the documentary;"[20] it promotes both distantiation and identification, cognition and emotion, belief and disbelief.

The production of doubt and ambiguity at so many different levels is deeply counter-hegemonic, both to Hollywood-style realism and to the Islamist politics of certainty. It is also thoroughly postmodernist, as doubt and uncertainty are part and parcel of postmodernism's ethos. Significantly, Kiarostami's attacks on these hegemons are offered at the level of filmic style, not content. Indeed, *Close-Up* is entirely about the lie at the heart of cinema, whereby actors pretend to be others, producing a sustained and complex treatise on the morality of the Iranian dichotomy between being and acting. It is also about the double consciousness with which disaffected Iranians approach the state and its diktats.

Many other art-house filmmakers employed self-reflexivity and other deconstructive devices: Baizai, Mehrjui, Mohsen Makhmalbaf, Panahi, Banietemad, and Farmanara. In Baizai's films self-reflexivity is clearly influenced by his deep knowledge and appreciation of *taziyeh*, about which he has written. Early on in his *Travelers* (*Mosaferan*, 1991), the lead actor announces to the camera that she and her family who are leaving for a wedding in another city will never get there, as they will all die in a car crash. As in *taziyeh*, the spectators know the story's outcome before the performance begins.

The surprise is in how it is told. As in *taziyeh*, the acting is often declamatory, and some of the main characters being mourned are missing. The elaborate wedding ceremony in opulent circular hallways resembles a *taziyeh* in which guests, bride, and groom mourn the death of their loved ones in the accident. Circularity, an important principle of *taziyeh* staging, is emphasized not only by the film's circular setting but also by the circular traveling of the camera as it covers the action, and by the characters' circular movements, particularly the bride as she spins around.

In his *Bashu, the Little Stranger*, too, Baizai inscribes *taziyeh* aesthetics powerfully but subtly. In one sequence, Bashu assumes the role of an amanuensis for Nai who dictates a letter to her husband. The scene is outdoors and Nai is hanging her wet clothes on the line, while Bashu is seated nearby. As she takes the washing from a tub, she walks left to hang it on the line while dictating the letter, the camera panning with her; she stops, picks up another piece of wet cloth, and continues her dictation as she walks left, eventually making a full circle, the camera following her arc. This circular space described by both protagonist and camera is that of the *taziyeh* arena, whose narrator is Nai, addressing her audience and her missing husband.

The shot's background is also inflected by *taziyeh*, using its capacity for suturing different times and places in the same setting: as the camera pans, we see helmeted soldiers among the lush bushes, reminding us of the war front hundreds of miles away on the Iran-Iraq border, which may be the cause of the husband's absence; when the camera continues its pan, helmeted construction workers are seen in the background, reminding us of those who were blowing up a tunnel in the mountains earlier, scaring Bashu.

In Mehrjui's family drama *Leila* (1997), a lead character breaks the fourth wall several times by speaking to the camera, while his *The Mix* (*Miks*, 1999) self-reflexively focuses on filmmaking, particularly postproduction. This and pre-production script approval are stages in which the influences of both capital and censorship are paramount. Postproduction censorship, which may necessitate new filming, editing, sound recording, and mixing, has been known to prevent important premieres. *The Mix* parodies this chaotic and stressful period in the life of the diegetic film director of a film-within-film (Khosrow Shakibai), a stand-in for Mehrjui, who works with his technicians to conquer crazily proliferating obstacles to their film's premiere, just three days away at the flagship national film festival, Fajr. The entire film takes place inside a studio complex, where voice actors dub the voices of characters, sound effects and music are recorded, various soundtracks are mixed, and an exhibition print is readied for festival screening.

To top it all, the censors require that several instances of improper *hejab* be removed from the film. The postproduction crew and director race against time, emphasized by intercut close-ups of a ticking clock. Such time pressures and censorship considerations often force filmmakers to make emergency compromises with which they may not be happy afterward (such as the ending of Mehrjui's *The Tenants*, or *Ejarehneshinha*, 1990). The film-within-film is not fully finished and its screening at the festival is sabotaged by technical problems; in the meantime, the director, who has gone mad under the pressure and has been bound by the crew with ropes to a big piece of sound equipment, collapses.

In another example of self-reflexivity, the lead character goes by the name of the actor who plays him, Khosrow, while some of the others are called by the names of the technical crew whose parts they play, creating confusion or parallels between the actors and the parts.

Unfortunately, the chaos of postproduction permeates not only the diegetic director's film but also that of the empirical director's film, *The Mix*. Mehrjui intercuts the postproduction chaos with clips from the movie in process, creating an incoherent intertextual density. This perhaps accounts for the tepid response the film received from Iranian spectators and critics. Nevertheless, it is an intensely personal and authorial film for Mehrjui: he co-produced the film, wrote the screenplay and directed it, and he co-designed the costumes and the sets. In another way, *The Mix* is a great film, emblematizing the speed, pressure, disruptions, and sensory overload of modernity and industrialization and the costs for their subjects.

Makhmalbaf used these deconstructive strategies in several of his mid-career and later films, including his trilogy on cinema. *Naser al-Din Shah, the Movie Actor* aka *Once Upon a Time, Cinema* (*Naser al-Din Shah, Aktor-e Sinema*, 1991) is his audacious and loving homage to the history of Iranian cinema through the eyes of its first filmmakers. In *Salaam Cinema* aka

Cinema, Cinema (*Salam Sinema*, 1994), he inscribes himself as an authoritarian director who puts out a casting call that brings in over 5,000 applicants. This enthusiastic group, who will do anything to get into the movies, forces Makhmalbaf to aggressively interview, interrogate, and harass the prospective cast members.

The trilogy's first film deals with the early filmmakers and their relationship to the court, the second deals with Iranian fans' cinephilia, while the third film, *The Actor* (*Honarpisheh*, 1993), deals principally with actors and their cinematic world. His *Gabbeh* (1996) is remarkable for its self-reflexive structure and counter-hegemonic uses of colors; it applies that recursion to one of the oldest arts in Iran, carpet weaving (and its variant, *gabbeh*), and one of the newest arts, filmmaking. As weavers weave not only standardized patterns but also their own personal signatures, preferences, and situations into their *gabbeh*, so does a postmodernist filmmaker like Makhmalbaf inscribe his own thoughts, concerns, and stylistic signatures into his films, including *Gabbeh*.

In Panahi's *The Mirror* (*Ayeneh*, 1997), the child protagonist (Mina Mohammadkhani) stops halfway through the film and, speaking to the camera, declares that she is not going to cooperate with the director. Banietemad, too, uses self-reflexivity and self-referentiality extensively, particularly in her *The May Lady* (*Banu-ye Ordibehesht*, 1997), which deals with the life and loves of a documentary film director.[21] In contrast to Kiarostami, Makhmalbaf, and Mehrjui, other directors' self-reflexivity did not involve self-inscription. Kiarostami's involvement with his films is so multi-layered and intimate that his films are about Kiarostami, as well as their nominal subjects and cinema. The following excerpt from an interview in *Gozaresh-e Film* magazine elucidates:

> Interviewer: Is *The Wind Will Carry Us* an image of yourself?
>
> Kiarostami: Yes, but you have to look for this image in the main character. I also see myself in the little boy. In *Close-up* I find myself in the character of Ali Sabzian and the Ahankhah family who are deceived. I'm like the character who lies, and at the same time I'm similar to the family who's been lied to. In all films, some characters are like the director, and in *The Wind Will Carry Us*, the woman in the café is like me, although she's a woman.[22]

Despite these associations, these characters are hardly autobiographical, as Kiarostami's various deconstructive strategies create uncertainties about their author and authenticity. However, Bahman Farmanara's film *Smell of Camphor, Fragrance of Jasmine* (*Bu-ye Kafur, Atr-e Yas*, 2000), made after twenty years' hiatus, was a bravura performance of self-inscription in which, like Kiarostami and Mohsen Makhmalbaf, the director did not shy away from casting himself in an unflattering light, taking the truthful but perhaps painful path to biographical self-representation—warts and all. As he relates it, Farmanara threw away the "whole vanity part," and decided that the only way that this character was going to be believable was to show him as he himself was: "[H]e smokes, he's fat, he doesn't care about himself, and he has a death wish."[23] He is no longer merely inscribing himself as an actor playing the part of his namesake, Bahman Farjami, but also as an actor who is playing himself in a story that to a large extent is about himself, about a fallow period in Farmanara's life when he was suffering from depression and unable to make movies.

The coincidence of actor, director, and part satisfies Phillipe Lejeun's classic definition of the autobiographical pact, one in which "the *author*, the *narrator*, and the *protagonist* are identical."[24] Most self-inscriptional and self-reflexive movies are not autobiographical, as Iranians' dual, hierarchical, and collective psychology and attendant social practices create slippery realms where the three terms of the autobiographical pact cannot reliably coincide. Farmanara's film is thus rare. Like the pre-modern or early modern Iranians in the Qajar period and the first Pahlavi era, he is not defensive about his own incomplete or unflattering image, nor about the image of his nation, and he does not try to keep up false appearances—or as the Persian saying goes, he does not try to keep his cheeks rosy by slapping himself. He is a self-conscious modern subject, with all the uncertainties and dualities that modern subjectivity entails.

Here, the traditional firewall between Iranian interior and exterior spheres is dissolved. He is willing to present himself (and by extension his nation) to insiders and outsiders as he is, as an autonomous agent in history, not as a mere subject of history's effects. He is willing to admit that he is not perfect, that he harbors doubts about himself, and that he makes fun of and criticizes himself. He is not afraid to hang his dirty individual or national laundry in public. In embodying individual subjectivity and responsibility, and in embodying the tenets of the autobiographical pact, *Smell of Camphor, Fragrance of Jasmine* is a triumph of modernity in late twentieth-century cinema.

With his haunting debut feature film, *Black Tape: The Videotape Fariborz Kamkari Found in the Garbage* (*Ravayat-e Maghshush*, 2002), Fariborz Kamkari contributes not only to the increasing output of Iranian Kurdish filmmakers but also to the roster of audacious experimental films. The conceit of the film (with dialogue in Persian and Kurdish) is that the director, Kamkari (who also wrote the screenplay), came across a videotape containing the film. The story the film tells in fits and starts is that of Parviz (Gholamreza Moasesi), an ex-army sergeant and torturer, married to his beautiful much-younger wife Goli (Shilan Rahmani), daughter of a Kurdish rebel. Their relationship is fraught with power imbalance, violent fights, voyeurism and sadomasochistic sex play, unusual in its candor for the normally demure arthouse cinema.

Goli is both a prized trophy wife and a slave, whom Parviz makes love to but treats like a prisoner. This is because he has acquired her in a manner that Kamkari says he heard in real testimonies of Kurdish refugees: poor parents sell their young daughters to rich Persians and Arabs as wives. The film dramatizes the violent crumbling of this family relationship with a brutal twist in the ending, and goes beyond the boundaries of the story, as there are frequent references to Parviz torturing and killing Kurds, including her family. It is told with "video diary" hand-held clips filmed primarily by the two protagonists, with stops, starts, false starts, and dropped cameras. The camera becomes a third character.

The point-of-view filming replicates the gendered power imbalance: Parviz films inside the couple's apartment, with frequent intrusive zoom-ins and claustrophobic framing that seem driven by the desire to "pin down and enclose the subject."[25] Goli's filming, on the other hand, is mostly exterior, with a looser and wider style allowing freedom of horizon and action. It's unclear if the contrast is due to the director's instructions, the exigencies of women's representation in cinema (forcing a tighter framing of women, particularly in intimate scenes, to avoid censorship), the circumstances of filming (which took place inside Kamkari's own apartment) or the real life background of the actors (particularly Rahmani, who had been a refugee herself living in camps). Perhaps all of these were factors.

That the film was mostly shot inside the director's apartment, that Rahmani had been a Kurdish refugee herself, that the primary relationship was based on the Kurds' real-life stories, that Parviz forbade Goli to speak her own language—all these anchor the film in reality, preventing it from flying into self-reflexive and fictionalized alternate worlds. The result is an audacious, powerful film told in a fresh style different from commercial movies and arthouse films. The film was banned in Iran.

A consequence of the strategies of metarealism for the film's reception is that spectators do not aggregate as a collective. According to Brecht, while Aristotelian drama creates a collective entity in the movie house "for the duration of the entertainment" on the basis of the "common humanity" that all the spectators share, self-reflexive drama is "not interested in the establishment of such an entity. It divides its audience."[26] Instead, each spectator responds subjectively and individually to the work of art.

While such an outcome of counter-hegemonic strategies may be celebrated as an empowering gift of modernity and postmodernism to artists and spectators, allowing them to engage in individualized, "cellular" resistance against mainstream culture and ideology, they may also be condemned as a disempowering curse, for these textual politics of playfulness, irony, and double-consciousness may undermine the films' social politics of certainty and collectivity. As Marxist literary critic Masud Zavarzadeh warned, the danger is that this "ludic postmodernism," in the name of "paradox, parody, and pastiche—complexity—places the most blatant instances of social exploitation and their naturalization in films and other texts of culture under interrogative immunity and grants them free play under the sign of immanent resistance."[27] This is what the best of the dissident exile filmmakers, critics, and intellectuals may be saying in their critique of the Islamic Republic art-house films that circulate in international film festivals, that they engage in ludic postmodernism. The damage that such ludic deconstructive textual strategies can cause in cinema and media exceeds the realm of national cinemas and politics. Strategies that emphasize the endless playfulness of the signifier without being anchored in what Derrida called a "transcendental signified," or social reality, favor global capitalism by flattening all social contradictions and oppositions as resistance or mere difference, thus reproducing "the ethos of the democratic pluralism that is the ideological underpinning of stateless corporate capitalism."[28]

What are the implications of this situation for the Iranian art cinema? Art-house filmmakers' use of these deconstructive textual strategies stems from a deep-seated yet contradictory impulse, which lies at the core of the work of intellectuals in the age of globalization, particularly among those who live in authoritarian states. On the one hand, their filmic deconstruction of reality stems from their desire to question, to counter, and even to deny the singular, state-sanctioned "social reality" of the Islamic Republic. On the other, they want to reach out to the globe, to be heard, and to break apart the self-imposed official certainties and sanctimonies in order to create another self-generated, alternate, "cinematic reality." This alternate filmic reality is contingent and open to multiple, even contradictory, interpretations. These emancipatory counter-hegemonic strategies at home, however, seem to feed into the dominant globalized and triumphalist capitalist postmodernism, which popularizes these films in the wider world and grants their makers the honor of being "auteur" directors. This sort of recognition is what every artist seeks. However, by commercially diffusing their works, global postmodernism may also defuse them politically, by softening their critical edge and coopting it as mere style.

10

THE RE-EMERGENCE AND EVOLUTION OF
POP MUSIC IN THE ISLAMIC REPUBLIC OF IRAN

FROM HEAVENLY TO EARTHLY LOVE

Nahid Siamdoust

This chapter traces the birth and evolution of state-approved pop music in post-revolutionary Iran. As Iran slowly emerged from the devastating emotional and economic impact of the Iran-Iraq war, its large youth population was eager for forms of cultural production that reflected its openness and optimism toward the world and the future. State officials responded to these shifts in demography and taste by opening the gates to pop music after nearly two decades of prohibition. The bulk of this article narrates this process, which was spearheaded by a number of young musicians and distinct individuals among state officials, attesting to the importance of personal agency within a politically authoritarian context. It also examines the evolution of this state-controlled *musiqi-ye pop* from its initial forms, with its un-provoking rhythms and innocuous content, drawing often on religious or natural themes, to its current forms, with its fast dance beats and themes of romance.

It is now often difficult to distinguish between pop music produced in Tehran and that produced in the capital city of the Iranian diaspora half a world away, dubbed *Tehrangeles*. Since the revolution and through to the mid-2000s, pop music produced by expatriates in Los Angeles often dominated Tehran's (private) party soundscapes, and was also prevalent in everyday spaces such as taxis and people's homes. This nearly unidirectional flow of production reversed by 2005, when some pop music made in Iran reached higher popularity even among expatriates. By then the Islamic Republic no longer policed against fast beats and love lyrics, and production and recording quality had vastly improved. This cultural exchange has now reached a sort of equilibrium, as both music scenes influence each other and collaborate. In fact, even the distinction between the two cities is now quite fluid as musicians inside Iran sometimes emigrate and continue their work in expatriate music production circuits. Ultimately, the Islamic Republic—insofar as there is a unified body of decision making on cultural production—has been pragmatic in its approach to pop. As long as the music does not pose an ideological or political threat to the regime, it is permitted, no matter how fast the beats or earthly the themes.

But this pragmatic stance was not policy from the start. It took the Islamic Republic's cultural bodies a decade to arrive at this—still sometimes volatile—position, since all these issues were at first contested. I argue that whereas the state initially regulated pop music based on "Islamic" sensibilities, it has allowed musicians in this field to push the boundaries in their beats and lyrics. Because the government as well as other non-elected ideological bodies strictly control Iran's public entertainment space, the state is not necessarily concerned about the potential of subversive fun. As Asef Bayat has argued, "Fear of fun [...] is not necessarily about diversion from the higher powers or noble values as such but about the fear of exit from the paradigm that frames and upholds the mastery of certain types of moral and political authorities, be they individuals, political movements, or states."[1] Within this controlled public space, the state has extended the limits on cultural expression, which over the years has led to a popular but shallow official musical culture. Although audiences always inject their own interpretations and subversions into the officially sanctioned or "public transcript,"[2] they never leave the state's "power paradigm" in this tightly controlled field. Thus, more than a decade after lifting the ban on pop music, the state allows most kinds of beats and lyrics as long as it can remain in control of production, and as long as the music doesn't pose a threat to its legitimacy.

The rebirth of pop music in Islamic Iran

> I just knew that a current would have to sweep in and eliminate this problem; pop music had to start again. I saw the music that entered Iran from overseas and most of it was no longer relevant to people's lives inside Iran, and still it was met with great public reception. People would play it in their houses and their cars, and this at a time when those tapes were considered a sin and one could be severely punished for having them. I was certain that we needed to talk to the country's officials and convince them that this ban on pop was a mistake.
>
> Khashayar Etemadi, August 2011, Tehran
> Singer of the Islamic Republic's first sanctioned pop song

The revival of Persian pop music from within the Islamic Republic's official state media was one of the most momentous events in post-revolutionary Iranian music.[3] From the start, the process was fraught with anxieties about national identity and state ideology.[4] After all, the revolutionary motherland had by now banned and de facto exiled its most famous creators of pop. Music itself has long been a contested art form within Islam[5] and all music was adversely affected following the revolution. Gradually, certain kinds of music were allowed, chiefly revolutionary anthems and march music.[6] Although Persian classical music was neglected, it was not completely banned, so that some of its most famous practitioners, such as Mohammad Reza Shajarian and Shahram Nazeri, could continue to publish records throughout the 1980s. In fact, Persian classical music started to "attract a mass audience for the very first time" due to a heightened sense of national identity at the time of the revolution.[7] But pop music, entangled as it was in webs of signification denoting "Westoxification," represented more than any other genre the "depraved" culture that the revolutionaries had fought to eliminate. Although pop had been "indigenized" and was quite "Iranian" in themes, vocal styles and even musical arrangements, Iran's complicated relationship with the West and the Pahlavi regime's inadvertent elevation of Western over Iranian culture meant that pop music and the cabarets of Lalehzar were some of the revolution's first casualties.[8] But household names like Googoosh, Dariush, Ebi, Hayedeh and Homeyra were barely silenced with the revolution as their songs—all now produced in Los Angeles—continued to stream into Iran via cassette and VHS (Video Home System) tapes, and remained for a long time the only Iranian pop legacy.[8]

Finally, after fifteen years of near prohibition, the first homegrown pop creations were broadcast into Iran's post-revolutionary soundscape through conservative state media, to much surprise. The very first attempts at pop music were mostly spontaneous productions by the first generation of young music academy graduates and their friends. These young musicians succeeded because they were supported in their efforts by music officials who were motivated by a variety of factors, chief among them to create "music for the youth" and stem the tide of "cultural invasion," a term that referred equally to Western and expatriate Iranian creations. Hence, to use Bourdieu's terminology, agents in the field of music with certain social positions—accrued through "revolutionary/ideological" cultural capital—were able to initiate what at that point might have seemed like an impossible task. Because of their positions, they were able to proceed without being stopped by hierarchically superior agents in other fields, such as the *ulama* or the *monkerat* (security). In mapping a sort of history of the creation of state-sanctioned pop music in post-revolutionary Iran, I draw mostly on my interviews to offer an account based on the narratives of those who were at the heart of this process, augmented by conversations over the years with other people working in music, and the little that exists in print.

There is still a lot of speculation about the reasons behind the government's decision to permit pop music. Many believe that the government decided to partake in a lucrative entertainment sector, as it was in any event powerless to stem the flow of expatriate pop music through the black market and through newly emerging technologies such as satellite TV and the Internet. But the generally accepted narrative is that the Islamic Republic, in a calculated move, launched young singers—often with voices and styles similar to popular *los ānjelesi* stars—in order to draw Iranians' attention away from what it considered to be degenerate expatriate content invading the country, and inward toward a state-controlled, conforming discourse.[9] While there is debate about the reasons behind this move, the outcome is clear, as Laudan Nooshin writes: "By legalizing certain types of pop music, not only has the government blunted the subversive potential of imported pop, but it has done so by appropriating the very form of cultural resistance used against it in the 1980s as its weapon of countersubversion".[10]

Throughout, suspicions about the government's intentions have been fueled not just by the common perception that anything that happens in state media must necessarily be orchestrated and directed from above, but also by what many perceived as uncanny similarities between the new voices and those of pre-revolutionary pop stars (referred to as *shabih-sāzi* or *shabih-khāni*, imitation). This view was often expressed in the conversations that I had about the subject, and in the literature. For example, in an interview conducted with one of the main revivalists of this genre, Fereydun Shahbazian, journalists pressed him about the similarities and asserted that, "It seems that a special policy wants this imitation to take place. The idea that this happened totally by coincidence is hard to believe. Even if we assume that this was the case, it is unexpected of state media to simply concur with [it] and for it to be able to continue without any problems."[11]

However, a confluence of factors—rather than a government-orchestrated effort—facilitated the rebirth of pop music in the late 1990s. For one thing, nearly a decade had passed since the grief-stricken years of the Iran-Iraq war and the somber atmosphere had lightened somewhat. Importantly, it was also around this time that the "children of the revolution," born around 1979, were coming of age. Although the country had been broken, this generation was too young to have experienced it first-hand and, with its entire youth still ahead of it, was now yearning for bigger, brighter horizons. For these young people, who would later prove intent on riding the digital wave, state-sanctioned fare did not embody their sense of openness and optimism.

This spike in the youth population necessitated new thinking about cultural production among policymakers. As it was, many of these youths listened mostly to *los ānjelesi* and Western music, even though neither of those reflected their lived realities as young people coming of age in post-revolutionary Iran. Dozens of bands across Iran were already contributing to a burgeoning underground rock scene. Meanwhile, the first generation of graduates from the state's music academy were out of school and looking for ways to make careers as musicians. These processes were happening toward the end of President Akbar Hashemi Rafsanjani's "reconstruction" period, when a new wave of expatriate Iranians with various kinds of cultural and/or material capital had started to return to Iran and contribute their skills and knowledge. Significant among these for the creation of pop music was the prominent producer Babak Bayat,[12] who produced the "first" pop album. Also importantly, the official in charge of music at state television, Mohammad Ali Moʿallem Damghani (henceforth referred to as Moʿallem), had both an artistic background (as a poet) and high revolutionary capital (as a confidant of the Supreme Leader Ayatollah Ali Khamenei), which meant that he could enable this process from deep within the state's conservative propaganda machinery, the Voice and Vision of the Islamic Republic of Iran (henceforth referred to by its English acronym IRIB, which stands for Islamic Republic of Iran Broadcasting). Hence, pop music's revival in post-revolutionary Iran happened through a convergence of factors that were circumstances of time, chance and personal agency rather than orchestrated attempts by a central body, as I will explore in more detail in this chapter.

Transitional forms of pop music

The "new" pop did not come out of nowhere, of course, but the cultural shift that allowed for its re-emergence was drastic enough that for many its appearance seemed quite sudden. In fact, in the interim years between the end of the 1980s—when the airwaves were filled with religious, war-related, and traditional music or national hymns—and about 1997, when the new pop really emerged, there existed what is now variably referred to as *"pop-e sonnati"* (traditional) or *"pop-e kelāssik"* (classical) in Persian, depending on the music. Most of this music could not be classified within the registers of the war decade, and presented something new. Bijan Bijani, for example, sung mostly classical or folkloric lyrics over Iranian music arranged to Iranian and Western instruments.[13] Hassan Homayunfal's work was often a combination of Iran's regional music with accessible lyrics and vocals that retained a sorrowful wartime tone.[14] Bijan Khavari's instrumentalization was poppy, but with *sorud* or anthem-like stretches and also simpler lyrics.[15] Similarly, Mehrdad Kazemi's music was based on pop rhythms but contained folkloric and spiritual lyrics.[16] This was not contentious music, and was aired on state media. When this music was broadcast on television, scenes of nature often provided the backdrop to middle-aged singers stiff as trees. They dressed in tan-colored suits, and sang into wireless microphones on sets decorated with colorful geometric forms and flowers. Almost all these songs drew on classical poetry, folkloric verses, nature or spiritual themes for content, and had an overall familiar and wholesome quality to them. Homayunfal's *"Nasim-e Sahari"* (Dawn's Breeze), frequently aired on television and radio in the mid-1990s, is representative of this genre. It's a sentimental song about seeking escape from the streets with the morning breeze, heavily instrumentalized on Iranian percussion instruments, flute and violin.

What differentiated the new pop was not just the music itself, which sounded decidedly more upbeat, but also the youthfulness of the new stars and how people were allowed to express themselves about the music. As Mo'allem, the director of IRIB during that period explained to me, due to religious sensibilities, most music was for a long time called *sorud*:

> There was an issue of naming (*tasmiyeh, nāmgozāri*) as music is one of those issues on which *fuqahā* [Islamic jurisprudents] can completely disagree. [...] All music was

called "*sorud*" but was divided into different categories of *sorud*; one was *sorud* for the youth, one for the elders, one for promoting the Persian language, one for children, and so on. We would use the word "*sorud*" but add other qualifying terms that would explain and define what was meant.[17]

The term *sorud* has been sanitized for over a century, denoting a sort of choir-like communal singing for higher purposes, be they patriotic, military or spiritual. In tracing a history of the *sorud*, Houchang Chehabi illuminates its prominence within Reza Shah's nationalist project, and later again within the Islamic Republic's revolutionary repertoire. In defining the term, he writes:

> Neither "hymn", nor "song", nor "march" fully capture the essence of pre-World War II Iranian *surūds*, for which reason the term is left untranslated. The tempo and rhythm of the *surūds* were those of a march, the melodies were in Western keys (although traces of the *radīf* could at times be found), and the lyrics expressed pride in one's country, province, school, vocation, and love of one's national history, flag, land, and the monarchy [...].[18]

The same characteristics still apply to the *sorud* in post-revolutionary Iran, except that pride in one's country and identity is expressed in specifically religious-nationalistic terms.

It is easy to see why the ambiguous but wholesome *sorud* would be considered the least problematic, at least as far as terminology is concerned; in form, content and impact it connotes the polar opposite of the kind of music that Islamic jurisprudents have considered *haram* (forbidden) for centuries. That music is best captured by the term *ghinā*, which revolutionary leader Ayatollah Ruhollah Khomeini described as "a singing that comes from the throat and can bring ecstasy and joy to the listener and is suitable for gatherings of amusement and vanity".[19] Hence, whereas *sorud* is choral, *ghinā* is throaty; whereas *sorud* brings pride and resolve to the listener, *ghinā* brings ecstasy and joy; whereas *sorud* is for the higher aims of unity and progress, *ghinā* is for amusement and vanity.

This strict bifurcation of music into *haram* and *halal* was slowly dissolved not long after reformist President Mohammad Khatami's landslide 1997 election. As Moʿallem explained, policy makers decided that "a return to the names of the past was not so faulty," considering "the completely conspicuous cultural changes that everyone was witnessing" and so "*sorud* once again came to mean *sorud* and the new music for the youth was once again called pop."[20] Needless to say, this does not mean that music was no longer contentious. The words "music" and "concert" are still problematic in certain circles, and many musicians find themselves using euphemisms. This is demonstrated in an anecdote relayed to

Farhad Khosrokhavar by one of his interviewees, in which he talks about the problematic status of music in Iran's main seminary town, Qom:

[...] if the word "music" is announced, it is a problem to [the authorities]. If we call [a musical occasion] "chanting" [*sorud*], this is more acceptable to them. If you want to do something publicly as music, you won't get authorization. If you call it "revolutionary songs" you'll get it. Hiding behind that word you can do what you want.[21]

In contexts where "music" itself is not fundamentally problematic, however, the term "pop music" no longer carries the burden of a Pahlavi past but embodies a post-revolutionary identity. The continuation of Pahlavi-era pop music in Los Angeles, and often even pre-revolutionary works created in Iran, are now generally referred to under the umbrella term *musiqi-ye los angelesi*.

The process of state pop music creation

Some of the first attempts at pop music that recalled Iran's pre-revolutionary pop heritage, with pop instrumentals and faster beats, were made by Khashayar Etemadi, then in his early twenties. Etemadi had studied music from an early age, and through his family had come into contact with prominent musicians, among them Babak Bayat. Etemadi was in a group of friends along with Shadmehr Aghili, Alireza Assar, and Fouad Hejazi, all of whom went on to make significant contributions to post-revolutionary pop music. They sometimes played together at weddings and other occasions, mainly performing covers of pre-revolutionary pop songs. Etemadi's voice had (and still has) a remarkable resemblance to the voice of Dariush Eqbali (whose stage name was shortened to "Dariush"), one of Iran's most famous and respected pre-revolutionary singers who still enjoys immense popularity. Etemadi's early attempts are emblematic of the difficulties involved in pop's emergence in the Islamic Republic.

Already in the early 1990s, Etemadi had submitted several pop songs to the IRIB, but they were all rejected. It was a few years before Mo'allem was director of music at the *sāzmān* ("organization," as the mammoth IRIB is referred to by its employees), and Etemadi was dealing mostly with Mehdi Kalhor, Fereydun Shahbazian, and a music council whose members he described as "showing goodwill but ultimately unwilling to green-light" his work. As he explained to me in a private recording studio, lodged in an apartment high in a residential tower in West Tehran's Sa'adatabad, "Because of my voice's similarity to Dariush, they would reject my work constantly. They would label me as doing *shabih-khāni* [imitation] and write me verdicts in green ink that read, "dismissed due to resemblance to one of the *khārej az keshvar* [overseas] singers." I kept arguing with them and saying that it was not my fault that my voice was the way it was, especially since it resembled one of the good singers who was never considered to be *mobtazal* [trite]."[22] Finally in March 1995, Etemadi received a permit for one song, titled "*Rāz-e Penhān*" (Concealed Secret), which was based on a Hafez poem that begins, "*Del miravad ze dastam/sāheb delān khodā-rā*" (My heart is rent/Oh, you men of heart advise!). This song ticked all the registers that had been applied to the "traditional pop" genre previously discussed, and so it was broadcast on radio and television for *Nowruz* (New Year) 1995.

Etemadi's success was short-lived. In the following two years, he approached state media with several more tracks, but was rejected on all counts. Throughout this time, the young musician was contemplating emigrating to Los Angeles and creating his work there. But part of him was certain that pop music would be allowed again because he believed that it was essentially unproblematic. As he told me, "I was certain that we needed to talk to the country's officials and convince them that this ban on pop was a mistake."[23]

During this time, Etemadi's association with the pop music veteran Babak Bayat motivated him to conceive of creating what he and others describe as "the first pop album after the revolution." The bureaucratic process for producing any music in those days was elaborate and extremely time-consuming. As Etemadi recounted, artists had to submit extensive paperwork about the professional and personal backgrounds and allegiances of those involved in the production, as well as the proposed scores and lyrics, to the Ministry of Culture and Islamic Guidance (or Ershād), which would then invite the applicant for a voice test. Following this test and an examination of all submitted criteria, Ershād would issue a permit for a test recording in a government-approved studio. Once recorded, the work could not be taken out of the studio until Ershād issued yet another permit, which solely permitted the work to be transported from the studio to Ershād. Only following this procedure and yet another ministry permit could the work for the actual recording begin, which was very expensive at the time due to analog technology and the scarcity of high-quality equipment and skilled operators.

By 1996, Etemadi had managed to sell an apartment in order to invest the money into recording the album, which he says cost him about 7 million toman.[24] Appropriately, he called the album *Delshureh* (Anxiety). In my interview with him in 2011, he still spoke with immense excitement about the project:

I really insisted that it had to be a great album to stand the test, as it was the first of its kind. Everyone was so enthusiastic. For the first time in more than fifteen years, the sound engineers were once again recording pop music, the capable players of the symphony orchestra who for long had only played anthems or film music had to suddenly play these really fast rhythms [...] We were all experiencing this kind of work again either for the first time or for the first time in a very long time. Even the graphic designers had to make big adjustments for the album cover and the posters. After all, the work was very different from what they had done for traditional or classical music.

Once the album was completed, it took Ershād nearly two years to approve the work and issue a permit for its production and release. Following approval, state radio and television broadcast tracks individually in 1997, leading up to the album's release.

Most first-generation pop musicians ascribe the opening of official airwaves to the efforts of the already mentioned Ali Moʿallem Damghani, poet and confidant of Ayatollah Ali Khamenei. Etemadi attributes his permit to Moʿallem, and has said that "if it was not for him, I and others like me would have never gotten anywhere. He is the only person to whom Iranian pop music will forever be indebted."[25] According to Moʿallem's deputy Fereydun Shahbazian, who was in charge of music at IRIB in the 1990s, he had long been interested in opening the gates to *"musiqi-ye pop-e fākher"* (fine pop music),[26] but it appears from most accounts that it was Moʿallem's weight and approval of permits that finally launched this process.

The six songs on Etemadi's first album are orchestral and have a sad filmic quality to them with themes of grief, nostalgia and longing. The first song that he had submitted to IRIB in his new application was *"Monji"* (Messiah), more commonly referred to as *"Mardi miāyad ze khorshid"* (A man will come from the sun), a spiritual/religious song in tune with the state's promotion of the culture of anticipation (*entezār*) for the *Mahdi*, the messiah of Shi'a Islam. The song was broadcast frequently on state radio starting in December 1997, coinciding with the birthday of the *Mahdi* during the annual *Nimeh-Shaʿban* celebrations, and got a lot of attention. It begins melancholically with fragile violin sounds and builds in tempo as a male choir hums, a distant female wail weaves in, and Etemadi's clear voice begins to sing words that herald the coming of the Messiah:

[...]
Mardi miāyad ze khorshid
Mardi miāyad setam-suz

[...]

Mardi az nasl-e Mohammad
Bar tanash sholā-ye tufān
Zin-o barg-e asbash az khun
Ākharin monji-ye ensān
Mardi az donyā-ye behtar
Ruhash az āyineh bartar
Dar galuyash neynavāyist
Owj-e parvāz-e kabutar

[A man shall come from the sun/A man shall come searing all injustice/[...]/A man from the generation of Mohammad/Wearing the storm as his cloak/Of blood his horse's armor/Humanity's last savior/A man from a better world/Clearer than a mirror his soul/In his throat the song of a flute/Reaching the highest trajectory of a dove's flight]

Despite the contextual discrepancy between pre-revolutionary Dariush and IRIB-aired Etemadi, there is not only a strong vocal resemblance to Dariush but Etemadi's mode of singing is also reminiscent of the Pahlavi pop era. The lyricist of this particular song, Akbar Azad, has also written for Dariush in the past, which may add to the similarity in styles. However, the interludes are a continuation of the march-like songs prevalent on Islamic Republic television. Hence, Etemadi had managed to create continuity with Iran's pop legacy while establishing a new framework. In the beginning, many who heard Etemadi's voice on state media for the first time were stunned, as Etemadi experienced in a taxi soon after the song's release: "The driver just froze and stepped on the brakes. He said he couldn't believe that Dariush had returned to Iran!" However, in contrast to the subversive political nature of Dariush's songs, this song was well aligned with the post-revolutionary state's promotion of religious ideology, as already mentioned. The *Mahdi* occupies an important place in Iranians' belief system, and strikes a chord with most Iranians regardless of their political inclinations. Etemadi's next songs were equally about spiritual or religious themes, including one sung for Imam Ali titled "Khāk-e Āstān-e Molā" (The soil on Imam Ali's court).

The transition to a fully-fledged pop music with light lyrics and faster rhythms was underway, but happened over several years. Although the "first" pop song by this account was Etemadi's "Monji," when people talk about Iran's first post-revolutionary pop song, they are almost always referring to the first song to be broadcast on state television, Etemadi's "Man o To, Derakht-o Bārun" (Me and You, Tree and Rain), based on a piece by the "dissident" poet Ahmad Shamlu. Its broadcast had a huge impact in Tehran, not only because of the song's visibility, but also due to the novelty of such a song on the otherwise taciturn state television. The song differs considerably from the traditional or classical pop discussed previously, as well as Etemadi's earlier songs. There are no vestiges of march songs, nor religious or spiritual lyrics. Musically, the song is reminiscent of the more sentimental, romantic pre-revolutionary songs of Googoosh and Dariush, and the words are an ode to a nurturing love, drawing on earthly natural allegories. Despite its risqué treatment compared to its precedents, it was perfect for state television, as its lyrics of trees and spring matched IRIB's practice of backing songs with nature footage:

> *Man bahāram to zamin*
> *Man zaminam to derakht*
> *Man derakhtam to bahār*
> *Nāz-e angoshtā-ye bārun-e to bāgham mikoneh*
> *Miyun-e jangalā tāqam mikoneh*
>
> [I am the spring, you the earth/I am the earth, you the tree/I am the tree, you the spring/The caress of your rain-like fingers makes of me a verdant garden/Engulfs me like an arch among forests]

Considering the Islamic Republic's uneasy relationship with the poet of the song, the track generated great curiosity and contributed to optimism that real changes, greater social and artistic freedoms, were about to happen.

Similarities in voice and style

The issue of *shabih-khāni* or imitation is fundamental to any discussion of the anxieties surrounding post-revolutionary pop music. The real or perceived similarity between Islamic Republic pop stars and pre-revolutionary ones had led to the commonly held view that the state was intentionally copying the style in order to draw the youth toward its own controlled creations. But contrary to common perception—as Etemadi has publicly confirmed—official agents of state television were disinclined to promote singers with voices and styles similar to pre-revolutionary stars.[27]

While the state's decision to allow the production of "sanitary" pop music for the growing youth population was intentional (though not initiated), the reasons for the similarity in vocals were more complex. Young singers with similar voices to pre-revolutionary stars may have been more strongly motivated to become singers, or been encouraged by listeners who were nostalgic for Iran's golden pop age and its era of greater social freedoms. This putative similarity in styles and voices may also have come from the desire to compare the two, rather than an assessment based on objective factors.[28] In cases where the similarity was evident, perhaps it was because the youth behind Iran's first wave of Islamic Republic pop music had no other role models to emulate. As a youth interested in singing, Etemadi did not care about Dariush's political allegiance, as he told me, "That's none of my business. Dariush has shown throughout the last forty years that he was not just an event, he is a legend. I respect him so much." When he met Dariush—whom he himself considers "a much better singer"—Etemadi told him, "I became a singer because of my love for your voice."

The two officials who did most to enable this revival at state TV both deny a conscious effort to simulate pre-revolutionary pop. In the above *Persian Art Music* piece, the interviewers remain skeptical that this pop revival could have happened without the systematic planning and approval of the highest bodies within IRIB. They keep pushing Shahbazian, claiming, "Until that day no one believed that if someday this happened, it would start at IRIB," whereupon Shahbazian replies, "I just believed that the youth can produce good music, and needs it. I don't know why but no one stopped me." His hierarchical superior Moʿallem, on the other hand, has an intriguing response to the question of imitation:

> Similarities in voice are accidental. [...] This here is the mother country. Rivers flow into the ocean and not the other way around. There is no problem if the singers here are imitating their own past. This has nothing to do with Dariush or Khashayar. They had a past that they liked, and they are imitating that past.[29]

The 1979 Revolution is a stark threshold in Iranian history and most have a tendency to view everything through the prism of "before" and "after" the revolution. Here, Moʿallem breaks down the pre- and post-revolutionary dichotomy and reclaims a past that has been entirely rejected by the Islamic Republic that he serves. In doing so, he claims agency and authenticity for the artists whom he promoted within state television at the cost of appearing to legitimize a past that for many revolutionaries represented the "depraved Occidentosis" they had fought to eliminate.[30] Indeed, without claiming part of that past, the creation of state-sanctioned pop music within IRIB may have never happened.[31] One could even argue that only Dariush's voice could offer that first transitional space, that first "imitation," as he was viewed as a revolutionary singer in his own time. The overlap was so evident that even the man who gave Etemadi his first permit confused him in his recollections with Dariush. In relating this first phase of pop music in post-revolutionary Iran Moʿallem told me: "The first youth who came to us ... by the name of Dariush, yes I think his name was Dariush, brought a very epic (*hemāsi*) and committed (*moteʿahhedeh*) pop song and we gave him a permit for the song to be broadcast from state radio." Uncertain about the singer's name, he then paused for a few moments and finally arrived at the name Khashayar Etemadi, and continued, "After him, slowly others came into the field and all sorts of pop music were produced, from pop that was sad to mystical to epic, all varieties of pop based on what Iran's music could offer."[32] At first, he couldn't even remember the name Dariush, and sought my help by saying, "you know, the guy who sang that song called *"Bu-ye gandom"* [Smell of wheat],"[33] conflating not just Etemadi and Dariush in his mind, but also the pre-revolutionary and post-revolutionary pop periods.

From heavenly to ambiguous love

After Etemadi's first releases, and a few concurrent semi-pop tunes by the singer Mohammad Esfehani mostly serving as television serial titles, other first-generation pop musicians received permits and released works that were aired on state media. Not surprisingly, most musicians' cautious first works were of a religious or spiritual nature. A 1998 album, *Fasl-e Āshenāyi* (Season of Acquaintance), released by IRIB's publishing arm Sorush, showcased all the singers of this first generation, except for Esfehani. The featured stars were Khashayar Etemadi, Qasem Afshar, Hossein Zaman, Alireza Assar, and Shadmehr Aghili.

Most popular among these was the heartthrob Aghili, whose professional trajectory is instructive. Had he appeared on the music scene five years later, he would have been able to remain inside Iran and continue his work. But at the time, he was too quick to offer fast rhythms and suggestive rhymes. An Elvis-lookalike with a trendy haircut and a mischievous look, Aghili came from a *khānevādeh-ye shohadā* (martyrs' family) background with two brothers lost to the Iran-Iraq war, and hence had the right revolutionary credentials. Although his first album, *Mosāfer* (Traveler), contained love songs, the two best promoted and most popular songs were of a sad, spiritual nature; one about a lost and eternal traveler, and another about the fate of a jasmine flower whose beauty was a thorn in the eye of the less beautiful, leading a "heavenly" gardener to transplant it to a special place from where its scent permeates every sunset. Both songs allude to intangible beings, recalling lost loved ones in a mournful voice over melancholic music. More importantly, the latter's symbolism of the jasmine flower alludes to Fatemeh, Prophet Mohammad's daughter, aligning the song with the state's Shia ideology of promoting the *ahl-e beyt*, the descendants of the Prophet.

But already on this first, approved, album, there are signs of the musical direction that Aghili would strike in his later records. Several are about love and heartache, sung over faster, lighter rhythms. In addition, Aghili's undeniable youthful charm contrasted to the other more serious singers in this first generation. In one video, Aghili performs his song "*Bitābi*" (Restlessness) with a full cast of young musicians moving slightly but rhythmically behind their guitars, percussions and keyboard.[34] Part of the song's lyrics are:

Bā khiāl-e to ageh bāsheh khiāli nadāram
Shab tā sobh geryeh va bi-khābi-ro kheili dust dāram
Midunam yeh ruz miyāy ʿomri-ye bi-qārāretam
Entezār-e to va bitābi ro kheili dust dāram

[Thinking of you, I have no other thoughts/All night I embrace vigil and tears/I know that you will come one day, a lifetime I've been waiting/This restlessness and waiting I embrace]

Although the song could be interpreted to be about the culture of "*entezār*" (anticipation) for the *Mahdi*, the playfulness of the music and Aghili's gaze and smile leave no doubt that he is waiting for a lover and not for the Messiah. Aghili's next album *Dehāti* (Villager) was banned on IRIB, but did receive a permit from Ershād, a move which stunned the public and got Ershād into trouble with other authorities. The album is full of fast beats and 6/8 rhythms, which had previously been considered impermissible. After the surprising official release of this much-anticipated album, Aghili decided to leave Iran for Los Angeles, where he joined pre-revolutionary singers in spirit and style.

When this first generation of pop singers started, earthly love matters seemed taboo and most singers either offered lyrics about spiritual love or other subjects entirely. There was then a period of transition when artists began to sing words that weren't easily pinned down to the earthly or heavenly realms. Teen idol Benyamin Bahadori best embodied this period of equivocation. By the mid-2000s, his albums were sold legally in stores, and he was promoted on state radio and television in part because his music was loyal to the state-imposed public transcript. His most famous song was in fact picked up by the scandalous *hezbollahi* panegyrist Abdol Reza Helali, who sang words of praise for Imam Hossein's most courageous companion warrior, his half-brother Abbas ibn-Ali, to Bahadori's melody.[35] However, Benyamin sings the song in a manner that would suggest it is sung for a lover, although nothing in the lyrics points to earthly love *per se*. Still, Benyamin calls his song

"*Khātereh-hā*" (Memories), and starts out by saying "I close my eyes and envision you," in an intimate way that seems to denote a personal experience with a real person.[36]

But Benyamin also sang religious pop songs that are unambiguously about religious figures or places, such as his track "*Āghām*" (My Master) about Imam Mahdi.[37] In a state TV interview in March 2007, Benyamin says he had "a very good feeling" when working on his new album 85. The presenter then prompts him to talk about his song for the Messiah. Benyamin takes the lead and says, "Considering my family mentality and everything [...] I have to say we all had a great feeling making that song," upon which the presenter asks rhetorically, "Is it at all possible that one would do work for the imams and not receive their aid and blessings and feel great?" Indeed the song, as well as treating the longing for the *Mahdi*, is a tribute to the most important Shia shrines. In the song Benyamin wonders whether he is a guest in the Medina of Fatima, the daughter of the Prophet Muhammad, or perhaps visiting Imam Hossein in Karbala, or whether he has gone to Damascus to visit Zeinab, "the lady of love," Imam Hossein's sister, or is spending the night at the shrine of Imam Ali in Najaf, or maybe in Samarrah, where Imam Mahdi's own shrine is situated. The lyrics draw on a purely Arab and Shia heritage, supporting Iranian state doctrine.

At the time, Benyamin was a novel phenomenon of hybridity in that he complied with the public transcript, but did not conform all the way, making him popular with Iranians of various religious and ideological persuasions. When he sang about religious themes, he couched them in modern techno and pop beats, or, he took religious melodies and secularized them into songs of romance. Similarly, while his MySpace homepage carried the Qur'anic declaration of faith, "*Lā Illah-al-il-allāh, Muhammad Rasul-allāh*" (There is no God but God and Muhammad is his Prophet), it also had slick photos of him as an urbanite with a fashionable haircut, trendy clothes and sunglasses, not to mention the half-naked girls who were his "friends."[38]

By now, stars like Benyamin no longer need to pretend to sing about God or his prophets and imams, playing sold-out concerts to hysterical crowds. In his song "'*Āsheq shodam*," Benyamin sings "I hope she won't find out [...] if she knows I know she won't stay." Most other pop songs also have themes either of romance with titles like "*Bi to mimiram*" (I'll die without you)[39] and "*Beh 'eshq-e to*" (For your love),[40] or of heartache with titles like "*Khiyānat*" (Betrayal)[41] or even anti-love songs like "*Injā jā-ye to nist*" (This is no place for you),[42] a popular genre where resentment and near-hatred is expressed for former lovers. Judging by the shallow uniformity of these themes, it appears that the authorities have made an unwritten decision that love songs are unproblematic and should be permitted. After all, Ershād must still sign off on every song and the prevalence of these songs suggests that they are easily passed.

Equally, the authorities now seem to find little fault with fast beats and dance rhythms. In fact, pop songs have become so unproblematic, and are so in demand, that even classical artists like Alireza Eftekhari and the conservative singer Mohammad Esfehani have dabbled in the genre. When I attended Esfehani's concert in July 2011 in Tehran, the star looked very much like an Islamic Republic official or bureaucrat, with a loose fitting grey suit, lemon shirt and tinted glasses. The person next to me commented in the middle of a song, "If there wasn't music you'd think he was a *nohe-khun* (eulogist) at a funeral." Yet Esfehani's music was what one would describe as "disco" music in Iran, with a fast tempo couched in elements of techno and reggae, accompanied by the thrilling riffs of a guitar player sporting a huge Afro.

The uncertain status of music

Despite this seeming freedom, even state-sanctioned pop music is not immune to criticism. For many years now, experts—especially those who agitate for *fākher* or elevated music—have condemned the enablers of this kind of pop music in the strongest terms. It sometimes seems as if the censors have lost control over the genre. In late 2012 the music director of the Ministry of Culture and Islamic Guidance resigned from his post officially citing his health, but had frequently admonished pop musicians to "Iranianize" their music, which he said had nothing but fast rhythms.[43] Many interpreted his resignation to be in protest against the impotence of his office to enforce new regulations.

In general, the guidelines for music production in Iran suffer from a lack of clarity. While the state's effort to police the cultural field means that most art forms are affected by various degrees of volatility, music suffers from a unique existential vulnerability. In examining the process of cinema's integration as a revolutionary art form, for example, Hamid Naficy illustrates how Iran's clerical government—led by Ayatollah Khomeini himself—transformed its view of cinema as a corrupting licentious Western import to one that should be used in the service of the revolution.[44] Already by the mid-1980s, remarks Richard Tapper, "the failure to establish an Islamic ideological cinema was evident."[45] In a way, the decision on cinema in Iran was similar to the one taken on classical music in Stalinist Russia. Both states determined that these art forms were not part of the ideological superstructure, and defined them as neutral infrastructure that could be imbued with Soviet ideology or Islamic culture, respectively.[46] Music, on the other hand, was problematic in Islam, and so whereas clear regulations were made on cinema early on, music still continues to occupy a grey zone of uncertainty or *belātaklifi*, which is often deplored in Iranian public discourse, especially among musicians.

This *belātaklifi* pervades every aspect of music in Iran, but is most apparent on state television. Although it relies on music for a great deal of its programming, it has always had a divided position vis-à-vis music. Its stance eased up slightly at the onset of reforms and the re-emergence of pop music. The first time Etemadi appeared on television, he sang live at a piano, with a large choir and orchestra, on Channel 5's "Shab bekheyr Tehran" (Goodnight, Tehran) program in 1999. This illustrates a surprising level of flexibility within state television at the time, considering its unofficial ban on showing musical instruments on domestic channels. Prior to this program, there were very few instances where the IRIB orchestra was shown on television with its instruments in view.[47] For this performance, Etemadi sang his track, "Az Pārs tā Khazar Irān neshasteh ast" (From the Persian Gulf to the Caspian, Iran is steadfast), which praises Iran, this "lion that has broken the claws of demons." It is not only a highly nationalistic song, but also very militaristic, with prominent passages of march music and self-aggrandizing, aggressive lyrics. The military nature of the song may in part explain this exception to the ban on showing musical instruments, since they are also visible on television at the annual Defense Week parades and marches. The song's optimistic and proud tones about Iran are an indication of the general national mood at the time:

Ey eftekhār-e Sharq
Dar bām-e in jahān
Pichideh nām-e to
Golvājeh-ye omid

[Oh you pride of the East/On the rooftops of this world/Your name echoes/A promise of hope]

This seems to have been a truly exceptional event, as I have not heard of any other such instances since then despite asking most everyone I have talked to or interviewed about music in Iran over the past six years. The absurdity of banning instruments on television while allowing people to see them in concerts is often commented upon, but as the most official medium channeling core Islamic Republic ideology, state TV upholds the most conservative standards.

Pop music today: love and fast rhythms, but that's not all!

Since the days of Etamadi's first shows, pop concerts have multiplied and unless it is a period of religious mourning, one can choose between various concerts to attend, especially ahead of joyous holidays such as *Nimeh-Sha'bān* (Birth of the *Mahdi*) or *Nowruz* (Persian New Year). Alone in the Iranian calendar year 1388 (2009/2010 CE), Ershād issued permits for nearly 300 pop concerts, and that in a year of minimal concert activity due to the election upheavals.[48] Often, the most popular stars will perform many nights in a row. The record is now held by Maziar Fallahi, who in November 2012 performed eighteen consecutive concerts, two per night, to more than 25,000 fans in total.[49] The fact that artists can give this many concerts is testament to remarkable audience interest. However, Mohammad Hossein Tutunchian, owner and manager of probably the most prominent events company, Qoqnus, told me the need to bunch so many concerts together—which he calls "*hojum-e lahzeh-i*" (moment's rush)—arises from the limited periods during the year when there are no religious mourning days, as well as the fact that the largest concert hall in Tehran holds only 3,200 seats.[50]

Still, multitude does not necessarily mean variety. For the past years, the top artists have remained more or less the same, with their images ubiquitous on the pages of pop culture and music magazines: Reza Sadeghi, Mohsen Yeganeh, Hamid Askari, Ehsan Khajeh-Amiri, Benyamin, Mohsen Chavoshi, Farzad Farzin, Ali Reza Assar, Arian Band, and more recently Maziar Fallahi and Behnam Safavi. For the most part, these artists have presented something original—whether in voice, persona or music—that differentiates them from the pack. However, many pop acts sound quite similar, and the concerts are sound and light extravaganzas of little originality or quality, where one can often hear variations of famous Western pop tunes integrated into the songs.

But not all Iranian pop songs are love songs, nor shallow. One of the most popular singers is Reza Sadeghi, whose biggest hit for a long time was "*Vāysā donyā*," (Stop, world!), in which he reprimands a world that is full of sadness and conflict and asks the world to stop so he can get off. Heavy-set and bearded like Assar, and also always dressed in black, Sadeghi is a messenger of love and kindness. Besides promoting love in his songs, at his concerts he also calls out dozens of times to his fans, "*Man 'āsheqetam*" (I love you), which is often reciprocated, to which he replies, "*Gholāmetam*" (I'm your servant).[51]

Judging by the joyous nature of the songs and atmosphere offered by the hundreds of pop concerts in Iran every year, one is tempted to read the immense audience attendance as a willful act of joy against the somber mood that prevails in the public sphere in Iran.[52] This is no doubt partly what is happening, though the restricted nature of music production and performance in Iran complicates any interpretation of audience support. Still, just as the heavy sadness of lyrics in some pre-revolutionary pop songs functioned as an oppositional idiom, I believe the generous promulgation of love in some post-revolutionary pop songs and concerts similarly functions as an idiom that opposes the officially promoted culture of grief.[53]

Conclusion

As I have discussed here, the mutual influence between Iranians and their expatriates has been instrumental to creative endeavors in music production. Two decades into the Islamic Republic, Iranians inside Iran were for the most part still listening to expatriate productions streaming in from Los Angeles, and the flow of music was largely unidirectional. By the mid-2000s, the flow had nearly entirely reversed, as music made in Iran had achieved such sophistication that expatriates were not only listening to music by the likes of Benyamin—who by now, like others such as Ehsan Khajeh-Amiri, goes on annual concert tours to Europe and the US—but were also collaborating with artists in Iran. Famous musicians have for years now commissioned their lyrics from poets like Maryam Heydarzadeh, and worked with prolific Iranian songwriters like Roozbeh Bemani. This flow has now somewhat reversed again as some of the most popular "underground" Iranian acts have migrated to Los Angeles and are broadcasting their work into Iran via satellite, including Sasy Mankan and Hossein Tohi.

Ultimately, Islamic Republic officials have often proven to be pragmatic rather than dogmatic in their approach to music. Policy decisions are made via negotiations between the various power centers, but the cumulative process that results in actions ascribed to "the Islamic Republic" led not only to a lifting of the ban on pop music after nearly two decades, but also to a retreat from unspoken prohibitions against fast beats and themes of earthly love. By now, one could argue that everything is allowed except for the solo female voice, explicit sexual lyrics, rhythmic movement on stage or among audiences, and most importantly, anything that the state considers a threat to its authority or legitimacy. By making some concessions, decision makers have revealed that they are most concerned with finding a balance between the need to allow for some form of entertainment for Iran's huge youth population as well as guarding the state's political interests and refraining from actions that could incense Iran's conservative strata and ulama. It took the Islamic Republic about ten years to gradually move from its initial trajectory of towing an Islamic line in pop music to insuring that it simply retained control over the pop music space, allowing for a "controlled fun" that permitted more but lacked the subversive nature of spontaneity. Rephrasing Bayat, the state has transitioned from preventing people from diverting from God to preventing them from challenging its power paradigm.[54] This does not mean that people do not find other ways of subverting existing power structures. In fact, they are very creative, as any observer of Iran will know.

PART IV

POLITICAL ECONOMY OF SOCIAL CHANGE

11

THE ECONOMIC AND POLITICAL ROLE OF BONYADS (PARASTATAL FOUNDATIONS) IN THE ISLAMIC REPUBLIC

Manochehr Dorraj

As significant as the ideological make up, psychological profiles, and self-perception of political actors might be in determining their political behavior, more salient are the larger social forces, structural and institutional frameworks, and policies and processes that allow them to maintain and manipulate power to remain politically relevant on the national and global stage.

Driven by a populist interpretation of Shi'ite Islam and a corporatist strategy that aspired to incorporate the support of the newly energized masses for the state, in the aftermath of the Iranian Revolution of 1979, the Islamic Republic established a number of significant new institutions to achieve these goals.[1] Bonyads were among the most significant of such organizations. Bonyads—parastatal foundations—are quasi-governmental organizations, used as vehicles for the dispensation of aid, services, and handouts to the lower classes, thus facilitating their recruitment and incorporation into the military and the security apparatus and the government bureaucracy. As such, close scrutiny of the political and the economic roles of Bonyads in the post-revolutionary era may shed light on the institutional and policy mechanisms employed by the Islamic Republic to build and consolidate its base of support and maintain power and political control.

In this chapter, I discuss the pre-revolutionary origins, the post-revolutionary evolution, and the political and economic dynamics that define the multiple functions of Bonyads. In this regard, I examine how Bonyads' original role as organizations of charitable giving and dispensation of aid and services to the poor have evolved into significant instruments of power for the clerical and para-military elites. I will dissect their simultaneous reliance on and autonomy from the state and the dynamics that govern their function as institutions running parallel to the formal economy and governmental bureaucracy. I will examine their impact on poverty and inequality in Iran since 1979. I will also discuss their expanding role in the Iranian economy as corporate entities and their significant impact on the political landscape, particularly in incorporating the underclass.

By shedding light on the multiple functions of Bonyads—as a microcosm of the modus operandi of the Islamic Republic in the economic as well as the political and cultural realms—some possible answers will emerge to the vexing question as to why, despite all the odds, the Islamic Republic has continued to survive.

The evolution and functions of Bonyads

The religious antecedent of Bonyads is rooted in a tradition of charitable giving and the institution of *awqaf* (religious endowments). One of the major tenets of Islam, *Khums* and *Zakat* (alms giving), obligates Muslims to pay a portion of their income to the clergy in taxes. The Shi'ite *'Ulama* (the learned clerics) have traditionally used a portion of these taxes to provide for the needy and to support themselves, and the rest was invested in land and other properties. This had a dual impact. On the one hand, it provided the clergy with a financial asset to be used at their discretion, thus lending them independence from the state. By distributing some of the funds among the poor, it also provided the clergy with a potentially captive army of supporters, thus lending them political muscle.[2]

There was historical precedence for principles that guided the creation of Bonyads in the Shi'ite culture of Iran, and during the Pahlavi monarchy, there were also institutions named "Bonyad-e Pahlavi." These had some limited humanitarian and patronage function but, for the most part, represented the monarch's estate and the enhancement of the value of its assets. Their post-revolutionary incarnation was informed by the prerogatives of establishing and consolidating the power of a revolutionary state guided by a Shi'ite populist ideology.

Due to the appeal of Marxist ideology among the intelligentsia, and the subsequent radicalization of Iranian political culture in the 1960s and 1970s, to remain salient in such a political landscape, increasingly, an ascendant populist Shi'ite discourse emerged to position Islamic organizations favorably, politically disarming the secular opposition, thus winning the contest for hearts and minds. The revolutionary uprising and its accompanying sense of empowerment had politicized and radicalized millions of Iranians. To remain in charge of the leadership of the mass movement that the revolution had unleashed, the clergy had to adjust its discourse. Thus, the politicization of Shi'ite Islam—represented by Shariati, Ayatollahs Taleqani, Khomeini, and Motahhari—provided the ideational fuel that led to the establishment of the Bonyads and determined their mission, not just as charitable institutions, but also as organizations with a political agenda, designed to solidify the power of the new government.

As one of the largest urban social movements of the twentieth century, the revolution had mobilized and energized millions and brought the hitherto unrepresented and impoverished masses into the political arena. The demand for social justice, a more equitable distribution of resources and political representation were prominent on the political agenda of contending revolutionary forces that dominated the political scene in the immediate aftermath of the revolution. It became abundantly clear that mobilizing and consolidating the support of the politicized populace, foremost among them, the urban and rural poor, would play a decisive role in the survival of the fragile new regime.[3]

Saddam Hussein's invasion of Iran in 1980, and the ensuing war (1980–1988), intended to overthrow the Islamic Republic and annex the oil fields of southern Iran, and the numerous coup plots in the early years of the revolution by remnants of the Shah's army, accentuated this prerogative. The newly empowered clerical elite sought to shield themselves from external and internal threats by consolidating public support through mobilization of millions of the underclass, channeling their political energy toward the reinforcement of the regime by establishing new formal and informal institutions of governance.[4] In this context, Bonyads were highly significant political instruments.

By providing a social safety net for the poor and facilitating their social mobility, the underclass—hitherto unrepresented and voiceless—was bestowed with a sense of empowerment. The downtrodden and the deprived, now armed and imbued with a sense that their cause was just and they were defenders of a sacred order, could be unleashed on internal and external political opponents.

In the immediate aftermath of the revolution, as the assets of the royal family and the former elite who had escaped the country were confiscated, a number of parastatal foundations were created—the most significant among them being Bonyad-e Mostazafan (the Foundation of the Deprived). After the onset of the Iran-Iraq war that left many dead, disabled, and wounded, the name of this organization was changed to Bonyad-e Mostazafan va Jan Bazan (The Foundation of the Deprived and the Disabled Veterans, or MJF). During the war, this organization took an active role in providing housing, rehabilitation, occupation, and direct assistance to the disabled and wounded war veterans and the family members of those who had died in battle. However, a separate foundation was also created that was exclusively devoted to the war veterans and their families. I discuss this organization separately below.

Known as the biggest holding company in the Middle East, and established in 1979, Bonyad-e Mostazafan is the largest among the foundations, inheriting the majority of the Shah's assets (approximately $3.2 billion) and many nationalized industries formerly belonging to the elite, which had been confiscated by the decree of Islamic revolutionary courts. Whereas its primary mission in the immediate aftermath of the revolution was defined as a charitable arm of the state, tasked with providing aid and assistance to those on a low-income—especially those who had sacrificed for the revolution and were ideologically committed to the Islamic Republic—by the 1990s, it had transformed into an economic conglomerate with a distinct dual function: one charitable and the other corporate. MJF also invests in twelve of the most impoverished Iranian provinces, building schools, medical clinics, mosques, and leisure facilities. They claim to provide financial aid and services for some half a million people.[5]

The business ventures of MJF are numerous. They include oil and gas, petrochemical, shipping, transportation, mines and metals, farming, horticulture, textiles, electricity, tourism, tires, tiles, hotels, housing, food and beverages, real estate and commodity trading. After the government, MJF is presumed to be the largest economic entity in Iran. They produce 80 per cent of all textiles and two-thirds of all glass in the country.[6]

Reportedly, their annual budget amounts to more than 10 per cent of the Iranian government's budget. They manage about 400 companies and factories, and employ more than 200,000 people. The financial assets of this organization are now estimated to be about $10 billion. This foundation is also very active in foreign investment, investing hundreds of millions of dollars primarily in the countries that maintain active economic relations with Iran, including China, Venezuela, India, Bangladesh, Pakistan, Turkmenistan, and Kazakhstan. They also engage in economic activities that involve some Western nations, trading crude oil on the global market through some British subsidiaries, operating a joint venture shipping company in Italy and England, conducting business through a German holding company and importing Japanese cars.[7]

While its creation was politically motivated, over the past three decades it has evolved into a powerful commercial entity which is simultaneously an instrument of dispensation to the lower classes and a vehicle for the enrichment of a segment of the politically connected elite. The new Director of MJF and former Defense Minister, Mohammad Forouzandeh (1999–present), who is said to be a respected establishment figure, has promised to curb corruption, de-ideologize the mandate of the organization by separating its charitable function from its business function, and bring about a new spirit of professionalism and transparency into its operation. Early in his tenure, announcing that 80 per cent of the companies and enterprises under the control of MJF were losing money, he took several initiatives, including removing 100 people from top management positions, streamlining and eliminating some of the enterprises that were losing money, further separating the operation of *Janbazan*—devoted to veteran affairs—from the *Mostazafan* relating to business ventures, and promising to privatize some of the holdings of MJF. He also declared his readiness to cooperate with elected government officials, allowing their auditors access to MJF's books and accounts. In recent years, there have even been suggestions to break up this Bonyad and distribute its assets and holdings among smaller cooperatives and foundations. However, the fact that the members of the board of trustees of Bonyad-e Mostazafan are all former secretary generals or leading members of the conservative religious party, Mo'talefeh, does not leave much hope that these reforms would be institutionalized and enduring. Given the entrenched power invested in maintaining the status quo and the past culture of the organization, it remains to be seen how successful Forouzandeh will be in implementing his proposed reforms.[8]

The second major foundation with an active profile is Komiteh-e Emdad-e Imam Khomeini (Imam Khomeini's Aid and Relief Committee). According to the official government website, this organization supports between 4 and

5 million of the most deprived by providing a wide array of aid, assistance, and services.[9] For example, according to one estimate, by 1995, 3 million people from the rural countryside and some 50,000 villages received benefits from the different organizations affiliated with Komiteh-e Emdad-e Imam Khomeini. By 1999, about 1.6 million of the elderly and underprivileged received benefits and subsidies from this organization.[10] The aid work of this foundation alongside the rural development work done by Jihad–e Sazandegi (Crusade for Reconstruction), and the rural development projects undertaken by a sector of the Basij para-military force, may partially explain why pockets of extreme rural poverty in Iran since 1979 have diminished, and, consequently, why the base of support for the Islamic Republic remains stronger in the rural areas than urban centers. This foundation also provides disaster relief and development assistance in such Islamic nations as Afghanistan, Tajikistan, Azerbaijan, Lebanon, and Kosovo.

The third major foundation that became particularly active after the onset of the Iran-Iraq war was Bonyad-e Shahid Va Omour-e Janbazan (The Foundation of Martyrs and Veterans Affairs). Established a month after the Islamic Revolution of 1979 to attend to the needs of those who had lost family members during the revolution and later on the war front, it has significantly contributed toward maintaining the loyalty of a sector that plays a key role in providing security and military support to the regime. It receives its funding directly from the national budget. Its director, Muhammad Ali Shahidi, is the former Islamic Revolutionary Guard Corp Air Force commander who was an adviser to Ahmadinejad. Reportedly, Bonyad-e Shahid has done considerable aid work to respond to the needs of the family members of those who lost their lives serving the state, and those who became disabled due to war and internal strife. The foundation provided aid for the family of "more than 188,000 people who had lost their lives during the war and gives specialized services such as in-kind transfers, educational support, and housing to widows, orphans, and victims of the war."[11] Bonyad-e Shahid has also done considerable charitable work in the Shi'ite communities of Lebanon.

During the war years, as the number of war casualties reached between 200,000 and 400,000, and many more were wounded and disabled, according to the statistics of the Iranian Central Bank, between 1981–1990, the resources allocated to this organization by the government increased annually by 29.3 per cent from 11.4 billion rials in 1981 to 115 billion rials in 1990.[12] Bonyad-e Shahid also provides home loans to the surviving family members of the martyrs and the Basij para-military members and their families. It has reportedly loaned 120 million rials to urban families and 150 million rials to the rural families.

To ensure that this organization continues to remain financially self-sufficient and profitable, like other foundations, it was encouraged to develop into a business enterprise. To safeguard its viability and invest the financial savings of the surviving relatives of war veterans and the disabled, in 1984, the foundation established the Shahid investment company with a capital of $10,000. In the following years, the company expanded its business activities in the domestic market as well as in Germany and the United Arab Emirates. By the 1990s, it had controlling stake in some fifty companies, and by 2010 its capital was estimated to be $72.16 million. The range of its business activities include industry, construction, agriculture, imports, exports, the energy sector, construction of refineries, fuel supplies, power plants, and brokerage services, including the establishing of Omid Bank. The trustee of this foundation is Ayatollah Khamenie. The Shahid foundation's chairman is Mr. Assadollah Kian Ersi whose formal education is in clerical studies. He is a former member of parliament (*Majlis*) and a former director of Imam Khomeini Relief Committee in Shahr-e Ray.[13] In addition to its domestic charitable activities and investments, the foundation also has philanthropic and business ventures abroad, most notably in the Shi'ite community of Lebanon under the auspicious of Hezbollah.

Another major foundation is Astan-e Qods-e Razavi (AQR) which is directly affiliated with a religious institution. This religious organization, rooted in the pre-revolutionary era, is in charge of managing the endowments of Imam-e Reza's shrine located in Mashhad, Khorasan, in the province of Razavi. Reportedly, this shrine is vaster than Vatican City and draws more pilgrims than Mecca, the birthplace of the prophet, drawing more than 12 million annual pilgrims from predominantly Shi'ite nations in order to pay homage to a ninth century Shi'ite martyr saint. The source of its funds are drawn from religious taxes, donations, and its many business ventures ranging from food and agriculture to auto plants, real estate, mines, industries, textile, pharmaceutical, engineering, construction, sugar refineries, dairy farms, bakeries, and many other enterprises. It owns one-third of the land in Mashhad, Iran's second largest city, and, apart from the state, is regarded as the largest landowner in the country. The total assets of this Bonyad are estimated to be worth about $15 billion.[14]

While the trustee of this organization is the current Supreme Leader, Ayatollah Khamenei, this foundation is headed by Ayatollah Abbas Vaez

Tabasi, known as a conservative cleric, a member of the Society of Combatant Clerics, who is also closely affiliated with the Mo'talefh party and the traditional merchants in the bazaar. He was appointed by Ayatollah Khomeini and has been in charge of the foundation since 1980. Tabasi is also a member of the influential national supervisory organization, the Assembly of Experts, since 1979, overseeing the activities of the supreme leader. In addition, Tabasi was also appointed as a member of the Expediency Council since 1997, which supervises the viability and suitability of policies proposed by all branches of government, particularly in the executive branch. Like other Bonyads, this foundation also has both charitable and business functions. The relationship between this organization and Ahmadinejad's administration was very tense. In 2006, the Agricultural Jihad Ministry reportedly confiscated some 400,000 hectares of farmland in Sarakhs, in northeastern Iran. Some observers have interpreted this initiative by Ahmadinejad's government as an attempt to reduce the power of the traditional clerical elite.[15] AQR is also involved in trade, construction, and joint ventures in Islamic countries such as Syria, Afghanistan, Turkmenistan, and a few other Central Asian countries. It is looking into economic opportunities in Europe, India, and North Africa as well. Given the enormous assets of this Bonyad, during the presidency of Khatami (1997–2005), when a new spirit of reform swept the country, provision of state subsidies to this foundation came under criticism. However, the old policy has persisted despite criticisms.

There are a number of other smaller foundations that are not as significant economically or politically. Among them are: The 15 of Khordad Foundation, which is named after the 1963 uprising against the Shah's regime led by Ayatollah Khomeini. Closely associated with Khomeini, outside Iran this foundation is best known for putting a bounty on Salman Rushdie's head, offering $1 million to the would-be assassin of the *Satanic Verses* author.

Bonyad-e Maskan (the Housing Foundation) worked hard in the first decade of the revolution to build low-cost housing for those on a low-income. Before its dissolution into the housing ministry, the Housing Foundation distributed twelve thousand plots of land to lower-income families in Tehran alone, built 7,576 small units, and assisted private builders with another 5,095 units.[16]

Yet another organization, known as Bonyad-e Noor (The Noor Foundation), which is headed by the former Director of the Mostazafan Foundation, Mohsen Rafighdoost, is involved in a number of enterprises, including sugar refineries, real estate, and pharmaceuticals. Lastly, Bonyad-e Isargaran (The Isargaran Foundation), which is controlled by the Revolutionary Guards

Corp, primarily focuses on providing relief to the families of those who were killed or taken prisoner during the Iran-Iraq war.

All of these organizations were intended to provide charitable aid, goods, and services to the poor, to war veterans and their family members, the handicapped, and those who had lost the head of their family due to war or in service of the Islamic Republic. In addition to the expropriation of assets from the Shah's regime and the former elite, some of these organizations also receive funding from the collected religious alms and the *awqaf* investments, and, in some cases, from, direct assistance from the central government's budget.

Bonyads, poverty, and inequality

While Bonyads are tax exempt, they deposit some of their profits and savings into a special account in the treasury that is exclusively allocated for charitable purposes. Over the years, the foundations have provided considerable aid to the rural and urban poor. However, exact statistics are often not publicly available. According to some accounts, in the first decade of the revolution, in part due to the impact of Bonyads' charitable activities, the conditions of the rural and urban poor improved. Given the immense challenges of structural poverty in the country, however, these charitable handouts and subsidies have not altered substantially the condition of the poor in Iran.[17]

Another scholarly view of the state of equality and social justice in Iran held that "immediately after the revolution, overall inequality fell substantially, by about 10 Gini points, from 0.56 to 0.46 but since has remained fairly stable at levels well above those observed in countries such as Egypt. It is nonetheless much lower than Latin America."[18] However, since 1995, "poverty has declined steadily to an enviable level for middle–income developing countries." In the first two years of the Ahmadinejad administration, however, while the levels of rural poverty remained the same, "urban poverty increased by 1.5 percentage points, or about 680,000 individuals." This is particularly striking in light of the fact that in the last decade, with the surge in oil prices and the influx of petro-dollars, income inequality in Iran has not improved. When looking at the economy as a whole, the larger "picture that emerges is a mixed one: success in improving the standard of living and the quality of life for the poor, and failure in improving the overall distribution of income."[19]

Several other observers concur with these conclusions. For example, in his empirical study of economic growth and income disparity in post-revolution Iran, Mohammad Ali Moradi, an economist, claims that "while the level of poverty has been reduced, income inequality is still high in Iran."[20] A report published by the United Nations Development Program in 2009 concludes that "between 1980 and 2007 Iran's Human Development Index rose by 1.23% annually from 0.561 to 0.782 in 2009."[21]

However, others paint a starkly different picture of poverty in Iran. In a recent conference organized by Markaz-e Amar-e Iran (The National Statistics Center of Iran), under the aegis of several ministries, Tehran University, and the United Nations Population Fund, three government researchers (Mansour Kiani, Khalil Attar, and Jila Habibi) have concluded that "between 44.5 per cent and 55 per cent of Iran's urban population live below the poverty line." This amounts to 23.3 million city dwellers, or more than one quarter of the country's population.[22]

The high rate of poverty in the major cities is in part due to the fact that since 1979, Iran's population more than doubled, reaching 80 million, but the ability of the government to create employment has not kept up. The mass migration from rural areas to the major cities has exacerbated over-crowding, shortage of housing and pressure on healthcare, and swelled the ranks of people living in slums and shanty towns, where poverty is mostly concentrated.[23]

The latest rounds of sanctions on Iran have had a deleterious impact on the economy in general and on the plight of lower-income people in particular. With Iran able to sell only one-third of its oil on the global market, and with energy constituting 78–80 per cent of total exports, the foreign currency inflow has diminished considerably, decreasing Iran's income from its energy export by $24 billion. According to the International Currency Fund, due to the impact of sanctions, Iran's non-oil exports may also decline by $7 billion. Coupled with the European Union's oil embargo and the US trade embargo on Iran, in the 2012 fiscal year, the government experienced a budget short-fall of $31 billion in its exports. The International Monetary Fund projected that the impact of sanctions reduced GDP by 2 per cent in 2013. Consequently, 40 per cent of the population now faces extreme poverty.[24] Due to the Ahmadinejad administration's reduction of food and energy sub-sidies and the high rates of inflation (about 42 per cent) and unemployment (about 18 per cent) in the country, sanctions have had a debilitating impact on the poorest and most vulnerable members of society.[25] Although President Rouhani has declared improving Iranian people's economic wellbeing remains his top priority, since late 2015 the major sanctions on Iran were not removed, and in the same period the price of oil on the global market declined substantially, it remains to be seen whether Rouhani's aspiration will be realized any time soon.[26]

These negative economic developments will have an impact on many businesses, including Bonyads, and their ability to provide for their patronage-based constituency. If the current economic problems become more chronic and sustained, in the absence of these foundations' ability to provide for the vulnerable—whose support for the regime has proven to be crucial for its survival—it remains to be seen what impact such developments will have on the Islamic Republic's political stability and longevity.

Since some of the foundations are poorly managed, and many of the enterprises in which they have invested have lost money and assets, the government has subsidized them in the past. This serves a dual purpose. The government is keen to see that the Bonyads continue their charitable function, which is regarded to be key to the legitimacy and security of the Islamic Republic. As pillars of the regime's power, the failure of these organizations can undermine the legitimacy of theocracy. To pre-empt the political fallout induced by the sanctions, declining oil revenues, and the severe devaluation of the rial, which began in August 2013 and continues to fall, the government has used its reserve currency fund to ensure that the price of basic necessities such as bread, meat, and gasoline, does not escalate sharply. It remains to be seen whether this temporary fix will be a long-term panacea. However, given the negative economic impact of sanctions, the ability of the government to subsidize Bonyads has been hampered and the profit margins of Bonyads have diminished as well. Thus, the effort to weaken the economy of the regime, spearheaded by the United States, Israel, and the European Union, is hurting both the government and the Bonyads, as well as the recipients of their aid and services. We are yet to witness the full political consequences of this unfolding drama.

Bonyads' impact on Iran's political economy

Parastatal foundations function like holding companies that are neither private nor totally state-owned. They are tax exempt, receive custom privileges, interest free loans, preferential rates of foreign exchange, their books and accounts are not audited by independent governmental agencies, they enjoy regulatory protection from private sector competition in addition to other benefits. They act as monopolies, are often the recipients of no-bid contracts from the state, their business activities, budgets, and book-keeping are shrouded in secrecy, and they are accountable only to the supreme leader and his representatives. They are estimated to account for 33 per cent of the Iranian economy and employ some 5 million people.[27] As such, these informal institutions have a significant impact on the Iranian economy and polity, and will continue to play an important role in shaping its future.

While since the 1990s several major sectors of the Iranian economy have been privatized, Bonyads have for the most part proven resilient to privatization and economic reform.[28] When mounting public criticism prompts some elected and representative institutions of the government to implement reforms, the Bonyads' powerful allies in other non-elected institutions of government step in, blocking such initiatives.[29] For example, the parliament (*Majlis*) in an attempt to expand the budget of the government, has tried to pass bills—as it did during 1999–2000—to remove the tax-exempt status of Bonyads, but "the Council of Guardians vetoed the bill on the grounds that they are non-governmental and their earnings were used for charitable purposes."[30] In this way, the foundations have used their economic power and political connections to maintain the status quo.

Bonyads have been criticized by some parliamentarians, journalists, and intellectuals for being the recipients of preferential treatment and tax exemptions. With the onset of privatization of the Iranian economy since the 1990s, Bonyads were given preferential access to the state-owned industries, cooperatives, and firms.[31] It is projected that by 2015, Bonyads and other semi-governmental economic entities and cooperatives "will become the largest bloc of shareholders in the Iranian economy and it is estimated by then 35 per cent of corporate Iran would belong to such entities." It is also estimated that by 2015 the private sector would be the second largest player in the economy and the government's role would assume the third position. Since 2000 the role of the government in the economy has decreased from 60 per cent to 35 per cent and this downward trend is projected to continue in the near future.[32]

The scholarly assessment of the role of Bonyads is diverse. Some argue that, since their inception, Bonyads have provided much needed aid and public service to the poor and underprivileged. In the institutional environment of a country such as Iran, they are best positioned for public service delivery and perform better than the private sector and government in this area. Insofar as persistence of poverty can hamper economic development, the poverty alleviation agenda of Bonyads is potentially conducive to economic development and growth.[33] Others suggest that Bonyads' lobbying for a reduced role of government in the economy, the removal of trade restrictions, and some subsidies, may be potentially beneficial to the Iranian economy. Hence, their support for Iran's stalled membership of the World Trade Organization (WTO), considering that such a membership would entail economic reforms, is still regarded to be a potentially positive development. More significantly, they can play the role of mediator between the state and the private sector in a transition process in which the role of the state in the economy is reduced even further.[34] However, others are not so sanguine about the future role of Bonyads and regard them as instruments of clientelism and crony capitalism, who maintain monopolistic control of key sectors of the economy, and serve as catalysts for economic stagnation.[35]

Looking back at their evolution from institutions intended to deliver social justice and provide a social safety net for the poor to conglomerates whose primary mission is to expand their margin of profit, reveals the profound contradictions in the Iranian economy as a whole. As Suzanne Maloney has observed, "In the absence of the fully articulated command economy or the unfettered ability of private capital, both domestic and foreign, to pursue opportunities, the economy of the Islamic Republic stagnated, dominated by rent-seeking interest groups and agencies, such as the parastatal foundations that concentrate on enhancing their own market positions."[36] Such an oligopolistic economic environment in which the Bonyads monopolize the market and stifle free competition is also inhospitable to foreign investment and deprives the country of much-needed capital required for investment and creating employment and economic prosperity.

Concerns with the privileges enjoyed by Bonyads and the deleterious impact of corruption on the economy escalated in the 1990s, and later during the presidency of Khatami (1997–2005). Under public pressure and calls for reform, foundations were prompted to come up with new schemes to mask their operations and maintain their advantageous position in the market. Some with ties to the state began establishing private companies attached to government ministries. As such, they were able to use government resources for private gains. These state-affiliated enterprises effectively remove state assets beyond its regulation and control, creating financial safe havens and enriching their owners.[37] Since the assets of most Bonyads originated in the confiscated property of the former regime, and their continued economic success depends on support from the government, they have become unproductive entities that engage in rent-seeking activities, attributes that hamper economic growth and development.

The Bonyads' key position of "authoritative allocation of scarce resources"— to borrow a phrase from David Easton on the essence of politics—lends them a central economic role often attributed to the state. What renders them powerful is not confined to their control of an estimated one-third of the Iranian economy; it is also their significant political connections and political function in buttressing support for the regime, especially among the rural and urban poor. As well as providing for the vulnerable, they also play a significant role in their indoctrination, socialization, and mobilization, thus garnering their support for the Islamic Republic. Through their multiple economic and political functions, Bonyads also play an important role in recruiting the lower and lower-middle class recipients of their aid and services to the security apparatus and the government bureaucracy.

The bureaucracy left over from the Shah's regime was not trusted by the Islamic Republic. Therefore, since the 1979 Revolution, there has been a concerted effort to purge members of the Shah's regime's bureaucracy and replace them with those who are ideologically loyal and committed to the regime. Bonyads have facilitated the achievement of this goal. A special quota is set aside for those organizations, giving lower classes preferential admission to universities throughout the country. They also receive preferential treatment in public sector placements that require the passing of "ideological and religious tests."

This policy is intended to provide the regime with the necessary technical and scientific expertise required to run the modern bureaucratic machinery of the state. In so doing, the Islamic Republic has effectively restructured the state apparatus, tightening its grip on power. In addition, this ideologically loyal constituency can be mobilized against internal and external opponents, as it was during the Iran-Iraq war and the uprising of 2009, dubbed the "Green Movement." As such, Bonyads are crucial institutional pillars on which the theocracy stands, and they constitute significant instruments of power and control.

Some Bonyads also have explicit cultural and educational functions intended to indoctrinate, propagate, and reproduce the official ideology of the state, contributing to the political consolidation of the regime. The most significant among them are Sazman-e Tablighat-e Islami (The Organization for Islamic Propaganda), the Farabi Foundation, mostly focused on production of Islamic cinema, and Resalat, an organization that publishes a major conservative newspaper.[38]

Due to the significant impact of cinema on Iranian cultural life, the role of Bonyad-e Mostazafan in the production and reproduction of Iranian cinema since 1979 merits a closer look. In the immediate aftermath of the revolution, when populist policies and ideological concerns were ascendant, non-fiction cinema was transformed to serve as an instrument of new political and religious orthodoxy. In collaboration with the Ministry of Culture and Islamic Guidance, the Voice and Vision of the Islamic Republic, the People's Cinema Society, and the Farabi Cinema Foundation during the Iran-Iraq war, "the Sacred Defense War movies" became a growth industry, producing both documentaries and fictional movies about the war.[39]

Closely associated with this phenomenon was the creation of "Jihad Cinema" and electoral campaign films. Both genres were driven by distinct political agendas and were designed for political mobilization. The resources of the state were employed to ensure these movies had a wide circulation. Led by Seyyed Morteza Avini, a theoretician and practitioner of Islamic cinema, numerous films such as *Soldiers of God* and *The Chronicle of Victory* extolled the virtues of martyrdom and portrayed martyrs as heroes of the nation who brought glory to their fate and the country, and, in the process, eternalized themselves. The use of religious metaphors and allegories lend these movies a distinct Islamic character. Hence, "Jihad TV" whose personnel were drawn from the ranks of the Reconstruction Crusade, Islamic Revolutionary Guards Corps, and the Basij para-military corps ensured that television was also serving state policies of proselytization and mass mobilization.[40]

After the war, Avini founded the Bonyad Revayat (Chronicle Foundation), which became an umbrella organization to collect all documents, including film documentaries, fiction, and other accounts of the war. However, with the war's end, as the populist phase of the revolution gave way to the post-populist policies of the early 1990s, Iranian cinema also experienced its own transformation and became more professional, and less subject to ideological manipulation. It is in this period that Farabi Cinema, the largest producer of films and owner of cinemas, began to promote "art-house films" at home and abroad. This initiative brought Iranian cinema global acclaim and recognition. Farabi Cinema particularly flourished under Khatami's tenure as the minister of culture and Islamic guidance until his resignation in 1992, and later during his two-term presidency (1997–2005). The relaxation of censorship and the open political space culminated in the production of many award-winning films and laid the foundation for the subsequent success of Iranian cinema on the global stage.[41]

Iranian cinema is just one of the ways that the state has attempted to socialize the population in the official interpretation of Islamic ideology, with the ultimate goal of creating a new generation of Muslim men and women dedicated to the task of serving and preserving the Islamic Republic for decades to come. MJF, for example, annually enrolls 150,000 young Iranians, mostly drawn from the lower middle classes, in youth camps. One of the priorities of such camps is to promote Islamic education designed to reinforce the dominant state ideology. Bonyads also help to mobilize the recipients of their handouts and financial aid in support of the regime. They call on recipients to participate in pro-government rallies, political sermons during Friday prayer, and exhort their support for speakers. These supporters play a key role in keeping opponents at bay and maintaining the status quo.

The privatization of state-owned enterprises, which has been taking place since the 1990s, did not include most Bonyads. Indeed, many state-owned enterprises were auctioned off to Bonyads on favorable terms, so that privatization has expanded their holdings and strengthened them financially and politically. Bonyads' freedom from governmental or parliamentary regulation and control has also rendered them more autonomous and powerful. This allows them to function outside of the formal institutional structure of state bureaucracy, constituting parallel centers of power.[42] As such, they have contributed to the creation of an institutional dualism in the Islamic Republic that many leaders, starting with Bazargan and Bani Sadr and continuing with Khatami, have lamented.

Given the financial strength and the political power of Bonyads, those who control these foundations control the real levers of power. While, during the first decade of the revolution, the offices of the president and prime minister supervised the activities of Bonyads, after Khomeini's death in 1989 and Khamenei's ascendance as the new supreme leader, and the phasing out of the office of prime minister, this oversight function was passed on to Khamenei and his office. Thus, Bonyads came under his direct control. This independent base of financial and political support enhanced the power of the supreme leader considerably and helped to position him at the center of a complex power structure that was hierarchical yet dispersed.

However, some Bonyads, such as MJF, pass on approximately 20 per cent of their profits to pay for the expenses of the office of supreme leader,[43] making this office equally dependent on them and creating a symbiotic relationship of co-dependence based on mutual interest. Additionally, the fact that an overwhelming majority of Bonyads' leaders come from the conservative wing of the Iranian political spectrum negatively predisposes them to the idea of reforming their institutions. Thus, the repeated calls by reformists in parliament or journalists to tax Bonyads and regulate their activities have been ignored.[44] This turn of events reinforces the conservative factions in the Iranian political spectrum and strengthens their hold on power.

Moreover, these parallel institutions of power enable the clerical elite to bypass and keep in check the elected and representative institutions and the public organs of power such as the parliament, local governments, municipal councils, and even the presidency, should the president be at odds with them. This ensures that the real power resides in unelected and ideologically loyal institutions that are free of the influence of civil society, and are committed to safeguarding the regime's survival as their top priority. The creation of these parallel centers of power, headed for the most part by the former military or para-military leaders, also militarizes the power structure, strengthening political authoritarianism. In the absence of structural reforms, therefore, the possibility of a peaceful democratic transition in the near future would be restricted.

Bonyads have emerged with a distinct interest and their own apparatus of power. By bypassing official governmental institutions and directly allocating money to their base, they buy loyalty for their distinct political agenda. This has led to the charge that they are a government within the government. Therefore, it is not clear how much power official political actors, including the president and the supreme leader, have over the operation of these organizations.

Conclusion

Since its inception in 1979, the Islamic Republic has employed a number of political, economic, and institutional instruments to mobilize and consolidate its base of support. The most significant of these are the Bonyads. During the first decade of the revolution, when revolutionary zeal and ideological politics were intense, the charitable functions of Bonyads superseded their business functions. With the ascendance of Rafsanjani to power, the gradual privatization of state-owned enterprises and the onset of a more pragmatic tone in Iranian politics, the emphasis has shifted to transforming these organizations into profitable enterprises.

There were several distinct factors responsible for this transformation. With a treasury drained by the Iran-Iraq war, and the continuing weakness of the private sector, induced in part by the massive expropriation of private property and nationalization of the major industries, the state needed entities such as Bonyads to assume a larger role in order to fill the economic vacuum. In addition, the Iranian government sought a way to demobilize military personnel in the aftermath of the war and diffuse the possibility of a military coup d'état. Bonyads were useful vehicles for the achievement of these goals. This partially explains the reason for the influential positions that the individuals with military and para-military backgrounds play in these organizations.

In light of these considerations, in time, their function was redefined not only as an instrument of distributive justice for those on a low income, comprising the primary constituency of the regime, but, increasingly, Bonyads were the new economic stakeholders of corporate Iran with considerable economic and political clout. Privatization initiatives for the most part have not included the assets of the Bonyads. Quite the contrary, many nationalized industries and enterprises were sold to Bonyads, often through no-bid contracts, empowering them further. Many question why these organizations should continue to be the target of preferential treatment from the government.

The evolution and transformation of Bonyads since 1979 from agents of distributive justice, providing a social safety net for the poor, to business conglomerates that relentlessly pursue capital accumulation, follows the pattern of gradual bureaucratization of revolutionary institutions that we have witnessed in many revolutions.[45] Once the idealist revolutionary spirit of self-sacrifice and the primacy of serving the deprived is exhausted, bureaucratic inertia and the politics of self-preservation come to the fore.

The expanding economic and political power of Bonyads since 1979 and their autonomy from the official economy and the elected institutions of government have generated a dual structure of power, culminating in both a lack of accountability and transparency, and exemption from the legal strictures that ordinarily govern economic transactions. As a powerful unelected elite, Bonyads have contributed to paralyzing elected government institutions, hampering the much needed rationalization and reform of the economic and the political system.

While a case can be made that the charitable role of Bonyads has helped to curb the levels of absolute poverty in Iran, the reality remains that handouts and subsidies for select groups of loyalists are no substitute for sound economic programs that address the structural flaws in the Iranian economy that are ultimately responsible for alarming levels of urban poverty. Only through careful consideration of systemic reforms will productivity rise and economic growth be fostered, generating prosperity for all. For this vision to become a reality, the opaque political system needs to be reformed as well.

12

RE-MAPPING OF THE CORPORATE LANDSCAPE
IN IRAN

Bijan Khajehpour

In 1989, when Ayatollah Khomeini died, Iran was just moving out of a closed war economy with a GDP (PPP)[1] below US$100 billion and a state-dominated economy. Today, Iran's PPP GDP is close to US$1 trillion[2] and it has a diverse economy that is trading with more than 150 countries.[3]

A simplistic explanation of the country's economic growth would refer to its resource wealth and also the fact that the country went through a post-war reconstruction during the past two decades. However, the actual picture is more complex, especially considering that the country has been under tightening external sanctions in the past decade. Experts agree that the Iranian economy has moved away from an economy focused on basic needs toward a growth economy. However, the central question is how the transformation and development of Corporate Iran contributed to this phenomenon.[4]

Analyzing the enterprise development in Iran is challenging, largely because of the existence of a growing sector known as the semi-governmental sector.[5] In fact, Iran is unique in the sense that its state sector is much larger than its governmental sector. In other words, a large number of entities that are considered as "state sector" are not under the government umbrella, that is, the religious, revolutionary, and military foundations are not controlled by the government, but rather by state institutions such as the Supreme Leader's Office.

Therefore, assessing business and enterprise development in Iran requires an understanding of the transformations that have taken place in three spheres (that is, government, semi-government and private sectors). This chapter's aim is to analyze the interaction of these three sectors as well as how each of these sectors has been influenced by the social, economic, internal and external political dynamics.

Toward that end, below we will look at the most significant trends in economic policy since 1989 as well as the country's privatization campaign, external sanctions and subsidy reforms that have shaped Corporate Iran throughout the past two decades. Finally, the chapter will conclude by identifying the sustainable trends in Corporate Iran to be able to project future processes including the impact of the corporate landscape on domestic, economic and foreign policy. The core focus of this chapter is to outline the benefits and problems that attend the transformation of Corporate Iran and to identify how this phenomenon could change Iran over the next decade.

Economic policy in the post-Khomeini era

In 1989, Iran's economy was heavily reliant on central planning and government dominance in all large enterprises with the private sector mainly focused on small-scale trading, service and agricultural ventures. However, Iran has witnessed different degrees of political and economic reform in three different administrations in the post-war era:

The **Rafsanjani administration** (1989 to 1997) was focused on post-war reconstruction and economic restructuring. His government introduced the concept of 5-year development plans and initiated the first post-revolutionary privatization attempts. He also invested heavily in the training of state managers to professionalize technocrats and state enterprise managers. However, Rafsanjani's economic adjustment policies were accompanied by high inflation as well as an external debt crisis that left a negative legacy of his approach to the Iranian economy.

The **Khatami administration** (1997 to 2005) shifted the overall theme from economic to political reform. It addressed legal and political shortcomings in areas such as civil society, liberalization of the media, and introduction of local councils. Khatami's administration appreciated the interdependency of different policy areas (social, political and economic) and tried hard to lay the legal and political foundations for the growth of the private sector, including the attraction of foreign investment.[6] However, Khatami's political reforms alienated the lower income classes who were unhappy about inflation and unemployment.

The **Ahmadinejad Administration** (2005–2013) has relied on populist policies and has attempted to redefine central planning. It reversed a number of policies that were introduced in the previous administrations and dissolved the Management and Planning Organization that was in charge of central planning. As will be explained later, privatization picked up pace in this administration for all the wrong reasons. Finally, the single most important shift in this era was the introduction of subsidy reforms that had a tremendous impact on Corporate Iran.

Since August 2013, the administration of Hassan Rouhani has been engaged in reversing the failed policies of the Ahmadinejad era. Symbolically, the Management and Planning Organization was revived in November 2014.[7]

Five-year development plans

The Iranian government's economic policy has revolved around a series of Five-Year Plans (FYPs) that have emphasized a gradual move toward a market-oriented economy and the development of the private sector. However, as will be explained below, political and social concerns have hampered the application of sound economic policies. Iran has now completed five FYPs and when one studies the objectives of these plans, the recurring themes are economic liberalization, granting more responsibility to the non-state sector, reducing government intervention, restructuring government finances, deregulation, privatization and empowering the private and cooperative sectors.[8]

None of these was successful in fully achieving its goals, but they made progress in the reversal of the economic situation of the 1980s. Well into the third FYP, it had become clear that government policies had not enticed the true private sector to engage in the privatization program. An analysis of the causes of private sector hesitation identified the following reasons for this phenomenon:

- **Absence of a competitive environment**: Government domination, especially the existence of semi-governmental entities intimidated the private sector;
- **Lack of legal and political stability**: Laws and regulations were not sustainable and would be adjusted based on ideological preferences rather than economic necessities;

- **Absence of real civil society institutions**: The private sector did not feel represented, especially due to a government dominated Chamber of Commerce, Industry and Mines.
- **Distorted market structures**: The private sector was put off by distortions through subsidies, price controls and government interventions.
- **Legal Barriers and Lack of Transparency**: The Iranian Constitution (see below), along with many Iranian laws (such as the labor law), posed serious impediments to real privatization.[9]

In short, Iran's legal and business environment were not conducive to private sector activity. The labor law was pro-employee and hampered growth in employment. Tax laws and more importantly government licensing requirements were all impediments to a healthy growth of private sector engagement.[10] Though a number of these shortcomings have been addressed through legal and administrative reforms, significant obstacles have remained in place.

A closer look at the annual data that the World Bank produces on "Doing Business" underlines the fact that Iran is producing poor results in most categories, especially in protection of investors, securing permits and with regard to the tax regime.[11] One major obstacle was the strict interpretation of Article 44 of the Iranian Constitution that had discouraged the private sector. Article 44 reads as follows:

> The economy of the Islamic Republic of Iran is to consist of three sectors: state, cooperative, and private, and is to be based on systematic and sound planning. The state sector is to include all large-scale and mother industries, foreign trade, major minerals, banking, insurance, power generation, dams and large-scale irrigation networks, radio and television, post, telegraph and telephone services, aviation, shipping, roads, railroads and the like; all these will be publicly owned and administered by the State. The cooperative sector is to include cooperative companies and enterprises concerned with production and distribution, in urban and rural areas, in accordance with Islamic criteria. The private sector consists of those activities concerned with agriculture, animal husbandry, industry, trade, and services that supplement the economic activities of the state and cooperative sectors. Ownership in each of these three sectors is protected by the laws of the Islamic Republic, in so far as this ownership is in conformity with the other articles of this chapter, does not go beyond the bounds of Islamic law, contributes to the economic growth and progress of the country, and does not harm society. The [precise] scope of each of these sectors, as well as the regulations and conditions governing their operation, will be specified by law.[12]

As such new efforts were needed to facilitate a true process of privatization. The re-interpretation of Article 44 of the Iranian Constitution paved the way for a different approach to privatization in the 4th FYP.[13] The main objectives of privatization stated in this re-interpretation included: accelerated growth of the national economy; promotion of broad-based public ownership to achieve greater social justice; enhancing the efficiency of economic enterprises and the productivity of human and material resources and technology; enhancing the competitiveness of the national economy; reducing financial and administrative burdens on the government, which is encumbered as a result of its controlling role in economic activities; and increasing the general level of employment.[14]

This necessary shift was endorsed by the Supreme Leader, Ayatollah Khamenei, and the government was instructed to facilitate private sector participation in the following sectors by the end of the 4th FYP (March 2010): all major industries, referred to in the law as "mother industries" (including downstream oil and gas), large mines (excluding oil and gas) and all international trade activities, unless the sector was a government monopoly by law. Consequently, any continued government role and participation in such industries would require permission from parliament. Furthermore, the decree instructed the government to prepare the grounds for the Iranian economy to interact with the global economy through "a gradual and targeted process."[15]

However, political, legal and administrative obstacles have remained and diverse political factions have implemented the privatization program based on their own reading and their own interests. For example, President Ahmadinejad introduced a populist plan in offering shares of government entities to the vulnerable social classes in a scheme called "Justice Shares." The concept of Justice Shares allowed the government to maintain partial control over some key entities as the government ended up "representing" the share blocs owned by private citizens as "Trustees."[16] In addition, as will be seen below, a significant number of government companies have been transferred to semi-governmental entities such as pension funds, revolutionary and religious cooperatives.

While the new interpretation showed the overall direction, it did not offer very clear instruction on the targets and methodologies of privatization. That gap was partly filled through the "Law on Implementation of Article 44."[17] The original decree as well as the corresponding laws obliged the government to sell off 80 per cent of the shares of most governmental entities, with the exception of upstream oil and gas companies, the Central Bank of Iran, Bank Melli Iran, all specialized banks as well as all companies where the government had a monopoly by law (e.g. Telecom Infrastructure Company) or those companies that played the role of regulatory bodies (e.g. Data Services of Iran).

The 20-year perspective document

In addition to the aforementioned FYPs, in 2005, the top leadership of the Islamic Republic published the outline of the 20-Year Perspective (the Document) of the country (also known as Vision 2025). The Document calls for Iran to develop to be the region's top technological and economic power by 2025 and describes Iran in 2025 as a "Knowledge-based Economy" that will be an inspiration for other nations as well as an active player in the global trade and economy.[18]

The Document sets out ambitious plans for the various sector activities in the Iranian economy. As far as Corporate Iran is concerned, the Document envisages the following general policies: a change in the role of government from direct ownership and management of enterprises to policy-making, guidance and overseeing; economic empowerment of the private and cooperative sectors, enabling them to enhance the competitiveness of their products in international markets; preparing Iranian enterprises to apply global trading rules intelligently and in a gradual and target-oriented manner; development of knowledge-based human capital; development and enhancement of national standards and endeavoring to conform quality assurance systems to international standards; planning privatization with the goal of improving efficiency, competitiveness and greater public ownership.[19]

Evidently, these ambitious objectives can only be achieved, if the country manages to empower the true private sector and create an investment regime in which private investors feel secure and protected. The first step in that direction would be a successful privatization program and a genuine withdrawal of the government from economic activity.

An analysis of privatization performance

The clear instructions of the privatization decree and its subsequent laws and by-laws paved the way for the genuine transfer of ownership of government entities to the non-governmental sector. In order to reduce the risk of corruption, the relevant laws and regulations foresaw that state companies would be organized in the form of Specialized Holding Companies (SHC) and their subsidiaries. SHCs would remain in government control whereas subsidiaries would be sold to non-governmental entities.[20] Key stakeholders in the privatization process have been the Iranian Privatization Organization (IPO)[21] and the High Council of Ceding,[22] which essentially took charge of the privatized companies in the interim period before deciding to whom the shares would be transferred. The executive by-laws of the privatization process obliged the government to offer the shares of privatized companies through stock exchanges. Should that not be possible due to issues such as a poor track record, IPO would be allowed to sell the shares through tenders and negotiations. According to IPO statistics, in the period from 2005 to 2012, some 68 per cent of company shares were offered through the Tehran Stock Exchange. See the following graph for a detailed breakdown of the channels that have been used for privatization.

Despite the fact that a large segment of transactions were conducted through the Tehran Stock Exchange, the process did not warrant for a fully transparent transfer of ownership. In fact, a number of business and political stakeholders have criticized the government's conduct in transferring shares to the non-governmental sector. In the process, business networks affiliated with the government set up cooperatives and other entities to benefit from the privatization campaign. According to Iranian Parliamentarian, Abbas Rejaei, who is the head of the Majlis Commission on Agriculture, Water and Natural Resources, the privatization campaign has mainly empowered semi-governmental entities and has essentially shifted ownership within the same circle.[23] In July 2012, the country's State Audit Organization[24] issued a report on the privatization performance that concluded:

> In the decade between 2001 and 2011, lack of a clear strategy in privatization policies led to two phenomena, i.e. creation of semi-governmental networks that have competed to own the privatized entities and also the creation of corrupt networks which aim to acquire government companies to be able to sell off their assets. Unfortunately, the actual share of the real private sector is so low in the process that it is not worth commenting in this report.[25]

Figure 16: Channels of Privatization, 2001–2012

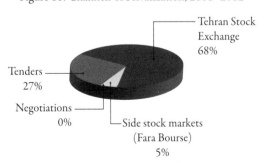

Tehran Stock Exchange 68%

Tenders 27%

Negotiations 0%

Side stock markets (Fara Bourse) 5%

Source: Iran Privatization Organization (www.ipo.ir), last accessed on 29 April 2013.

Consequently, the main beneficiaries of the privatization process were business networks close to the government as well as semi-state institutions that had access to government assets. Incidentally, among these business networks ideology is rarely as significant as vested economic or political interests, and political allegiances are based primarily on networks of patronage and mutual self-interest. However, the patronage links are not just structured around clerical networks, but also around military organizations, provincial interest groups and regional affiliations.

In terms of quantitative performance, the privatization campaign in Iran started at a slow pace—on average, only US$100 million of government shares per year were sold off during 1991–2007. The pace finally picked up after the re-interpretation of Article 44 and the establishment of processes that accelerated the required formalities. The following graph depicts the actual sale of government shares to the diverse categories of non-governmental buyers.

The following assessments can be made about the privatization effort so far:

- The category described as "private entities" includes a number of semi-governmental organizations that were set up to profit from privatization as opposed to the genuine private sector;
- Considering the fact that Justice Shares did not generate any revenue for the government (they should be understood as a populist move to transfer

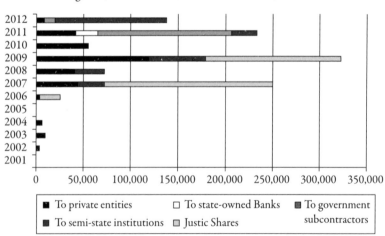

Figure 17: Privatization Sales since 2001[26] in Billion Rial

Source: Iranian Privatization Organization (www.ipo.ir), last accessed on 29 April 2013.

government assets to lower income classes) the peak year in terms of actual revenue was 2011, when the government pocketed Rial 232,647 billion (or US$19 billion at 2011 rates);

- It should be noted that the category "semi-state institutions" mainly consists of cases where the government sold companies to semi-state institutions in lieu of the government's debt to those entities (such as the Social Security Organization);

- In the period between 2001 and 2012, some 24 per cent of the shares have been sold to the semi-governmental sector, while 45 per cent have been transferred to the private sector. However, as the above report by the State Audit Organization indicates, the bulk of the transfers have gone to the semi-governmental entities;

- The peak of the so-called "private sector participation" was in 2009 reflecting two important trends: deteriorating political and economic conditions following the 2009 elections as well as the intensification of external sanctions led to a lower participation by the non-governmental business networks; and the low hanging fruit had already been absorbed, leaving the more challenging cases for privatization that have been sold to the semi-state institutions—in fact, the highest level of transfer of shares to the semi-state institutions took place in 2012.[27]

The government decided to withdraw from the economy only half-heartedly. By maintaining a 20 per cent stake in all major companies, the government has remained one of the largest shareholders of key companies (in most cases, the privatized share bloc would be broken into smaller segments). Furthermore, in many companies, an additional 20 per cent of the shares would be awarded to lower income classes in the form of Justice Shares—this share bloc is also represented by the government on behalf of the lower income classes.[28] Essentially, by controlling or representing the shareholders of 40 per cent of key companies, the government controls in most cases two out of five board seats. Therefore, how independent each "privatized" company can act, depends fully on the self-confidence and power of the remaining shareholders. This may explain why the true private sector preferred not to acquire the shares of such companies paving the way for the semi-governmental entities to take advantage of privatization opportunities.

Although the true private sector has not actively participated in the privatization process, private investment has grown in the Iranian economy, mainly due to the re-interpretation of Article 44 that redefined the boundaries of the state sector versus non-state players. In other words, private sector investors feel that the re-interpretation of Article 44 has granted them enough protection to initiate new companies in those sectors that were dominated by the governmental sector in the past.

Veteran industrialist Mohsen Khalili, who is known as the father of Iranian industry, believes that the main cause for the private sector's lack of participation in privatization is "the mutual distrust between the government and the private sector with regard to monopoly behaviors." His remedy is to "structure the companies in a way that there would be no private sector monopoly after privatization."[29] Evidently, the rebuilding of mutual confidence by these two key players in the economy will require time and commitment on multiple levels—in the meantime, the semi-governmental sector is benefiting as the third player with the political and financial muscles to take over key governmental entities.

Composition of corporate Iran

Despite its quantitative success, the process of privatization has not been smooth. There have been many layers of resistance starting from the parliament itself, but also resistance from the middle managers in state entities. The motivations for opposition to the way the current government has handled privatization were varied and many. These include, among others, political stakeholders such as parliamentarians, who object that most of the interests are going to semi-governmental entities—including military organizations and managers of state companies—which do not have the expertise to manage complex organizations that have been in state ownership for a long period. Furthermore, intellectuals argued that the process would pass on government monopolies to private sector monopolies, not producing any tangible benefits for the society as a whole, while economic experts favored a much slower process in which the government could duly prepare the various companies for privatization to achieve a smoother process with fewer job losses and a greater value for the privatized firms.[30]

Nonetheless, the process is changing the composition of ownership in the Iranian economy. The following table indicates the changing structures of ownership since the beginning of the process in the year 2000:[31]

There is no doubt that the changing composition will influence behavior patterns in Corporate Iran. The growth of the semi-governmental sector (along with the cooperatives sector that is directly affiliated with the same groups) will dramatically change the business culture and will cultivate the empowerment of the opaque business networks that have been shaped in recent years around traditional and new patronage structures. Dominated by military, religious and provincial affiliations, Iran is witnessing the emergence of many competing business networks that will dominate the business environment and overshadow the true private sector.

Table 7: Division of Ownership in the Iranian Economy, 2000–2015

	Year 2000	Year 2005	Year 2010	Year 2015 (projected)
Government	60%	50%	35%	25%
Semi-govern-mental entities	20%	25%	30%	35%
Private sector	17%	20%	28%	30%
Cooperatives	3%	5%	7%	10%

The empowerment of trusted circles during the Ahmadinejad tenure initially translated into the marginalization of those business circles that had benefitted from the Rafsanjani and Khatami eras. Consequently, many such companies had to downsize and/or look for business outside Iran to compensate for lost opportunities. Government projects started flowing to companies and entities that were closer to the administration as well as to the business circles around the Islamic Revolutionary Guards Corps (IRGC). More importantly, new licenses were mainly issued to trusted individuals, restricting new business opportunities (such as new services, banking, insurance and others) to a limited circle of entrepreneurs. As explained above, the process of privatization during the Ahmadinejad administration focused on opaque ownership structures, usually through the promotion of "cooperatives".[32]

President Hassan Rouhani has tried to reduce the tensions between the semi-state and the private sectors. In a speech in September 2013, Rouhani urged the IRGC (as the largest bloc within the semi-state sector) to "take on important projects that the private sector is unable to take on."[33] Nonetheless, semi-governmental entities are gradually becoming the largest stakeholders in Corporate Iran. Even though the genuine private sector will grow in the coming years, all economic players will have to get used to dealing with a corporate landscape influenced largely by religious, revolutionary and military organizations.

One needs to take a look at the shareholders and executives in Iran's growing telecommunications sector to fully grasp the transformation. The sector was firmly in government hands before the re-interpretation of Article 44 of the Constitution, but is now owned by companies affiliated with the IRGC, the Mostazafan Foundation,[34] religious foundations and cooperatives (including the Cooperative of the Revolutionary Guards). Almost all executives of this industry are former Revolutionary Guards commanders who have gone from fighting the Iran-Iraq war in the 1980s to managing reconstruction projects in the 1990s and managing semi-governmental organizations in the 2000s. Today, they are becoming internationally savvy businesspeople. As one private sector consultant told the author, "The same person who used to only talk about ideological issues and experiences, is now more interested in SWOT analyses and his company's strategic positioning."

In the meantime, the true private sector is also growing, not because it has secured investment opportunities in the privatization process, but rather because the new interpretation of Article 44 has provided private sector investors with more security about the country's economic structure. The growth of private sector activity in banking, insurance, light industries, telecommunications and even manufacturing and heavy industries can be considered the most significant driver of economic growth in the past few years.[35] Nonetheless, most capital-intensive sectors remain in government control (either directly or through semi-governmental entities) and the private sector is focused on labor-intensive sector activities, hence the necessary employment opportunities in the economy will be provided by the private sector.[36] Another area of significance for the private sector relates to the Total Factor Productivity (TFP), which is relatively low in Iran. Based on official estimates, HR efficiency has grown at a rate of about 1 per cent in the past few years, while capital efficiency has declined by about 1 to 2 per cent leading to a negative TFP growth rate up to 2013 (please see Table 8 below). The trend seems to have been reversed as of 2014 and it remains to be seen whether the economy can improve TFP in the light of the emerging removal of sanctions. In the meantime, Iranian planners had hoped to achieve a 2.5 per cent TFP growth annually between 2005 and 2010.[37]

However, challenges in the field of Human Resources have also extensively influenced the development of Iranian enterprises. A thorough study from the year 2007 summarizes key challenges faced by Iranian enterprises. Issues such as "low productivity and performance, lack of motivation, lack of necessary skills and work ethics" were highlighted. However, the biggest challenges for the private sector were seen as "the instability of the business environment" and "the Iranian labour law."[38]

Table 8: Efficiency Growth in Iran

Efficiency growth—in %	2011	2012
Human Resources	1.2%	1.1%
Capital	−0.2%	−0.1%
Total Factor Production	0.6%	0.6%

Source: Table on "Economic Indicators," Iran Economics Magazine (Eghtesad-e Iran), Jan. 2013.

The impact of external sanctions

Iran has been under various waves of sanctions over the past three decades. Though an interim nuclear deal signed on 24 November 2013 has suspended some of the sanctions and has also put a halt to the introduction of new sanctions, the country's economy continues to be burdened by external restrictions.[39] The conclusion of the nuclear negotiations between Iran and the so-called P5+1 (US, UK, France, Russia, China and Germany) on 14 July 2015 and the eventual implementation of the so-called Joint Comprehensive Plan of Action[40] (JCPOA) will lead to the lifting of most external sanctions in the course of 2016. Nonetheless, the prevalence of sanctions has already negatively influenced enterprise development in Iran and a continuation of sanctions would undermine the development of Corporate Iran.

Historically, sanctions have restricted Iran's access to Western technology and international financial flows. The most significant impact of the wave of sanctions until 2013 had been a recessionary development in the country that further complicated the management of the economy. This led to a greater degree of debate on what economic policies should be adopted. The regime principals have termed Iran's response to draconian external sanctions the "economy of resistance," and some even believe that the concept of "economy of resistance" can help Iran solve some of its structural and longstanding economic problems such as over-reliance on oil revenue, low productivity rates, and lack of a strong private sector. In February 2014, a decree signed by the Supreme Leader, Ayatollah Khamenei, outlined the core objectives of the "economy of resistance," focusing on domestic capacity building and export-led growth.[41]

As far as Corporate Iran is concerned, it is valid to state that Iranian enterprises have suffered extensively as a result of sanctions. Smaller industrial units have been sandwiched between sanctions-related impediments and increased energy prices as well as inflation.[42] Even large industrial units (such as the automotive companies) have reduced production (by up to 40 per cent) and have had to make staff redundant.[43] Though the interim deal suspended some of the sanctions on selected industries, including the automotive sector, key restrictions have remained in place. Companies are facing additional challenges in the field of Human Resource Management, especially as sanctions and deteriorating economic conditions are reducing the human resource pool in the country.[44] The representatives of industry are demanding greater support from the government in the form of settling past dues, tax relief and hard currency allocations.[45]

Furthermore, banking and other sanctions have shifted a significant section of the Iranian trade away from official banking to the network of foreign exchange bureaus. Most importantly, external sanctions have inhibited a large segment of the true private sector in Iran as the government and semi-governmental sectors have more resources to circumvent sanctions. In fact, according to Mohammad Ilkhani, deputy director of the Headquarters to Combat Smuggling, the annual value of goods smuggled into the country amounts to $25 billion.[46] If one adds this volume to the official imports per annum (about $60 billion in the year ending on 20 March 2014), one can conclude that about 28 per cent of the country's trade goes through unofficial channels.[47] The prevalence of banking sanctions is paving the way for a growth of transactions into and out of Iran being organized by unofficial financial networks, increasing the chance of money laundering and illegal financial dealings.

The above phenomena have hampered the integration of Corporate Iran in the global economy and have compelled Iranian businesses to engage in trade and partnerships with eastern trading partners, especially China, India, Russia and Turkey.[48] This will mean that Iranian enterprises will imitate some of the developments of enterprises in the aforementioned countries. Especially, an imitation of the Russian experience would further consolidate semi-state institutions and opaque business networks. All in all, sanctions and the economic hardship they bring have further empowered the semi-governmental sector and challenged the private sector. A potential lifting of external sanctions which could happen, should Iran and the international powers reach a comprehensive agreement, could ease some of these tensions, but for now Corporate Iran has to deal with the negative impacts of external sanctions.

The response of the private sector and domestic industry has been to lobby for further economic liberalization with the objective of easing some of the existing tensions in business activity. One initiative has been the issuance of a decree on boosting domestic production. This decree focuses on "improving efficiency of production systems, offering incentives to leading producers, expanding research and development projects, supporting cooperatives and private sector as well as small-scale enterprises, boosting cooperation between universities and industry, promoting the culture of consuming domestically manufactured products and streamlining fiscal and monetary procedures."[49]

The central entity that represents Corporate Iran in such bargaining processes is the Iran Chamber of Commerce, Industry, Mines and Agriculture (the Chamber). One important initiative by the Chamber revolves around the "Law for the Continuous Improvement of the Business Environment," which aims to remove "all parallel laws as well as outdated and irrelevant regulations so that the private sector can operate more freely." In the words of Dr Mohammad Nahavandian, former president of the Chamber, the objective of this campaign is "to promote private sector economic activity and investment in an economy that is hit hard by external sanctions."[50] Mohammad Nahavandian has now moved to the government and plays an important executive role as the chief of staff in Hassan Rouhani's administration. Incidentally, the private sector continues to hope for further reforms to improve business climate, but also for an easing of external sanctions.[51]

Other phenomena influencing corporate Iran

In addition to the above developments, Iran's enterprise development has been influenced by demography, corruption and mismanagement, subsidy reforms and the development of regional export markets. These phenomena have had the following consequences for Iranian companies:

Impact of demography

Iran has a relatively young and dynamic population. Based on the latest Census in 2011,[52] 70.9 per cent of the Iranian population is between the ages of 15 and 64 (working population) and 31.5 per cent is between the ages of 15 and 29 (youth population).

Other important facts about the Iranian population are: Some 70 per cent of the Iranian population are now considered urban citizens. There are a total of 10.5 million citizens (14 per cent of the population) with higher educational degrees. Some 4 million young citizens (5.3 per cent of the population)

Figure 18: Iran's Demographic Profile Based on the 2011 Census

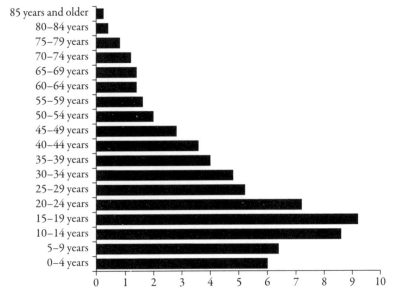

Source: Statistical Center of Iran, www.amar.org.ir, last accessed 29 April 2013.

are studying at Iranian universities—women comprise the majority of the university population (about 63% based on 2011 statistics). Youth unemployment stood at 26.5 per cent in 2011.[53]

All in all, the demographic realities mean that Corporate Iran is faced with the following phenomena: consolidation of a young, dynamic and educated society that is faced with economic ills such as youth unemployment; availability of a young, urbanized and educated workforce; growing demand for modern, urbanized products and services (such as modern distribution, e-commerce etc.); brain drain caused by economic and political uncertainties and existence of generational tensions and differences inside the workforce.

The existing demographic realities present opportunities for some businesses (such as the IT and technology sectors), and threats or disruptions to others (the more traditional segments of the Iranian business community). The young demographic profile has turned attitudes in Corporate Iran toward more modern, technology-driven solutions and approaches. The author has repeatedly observed the impact of the generational shift on trading enterprises, industrial units and family businesses. The new generation is more modern, more educated and also more risk-taking in new investment initia-tives. Consequently, the average Iranian company is moving from a traditional trading company toward an international, modern investment entity that is looking at integrating diverse sector activities.

Impact of corruption and mismanagement

The Iranian state bureaucracy has always been subject to administrative cor-ruption, but there is agreement among analysts that corruption and misman-agement rose enormously during the Ahmadinejad administration. According to Transparency International, Iran currently ranks 136 out of 175 countries in the corruption index.[54] A recent survey revealed that the main shift in recent years has been the open nature of corrupt dealings, that is, the emer-gence of an "over the table corruption" as opposed to the previous levels of "under the table corruption."[55] It should be noted that the Rouhani adminis-tration has embarked on a new effort to fight corruption.[56] It is too early to gauge whether the new campaign will bear fruit, but at least there is a high level acknowledgement of the issue.

Mismanagement is yet another phenomenon that is undermining Corporate Iran. Short-term orientation in government policies, politicization of decisions, and unprofessional approaches to economic programs have all undermined a healthy development in Iranian enterprises. One case of mismanagement was witnessed in the country's foreign exchange policy. In fact, the Iranian Rial was devalued heavily in 2012 with most of the external trade being conducted at a so-called "currency exchange rate" that was more than double the official exchange rate. The consequent establishment of a multi-tiered exchange rate system is in itself a cause for concern as it opens up avenues for corrupt deal-ings and an abuse of the existing differentials between official exchange rates.[57]

Furthermore, high profile embezzlement cases and public accusations of high-level politicians against each other are all indicative of the existence of a trend of corrupt dealings in government and administrative circles.[58] Such phenomena add further uncertainty to the external environment of Iranian businesses, making healthy development impossible.

Impact of subsidy reforms

The Iranian government introduced the first phase of a subsidy removal plan in December 2010 as a result of which Iranian households and business faced a major hike in energy prices. The second phase of price hikes was introduced in April 2014. The policy has had a negative impact on Corporate Iran due to short term adjustment processes. Higher energy prices have increased the final production cost, changed the level of optimum production levels in some industries and also altered consumer behavior and demand. Furthermore, the government's failure to subsidize many industries for the sudden increase in energy costs has led to a negative cash flow.

In the medium term, Corporate Iran could potentially benefit from the subsidy reforms. Obviously different economic sectors will benefit to varying degrees, but in general the subsidy reforms have compelled Corporate Iran to look for ways to increase efficiency, cut costs and also to look for more creative ways to generate revenues to compensate for the impact of price shifts. Coupled with appropriate trade and foreign exchange policies, the new situation could help Corporate Iran consolidate export opportunities and penetrate global markets.

Impact of regional markets

Finally, Corporate Iran has benefitted from the emergence of some regional markets in its neighborhood that have paved the way for a growing export orientation in the country. The emergence of oil and gas rich markets such as Iraq, Turkmenistan, Kazakhstan and Azerbaijan—all Iran's direct neighbors—have presented Corporate Iran with a welcome opportunity. In fact, based on the latest export statistics, Iraq is now Iran's top export market for non-oil products with the volume of trade between the two countries standing at US\$12 billion in 2013.[59] Though regional crises such as the situation in Syria and the rise of *Daesh* (also known as ISIS) have injected some uncertainty into these regional markets, Corporate Iran is consolidating itself as an important exporter to its neighbors.

Evidently, the emergence of export markets in the immediate region has helped Iranian enterprises to position themselves as exporters and consequently paved the way for a greater tendency toward exporting to international markets. Therefore, one can also identify a transformation of Corporate Iran from a business community focused on imports and production for domestic consumption toward an export-oriented economy.

Transformation of Corporate Iran

The shift of ownership away from the central government toward religious, revolutionary, military and provincial entities and cooperatives has a number of implications for Corporate Iran. These new owners belong to the state, but are not controlled by the government. The duality of state versus government is in itself one of the complexities. The state as a whole includes many organizations that are accountable to religious authorities (mainly the supreme leader) and not to the government. Evidently, these shifts influence attitudes, business decisions and enterprise developments.

To understand the extent of change in the sphere of enterprise development, we need to take into account that the country has transformed on various fronts in the past two decades. Most significantly, Iran has moved from a government-run closed war economy to a diverse growth economy by leaving behind its government-centric economic structure and heading toward a diverse and decentralized economic structure. At the same time, the country has experienced a generational shift within its society, business community and state technocracy. Governance structures have evolved from an ideological mindset (shaped by revolutionary forces) through a technocratic mind (driven by technocrats during the country's post-war reconstruction) toward a technological-nationalistic mindset (pursued by military commanders and organizations). In other words, the country in general and the business community in particular have become more pragmatic and less ideological. This phenomenon has also paved the way for the transformation of business culture from state technocracy to a military-nationalistic mindset. Within Corporate Iran, this transformation, alongside phenomena such as subsidy reforms, has compelled businesses to become more efficient and modern. Finally, the growth of an export economy has helped Corporate Iran to integrate in regional and international trade, paving the way for greater interaction between Iranian and international businesses.

Shifts in attitude

All the aforementioned transformations influence attitudes in Corporate Iran. While companies owned by the government would mainly fall back on government networks, the changing ownership will also change the networks—there will be a growing move toward semi-governmental networks in areas such as banking, insurance and subcontracting. The new networks would rely largely on traditional and new patronage structures, or their affiliation with institutions such as the IRGC and Basij.[60]

Another distinction can be found in attitudes toward international business: Prior to major privatization efforts government ministries and governmental circles were more in tune with Iran's conventional trade approach, as in the export of crude oil and the importation of goods and services. However, among the new owners of Corporate Iran, there is a stronger tendency toward revolutionary ideals such as self-sufficiency and national capacity building. These attitudes are also reflected in the new "economy of resistance." The military and even revolutionary organizations are dominated by former military commanders whose psychological mindset is influenced by their experiences in the Iran-Iraq war, leading to a deep mistrust of Western values and enterprises, as well as a desire to fully control all processes. While this mindset can lead to inherent tensions in enterprises, an upside in many organizations, especially those affiliated with military entities, is their growing inclination toward a disciplined and modern approach to management. In contrast to the traditional values of age, experience and hierarchy, the new model is based on efficiency, accountability and performance. This culture also appreciates the value of technology and knowledge, but can also encourage overconfidence in what a military commander can achieve on their own.

Evidently, the current process is shifting the balance of power away from the governmental sector toward the semi-state sector. Consequently, the emergence of a new balance of power between government on the one side and the semi-governmental entities on the other will have a direct impact on medium-term economic and political developments. Private sector players as well as international investors will have to analyze the changing dynamics and understand risks and opportunities in the new enterprise environment.

The increasingly economic nature of these semi-state entities may help them to become more profit-driven and pragmatic in the future. If such organizations move toward an economic justification rather than justifications based on ideology or security, it may lead to better regional and international cooperation. At the same time, the majority of economic organizations in Iran are experiencing changes and shifts, especially in the way they are structured and managed. There is greater attention to professionalism and modern management and there is also the impact of the younger generation of managers who are more educated and more international. As such, one needs to revisit perceptions and assessments of all these entities on a regular basis, especially as so much is influenced by personalities who lead these organizations.

Looking ahead, a number of determinant factors (such as the domestic composition of power, foreign relations, the implementation of the JCPOA and regional developments) are still in flux. Nonetheless, if one projects the trajectory of the past developments, one can identify a number of future trends in shaping Corporate Iran including a continued struggle between the government and semi-state companies to dominate the Iranian business scene, as well as a tendency toward more competition, professionalization and internationalization. These changes won't be free of tensions, but they will help Iran develop a more pragmatic approach to the rest of the world, which will help to realize the country's economic potential.

Perceptions of private business

When gauging the impact of these developments on Corporate Iran, we need to understand the relationship of the private sector with the semi-state sector. There is no doubt that the country's genuine private sector is in a very challenging position and one of the root causes of their dissatisfaction is the growing role of the semi-governmental sector. The private sector is faced with a number of challenges, especially given that lucrative government opportunities are essentially closed to the private sector, due to the distrust between the government and the private sector. It is important to note here that semi-state institutions continue to attract former government officials as their board members, advisors and beneficiaries. Finally, the few contracts that are secured by the private sector face an array of obstacles such as lack of access to financing resources, non-allocation of needed raw materials or subcontracting services, and pressure from governmental regulators or provincial and municipal licensing bodies.

The majority of private sector players have a negative perception of the semi-governmental companies. Nonetheless, such entities are an important part of the Iranian economy and the private sector has to deal and also partner with them on a regular basis. At the same time, key private sector players believe that semi-governmental entities have corrupt and opaque links with the networks of power, hence their ability to navigate through the opaque system of economic benefits in the country. However, the private sector appreciates that the new entities have a more disciplined approach to managing projects and a greater commitment to modern concepts such as efficiency. Furthermore, private sector players know that semi-governmental entities can rely on a very extensive business network, especially due to their vast involvement in the Iranian economy and their presence in major economic and business institutions of the country. Such networks are very valuable in the implementation of major projects and sometimes the private sector can benefit from the same networks if they end up in a partnership with semi-state institutions. Finally, the private sector realizes that such entities have an easier access to state privileges, from funding to technological access as well as ability to import needed goods and services.

Despite its reservations, the Iranian private sector recognizes that the semi-governmental companies will be a permanent reality in the Iranian economy. However, in most cases, they would avoid a longer term partnership and would favor short-term, project-based agreements with such organizations. Consequently, Corporate Iran will increasingly be influenced by a tense, but growing cooperation and partnership between semi-state institutions and private sector companies. Analysts tend to believe that the private sector will gradually compel the semi-state institutions to become more open and sophisticated in their approaches. However, it is more realistic to anticipate a growing interdependency between these two groups with varying degrees of cross influence and cross fertilization, though it remains to be seen what kind of a business culture will emerge eventually.

Conclusions

The characteristics of today's corporate landscape in Iran are heavily dependent on the country's political, economic and social realities. Considering the major upheavals of post-revolution Iran (revolution, war, reconstruction, internal and external uncertainties) and the consequent internal and external transformations, Corporate Iran is still in a state of flux. Nonetheless, if one projects the trends of the past two decades, one can identify a number of future trends.

Privatization along with the consolidation of diverse, decentralized networks of power will create a more complex set of stakeholder relations for Iranian enterprises. While previously an enterprise needed to develop a good working relationship with the government as the largest economic player, it will now need to understand the complexity of relations and competitions between networks around its business. This means that Iran will witness the emergence of new formal and informal entities (guilds, industry associations, regional chambers of commerce, cooperatives etc.) that will represent the interests of Corporate Iran. Eventually, a number of such entities will convert to political parties and potentially pave the way for a more democratic interaction between Corporate Iran and the branches of power. In fact, there is precedence for this phenomenon: The Islamic Motalefeh (Coalition) Party was originally an association of traditional merchants, but it became a political party that has participated in bargaining processes with the government. Furthermore, the Society of Industrial Producers (*Jamiayate Tolidgarayan*) is another example of a business interest group that has become a political entity. Projecting this into the future, Iran will witness a greater diversity of entities representing the interests of Corporate Iran in political decisions. However, it is uncertain whether this political representation will help the country's democratization or whether they will set the stage for an opaque set of informal relationships that would empower mafia-style interdependency between politics and business. The negative impact of the external sanctions on the private sector and the actual empowerment of the semi-state institutions could strengthen the likelihood of the latter.

Parallel to these developments, the central government will gradually lose significance in operational business activities, focusing more on regulatory functions with most large scale enterprises being controlled by semi-state institutions. As such, the regulatory framework will become the central instrument of the government in controlling economic activity. However, on the one side, the government's continued presence as a minority shareholder and the representative of Justice Shares will overshadow the operation of Corporate Iran. On the other side, a number of semi-state entities will empower provincial governments and municipalities who will be a part of the emerging business networks, maintaining a certain degree of government control in business activities.

Nonetheless, as long as the Iranian government remains a key player due to its monopoly on oil and gas revenues, Iran's political economy will continue to be torn between market economy impulses and revolutionary ideals such as social justice as well as rentier-economy mentality.

The genuine private sector will continue to be overshadowed by the semi-governmental organizations and business networks. Nonetheless, each will find their own sphere, especially as small to medium sized private companies will be more capable of reaping the benefits of new business opportunities. At the same time, the need for increased efficiency and professionalism will push private sector and semi-state enterprises toward long-term planning and cooperation, particularly if they wish to contain the negative impact of political uncertainties emerging from the central government.

Finally, modern management concepts will have to become an integral part of enterprise development in Iran—this will partly be driven by the generational shift and partly also through increased competition and a desire to be present in regional and international markets. There will be a greater emphasis on human resource management and skills development that will potentially become a differentiating factor between successful private companies and semi-state enterprises.

Evidently, some of these trends are contradictory and diverse segments of Corporate Iran will be dominated by one or the other trend. However, the core trend seems to be the emergence of more professional management concepts as well as the shaping of a corporate landscape in which business interests are increasingly represented by diverse formal and informal entities. There is no doubt that this representation will leave its footprint on Iran's domestic and foreign policy developments. If professionalism and pragmatism eventually become the core themes of Corporate Iran, it will be a question of time until they also influence the political development of the country. It remains to be seen whether this influence will favor a transparent and democratic development or one that will push Iran deeper into a culture of opaque, informal business networks.

Key determinants of this trajectory will be Iran's overall political direction, her relations with Western nations and the economy's interaction with international companies that hold democratic values; the overall wellbeing of the country's private sector, which is currently undermined by sanctions and government policies; and the potential role that the Iranian diaspora could play in encouraging and helping Corporate Iran to choose the path of transparency, accountability and responsibility, paving the way for impulses toward an open and democratic political development.

CONCLUSION

Mahmood Monshipouri

Although many scholarly works in recent years have focused on Iran's foreign policy, a systematic and thorough examination of the internal dynamics of social and cultural change in a country of such a rich history and civilization, complex social forces, and diverse ethnic population has largely escaped the proper global attention that it deserves. While much has been made of the meanings and implications of the 1979 Iranian Revolution, one of the most complicated revolutions of the twentieth century, it is especially true that Iran's "Green Movement" and the "Arab Spring" have dramatically shifted the spotlight from foreign policy to the domestic politics of the region.

The interplay of the Iran-Iraq War, protracted power struggles and internal squabbling, deteriorating economic conditions, and rising public disillusionment and social disempowerment in the 1990s led to increased tensions within the Islamic Republic. In the early 1990s, President Akbar Hashemi Rafsanjani pushed for privatization programs by reviving the stock market and subsidy cutbacks. His proposals were effectively blocked by Parliament. In the late 1990s, President Mohammad Khatami's economic proposals fell on deaf ears, as he soon realized that the "economy was an issue on which he wouldn't win against the conservatives."[1] All the signs indicate that current President Hassan Rouhani is not likely to have a smooth path ahead of him. Rouhani could face many similar—if not identical—challenges in implementing significant policy changes in the social, economic, and political spheres.

Perhaps the most contentious aspect of social change in Iran is related to the country's shifting internal dynamics in the post-Khomeini era, a time marked by profound and at times conflicting changes in politics, economics, and society. As shown in this book, social change in Iran cannot be categorized into traditional cases by simply examining material forces determining power, status, and prevalence in society as well as their consequences for the country at large. When investigating the specific tactics used by social movements, for instance, we should not let a focus on Islamic doctrines, hierarchy of power, and *Sharia* blind us to the increasing social change that is occurring in today's Iran. Increasingly, the Islamic Republic has found it difficult to privilege strictly conservative Islamist values over the policy needs of Iran's changing society.

Education has opened new opportunities to the masses, dramatically improving literacy rates for both males and females. Access to health care and social services has been expanded. Women have gained unprecedented advantages in educational and job opportunities, as well as in divorce cases, where they can recover the value of a wife's labor over the duration of the marriage.[2] Yet it is equally important to turn to ideational forces of change as a useful first step in any systematic attempt to understand and evaluate the breadth and depth of change and its implications for Iran as well as for the Middle East and North Africa (MENA) region at large.

This book provides a view into the social change, development, and construction of new ideas and realities through emerging identities, meanings, interests, and practices inside the Islamic Republic of Iran since 1989, the year in which Iran's revolutionary leader Ayatollah Rohullah Khomeini died. To grasp the process as well as the potential outcome of social change in Iran, it is crucial to examine the emergence of new dynamic and influential actors on Iran's domestic scene and their contribution to building social capital, while dispelling myths and stereotypes regarding Iranian women, youth, journalists, lawyers, academics, activists, and artists.

There is an increasing need for adopting new foci and alternative ways of viewing the dynamic relationship between ideas and material forces that have come to shape the underlying social norms, culture, and the aspirations of its youthful population for change. Although a wide spectrum of ideas and actions has characterized the process of social change, the contributors to this volume have underscored the importance of the central features of politics and society, including political power and the economy, demographic realities, gendered perspectives within the context of evolving social roles, dynamic culture, and changing norms and laws.

Iran has experienced dramatic social change, including the largest mass protests in the post-Khomeini era—in part reminiscent of its political history, but also in part due to the dynamics of seismic societal change that have transpired there, as has been the case in much of the MENA region more recently. The history of political rallies and protests in Iran certainly predates the Islamic Republic, but in recent decades many socioeconomic and political developments have challenged the imposed Islamic vision of state and society, exposing the complexities and internal contradictions of a regime ruled by fragmented elites, in a country in the throes of economic crisis, and a society in the midst of this rapid social transformation.[3]

As we have seen in this book, the forces behind social change are too complicated to be placed at the feet of any single source or parameter. A confluence of factors unique to the country's political history, geography, demographics, governance, gender issues, and evolving movie and music industries, have made Iranian politics the battleground for contending views and visions. It is an extremely difficult task to build consensus in a pluralistic system like Iran, as Arshin Adib-Moghadam has shown, in which several power blocs compete for economic and political leverage. Yet, the governmental institutions of the Islamic Republic, as William O. Beeman argues, reflect the need for the pragmatism and practicality that allow both continuity and change. Some experts, however, including Mansoor Moaddel, question the decades of the absolutist rule, arguing that the Iranian public has become less religious and grown more individualistic in their personal identity, liberal in their national identity, and vehemently opposed to the clerical authoritarianism of the Islamic Republic.

Over the decades, Iran's authoritarian governments have used the convenient argument that Western governments are constantly hatching plots to overthrow the Islamic Republic in order to maintain their stranglehold over the lives of its citizens and keep opposition movements from gaining sufficient traction to threaten the status quo. The women and youth, known to be among the most urbanized and educated segments of the population, have understandably constituted the bulwark of opposition to the Islamic Republic, in large part because both these social classes have sought employment opportunities and basic freedoms far exceeding the state's expectations and intentions. Although there have been noticeable advances in educational levels for both women and men, and there has been progress in rural development, literacy rates, and the reconstruction of the economy and infrastructure in the aftermath of the Iran-Iraq War, broader freedoms and social reforms have not been facilitated or allowed by the conservative government hierarchy.

The US and UN sanctions, however, have put tremendous pressure on Iran economically and politically, while successfully limiting the international and domestic options for the Iranian leadership.[4] As a result, Iran's economy has faced colossal obstacles since the mid-1990s, while suffering from poor performance and surging widespread public discontent and disillusionment with the regime. Whereas in the past, the sanctions policy has put Iranian rulers in a better position to bargain with the United States, using a jingoistic rationale to protect the country's sovereignty in the face of external threats and pressure, today's sanctions have proven lethal to Iran's economy.

In the meantime, Islamic doctrines have become increasingly flexible and accommodating to women's issues. As Arzoo Osanloo finds, women can question the government's validity with an assessment of how the legal system treated them. Iranian women, according to Farzaneh Milani, have expressed their identities and aspirations through literary movements, challenging established familial and political hierarchies, archaic religious traditions, and inequitable social conditions. The three decades of transformation since the revolution, as Djavad Salehi-Isfahani has compellingly demonstrated, have narrowed the gender gap in many areas, especially in education. Equality in education, along with a lower fertility rate, has noticeably enhanced women's power within the family, resulting in the allocation of more family resources to, for instance, child education.

This is not to argue that women's struggle for political power has fully succeeded. The issue of women and their rights has remained a thorn on the side of the Islamic Republic. The granting of the 2003 Nobel Peace Prize to Shirin Ebadi, a female Iranian lawyer, opened a new chapter in Iran's political drama. Iran's conservative and orthodox Muslims felt threatened and shunted aside by the lasting echoes of this recognition. Their immediate reaction to this prize was to decry it as external interference in Iran's internal affairs.

The greatest threats to human rights are not religious but political. Relying on the separation of church and state argument is not a plausible explanation for how politically motivated human rights abuses are often given religious disguise or rationale. Human rights advocates have insisted that women's empowerment can be the best antidote to extremism and that freedom and hope will undercut any popular support and sympathy for terrorists. Will Iranian women's greater presence in civil society and non-governmental organizations compel the government to effect necessary social changes? The answer has much to do with politics and little to do with the Islamic faith. Many Muslim countries, including Iran, Oman, Qatar, Somalia, Sudan, Syria, and the United Arab Emirates, have yet to ratify the UN Convention on the Elimination of All Forms of Discrimination Against Women (CEDAW). It is important to remember that, in this context, external pressure and support for women's struggles is indispensable.

As a female lawyer who for the past quarter century has fought the Islamic penal code and other archaic laws while defending the rights of women and children, Ebadi epitomizes a new generation of Muslim feminists. The awarding of the Nobel Peace Prize to her has already revealed the inherent contradictions in Iran's conservative ideology, and may foster the convergence of Muslim and secular feminists. What is perhaps most noteworthy is the increasing range of Iranian women who have embraced human rights as an empowering tool.

Islamic and secular women alike have questioned their traditional confinement to the home and moved toward broadening their participation in the public and social spheres. Secular women have also created solidarity networks with their Islamic counterparts in order to construct a new identity for themselves while building their social capital. This may explain why Iranian women have consistently pushed for shifting societal norms and legal and socioeconomic reforms—changes that have called into question the male-centered policies and patriarchal cultural practices that have historically limited public space for women's activities beyond domestic domains and rendered women subservient to men. Acutely aware of this significant social capital, President Rouhani supported wide-ranging social and political freedoms, including women's rights. This shrewd move helped him win the presidency in 2013.

Furthermore, the struggle for human rights in Iran has received a major boost as many young Iranians today have become more connected to the outside world through the Internet, social media, and contacts with Iranians living abroad. The youth were largely responsible for the watershed moment for Iran's diverse and courageous opposition movement, the Green Movement, invoking a nationwide reaction to Iran's disputed 2009 presidential elections. The movement initially shook the foundation of the Islamic Republic with mass public protest but was subsequently quashed by the regime. One of the most dramatic aspects of the Green Movement was a cleavage that opened up within the conservative Islamic Republic leadership. Many observers, including Monshipouri and Zakerian, have noted that Iran has suffered unprecedented political fissures, signaling that the religious establishment has become a divided house. Described as a "grassroots civil rights movement a century in the making," the Green Movement became emblematic of a crisis of legitimacy.[5]

While the Islamic Republic has survived several student protests, its confrontational approach toward such uprisings has undermined the vibrant public space that was once available under President Mohammad Khamati. Moreover, the resurgence of the power of the quasi-governmental actors, such as the Foundation for the Disinherited (also known as the "Bonyads") and Islamic Revolutionary Guards Corp (IRGC), has further reinforced its clientelistic and patrimonial system. Yet at the same time, as has been shown in this book, the Islamic Republic faces both material and ideational challenges that stem from within. The current regime has thus far failed to effectively cope with them and its broader inability to improve the lives of the vast majority of its citizens has led to a lingering crisis of legitimacy.[6]

Further fueling this crisis of legitimacy has been the performance of the Revolutionary Courts, one of the most controversial institutions of the state structure. These courts are broadly responsible for judging offenses such as crimes against national security, insulting the supreme leader, terrorism, espionage, conspiracy, armed insurrection against the state, narco-trafficking, or any act that could potentially undermine the regime of the Islamic Republic of Iran.[7]

Moreover, hard-core religious vigilantes, known as the Basij, who are recruited mainly from the ranks of the urban poor, the *bazaaris*, and petty criminals, serve as the unofficial watchdogs and storm troopers of the clerical establishment. These groups, who are typically tasked with assaulting dissidents on the street and who often resort to harassment of women who bend the rules of Islamic attire, are rarely if ever prosecuted by Iran's legal machinery. The Iranian judiciary has been rebuked by several international human rights organizations for such abuses. The court system also frequently enforces censorship laws to curtail public debate and crack down on the press, even if the parameters of political admissibility and tolerance are not clearly drawn.[8]

The Iranian diaspora community in the United States has served as a conduit through which new identities and lines of communication have been formed between Iranians living abroad and those residing in the country, affecting the latter and informing their perceptions of the United States and Americans at large. This line of communication did in fact contribute to the rise of the Green Movement over time, although a case can be made that Iran's Green Movement was to a large extent indigenous, authentic, diffuse, youth-driven, and organic.

The support from the Iranian diaspora community for such a movement, as Mohsen Mobasher rightly asserts, was crucial and noticeably fostered the protest movement in Iran. Social media and new modes of communication, which were prevalent at least outside the country, became relevant in a digitally interconnected world. Equally relevant was the way in which the resurgent political tensions between the US and Iran since the 1979 Iranian Revolution have affected the Iranian diaspora community in the United States and the way in which such reactions have traveled back and forth, whether through traditional or new media channels, between the public of these two countries.

Consistent with Moaddel's findings, many experts on the Middle East have observed that these young people generally tend to be less loyal to the Islamic regime and more interested in reform and social freedoms.[9] As elsewhere in the MENA region, Iran's youth movement has historically been at the forefront of the opposition to the regimes in power. Today, two-thirds of the population in the MENA region is under eighteen. This segment of the population faces one of the highest unemployment rates in the world—around thirty per cent—as the region ranks among the worst for youth unemployment.[10]

The youth's attention to the output of the movie and music industries stands in blatant disregard for archaic Islamic traditions and culture. Art, cinema, and pop music have played a creative and critical role in bringing into the open the social issues that the Iranian population has faced in recent decades. Iranian cinema has become an internationally recognized medium of expression for Iranian society. Many Iranian artists have embraced the notion that filmmaking can free an artist from authoritarian and absolutist state ideology. Modernization of the industry, as Hamid Naficy rightly notes, has involved a wide spectrum of activities, including the emergence of a new cadre of post-revolutionary filmmakers that has embraced women and ethnic minority directors as well. But more importantly, as Naficy has shown, a focus on humanism and intimacy has been adopted by Iranian filmmakers, presenting a stark contrast to the pervasive view abroad of the Islamic Republic as prone to violence, intolerance, and terrorism.

Likewise, the open climate of post-revolutionary Iran and a young generation of Iranians enthusiastic about promoting independent music rather than government-inspired productions have led to the emergence of pop music. While the sadness of lyrics in some pre-revolutionary pop songs served as an oppositional expression toward the Pahlavi regime, according to Nahid Siamdoust, the plethora of love songs in some post-revolutionary pop music has similarly functioned as an idiom that opposes the officially sanctioned culture of grief.

On the economic side, the disappearing gap between city and countryside amid this process of social change merits particular attention. The government's performance in helping the poor in rural areas has been encouraging. Rural-urban disparities, according to one study, have narrowed under the Islamic Republic of Iran. In 1976, for example, the mean per capita household income in rural areas was 44 per cent of that in urban areas. By 2005, it had increased to 63 per cent.[11] Several other indicators support this trend. The share of the urban population has soared from 49 to 67 per cent between 1979 and 2005. The rural-urban gap in household incomes has narrowed. Both rural and urban human development indicators have noticeably improved. Between 1976 and 1996, the female literacy rate rose from 17 to 62 per cent. Overall poverty has fallen. The national poverty rate was at 8.1 per cent in 2005, with relatively small differences in rural and urban poverty of 10 and 7.1 per cent, respectively.[12]

The country's economy, however, has been largely influenced by the conflicting push and pull of a patronage system on the one hand and modern privatizing forces on the other, making Iran's political economy discordant at best. Of the several key institutions that have played an important role in Iran's modern economy and society, one has to mention the Revolutionary Guard as well as the Bonyads that serve more or less as a corporate financial entity. As parallel institutions of power, Bonyads have fortified the position of the clerical elite and diminished that of elected institutions and other governmental structures, including the parliament, local governments, municipal councils, and even the presidency. Manochehr Dorraj is most insightful when he argues that by directly allocating money to their base, Bonyads have promoted a clientelistic system not restricted to Iran but now endemic in the region.

Similarly, privatization, along with the diverse and decentralized networks of power, has created a new and more complex set of stakeholder relations for Iranian enterprises. The emergence of new formal and informal entities is likely to promote the interests of corporate Iran. Ultimately such entities can potentially be converted into political parties and pave the way for a more democratic interaction between corporate Iran and the branches of power. All this, as Bijan Khajepour so poignantly notes, may bode well for a greater focus on human resource management and skills development that could mark a difference between successful private companies and semi-state enterprises.

Future prospects

There is still the unsettled question of just how far President Rouhani and his moderate camp are willing or able to go without being sidelined by conservative groups in Parliament and the Judiciary branch. As Rouhani faces new challenges and difficulties, resolving some of them seems to be a daunting task, he appears fully cognizant of how meeting the people's demands and aspirations is invariably connected to tackling one of the greatest foreign policy challenges ever facing Iran—namely, resolving Iran's nuclear dispute with the West—at a time when tough economic sanctions have brought the Islamic Republic's economy to a standstill. The Rouhani administration has vowed to shut down some credit institutions affiliated with the Revolutionary Guards and other power centers, increase supervision on the banking system, terminate the confiscation of land by powerful bodies and individuals, and levy taxes on organizations that currently enjoy tax exemptions, including companies affiliated with the armed forces and Astan-e Qods, a potent, conservative religious foundation.[13]

Although this book has sharpened our focus on conditions within the Islamic Republic, including economic, social, and political circumstances, the assumption that domestic politics and factors play a minor role in shaping foreign policy is completely erroneous. In fact, given the constitutive relationship between identity and foreign policy, attention to the latter becomes just as significant. It is worth noting that President Rouhani's approach to foreign policy stands in stark contrast to that of his predecessor, President Mahmoud Ahmadinejad. The latter's ideological-populist stance was premised on increasing rather than diminishing tensions with the West. Ahmadinejad often sought confrontation with the West to galvanize a nationalist constituency and warn of the threat the West posed to the very fabric of the Iranian nation.[14] Rouhani, by contrast, has pursued a centrist-pragmatic agenda based on a policy of engagement. His vision has revolved around resolving the nuclear dispute with the West through negotiations, reducing regional conflicts, and prioritizing the country's economic recovery and the general wellbeing of its people.

It is still too early to say whether Rouhani will be able to implement this vision, considering the structural, institutional, and strategic barriers to his success. If his tenure in office is to be more successful than his predecessor's, however, his administration will have to tackle many problems, while providing the perspective and political flexibility necessary to break away from the futile approach of the past. An obvious paradox for the foreign policy of

Tehran is that Iran has found itself an ally of the West in its struggle against the Islamic State in Iraq and Syria (ISIS) in the broader Middle East, but at the same time has remained on the US list of terrorist states due to its close association with Hezbollah in Lebanon and support for rejectionist Palestinian groups.[15] With the United States bent on breaking free of its previous regional commitment, Iran is poised to take advantage of the region's changing geopolitical realities.

Furthermore, the new volatility injected into the region since the 2011 Arab uprisings has underlined Tehran's absence of control over the unfolding of events in its neighborhood, dramatically increasing the regime's apprehensions about its own—real or perceived—vulnerabilities. As the Islamic Republic approaches its middle age, it seems far from certain that Iran will soon "find a sufficiently stable regional environment in which to establish its 'natural' place."[16] What is certain, however, is that Iran's complex relationship with the West needs to be placed in the broader context of coping with a potentially even more significant threat: the rise of the Islamic State. The Islamic State has captured oil fields in Syria and Iraq and threatens to spread its influence throughout the Arabian Peninsula. Following the 13 November 2015 terrorist attacks on Paris, Rouhani condemned them as "crimes against humanity" and offered his condolences to the grieving French people and government. Mohammad Javad Zarif, Iran's Foreign Minister, called these attacks an "inhumane crime," adding that "We are hopeful that in negotiation with other foreign ministers we can find ways to fight against the Islamic State and extremist threats and stop incidents like this."[17] The reality of a common threat has understandably drawn Iran and the United States closer to an agreement to contain, defeat, and eventually dismantle ISIS.

No clear path has yet emerged as to how the Islamic Republic and the West can reconcile their differences in the long term, nor is it clear what new foreign policy approach Tehran will adopt in the face of a region torn by war, shaken by political and economic uncertainty, and threatened by the rise of ISIS. The economic uncertainty has been aggravated by the recent dramatic fall in oil prices.[18] For now, Rouhani has staunchly supported the nuclear deal despite facing serious internal wrangling over the issue. Although this deal's implications remain to be seen, and may include the lifting of sanctions and ensuring Iran's future ability to enrich uranium for peaceful purposes, the Rouhani administration continues to push for the recalibration of Iran's foreign policy strategy and its emerging national security and defense priorities.

NOTES

INTRODUCTION: SOCIAL CHANGE IN POST-KHOMEINI IRAN

1. Craig Calhoun, "Social change," in Edgar F. Borgatta and Rhonda J.V. Montgomery, eds, *Encyclopedia of Sociology*, Second Edition, Vol. 4, New York: Macmillan Reference, 2000, pp. 2641–9; see p. 2643.

2. David W. Lesch, "The Iranian Revolution and its consequences," in Karl Yambert, ed., *The Contemporary Middle East: A Westview Reader*, Boulder, CO: Westview Press, 2013, pp. 247–58; see pp. 248 and 253.

3. Arshin Adib-Moghadam, "Iran-Iraq War," in Mehran Kamrava and Manochehr Dorraj, eds, *Iran Today: An Encyclopedia of Life in the Islamic Republic*, Vol. 1, Westport, CT: Greenwood Press, 2008, pp. 250–8; see especially pp. 251–252.

4. Arshin Adib-Moghaddam, *The International Politics of the Persian Gulf: A Cultural Genealogy*, New York: Routledge, 2006, p. 59.

5. Larry Potter and Gary Sick, eds, *Iran, Iraq, and the Legacies of War*, London: Palgrave, 2004.

6. Ibid.

7. Tareq Y. Ismael and Jacqueline S. Ismael, *Government and Politics of the Contemporary Middle East: Continuity and Change*, New York: Routledge, 2011, pp. 141–2.

8. Mehran Kamrava, *The Modern Middle East: A Political History Since World War I*, Berkeley, CA: University of California Press, 2013, pp. 167 and 374.

9. Alidad Mafinezam and Aria Mehrabi, *Iran and Its Place Among Nations*, Westport, CT: Praeger, 2008, pp. 108–9.

10. "Why They Left," Human Rights Watch, http://www.hrw.org:8080/de/node/112004/section/6, last accessed on 15 Nov. 2014.

11. Freedom House, *Countries at the Crossroad (2007): A Survey of Democratic Governance*, New York: Rowman and Littlefield Publishers, 2008, p. 350.

12. Said Amir Arjomand, *After Khomeini: Iran Under His Successors*, New York: Oxford University Press, 2009, p. 93.

13. Ibid.

14. Suzanne Maloney, "The Revolutionary Economy," *The Iran Primer*, US Institute of Peace, http://iranprimer.usip.org/resource/revolutionary-economy, last accessed 16 Nov. 2014.

15. Ibid.

16. Ray Takeyh, "Iran at Crossroads," *Middle East Journal*, Vol. 57, No. 1, pp. 42–56.

17. Mahmood Monshipouri, "Iran from 1979," in David P. Forsythe, ed., *Encyclopedia of Human Rights*, Vol. 3, New York: Oxford University Press, 2009, pp. 195–206; see p. 198.

18. Vali Nasr. "Iran," in Jeffrey Kopstein and Mark Lichback, eds, *Comparative Politics: Interests, Identities, and Institutions in a Changing Global Order*, 2nd ed., New York: Cambridge University Press, 2005, pp. 394–430; see p. 423.

19. Augustus Richard Norton, "Future of Civil Society in the Middle East," *The Middle East Journal*, Vol. 47, No. 2, Spring 2003, pp. 205–16.

20. Thomas Erdbrink, "President of Iran Vows a Deal," *The New York Times*, 16 Dec. 2014, p. 6.

21. Mahmood Monshipouri, "Diplomacy with Iran: A 'Win-Win' Situation," The Berkeley Blog, http://blogs.berkeley.edu/2014/11/18/diplomacy-with-iran-a-win-win-situation, last accessed 12 Dec. 2014.

22. Mahmood Monshipouri and Manochehr Dorraj, "Iran's Foreign Policy: Shifting Strategic Landscape," *Middle East Policy*, Vol. XX, No. 4, Winter 2013, pp. 133–47.

23. Lisa Pollard, "The role of women," in Jillian Schwedler, *Understanding Contemporary Middle East*, Fourth Edition, Boulder, CO: Lynne Rienner Publishers, 2013, pp. 345–76; see pp. 359–68.

24. Mark Gasiorowski, "Islamic Republic of Iran: political dynamics and foreign policy," in Karl Yambert, ed., *The Contemporary Middle East: A Westview Reader*, Boulder, CO: Westview Press, 2013, pp. 259–69; see pp. 261–2.

25. Alan Richards, John Waterbury, Melani Cammett, and Ishac Diwan, *A Political Economy of the Middle East*, Third Edition, Boulder, CO: Westview Press, 2014, pp. 321–2.

1. WHAT IS POWER IN IRAN? THE SHIFTING FOUNDATIONS OF THE *VELAYAT-E FAQIH*

1. Some sections of the article have been adapted from the introduction to Arshin Adib-Moghaddam, ed., *A Critical Introduction to Khomeini*, Cambridge: Cambridge University Press, 2014.

2. See among others Said Amir Arjomand, *The Turban for the Crown: The Islamic Revolution in Iran*, Oxford: Oxford University Press, 1989.

3. Asghar Shirazi, *The Constitution of Iran: Politics and the State in the Islamic Republic*, trans. John O' Keane, London: I.B. Tauris, 1997, p. 304.

4. Ibid., p. 302.

5. I am using the term "Islams" because there is no all-encompassing consensus about the meaning of "Islam" in the social and political realm. Islam is what people make of it. See further Arshin Adib-Moghaddam, *A Metahistory of the Clash of Civilisations: Us and them beyond Orientalism*, London and New York: Hurst and Oxford University Press, 2011).

6. Ibid. See also Ali Mirsepassi, *Political Islam, Iran and the Enlightenment: Philosophies of Hope and Despair*, Cambridge: Cambridge University Press, 2010.

7. See Arshin Adib-Moghaddam, *The International Politics of the Persian Gulf: A Cultural Genealogy*, London: Routledge, 2006.

8. The term "Irans" is meant to illustrate that there are many interpretations about the meaning of the country and that there is no consensus about the idea of Iran. I have expressed this hybridity of the imagined national narrative constituting the different meanings of the country in theoretical form in *Iran in World Politics: The Question of the Islamic Republic*, London and New York: Hurst and Oxford University Press, 2008. See especially the introduction and conclusion.

9. For a detailed account of the linkage between Ibn Arabi and Khomeini, see Latife Reda Ali, "Khomeini's Discourse of Resistance: The Discourse of Power of the Islamic Revolution," Ph.D. diss., London: School of Oriental and African Studies, 2012.

10. Baqer Moin, *Khomeini: Life of the Ayatollah*, London: I.B. Tauris, 1999, p. 40 ff.

11. Ibid., pp. 274–6.

12. See Alexander Knysh, "*Irfan* Revisited: Khomeini and the legacy of Islamic mystical philosophy," *The Middle East Journal*, Vol. 64, No. 4, 1992, p. 652 (footnote 81).

13. See Rula Jurdi Abisaab, *Converting Persia: Religion and Power in the Safavid Empire*, London: I.B. Tauris, 2004, p. 24. For Karaki's writings see Muhaqiq al-Karaki, *Jamealmaqasid*, Vol. 2, Qum: Ahlol Bayt Publication, 1365 [1986].

14. See Mohammad Ali Amir-Moezzi, *The Divine Guide in Early Shi'ism: The Sources of Esotericism in Islam*, trans., David Streight, Albany, NY: State University of New York Press, 1994, pp. 138–9.

15. For a full history of the idea of *marjaiyat*, see Abdulaziz Abdulhussein Sachedina, *The Just Ruler in Shi'ite Islam: The Comprehensive Authority of the Jurist in Imamite Jurisprudence*, Oxford: Oxford University Press, 1998; see also Linda Walbridge, *The Most Learned of the Shi'a: The Institution of the Marja' Taqlid*, Oxford: Oxford University Press, 2001, in particular pp. 1–12.

16. See William C. Chittick, *The Sufi Path of Knowledge: Ibn Al-Arabi's Metaphysics of Imagination*, Albany, NY: State University of New York Press, 1989.

17. See Adib-Moghaddam, *A Metahistory of the Clash of Civilisations*, p. 246. On Farabi's political thought see Muhsin S. Mahdi, *Al-Farabi and the Foundation of Islamic Political Philosophy*, Chicago, IL: University of Chicago Press, 2010.

18. Ruhollah Khomeini, *Shou'nva Ekhtiyarate Valiye Faqih*, Tehran: Vezarat-e Ershade Islami, 1986, pp. 29–30.

19. Khomeini, *Islam and Revolution: Writings and Declarations of Imam Khomeini*, trans. and ed. Bagher Moin, London: Mizan Press, p. 169.

20. Ruhollah Khomeini, *Al Makaseb al Muharrama*,Vol. ii, Tehran: The Institute for Compilation and Publication of Imam Khomeini's Work, 1995, p. 160; see also Khomeini, *Sahifeh-ye Noor*, Vol. x, Tehran: Markaz-e Nashr-e Asar-e Emam Khomeini, 2004, p. 308.

21. Khomeini, *Sahifeh-ye Noor*, Vol. xi, p. 403; Khomeini, *Al Makaseb al Muharrama*, Vol. ii, p. 160.

22. Ali Rahnema, "Ayatollah Khomeini's Rule of the Guardian Jurist: From Theory to Practice," in Arshin Adib-Moghaddam, ed., *A Critical Introduction to Khomeini*, Cambridge: Cambridge University Press, 2014.

23. Olivier Roy, *The Failure of Political Islam*, trans. Carole Volk, Cambridge, MA: Harvard University Press, 1996, p. 180.

24. See Arshin Adib-Moghaddam, *On the Arab Revolts and the Iranian Revolution: Power and Resistance Today*, London: Bloomsbury, 2013.

25. Ali Khamenei, "Biography," http://www.leader.ir/langs/en/index.php?p=bio, last accessed 21 Mar. 2013.

26. Ibid.

27. Ibid. In order to explain this particular issue further the following section is added: The Leader's refusal of the responsibility of becoming marji' for the people in the Islamic Republic of Iran, does not mean that the people inside the country are not allowed to follow him as a marji'. Consequently, multitudes of letters containing questions about religious issues come from inside the country and from abroad. Besides, a very large number of the noble people in Iran have selected the Supreme Leader as their marji'. There was a pressing issue in addition to the constant pleading by many great figures.

28. Speech given on Iran's national television, 6 June 1989.

29. "Khamenei challenged by Senior Cleric," Asia Times Online, 2 Nov. 2010, http://www.atimes.com/atimes/Middle_East/LK02Ak02.html, last accessed 11 Nov. 2012.

30. Ibid.

31. "Leader's Address to Army Cadets at Imam Ali Military Academy," http://www.leader.ir/langs/en/index.php?p=bayanat&id=3488, last accessed 12 Apr. 2013.

32. "Leader's Statement at the Tehran Friday Prayers," 19 Aug. 2005, http://www.leader.ir/langs/en/index.php?p=bayanat&id=3476, last accessed 19 Mar. 2013.

33. "Leader's Speech to the Residents of the Eastern Azarbaijan Province," 17 Feb. 2007, http://www.leader.ir/langs/en/index.php?p=bayanat&id=3595, last accessed 12 Apr. 2013.

34. Ibid.

35. Ibid.

36. "Supreme Leader's Address to Academics," 24 Sep. 2008, http://www.leader.ir/langs/en/index.php?p=bayanat&id=4058, last accessed 11 Apr. 2013.

41. Ibid.

38. "Hundreds of Ulama, Scholars, Clergymen, and Theology Students of Yazd Province Call on the Leader," 2 Jan. 2008, http://www.leader.ir/langs/en/index.php?p=bayanat&id=3659, last accessed 8 Apr. 2013.

39. The Expediency Council entrenched the *maslahat* principle even further. It is mandated to arbitrate disputes between the elected parliament and the Guardian Council in favor of the interest (and stability) of the system. These institutional changes demonstrate the importance of regime survival in the doctrines of the Islamic Republic. This is, of course, in tune with the interest of any other state.

40. Quoted in Shirazi, *The Constitution of Iran*, p. 230.

41. See further Arshin Adib-Moghaddam, "Islamic Utopian Romanticism and the Foreign Policy Culture of Iran", *Critique: Critical Middle Eastern Studies*, Vol. 14, No. 3 (2005), pp. 265–292.

42. See further Arshin Adib-Moghaddam, "The Pluralistic Momentum in Iran and the Future of the Reform Movement", *Third World Quarterly*, Vol. 27, No. 4 (2006), pp. 665–674.

2.   POST-REVOLUTIONARY IRAN: DEMOCRACY OR THEOCRACY?

1. Jim Lobe, "IRAQ: Neo-Cons See Iran Behind Shiite Uprising", Inter Press Service (9 April 2004), http://www.ipsnews.net/2004/04/iraq-neo-cons-see-iran-behind-shiite-uprising/, last accessed 28 October 2015.

2. Seyed Hossein Mousavian, with Shahir Shahidsalessm, *Iran and the United States: an Insider's View on the Failed Past and the Road to Peace*, New York and London: Bloomsbury, 2014. See also Shireen T Hunter, *Iran Divided: The Historical Roots of Iranian Debates on Identity, Culture, and Governance in the Twenty-First Century*, New York: Rowman & Littlefield Publishers, 2014, for an extended discussion of Iran's modern internal politics.

3. Michel Foucault, "Governmentality," trans. Rosi Braidotti and revised by Colin Gordon. In Graham Burchell, Colin Gordon and Peter Miller, eds, *The Foucault Effect: Studies in Governmentality*, Chicago, IL: University of Chicago Press, 1991, pp. 87–104.

4. Ibid., pp. 102–3.

5. See William O Beeman, *Language, Status and Power in Iran*, Bloomington, IN: Indiana University Press, 1986.

6. Elliott Abrams, "Rouhani in the Big Apple," National Review Online (20 September 2013), http://www.nationalreview.com/corner/359152/rouhani-big-apple-elliott-abrams, last accessed 28 Oct 2015.

7. Nayereh Tohidi, "Iran: Small Window of Hope," Open Democracy, 1 July 2013, www.opendemocracy.net/5050/nayereh-tohidi/iran-small-window-of-hope, last accessed 28 October 2015.

8. "Iranians celebrate Hassan Rouhani's election as president," BBC, 16 June 2013, http://www.bbc.com/news/world-middle-east-22924038, last accessed 26 November 2015.

9. Cf. Beeman, *Language, Status and Power in Iran*; Beeman, "Iran's Religious Regime: What Makes it Tick? Will it Ever Run Down?", *Annals of the American Academy of Political and Social Science*, 483 (1986), pp. 73–83; and Beeman, *The 'Great Satan' Vs. the 'Mad Mullahs': How the United States and Iran Demonize each Other*, Chicago: University of Chicago Press, 2008.

10. Cf. Beeman, *Iranian Performance Traditions*, Costa Mesa, CA: Mazda Publishers., 2001; and Peter J. Chelkowski, "*Ta'ziyeh*: Indigenous Avant-Garde Theatre of Iran," *Performing Arts Journal* 2 (1) (1977), pp. 31–40.

11. Cf. Michael M. J. Fischer, *Iran: From Religious Dispute to Revolution*, Vol. 3. Cambridge, Mass.: Harvard University Press, 1980.

12. See Yitzhak Nakash, *The Shi'is of Iraq*, 2nd paperback edition. Princeton, N.J.: Princeton University Press; Nakash, *Reaching for Power: The Shi'a in the Modern Arab World*, Princeton, N.J.: Princeton University Press, 2006; and Juan Ricardo Cole, *Sacred Space and Holy War: The Politics, Culture and History of Shi'ite Islam*, London: I.B. Tauris, 2002.

13. Cf. Michael M. J. Fischer and Mehdi Abedi, *Debating Muslims: Cultural Dialogues in Postmodernity and Tradition*, Madison, Wis.: University of Wisconsin Press, 1990.

14. Princeton University Iran Data Portal, 2000–2013, Elections, http://www.princeton.edu/irandataportal/elections/, last accessed 6 October 2013.

15. Cf. Beeman, *The 'Great Satan' Vs. the 'Mad Mullahs'*, and Beeman, "Iran's Islamic Republic", in John Esposito and Emad El-Din Shahin, eds, The Oxford Handbook of Islam and Politics, Oxford: Oxford University Press, 2013, pp. 399–410.

16. "Iran moves to ban stoning", *The Telegraph*, 13 February 2012, http://www.telegraph.co.uk/news/worldnews/middleeast/iran/9078684/Iran-moves-to-ban-stoning.html, last accessed 26 November 2015.

3. AFTER RELIGION: ASSESSING A LIBERAL SHIFT AMONG IRANIANS IN THE POST-KHOMEINI PERIOD

1. The surveys can be found at www.mevs.org

2. The data used in this chapter are drawn from comparative cross-national survey projects funded by the national science foundation.

3. Mehrzad Boroujerdi, *The Iranian Intellectuals and the West: The Tormented Triumph of Nativism*, Syracuse, NY: Syracuse University Press, 1996; Farzin Vahdat, *God and Juggernaut*, Syracuse, NY: Syracuse University Press, 2002; Ramin Jahanbegloo,

ed., *Iran: Between Tradition and Modernity*, Lanham, MD: Lexington Books, 2004; Farhang Rajaee, *Islamism and Modernism: The Changing Discourse in Iran*, Austin, TX: University of Texas Press, 2007; Mehran Kamrava, *Iran's Intellectual Revolution*, Cambridge: Cambridge University Press, 2008; Mojtaba Mahdavi, "Post-Islamist trends in post-revolutionary Iran," *Comparative Studies of South Asia, Africa and the Middle East*, 31: 1, 2011, pp. 94–109.

4. One exception is that hostility toward immigrant workers has increased, shown in Table 1.

5. Some scholars prefer to apply the term nationalism only to territorial nationalism and such other cases as pan-Arab nationalism, religious nationalism, or pan-Africanism, which cut across national boundaries and are rooted in race, ethnicity, or religion, as alternatives to nationalist movements; see Ronald Aminzade, *Race, Nation, and Citizenship in Post-Colonial Africa*, Cambridge: Cambridge University Press, 2013. Other scholars, by contrast, have used the term pan-Arab nationalism and religious nationalism. Religious nationalism, in particular, has been employed to capture the political specificity of the Islamic fundamentalist movements that have emerged in the Middle East in recent decades; see Mark Juergensmeyer, *The New Cold War? Religious Nationalism Confronts the Secular State*, Berkeley: University of California Press, 1993; Roger Friedland, "Religious nationalism and the problem of collective representation," *Annual Review of Sociology*, 2, 2001, pp. 125–52; "Money, sex, and God: the erotic logic of religious nationalism," *Sociological Theory*, 20: 3, Nov. 2002, pp. 381–425; Jonathan Fox, "The rise of religious nationalism and conflict: ethnic conflict and revolutionary wars, 1945–2001," *Journal of Peace Research*, 41: 6, Nov. 2004, p. 715–31.

6. Anthony David Smith, *Nationalism and Modernism*, London: Routledge, 1998, p. 1.

7. Nadav Safran, *Egypt in Search of Political Community*, Cambridge, MA: Harvard University Press, 1961, p. 87.

8. William L. Cleveland, *The Making of an Arab Nationalist: Ottomanism and Arabism in the Life and Thought of Sati' al-Husri*, Princeton: Princeton University Press, 1971, p. 130.

9. Cited in Emmanuel Sivan, *Radical Islam: Medieval Theology and Modern Politics*, New Haven, Conn.: Yale University Press, 1985, p. 31.

10. Ruhollah Khomeini, *Islam and Revolution: Writings and Declarations of Imam Khomeini*, trans. Hamid Algar, Berkeley: Mizan Press, 1981, p. 38.

11. Maurizio Viroli, *For Love of Country: An Essay on Patriotism and Nationalism*, Oxford: Clarendon Press, 1995, p. 6; and Aminzade, *Race, Nation, and Citizenship*.

12. Figueiredo and Elkins further measure the concept of national pride against nationalism and patriotism. Assessing the relations of these dimensions with attitudes toward immigrants, they conclude that "while nationalists have a strong predilection for hostility toward immigrants, patriots show no more prejudice than does the average citizen." See Rui J.P. de Figueiredo Jr and Zachary Elkins, "Are patri-

ots bigots? An inquiry into the vices of in-group pride," American Journal of Political Science, 47: 1, Jan. 2003, p. 171.

13. Mansoor Moaddel, "The Iranian Revolution and its nemesis: the rise of liberal values among Iranians," *Comparative Studies of South Asia, Africa and the Middle East*, 29: 1, 2009, pp. 126–36.

14. Ayatollah Khomeini "considered governmental rules higher than the primary and secondary religious rules." See "General principles of Imam Khomeini's political thought," http://www.al-islam.org/message-thaqalayn/vol2-n2–3/general-principles-imam-khumaynis-political-thought-kazem-ghazi-zadeh-0, last accessed 27 Dec. 2014.

15. Friedland, "Religious nationalism and the problem of collective representation."

16. See Mansoor Moaddel, Julie de Jong and Munqeth Dagher, "Beyond sectarianism in Iraq," *Contexts*, 10: 3, 2011, pp. 66–7; and Moaddel, *Islamic Modernism*.

17. Mansoor Moaddel, Mark Tessler and Ronald Inglehart, "Foreign occupation and national pride: the case of Iraq," *Public Opinion Quarterly*, 2008, pp. 1–29; Ronald Inglehart and Christian Welzel, *Modernization, Cultural Change, and Democracy: The Human Development Sequence*, Cambridge: Cambridge University Press, 2005; and Moaddel, Tessler, and Inglehart, "Foreign occupation and national pride."

18. See, for example, Rui J. P. de Figueiredo, Jr. and Zachary Elkins, "Are patriots bigots? An inquiry into the vices of in-group pride," *American Journal of Political Science*, 47: 1, Jan. 2003, pp. 171–88.

19. See Bruce Koepke, "The situation of Afghans in the Islamic Republic of Iran nine years after the overthrow of the Taliban regime in Afghanistan," Middle East Institute, 4 Feb. 2011, http://www.refugeecooperation.org/publications/Afghanistan/03_koepke.php, last accessed 21 June 2013.

20. The relationships between democracy and other variables do not display a consistent empirical pattern. As shown in Table 2 (not shown in Table 3), democracy does not have consistent relationships with liberal or conservative values. This lack of consistency may be because the idea of democracy has been appropriated by both the ruling authoritarian Islamic regime and the opposition. The concept may have different meanings to different people. It certainly means totally different things for the followers of clerical absolutism and for the supporters of liberal values. In the Iranian current context, therefore, the concept of secular politics may be a more effective tool to distinguish "authoritarian" democracy from liberal democracy. In other words, it is a better measure of people's orientation towards liberal democracy.

21. According to experts, the root mean square error of approximation (RMSEA) should be less than 0.06 and Comparative Fit Index (CFI) larger than 0.95. See James B. Schreiber, Frances K. Stage, Jamie King, Amaury Nora and Elizabeth A. Barlow, "Reporting structural equation modeling and confirmatory factor

analysis results: a review," *The Journal of Educational Research*, 99: 6, July/August, 2006, pp. 323–37.

4. WOMEN AND CRIMINAL LAW IN POST-KHOMEINI IRAN

1. I would like to express my gratitude to CIRS, especially Mehran Kamrava and Zahra Babar, for organizing the Working Group on Social Change in Post-Khomeini Iran, and to the colleagues who participated. The ideas for this chapter benefited from our insightful round-table discussions. I would also like to thank Mahmood Monshipouri for his editorial guidance. Finally, I gratefully acknowledge the support of The Fetzer Institute for funding the research for this project.

2. The decree was not legally binding, so a few judges did continue to issue the sentence, as in Ashtiani's case.

3. This statement was widely reported in the English language press. See, for instance, Ian Black, "Iranian media warned after paper calls Carla Bruni-Sarkozy a 'prostitute,'" *Guardian*, 31 Aug. 2010, http://www.guardian.co.uk/world/2010/aug/31/carla-bruni-sarkozy-iranian-media, last accessed 8 Dec. 2014).

4. Ibid.

5. "Iran: 'Confession,' Stoning Sentence a Mockery of Justice," Human Rights Watch, 10 Apr. 2010, http://www.hrw.org/news/2010/08/13/iran-confession-stoning-sentence-mockery-justice, last accessed 14 Dec. 2014. While the judiciary did not explain the grounds on which it dispensed with the stoning sentence, it did make clear that the prison sentence was issued for the charge of disrupting public order.

6. "Javad Larijani gives news of Sakineh Mohammadi's pardon," Radiozamaneh, 18 Mar. 2014, http://www.radiozamaneh.com/130752, last accessed 14 Dec. 2014.

7. Arzoo Osanloo, "The Measure of Mercy: Islamic Justice, Sovereign Power, and Human Rights in Iran," *Cultural Anthropology*, 21, 2006, pp. 570–602.

8. The 25 Oct. 2014 execution of Reyhaneh Jabbari ignited debates among activists outside of Iran as to the effects of international advocacy, especially in cases of retribution where the family of the victim is the ultimate decision-maker and not the state. Larijani placed the blame on the international "media blitz." See "Iran blames Western 'media blitz' for execution of Reyhaneh Jabbari," UN Watch, 31 Oct. 2014, http://blog.unwatch.org/index.php/2014/10/31/iran-blames-western-for-execution-of-reyhaneh-jabbari/, last accessed 4 Jan. 2015. For debates among activists, see Shadi Sadr, "Why did the international campaigns to save Reyhaneh fail?" BBC Persian Blogs, 4 Jan. 2015, http://www.bbc.co.uk/persian/blogs/2015/01/150104_l44_nazeran_jabbari_reihaneh_execution, last accessed 4 Jan. 2015; Mina Ahadi, "Ms. Sadr, Would it not have been better that you maintained the grandiloquent silence in the case of the fate of Reyhaneh?" International Campaign Against Execution, 4 Jan. 2015, http://notonemoreexecution.org/1393/10/6055/, last accessed 4 Jan. 2015.

9. The lock on law-making and *Shari'a* interpretation claimed by the conservative factions has broad consequences for authority and social control, while limiting the possibilities for popular and political mobilization.

10. For instance, just after the revolution, virtuous women were asked to stay home to perform their primary roles as mothers and wives. During the war, virtuous women were called upon to enter into the public and private work sectors while the men participated in the front. Throughout the reform period, virtue also meant civic and political engagement.

11. I have explored the post-revolutionary amendments to the civil codes on marriage and family and compared them to the pre-revolutionary family law code. See Arzoo Osanloo, "Framing Rights: Women and Family Law in Pre- and Post-Revolutionary Iran," *New Middle Eastern Studies* 5(2015): 1–18.

12. Since 2007, I have been conducting a research project on the Islamic mandate of forgiveness (*bakhshesh*) in Iran's system of criminal sanctioning, where it is codified as forbearance (*gozasht*). In annual research trips to Iran, lasting between one to four months, I have been conducting interviews, archival research, and participant-observation in numerous settings related to this topic. In particular reference to this chapter, in July of 2012, I conducted participant-observation in Tehran's Provincial Criminal Court. With the Court's permission, I sat in on criminal trials, interviewed various parties to cases, reviewed rulings, met with judges, and studied the provisions of the revised Penal Code with the Court's research committee.

13. Arzoo Osanloo, "Contesting governance: authority, protest, and rights talk in post-republican Iran," in Steven Heydemann and Reinoud Leenders, eds, *Comparative Authoritarianisms: Syria and Iran*, Stanford, CA: Stanford University Press 2012, pp. 127–42.

14. Valentine Moghadam, *Modernizing Women: Gender and Social Change in the Middle East*, Boulder, CO: Lynne Rienner, 1993, p. 59.

15. Minoo Moallem, *Between Warrior Brother and Veiled Sister: Islamic Fundamentalism and the Politics of Patriarchy in Iran*, Berkeley, CA: University of California Press, 2005, p. 90.

16. From a speech given on 12 Mar. 1985. See *Sahifa-yi Nur*, Vol. 19, p. 120, cited in Ruhollah Khomeini, *The Position of Women from the Viewpoint of Imam Khomeini*, trans. Juliana Shaw and Behrooz Arezoo, Tehran: Institute for the Compilation and Publication of Imam Khomeini's Works, 2001, p. 14.

17. Constitution of the Islamic Republic of Iranian 1979, rev. 1989.

18. Mohammad Tavana, "Three decades of Islamic criminal law legislation in Iran: legislative analysis with emphasis on the amendments of the 2013 Islamic penal code," *Electronic Journal of Islamic and Middle Eastern Law*, Vol. 2, 2014, pp. 24–38. This constituted a major undertaking that increased the number of provisions in the penal code by one-third.

19. Amin Banani, *The Modernization of Iran, 1921–1941*, Stanford: Stanford University Press, 1961; Husain Gholami, "The Islamisation of criminal justice and its developments in Iran," *Tilburg Foreign Law Review*, 7, 1999, p. 213. The codification of *Shari'a* into a comprehensive state law began as early as 1905 and spanned many substantive areas of law.

20. Majid Mohammadi, *Judicial Reform and Reorganization in 20th Century Iran: State-Building, Modernization, and Islamicization*, New York: Routledge, 2008, p. 230.

21. Despite the apparent popular support suggested by a referendum, the bitter disputes that took place during the drafting of the constitution revealed vast differences in how coalition leaders understood this new system of governance.

22. Article 4 of the Constitution of the Islamic Republic (1979) established the Council of Guardians to determine whether legislative acts conformed to the *Shari'a*.

23. Gholami, "Islamisation of Criminal Justice in Iran," p. 214.

24. In 1979, a separate Revolutionary Court was also created to prosecute people charged with violating the principles of the revolution, thus acting against the values of the Islamic Republic. Such crimes were tantamount to treason and included a wide range of offenses, including terrorism, inciting violence, blasphemy, insulting the leader of the Islamic Republic, and smuggling.

25. Rudolph Peters, *Crime and Punishment in Islamic Law: Theory and Practice from the Sixteenth to the Twenty-First Century*, New York: Cambridge University Press, 2005, p. 161.

26. Legislators also revised the codes of criminal procedure. Judges began to implement the new criminal procedures on 22 June 2015.

27. These are referred to as Article 612 cases, indicating the provision in the code that provides jurisdiction.

28. Peters, *Crime and Punishment in Islamic Law*, p. 163.

29. A note to Article 211 (1392) specifies acceptable sources of judge's knowledge (including, expert opinions, site inspection, local investigation, witness statements, and reports by law enforcement officers) and further clarifies that judge's knowledge cannot be derived from generic perception.

30. For a discussion on the theories behind *hudud* laws, see Wael Hallaq, *Shari'a: Theory, Practice, Transformations*, Cambridge, UK: Cambridge University Press, 2009, p. 311. Hallaq notes that the deterrent value of such crimes serves on a psychological level by becoming engrained in the mindset of potential offenders that their acts, even if not punished in this world, would leave them in "eternal Hellfire" in the next.

31. Article 167 of the Constitution of the Islamic Republic of Iran states:

    The judge must endeavor to judge each case on the basis of the codified law. In case of the absence of any such law, he must deliver his judgment on the basis of authoritative Islamic sources and authentic *fatwa*. He, on the pretext of the silence of or deficiency of law in the matter, or its brevity or contradictory nature, cannot refrain from admitting and examining cases and delivering his judgment.

32. The General Penal Code of 1926 was first amended in 1928 and saw a series of revisions up to 1973.

33. For an overview of women and criminal sanctioning from the pre-revolutionary to post-revolutionary period, see Maryam Hosseinkhah, "The execution of women in Iranian criminal law: an examination of the impact of gender on laws concerning capital punishment in the new Islamic penal code," Iran Human Rights Documentation Center, 7 May 2012, http://www.iranhrdc.org/english/publications/legal-commentary/1000000102-the-execution-of-women-in-iranian-criminal-law.html, last accessed 12 Dec. 2014.

34. Article 199, Iranian Penal Code (2012). For the punishment of flogging, the eyewitness testimony of two men and four women is sufficient. For punishments other than flogging, the testimony of three men and four women is needed.

35. Reza Ansari-Rad, "The conditions of proving the crime of *zina* are extremely difficult," *Zan*, 30 Nov. 1998 (9 Azar 1377), p. 9.

36. See, for instance, Mohammad Hashim Kamali, *Shari'ah Law: An Introduction*, Oxford, UK: Oneworld, 2008, p. 312. Kamali notes that the *hadith* that reference *rajm* do not prescribe it as a punishment to be carried out, but rather cite it as an example of a kind of practice carried out by Jewish law.

37. This final point seems to be the compromise reached by the Council of Guardians in the latest amendment to the penal code. See "In place of stoning, can we implement a different order?" Iranian Students' News Agency, 10 Apr. 2012 (22 Farvardin 1391), http://www.isna.ir/fa/news/91012206145, last accessed 17 Dec. 2014.

38. Amnesty International's report indicates that "no executions by stoning were known to have occurred but at least ten people remained under sentence of death by stoning." See "Annual Report: Iran 2013," Amnesty International, 23 May 2013, http://www.amnestyusa.org/research/reports/annual-report-iran-2013, last accessed 12 Dec. 2014. An earlier Amnesty report estimated that seventy-seven executions by stoning were known to have been carried out in Iran since the revolution, with eight since the 2002 memorandum by then-Head of the Judiciary, Ayatollah Shahroudi. The last stoning known to have taken place in Iran was in 2007. A number of defendants had their sentences commuted from stoning to hanging, while some are in legal limbo awaiting punishment. See "Iran's New Penal Code Retains the Punishment of Stoning," Justice for Iran, 18 May 2013, http://justiceforiran.org/call-for-action/stoning-new-penal-code, last accessed 12 Dec. 2014.

39. "Codifying repression: an assessment of Iran's new penal code," Human Rights Watch, Aug. 2012, http://www.hrw.org/reports/2012/08/28/codifying-repression, last accessed 12 Dec. 2014.

40. Note 3 of Article 132 specifies that the punishment for *zina* is "either" execution or stoning.

41. Mohammad Hossein Nayyeri, "The question of 'stoning to death' in the new penal code of the IRI," Iran Human Rights Documentation Center, Feb. 2012, p. 4, http://www.iranhrdc.org/english/publications/legal-commentary/1000000059-the-question-of-stoning-to-death-in-the-new-penal-code-of-the-iri.html, last accessed 17 Dec. 2014.

42. Mohammad Mostafaei, "Crime of adultery and stoning punishment in Iran's new criminal code; skills of defense in Hodud crimes," Universal Tolerance Organization, 1 June 2013, http://www.universaltolerance.org/en/what-we-do/articles/item/126-crime-of-adultery-and-stoning-punishment-in-iran-s-new-criminal-code, last accessed 22 Dec. 2014).

43. In Article 224 of the new penal code, *zina* that carries with it the death penalty, but not by stoning, is defined as: incestuous intercourse, intercourse with a step-mother, intercourse between a non-Muslim man and a Muslim woman (in which case the non-Muslim man will be sentenced to death), and finally, forcible rape.

44. Mostafaei, "Crime of adultery and stoning punishment in Iran's criminal code."

45. Article 49, Islamic Penal Code (1996). Youth who were exempted from criminal responsibility were sent to "Correction and Rehabilitation Centers" charged with providing juvenile reform and discipline.

46. Note 1 to Article 49, Islamic Penal Code (1996).

47. The old penal code referred to Article 1210 of the Civil Codes to state that the age of maturity is nine lunar years for girls and fifteen for boys.

48. Criticisms for this age of maturity for criminal responsibility abound, as numerous other areas of civic life regard the age of maturity as eighteen, such as obtaining a driver's license or passport.

49. Article 91, Iranian Penal Code (2012), author's translation.

50. Personal interview, 15 July 2012.

51. Personal communication, 28 Sep. 2012.

52. Personal communication, 19 July 2012.

53. This section is updated and revised from a section of a previously published article. Arzoo Osanloo, "When Blood Has Spilled: Gender, Honor, and Compensation in Iranian Criminal Sanctioning," *Political and Legal Anthropology Review*, 35, 2, 2012, pp. 307–25.

54. These were found in Articles 209 and 258 of the earlier (pre-2013) penal code.

55. Tavana, "Three Decades of Islamic Criminal Law Legislation in Iran," p. 36. Tavana interestingly hints at the possibility of gender equality in compensation for murder. However, during my fieldwork in Tehran's criminal court in 2014 and 2015, I confirmed that Article 551 does not apply to the *diya* that must be paid to account for gender imbalance in *qisas*. That is, when the family of the victim seeks to execute a man who killed a woman, that family must still pay one half of the diya in order to carry out the sentence.

56. Mashood A. Baderin, *International Human Rights and Islamic Law*, Oxford, UK: Oxford University Press, 2003, p. 83.

57. Peters, *Crime and Punishment in Islamic Law*, p. 7.

58. Mohammad E. Shams Nateri, "Formal and informal means of conflict resolution in murder cases in Iran," in Hans-Jorg Albrecht, Jan-Michael Simon, Hassan Rezaei, Holger-Christoph Rohne, and Ernesto Kiza, eds, *Conflicts and Conflict Resolution in Middle Eastern Societies—Between Tradition and Modernity*, Berlin: Duncker & Humblot, 2006, pp. 401–9.

59. *Holy Qur'an*, 2:178–9.

60. Baderin, *International Human Rights and Islamic Law*, p. 73.

61. Hamid Kusha, *The Sacred Law of Islam: A Case Study of Women's Treatment in the Islamic Republic of Iran's Criminal Justice System*, Aldershot, Hampshire, UK: Ashgate, 2002, p. 261.

62. Baber Johansen, "Contingency in a sacred law: legal and ethical norms in the Muslim fiqh," *Studies in Islamic Law and Society*, 7, Leiden: Brill, 1999, p. 206.

63. Cited in Ziba Mir-Hosseini, *Islam and Gender: The Religious Debate in Contemporary Iran*, Princeton, NJ: Princeton University Press, 1999, p. 61.

64. Ibid.

65. Although parliament has thus far lost the debate on gender parity in *diya*, in 2002, advocates were successful in passing a law that made an equal amount of *diya* payable to Muslims and Iran's recognized religious minorities, that is, Christians, Jews, and Zoroastrians.

66. "Islamic teacher responds to questions about difference of blood money and heritage between men & women," 31 Mar. 2013, http://lenziran.com/2013/03/31/islamic-teacher-respond-to-questions-about-difference-of-blood-money-and-heritage-between-men-women/, last accessed 6 Jan. 2015.

67. "Different *diya* between a man and a woman is not the basis for according privilege to a man," ISNA, 11 May 2013 (21 Ordibehesht 1392), http://www.isna.ir/fa/news/92022113645, last accessed 6 Jan. 2015).

68. "A man and a woman's *diya* in bodily compensation will be remitted equally," ISNA, 15 May 2013 (25 Ordibehesht 1392), http://www.isna.ir/fa/news/92022517172, last accessed 6 Jan. 2015.

69. 2:178 and 179, and 5:45.

70. Reza Ansari-Rad, "*Hooqooq-e jazaee Islami va masalleh-ye qisas va diya ye zan*" (Islamic criminal law and the issue of retribution and compensation for women), *Zan*, 23 Sep. 1998 (1 Mehr 1377), p. 9. Months later, *Zan* published another article critical of the gender disparity in *diya*. The essay was complemented by a caricature depicting a would-be criminal conjuring up the image of half of a woman, since his punishment for assaulting her would only amount to half that of a man's. Reza Ansari-Rad, "*Diya va nakhsh-e zan dar jame'eh ye emrooz*" (Diya and the role of women in society today), *Zan*, 10 Feb 1999 (21 Bahman 1377), p. 5. Later, the

newspaper published another satirical cartoon depicting a burglar inside a couple's house. The cartoon depicts the husband pointing to his wife with the caption: "Her *diyeh* is half of mine." Soon after, state officials shut the paper down.

71. Cited in Tim Elliot, "Blood money: women take on hard-line Islam in a campaign for equal rights," *New Internationalist*, 1 Feb. 2004, http://newint.org/columns/currents/2004/02/01/blood-money/, last accessed 12 Dec. 2014.

72. Manal Lutfi, "The woman's mufti: interview with Grand Ayatollah Saanei," *Asharq-Al Awsat*, 6 Apr. 2007, http://www.asharq-e.com/news.asp?section= 3&id=8554, last accessed 12 Dec. 2014.

73. Nader Karami, "Grand Ayatollah endorses end to gender discrimination," Roozonline, 3 June 2007, http://www.roozonline.com/english/news3/newsitem/article/grand-ayatollah-endorses-end-to-gender-discrimination.html, last accessed 17 Dec. 2014.

74. Ibid.

75. As of Dec. 2015, the rate of *diya* was 165 million Iranian rials, plus an additional one-third for deaths that occur during a Muslim holy month. "The Rate of *Diya* for 1394 has been Announced," Hamshahri Online, 25 Mar. 2015, http://www.hamshahrionline.ir/details/290575, last accessed 12 Nov. 2015.

76. "Iran women to get equal 'blood money' in car crashes," Reuters, 27 May 2008, http://in.reuters.com/article/2008/05/27/idINIndia-33787420080527, last accessed 7 Jan. 2015.

77. "Girls of Shin Abad receive *diya* equal to that of men," Human Rights Activists News Agency, 29 Nov. 2014, https://hra-news.org/fa/children/diye-2, last accessed 4 Dec. 2014.

78. Osanloo, *Politics of Women's Rights*.

5. A REVOLUTION WITHIN TWO REVOLUTIONS: WOMEN AND LITERATURE IN CONTEMPORARY IRAN

1. "Khamenei: Forugh Farrokhzad's death was her saving grace," www.peykeiran.com/Content.aspx?ID=51403, last accessed 12 November 2015.

2. Forugh Farrokhzad, "Tanha Sedast Ke Mimanad" ("It is Only the Voice that Remains"), in *Iman Biyavarim beh Aghaz-e Fasl-e Sard* (*Let Us Believe in the Dawning of the Cold Season*), Tehran: Morvarid, 1974, p. 86.

3. Simin Behbahani, "Gypsiesque (13)," in *A Cup of Sin: Selected Poems*, trans. Farzaneh Milani and Kaveh Safa, eds, Syracuse: Syracuse University Press, 1999, p. 75.

4. The Iranian government's tightening grip was not reserved only for writers and poets. Artists of all stripes, human rights activists, journalists, and film directors were subjected to a new wave of repression. For instance, Ja'far Panahi, a prize-winning, internationally acclaimed filmmaker and Muhammad Rasoulof, another filmmaker, were imprisoned. Narges Kalhor, a film director, and the daughter of a senior

cultural and media adviser to President Ahmadinejad, sought political asylum in Germany where she was presenting her film about torture at the Nuremberg film festival.

5. Unsurprisingly, this physical and spatial literary desegregation is mirrored online. Iran has one of the fastest-growing rates of Internet usage in the Middle East, and, here, too, women play an active and defiant role. Indeed, the new technology is a powerful desegregator. It does not recognize traditional walls, veils, and codes of segregation. It needs no passport and no written permission from a male legal guardian to leave the country. Nor does it need a visa to enter the country. Like a magic carpet or witch's broomstick, it is a miraculous means of transportation. In the words of one female blogger, Saïdeh Pakravan, "A blog gives me the perfect tool. I can stand tall on the parapets of my personal fortress, see old and new enemies of reason and logic and send out my own arrows as counter-arguments." See "By Way of Intro," *The Counter Argument Blog*, http://thecounterargument. wordpress.com/about/, last accessed 28 October 2015.

6. For a more detailed analysis of this literary renaissance, see Farzaneh Milani, *Words, Not Swords: Iranian Women Writers and the Freedom of Movement*, Syracuse: Syracuse University Press, 2011.

7. For translation of the autobiographical vignette, "Avvalin Ruz," see Goli Taraghi, "The First Day," http://www.wordswithoutborders.org/article/the-first-day, last accessed 28 October 2015; quotes come from this translation. See also Goli Taraghi, *Dow Donya (Two Worlds)*, Tehran: Niloofar, 2002.

8. Ibid.

9. Cynthia Haven, "Iran's leading poet receives new Stanford Literature Prize," *Stanford Report*, 5 Mar. 2008, news.stanford.edu/news/2008/march5/simin-030508.html

10. Simin Behbahani, "Pine Tree," in *Yek Dariche-ye Azadi (A Window to Freedom)*, Tehran: Sokhan, 1995, p. 175.

11. Ali Akbar Moshir-Salimi, *Zanan-e Sokhanvar az yek Hezar sal-e Pish ta Emruz (Persian Women Writers from a Thousand Years Ago until Today)*, Tehran: Elmi, 1956–1958.

12. Keshavarz-e Sadr, *Az Rabe'e ta Parvin (From Rabe'e to Parvin)*, Tehran: Kavian, 1956.

13. Farzaneh Milani, *Veils and Words: The Emerging Voices of Iranian Women Writers*, Syracuse, NY: Syracuse University Press, 1992.

14. Emineh Pakravan, born in 1890 in Istanbul, was the daughter of an Iranian diplomat (Hassan Khan) and married an Iranian diplomat, Fathollah Pakravan. She taught Persian art and history at the Daneshkadeye Honarhaye Ziba (The College of Fine Arts) for many years. Pakravan was a prolific writer and published, among others: *Destinées Persanes (Persian Fates)*; *Le Prince Sans Histoire (The Prince without a Story)*; *Abbas Mirza*; *La Quatrième Génération*; *Vieux Téhéran*; and *Téhéran*

de Jadis (*Tehran of Yesteryears*). I am grateful to Saïdeh Pakravan, Emineh Pakravan's granddaughter, for opening her personal library to me and answering all my questions.

15. These statistics are mainly taken from Hassan Mirabedini, "Dastan nevisiy-e zanan: gam hay-e larzan-e avaliy-e" ("Women's Fiction Writing: First Wobbly Steps"), *Zanan*, Mar. 2007; and Nazila Fathi, "Women writing novels emerge as stars in Iran," *New York Times*, 29 June 2005.

16. The overwhelming majority of these works have not been translated into English. The multi-billion-dollar publishing industry in the US is dominated by a few conglomerates driven by an obsession with blockbusters. The not-so-lucrative business of translating books from other languages into English, a cornerstone of intercultural communication and better understanding among nations, has no real place in such a market. The number of translations, regardless of genre, has dropped steeply in the past two decades.

17. Gina Nahai, "So What's with All the Iranian Memoirs?" *Publisher's Weekly*, 26 Nov. 2007, http://www.publishersweekly.com/pw/by-topic/columns-and-blogs/soap-box/article/4048-so-what-s-with-all-the-iranian-memoirs.html

18. Homa Sarshar, *Sha'ban Ja'afari*, Beverly Hills, CA: Naab, 2002.

19. Firoozeh Dumas, *Funny in Farsi: A Memoir of Growing up Iranian in America*, New York, NY: Random House, 2004.

20. "The eight-year war between Iran and Iraq also led to the emergence of a literature of war. Ranging between personal testimonials, short stories, and novellas this literature spoke to the experiences of a large number of young Iranians and captured the harsh realities of a devastating war with whose aftermath Iran continues to grapple, long after the end of the hostilities in 1988," writes Nasrin Rahimieh in "Literary Voices," *Middle East Institute*, 29 Jan. 2009, http://www.mei.edu/content/literary-voices

21. Western travelers to Iran in the eighteenth and nineteenth centuries commented on the uncanny absence of women from the public domain. For instance, Lady Sheil, wife of the then-British ambassador, who arrived in Iran in 1849, observed that during the welcoming ceremonies, "It was difficult to say how many thousands of people had assembled, or what class of persons had not come forth to do honor to the Queen of England's representative... but there was not a single woman," *Glimpses of Life and Manners in Persia*, New York, NY: Arno, 1973, p. 85; It is in the context of this glaring historical absence of women in the public domain that their massive participation in the current events in Iran must be understood.

22. Farid Ud-Din Attar, *The Speech of the Birds*, trans. Peter Avery, Cambridge, UK: The Islamic Texts Society, 1998, p. 69.

23. Shahrnush Parsipur, *Touba va Ma'nay-e Shab* (*Touba and the Meaning of the Night*), Tehran: Spark, 1989, translated into English by Havva Houshmand and Kamran Talatoff, New York, NY: Feminist Press at the City University of New York, 2006, p. 423.

24. Shahrnush Parsipur, *Zanan bedun-e Mardan* (*Women Without Men*), Tehran: Noqreh, 1989, translated into English by Kamran Talatoff and Jocelyn Sharlet, Syracuse, NY: Syracuse University Press, 1998, p. 28.

25. Suffragettes and early women's rights advocates in the US knew the liberating power of the bicycle and called it a "freedom machine."

26. Mo'in ed-Din Mehrabi, *QorratolʿAyn*, Cologne: Ruyesh, 1989, p. 149.

27. Forugh Farrokhzad, "Only the Voice Remains," in *Iman Biavarim be Aghaz-e Fasl-e Sard* (*Let's Believe in the Dawning of a Cold Season*), Tehran: Morvarid, 1974, pp. 76–81.

28. Mojdeh Daghighi, "Goft-o-gu ba Shiva Arastui (A Conversation with Shiva Arastui), *Zanan* (July 2004): 66.

29. Deniz Kandiyoti, "Bargaining with Patriarchy," *Gender & Society*, 2: 3, 1988, pp. 274–90.

30. Sattareh Farman Farmaian, *Daughter of Persia: A Woman's Journey from her Father's Harem through the Islamic Revolution*, New York, NY: Crown Publishers, 1992.

31. Amir and Khalil, *Zahra's Paradise*, New York, NY: First Second Books, 2011.

32. There is a vast discrepancy between Western, in particular North American, perceptions of Iranian women—victims of stern Ayatollahs, prisoners of their faith and their veil—and their representation inside the country. Remarkably, the long tale of the oppressed Iranian Woman in the US, and the aggressive, emasculating one inside the country is matched by another one-dimensional stereotype of the oppressive, violent Iranian Man abroad and the pushover at home. It is fascinating to compare the portrayal of emasculated men with the prevalent image of Iranian men as violent and degenerate. Take Dr Bozorg Mahmoody, the infamous husband of the blockbuster, *Not Without My Daughter*, the most popular book ever published in the West about Iran. This personal memoir received as a work of ethnography presented Dr Mahmoody as a violent hostage-taker. He not only lost all his property in the US, he was also denied even sporadic visitation rights with his only child. In 2003, fifteen years after the publication of *Not Without My Daughter*, Dr Mahmoody chronicled his side of the story in a documentary produced in Finland. In this film, *Without My Daughter*, a beleaguered father laments his slander and describes in poignant detail his desperate and unsuccessful attempts to be reunited with his daughter. "I am a beast and a criminal in the eyes of the world," says Dr Mahmoody. "I have been portrayed as a liar, a woman-beater, and a kidnapper. Even the courts of law have not seen any need for my presence to divide my family and give away my belongings. I have been denied the right to see my daughter for fifteen years or even to talk to her. My sin, my only sin was that I loved my child, my daughter, Mahtob." In his written version of the saga, an unpublished manuscript, Dr Mahmoody, who calls his divorce and child custody hearing a "travesty," claims that "within weeks Betty had claimed all our US assets, divorced me, won sole custody of Mahtob, and filed a restraining order against

me. I received notice of my court date in February 1992, via a letter sent to my sister eight months after the hearing had taken place." *Lost Without My Daughter*, written in English and addressed to a Western audience, has not found a publisher. According to Kris Hollington, the co-author of the memoir, in a personal communication, "The reason for the UK and US publishers' reluctance is, they say, 'it was all such a long time ago' and 'a Western audience will have no sympathy for Mr Mahmoody.'"

33. "We think back through our mothers if we are women," said Virginia Woolf in *A Room of One's Own*, and many Iranian women writers, especially in the Diaspora, have done that. *Moonlight on the Avenue of Faith* by Gina Nahai, New York: Washington Square Press, 1999, *The Good Daughter* by Jasmin Darznik, New York: Grand Central Publishing, 2011, *Things I've been Silent About* by Azar Nafisi, New York: Random House, 2008, and *The Dance of the Rose and the Nightingale* by Nesta Ramazani, Syracuse, NY: Syracuse University Press, 2002, among others, revolve around mother-daughter relationships. In Nahai's masterpiece, the protagonist, Lili, goes looking for her mother and foremothers and finds that they are missing in action. Lili forges alternative models for feminist biographical writing as a process in which new relational metaphors such as fostering and adoption open fresh insights on the role of mothers and foremothers as precursors.

34. Forugh Farrokhzad, *Asir* [Captive], 1955; reprint, Tehran: Amir Kabir, 1974, p. 74.

35. Faribah Vafi, *My Bird*, trans. Nasrin Jewell and Mahnaz Kousha, Syracuse, NY: Syracuse University Press, 2009, p. 25. For a more detailed analysis of this book, see my Afterword to the English translation of *My Bird*.

36. Ibid., p. 91.

37. Ibid., p. 90.

38. Ibid., p. 111.

39. Ibid., p. 133.

40. The *Qur'an* proclaims in chapter 33, verses 4 and 5: "God did not make your adopted sons as your own sons. To declare them so is empty claim... Proclaim their real parentage. That will be more equitable in the sight of Allah."

41. Simin Daneshvar, *Be Qui Salam Konam?* (*Whom Should I Salute?*), Tehran: Kharazmi, 1980.

42. Jalal Al-e Ahmad, *Sangi bar Gouri* (*A Tombstone on a Tomb*), Tehran: Ravaq, 1981. For a translation of the book, see *A Stone on a Grave*, trans. Azfar Moin, Costa Mesa, CA: Mazda Publishers, 2008.

43. With the introduction of the Family Protection Law of 1967 (later amended in 1975), among others, the following measures were implemented: the minimum age of marriage was increased to eighteen for women and twenty for men; polygamy was restricted (and required the explicit permission of the first wife); all divorce requests were required to be processed through the courts (no extra-judi-

cial divorce). Both men and women could also now file for divorce for a variety of reasons including: mistreatment or abuse; a prison sentence of more than five years; infertility of either partner; drug addiction; or insanity. Immediately following the Islamic Revolution of 1979, the law was repealed, and new measures implemented included: the minimum age of marriage for girls was reduced to nine years old (later amended to puberty); restrictions on polygamy were relaxed, and temporary marriages were once again permitted and encouraged; divorce was once again granted to the man as his unilateral right. See "Legal Profile of Iran," Emory School of Law, http://www.law.emory.edu/ifl/legal/iran.htm

44. Shirin Ebadi and Azadeh Moaveni, *Iran Awakening: A Memoir of Revolution and Hope*, New York, NY: Random House, 2006, p. 209. The adoption of a model of non-violent, civil disobedience crosses continents, centuries, and literary genres. It goes back to a literary foremother who declined to be complicit in the ruler's vindictive fury. At a time of national crisis, Scheherazade did not remain silent or uninvolved. Nor did she look the other way and leave the dictator to continue. On the contrary, she engaged in public service of the highest order. Leaving the opulent palace of her father, the grand vizier, she put her life at risk to save the lives of other innocent citizens. She volunteered—against the advice of family and well-wishers—to marry a man who was not only wicked, but also driven to murderous reprisal. Already recognized as a consummate storyteller, Scheherazade should also be celebrated as a master strategist and an accomplished negotiator.

45. Adam Shatz, "A Little Joie de Feu," *London Review of Books*, 35: 8, 25 Apr. 2013, http://www.lrb.co.uk/v35/n08/adam-shatz/a-little-feu-de-joie

46. Two of the most highly acclaimed masterpieces of modern Persian fiction, *Buf-e Kur* (*The Blind Owl*) and *Shazdeh Ehtejab* (*The Prince*) focus on the crisis of masculinity. For an analysis of both books from this vantage point, see my book *Words, Not Swords*.

47. Jalal Al-e Ahmad, *Weststruckedness*, trans. John Green and Ahmad Alizadeh, Lexington, KY: Mazda, 1982, p. 80.

48. Women writers' anti-apartheid, moderating, and modernizing role is being honored by a large number of people. For instance, the "Campaign for One Million Signatures," launched on 27 Aug. 2006, following several peaceful protests, has chosen the words of a pioneering woman poet as its motto: "Face-to-face, street-to-street." This is borrowed from one of the most anthologized poems of a mid-nineteenth-century poet, Tahereh Quorratol'Ayn. The aim of this non-violent, non-partisan, and non-religious civil society initiative is to collect one million signatures to protest discriminatory laws against women, and to raise awareness and educate Iranians. To achieve this, women and men took the message of the campaign to the streets. They wanted not only to challenge discriminatory laws and consolidate the physical presence of women in the public square, but also to celebrate the freer and more equitable world envisioned by their literary predecessors.

6. THE IRANIAN FAMILY IN TRANSITION

1. Afary makes a similar point when she notes how political Islam can be "a way to cultivate the Shia-Muslim style of modernity and freedom from the yoke of parents." See Janet Afary, *Sexual Politics in Modern Iran*, Cambridge: Cambridge University Press, 2009, p. 292.

2. Gary S. Becker *A Treatise on the Family*, Cambridge, MA: Harvard University Press, 1993.

3. Robert E. Lucas, Jr. *Lectures on Economic Growth*, Cambridge, MA: Harvard University Press, 2002.

5. John C. Caldwell, "Toward a restatement of demographic transition theory," *Population and Development Review*, 2, 1976, pp. 321–66.

6. "World Development Indicators database," World Bank, http://data.worldbank. org/products/wdi, last accessed 2 Feb. 2012.

7. Ibid.

8. Akbar Aghajanian, "A new direction in population policy and family planning in the Islamic Republic of Iran," *Asia-Pacific Population Journal*, 10, 1995, pp. 3–20.

9. Djavad Salehi-Isfahani, "Growing up in Iran: challenging times for the Revolution's children," *The Brown Journal of World Affairs*, 15, 2008, pp. 63–74.

10. Mohammad J. Abbasi-Shavazi, Peter McDonald, and Meimanat Hosseini-Chavoshi, *The Fertility Transition in Iran: Revolution and Reproduction*, New York: Springer, 2009; and Djavad Salehi-Isfahani, Mohammad J. Abbasi, and Meimanat Hosseini-Chavoshi, "Family planning and fertility decline in rural Iran: the impact of rural health clinics," *Health Economics*, 19, 2010, pp. 159–80.

11. Abbasi-Shavazi et al, *Fertility Transition*.

12. Salehi-Isfahani et al, "Family Planning"; see also Ali Hashemi and Djavad Salehi-Isfahani, "From health service delivery to family planning: the changing impact of health clinics on fertility in rural Iran," *Economic Development and Cultural Change*, 61, 2013, pp. 281–309.

13. Sergei Guriev and Djavad Salehi-Isfahani, ""Microeconomic determinants of growth around the world", in *Explaining Growth: A Global Research Project*, Gary McMahon and Lyn Squire, eds, IEA Conference Volume No. 150. London: Palgrave/MacMillan, 2003.

14. Ministry of Health and Medical Education, *Simaye Salamat va Jamiat dar Iran* (The pattern of health and population in Iran), Tehran: Ministry of Health and Medical Education, 2012.

15. Abbasi-Shavazi et al, *Fertility Transition*, p. 61.

16. Ester Duflo, "Women's empowerment and economic development," *NBER Working Paper 17702*, Cambridge, MA: National Bureau of Economic Research, 2011.

17. Lawrence Haddad, and John Hoddinott, "Women's income and boy-girl anthro-

pometric status in the Cote d'Ivoire," *World Development*, 22, 1994, pp. 543–53; John Hoddinott and Lawrence Haddad, "Does female income share influence household expenditures? Evidence from Cote d'Ivoire," *Oxford Bulletin of Economics and Statistics*, 57, 1995, pp. 77–96; John Strauss and Duncan Thomas, "Human resources: empirical modeling of household and family decisions," in Hollis Chenery and T. N. Srinivasan, eds, *Handbook of Development Economics*, Ed. 1, Vol. 3, Ch. 34, New York: Elsevier, 1995.

18. Quoted in Nancy Gibbs, "To fight poverty, invest in girls," *Time Magazine*, 14 Feb. 2011.

19. Ministry of Health and Medical Education, *Simaye salamat*.

20. Djavad Salehi-Isfahani and Daniel Egel, "Beyond statism: Toward a new social contract for Iranian youth," in Navtej Dhillon and Tarek Yousef, eds, *Generation in Waiting: The Unfulfilled Promise of Young People in the Middle East*, Washington, DC: Brookings Institution Press, 2009; Djavad Salehi-Isfahani, "Iranian youth in times of economic crisis," *Iranian Studies*, 44, 2011, pp. 789–808; and Fatemeh Torabi, Angela Baschieri, Lynda Clarke and Mohammad J. Abbasi-Shavazi, "Marriage postponement in Iran: accounting for socio-economic and cultural change in time and space," *Population, Space and Place*, 19, 2012, pp. 258–74.

21. Salehi-Isfahani, "Iranian youth."

22. Ziba Mir-Hosseini, *Marriage on Trial: Study of Islamic Family Law—Iran and Morocco Compared*, New York and London: I B Tauris, 1997.

23. Fatemeh Moghadam, "Commoditization of sexuality and female labor force participation in Islam: implication for Iran, 1960–90," in Mahnaz Afkhami and Erica Fiedl, eds, *In the Eye of the Storm: Women in Post-Revolutionary Iran*, New York: I B Tauris, pp. 80–97.

24. Ministry of Health and Medical Education, *Simaye Salamat*.

25. Navtej Dhillon and Tarek Yousef, eds, *Generation in Waiting: The Unfulfilled Promise of Young People in the Middle East*, Washington, DC: Brookings Institution Press, 2009.

26. Salehi-Isfahani, "Iranian youth."

27. Ibid.

28. Ibid.

7. THE STATE OF HUMAN RIGHTS IN IRAN

1. Mahmood Monshipouri, "The Green Movement and the Struggle for Human Rights in Iran," in Lucia Volk, ed., *The Middle East in the World: An Introduction*, New York: Routledge, 2015, pp. 195–208.

2. The issue of religious minorities and their status in Iran is not thoroughly addressed in this chapter due to the space allowed to each contributor. The authors have dealt with this issue in numerous publications elsewhere.

3. Mary Gillis, "Iranian Americans," http://www.everyculture.com/multi/Ha-La/Iranian-Americans.html, last accessed 28 Oct 2015.

4. Ann Elizabeth Mayer, *Islam and Human Rights: Tradition and Politics*, 3rd ed., Boulder, CO: Westview Press, 1998.

5. Richard Falk, *On Humane Governance: Toward a New Global Politics*, University Park, PA: Pennsylvania State University Press, 1995.

6. Alison Dundes Renteln, *International Human Rights: Universalism Versus Relativism*, Newbury Park, CA: Sage Publications, 1990.

7. Abdullahi Ahmed An-Na'im, *Muslims and Global Justice*, Philadelphia, PA: University of Pennsylvania Press, 2011.

8. Abdulaziz Sachedina, *Islam and the Challenge of Human Rights*, New York, NY: Oxford University Press, 2009, p. 71.

9. Anthony Tirado Chase, *Human Rights, Revolution, and Reform in the Muslim World*, Boulder, CO: Lynne Rienner Publishers, 2012, p. 119.

10. Ibid., p. 142.

11. "President's daughter rallies for women's sports in Iran," *Christian Science Monitor*, 28 March 1995, http://www.csmonitor.com/1995/0328/28071.html/%28page%29/2, last accessed 28 Oct 2015.

12. *Iran Times*, 15 Nov. 1996, p. 1.

13. Mehran Kamrava, "The civil society discourse in Iran," *British Journal of Middle Eastern Studies*, 28, 2001, pp. 165–85.

14. Farhad Kazemi, "Models of Iranian politics, the road to the Islamic revolution, and the challenge of civil society," *World Politics*, 47, 1995, 575–605.

15. Eliz Sanasarian, *Religious Minorities in Iran*, Cambridge: Cambridge University Press, 2000.

16. A Christian van Gorder, *Christianity in Persia and the Status of Non-Muslims in Iran*, UK: Lexington Books, 2010, p. 229.

17. Mahmood Monshipouri, "The politics of culture and human rights in Iran," in Mahmood Monshipouri, Neil Englehart, Andrew J. Nathan and Kavita Philip, eds, *Constructing Human Rights in the Age of Globalization*, Armonk, New York: M.E. Sharpe, 2003, pp. 113–44; see pp. 135–7.

18. Human Rights Watch, *World Report 2005: Events of 2004* (New York, NY: Human Rights Watch, 2005), 460.

19. Ibid., pp. 461–462.

20. Mehrangiz Kar, "Focusing on women in the internal politics of Iran," *The Brown Journal of World Affairs*, Vol. xv, No. 1, 2008, pp. 75–86; see pp. 83–4.

21. Haleh Esfandiari, "The politics of the 'women's question' in the Islamic Republic, 1979–1999," in John L. Esposito and R. K. Ramazani, eds, *Iran at the Crossroads*, New York, NY: Palgrave, 2001, pp. 75–92.

22. Nayereh Tohidi, quoted in Arshin Adib-Moghaddam, *Iran in World Politics: The Question of the Islamic Republic*, New York, NY: Columbia University Press, 2010, pp. 160–161.

23. Valentine M Moghadam, *Modernizing Women: Gender and Social Change in the Middle East*, 2nd ed., Boulder, CO: Lynne Rienner Publishers, 2003, pp. 211–12.

24. Ibid., pp. 212–15.

25. Fen Monataigne, "Iran: testing the waters of reform," *National Geographic*, 196: 1, July 1999, pp. 1–33; see p. 18.

26. United Nations, "Women in the Islamic Republic of Iran: a country profile," *Statistical Profiles*, 15, New York, NY: Economic and Social Commission for Asia and Pacific, 1998, pp. 4–17.

27. Azadeh Kian-Thiebaut, "Women and the making of civil society in post-Islamist Iran," in Eric Hooglund, ed., *Twenty Years of Islamic Revolution: Political and Social Transition in Iran Since* 1979, Syracuse, NY: Syracuse University Press, 2002, pp. 56–73; see especially p. 62.

28. "Iran," World Factbook, Central Intelligence Agency, 2008, available online: https://www.cia.gov/library/publications/the-world-factbook/geos/ir.html, last accessed 26 November 2015.

29. Mahmood Monshipouri, "Iran from 1979," in David P. Forsythe, ed., *Encyclopedia of Human Rights*, Vol. 3, New York: Oxford University Press, 2009, pp. 195–206; see p. 203.

30. Barbara Ann Rieffer-Flanagan, *Evolving Iran: An Introduction to Politics and Problems in the Islamic Republic*, Washington, DC: Georgetown University Press, 2013, pp. 129–30.

31. Ibid., p. 130.

32. Ibid., p. 130.

33. Mehrzad Boroujerdi, "Iran," in Ellen Lust, ed., *The Middle East*, Washington, DC: CQ Press, 2014, pp. 478–506; see p. 506.

34. Ibid., p. 499.

35. Mahmood Monshipouri and Ali Assareh, "The Islamic Republic and the 'Green Movement': coming full circle," *Middle East Policy*, Vol. XVI, No. 4, Winter 2009, pp. 27–46.

36. Quoted in Nick Cumming-Bruce, "UN rights investigator given Iran harsh review," *The New York Times*, 13 Mar. 2013, p. 11.

37. Hamid Dabashi, "Sattar Beheshti: When an Islamic Republic goes to the abyss of hell," Al Jazeera, 20 Nov 2012, http://www.aljazeera.com/indepth/opinion/2012/11/20121120853499130.html, last accessed 28 Oct 2015.

38. Mahmood Monshipouri, "Rowhani's [sic] election: promise of change or more of the same," *Insight Turkey*, 15:3, Summer 2013, pp. 45–50.

39. Robert Tait, "Iran pardons eighty political prisoners on eve of President Rouhani's visit to US," *Telegraph*, 23 Sep. 2013, http://www.telegraph.co.uk/news/worldnews/middleeast/iran/10328961/Iran-pardons-80-political-prisoners-on-eve-of-President-Rouhanis-visit-to-US.html, last accessed 21 Oct. 2013.

40. "Germany: human rights has not improved under Hassan Rouhani in Iran," Iran

News Update, 13 Mar. 2014, http://irannewsupdate.com/news/human-rights/792-germany-human-rights-has-not-improved-under-hassan-rouhani-in-iran.html, last accessed 3 Jan. 2015.

41. Ibid.
42. Ibid.
43. Ibid.
44. "As Rouhani comes to New York, domestic repression in Iran remains unabated," International Campaign for Human Rights in Iran, 17 Sep. 2014, http://www.iranhumanrights.org/2014/09/rouhani-video/, last accessed 4 Jan. 2015.
45. Ibid.
46. Hooman Majd, "The Day After a Nuclear Deal: How Will Iranian Politics Change?", Politico magazine, 22 June 2015, available at http://www.politico.com/magazine/story/2015/06/the-day-after-a-nuclear-deal-119291, accessed on 31 Oct. 2015.
47. The Daily Beast, "Iran Hardliners Trying to Kill Nuke Deal Arrest Western 'Infiltrators,'" 4 November, 2015, available at http://www.thedailybeast.com/articles/2015/11/04/iran-hardliners-trying-to-kill-nuke-deal-arrest-western-infiltrators.html, accessed on 4 November 2014.
48. Thomas Erdbrink, "Backlash Against US Seems to Gather Force in Iran," *The New York Times*, 4 November 2015, p. A3.
49. Thomas Erdbrink and Rich Gladstone, "President of Iran Takes Issue with Arrests," *The New York Times*, 5 November 2915, p. A4.
50. Mahmood Monshipouri, *Terrorism, Security, and Human Rights: Harnessing the Rule of Law*, Boulder, CO: Lynne Rienner Publishers, 2011, pp. 275–6.
51. Barbara Ann Rieffer-Flanagan, "The Janus nature of human rights in Iran: understanding progress and setbacks on human rights protections since the revolution," in Mahmood Monshipouri, ed., *Human Rights in the Middle East: Frameworks, Goals, and Strategies*, New York, NY: Palgrave Macmillan, 2011, pp. 111–27; see especially pp. 123–4.
52. *Human Rights Watch*, 2005, p. 464.
53. Thomas Erdbrink and Rick Gladstone, "Fearing price increases, Iranians hoard goods," *The New York Times*, 24 Apr. 2013, p. 7.
54. Gregory Newbold, Thomas Pickering, William Reinsch, and George Perkovich, "Weighing benefits and costs of international sanctions on Iran," Carnegie Endowment for International Peace, 6 Dec. 2012, http://carnegieendowment.org/2012/12/06/weighing-benefits-and-costs-of-international-sanctions-on-iran/emyo, last accessed 28 Oct 2015.
55. Julie A. Mertus, *The United Nations and Human Rights*, New York, NY: Routledge, 2005, p. 106.
56. Ibid.
57. Shadi Mokhtari, "The New Politics of Human Rights in the Middle East," *Foreign*

Policy, 30 Oct. 2012, http://mideast.foreignpolicy.com/posts/2012/10/30/the_new_politics_of_human_rights_in_the_middle_east

58. Mertus, *The United Nations and Human Rights*, p. 8.

59. Danny Postel, "Counter-revolution and revolt in Iran: an interview with Iranian Political Scientist Hossein Bashiriyeh," in Nader Hashemi and Danny Postel, eds, *The People Reloaded: The Green Movement and the Struggle for Iran's Future*, New York, NY: Melville House, 2010, pp. 82–105; see especially pp. 88–9.

60. Anthony Tirado Chase, *Human Rights*, p. 16 and 144.

61. Kurt Shillinger, "In 2013, world must focus on democracy hopes," *Christian Science Monitor*, 31 Dec. 2012 and 7 Jan. 2013, p. 34.

62. Rieffer-Flanagan, *Evolving Iran*, p. 129.

63. Mehdi Zakerian, *Toward a Conceptual Framework for the Internationally Recognized Human Rights* (Iran, Tehran: Mizan Publication, 2005). Available in Persian only.

8. US-IRAN TENSIONS IN POST-KHOMEINI IRAN AND IRANIAN IMMIGRANTS IN THE UNITED STATES

1. Alejandro Portes and Ruben. Rumbaut, *Immigrant America: A Portrait*. 3rd ed., Berkeley and Los Angeles: University of California Press, 2006.

2. Abdoulmaboud Ansari, *Iranian Immigrants in the United States: A Case of Dual Marginality*, New York: Associated Faculty Press,1988.

3. Mohsen Mobasher, *Iranian Immigrants in Texas: Migration, Politics, and Ethnic Identity*, Austin: Texas University Press, 2012.

4. The main reason for the lack of accurate official data on the number of Iranians in the diaspora is the illegal and undocumented flight of some Iranians, including high ranking members of the former regime and political activists, during and immediately after the revolution, as well as exodus of many young Iranian men during the 1980–88 Iran-Iraq war. Another reason for the paucity of reliable data is the lack or inadequacy of official statistics on immigration in non-Western societies where some Iranians have been residing in the past three decades.

5. Shirin Hakimzadeh, "Iran: a vast diaspora abroad and millions of refugees at home," Migration Information Source, http://www.migrationinformation.org/profiles/print.cfm?ID=424, last accessed 2006.

6. Mammad Aidani, "Displaced narratives of Iranian immigrants and refugees: construction of self and the struggle for representation," unpublished Ph.D. dissertation, Victoria University, 2007.

7. Mohsen Mobasher, "Class, ethnicity, gender, and the ethnic economy: the case of Iranian immigrants in Dallas," unpublished Ph.D. dissertation, Southern Methodist University, 1996.

8. Hakimzadeh, "Iran: a vast diaspora."

9. Lorentz, John and John T. Wertime, "Iranians," In Stephen Thernstrom, ed., *Harvard*

Encyclopedia of American Ethnic Groups, Cambridge, MA: Harvard University Press, 1980.

10. Mobasher, *Iranians in Texas*, 2012.

11. Nikki R. Keddie, *Modern Iran: Roots and Results of Revolution*, New Haven: Yale University Press, 2006.

12. Mobasher, *Iranians in Texas*, 2012.

13. Ibid.

14. Immigration and Naturalization Service, *1970–1977 Annual Reports*, US Department of Justice: Washington, DC.

15. Ibid.

16. CISNU was the only open opposition movement that survived the political repression of the Shah, which extended outside Iran. The organization had grown out of a number of Iranian student circles in Europe during the 1950s. The United States chapter joined the Confederation when the second congress of the European Confederation met in Paris in January 1962 and formed the World Confederation. In 1965, CISNU began to publish *Shanzdahom-e Azar* (the 16th of AZAR) as its official monthly newsletter and *Nameh-ye Paris* as a cultural quarterly. By 1972, CIS had as many as 5,000 active student members in eighty-five chapters all over the world. See Afshin Matin-Asgari, "Iranian student opposition to the Shah," California: Mazda, 2001.

17. Nikki R. Keddie, *Modern Iran: Roots and Results of Revolution*, New Haven: Yale University Press, 2006.

18. For example, before April of 1980, an estimated one half of Iran's 70,000 Jews had left Iran for either Israel or the United States (Allen and Turner 1988).

19. Mobasher, *Iranians in Texas*, 2012.

20. Ibid.

21. Between 1990 and 2000 as many as 133,389 Iranians were naturalized citizens; see Immigration and Naturalization Service, *Statistical Yearbook, 1986–2008*.

22. Ibid.

23. Mobasher, *Iranians in Texas*, 2012.

24. US Committee for Refugees and Immigrants, *1988 World Refugee Survey Report*, Washington DC, United States. Department of State. Bureau for Refugee Programs 1988.

25. US Census Bureau, *The 2011 American Community Survey 1-Year Estimates*, Washington DC: Department of Commerce, 2011.

26. Mohsen Mobasher, "Class, Ethnicity, Gender, and the Ethnic Economy: The Case of Iranian Immigrants in Dallas," unpublished Ph.D. dissertation, Southern Methodist University, 1996.

27. Ibid.

28. Hamid Naficy, "Narrowcasting and nationality: Middle Eastern television in Los Angeles," *Afterimage*, 20, 1993, pp. 9–12.

29. George H. Gallup, *The Gallup Poll, Public Opinion 1972–1977*, Vol. 2, Wilmington, Delaware: Scholarly Resources Inc., 1977.

30. Jimmy Carter, *Keeping Faith: Memoirs of a President*, Fayetteville: University of Arkansas Press, 1995, p. 445.

31. Fawaz A. Gerges, "Islam and Muslims in the Mind of America: Influences on the Making of US policy," *Journal of Palestine Studies*, 26, 1997, pp. 68–80, cf. 70.

32. "Americans take to the streets to vent wrath over events," *Houston Post*, 10 Nov. 1979; "Nationwide, Americans vent anger with rallies," *Houston Post*, 11 Nov. 1979.

33. "Action lauded here; some from Mid-East report harassment," *Houston Post*, 12 Nov. 1979.

34. "Americans take to the streets," *Houston Post*; "Iranian students' claims taunted at TSU rally," *Houston Post*, 10 Nov. 1979.

35. "Americans take to the streets," *Houston Post*; "Iranian students' claims taunted," *Houston Post*.

36. "Protesters demand Iranian students leave United States," *Houston Post*, 12 Nov. 1979; "Action lauded here," *Houston Post*.

37. "Americans take to the streets," *Houston Post*; "Iranian students' claims taunted at TSU rally," *Houston Post*, 10 Nov. 1979.

38. "Few Iranian students deported, INS chief tells Senate panel," *Houston Post*, 3 Apr. 1980.

39. George Gallup, Jr, *The Gallup Poll 1989*, Wilmington, Delaware: Scholarly Resources Inc., 1989.

40. Fawaz Gerges, "Islam and Muslims in the mind of America: influences on the making of US policy," *Journal of Palestine Studies*, 26, 1997, pp. 68–80.

41. Ibid.

42. Edward Said, *Covering Islam: How the Media and the Experts Determine How We See the Rest of the World*, New York: Vintage, 1997.

43. Sam Fayyaz and Rozbeh Shirazi, "Good Iranian, Bad Iranian: representation of Iran and Iranians in *Time* and *Newsweek* (1998–2009)," *Iranian Studies*, 46:1, 2013, pp. 53–72.

44. Jane Campbell, "Portrayal of Iranians in US motion pictures," in Yahya R. Kamalipour, ed., *The US Media and the Middle East: Image and Perception*, Westport: CT. Praeger Publishers, 1997.

45. John S. Lapinski, Pia Peltola, Greg Shaw and Alan YangSource, "Trends: immigrants and immigration," *Public Opinion Quarterly*, 61: 2, 1997, pp. 356–83.

46. Kathleen H. Sparrow and David M. Chretien, "The social distance perceptions of racial and ethnic groups by college students: a research note," *Sociological Spectrum*, 13:2, 1993, pp. 277–288.

47. Emory S. Bogardus, "Social distance in the city," *Proceedings and Publications of the American Sociological Society*, 20, 1926, pp. 40–6.

48. Bogardus' seven-item Social Distance Scale was based on the following associational networks: 1) kinship by marriage; 2) club as personal chums; 3) street as neighbors; 4) company as employees; 5) country as citizens; 6) country as visitors; 7) exclusion from the country. A score of 1 for any group would indicate no social distance and therefore no prejudice and the score of 7 would indicate greater social distance and prejudice.

49. Iranian Studies Group at MIT, 2005, http://web.mit.edu/isg/publications.htm

50. A complete review of the survey results is provided in Darious Zahedi, "Political attitudes and patterns of political participation of Iranian Americans in California," Berkeley: University of California, 2008, available http://repositories.cdlib.org/igs/WP

51. USC Annenberg, School of Communication, Bendixen and Amandi International, Miami, Florida, http://bendixenandamandi.com/wp-content/uploads/2010/08/NCM-Arab-American-poll-2004.pdf

52. Dale S. McLemore and Harriett D. Romo, *Racial and Ethnic Relations in America*, Boston: Allyn and Bacon, 2005.

53. Joe R. Feagin and Clairece Booher Feagin, *Racial and Ethnic Relations*, Upper Saddle River, New Jersey: Prentice Hall, 1999.

54. McLemore and Romo, *Racial and Ethnic Relations*.

55. Abdoulmaboud Ansari, *The making of the Iranian community in America*. New York: Pardis Press, 1992.

56. Nilou Mostofi, "Who we are: the perplexity of Iranian-American identity," *The Sociology Quarterly*, 44, 2003, pp. 681–703.

57. B. Blair, "Personal name changes among Iranian immigrants in the USA," in A. Fathi, ed., *Iranian Refugees and Exiles Since Khomeini*, Costa Mesa, CA: Mazda, 1991, pp. 145–60.

58. Mobasher, *Iranians in Texas*.

59. Ibid.

60. Ibid.

61. A. Portes and R. Rumbaut, *Immigrant America: A Portrait*, 3rd ed., Berkeley and Los Angeles: University of California Press, 2006.

9. THE POLITICS AND POETICS OF IRANIAN ART-HOUSE CINEMA

1. Hamid Naficy, *A Social History of Iranian Cinema v.3: The Islamicate Period, 1978–1984*, Durham, NC: Duke University Press, 2012, p. 171.

2. Hamid Naficy, *A Social History of Iranian Cinema v.4: The Globalizing Era, 1984–2010*, Durham, NC: Duke University Press, 2012, p. 176.

3. Naficy, *A Social History of Iranian Cinema v.4*, pp. 229–33.

4. Jane Howard, *Inside Iran: Women's Lives*, Washington, DC: Mage Publishers, 2002.

5. Mohammad Tahaminejad, *Sinema-ye Iran*, 2nd ed., Tehran: Daftar-e Pazhuheshha-ye

Farhangi, 2001/(1380), p. 85; Hamid Reza Sadr, *Dar Amadi bar Tarikh-e Sinema-ye Siasi-ye Iran (1280–1380)*, Tehran: Nashr-e Nay, 2003 (1381), p. 261.

6. Andrew Sarris, "Notes on the Auteur Theory in 1962," in Barry Keith Grant, ed., *Auteurs and Authorship: A Film Reader*, Malden, MA: Blackwell, pp. 35–45.

7. Philip Lopate, "Interview with Abbas Kiarostami," in *Totally, Tenderly, Tragically: Essays and Criticism from a Lifelong Love Affair with the Movies*, New York, NY: Anchor Books, 1998, pp. 352–3.

8. A different version of this section was published in Hamid Naficy, "Neorealism Iranian Style," in Saverio Giovacchini and Robert Sklar, eds, *Global Neorealism: The Transnational History of a Film Style*, Jackson, MS: University Press of Mississippi, 2011, pp. 226–39.

9. Quoted in Millicent Marcus, *Italian Film in the Light of Neorealism*, Princeton, NJ: Princeton University Press, 1986, pp. 21–2.

10. See Naficy, "Neorealism Iranian Style," pp. 231–2.

11. Michael Slackman, "Iranian Filmmakers Keep Focus on the Turmoil," *New York Times*, 3 Jan. 2010.

12. For more on the new wave films, see Hamid Naficy, *A Social History of Iranian Cinema v.2: The Industrializing Years, 1941–1978*, Durham, NC: Duke University Press, 2011, chapter 6.

13. For silent and early Iranian films, see Hamid Naficy, *A Social History of Iranian Cinema v.1: The Artisanal Era, 1897–1941*, Durham, NC: Duke University Press, 2011.

14. Mohammad Tahaminejad, "Kamran Shirdel, Coeur de Lion," *Forum des Images* (10 Sep. to 19 Oct.), Paris: 2003, p. 37.

15. Bahram Baizai, "Pas az Sad Sal," *Iran Nameh*, 14: 2, 1996, p. 379.

16. Author's personal interview with Abbas Kiarostami, Washington, DC, 19 Apr. 2001.

17. *Close-Up* is an exception, for Sabzian has subjectivity and undergoes change when he admits to his fraud, confesses to his love for Makhmalbaf's movies, and meets up with his idol.

18. Karbala paradigm refers to the knowing and willing self-sacrifice of Imam Hussein, the third Shiite imam and the grandson of Prophet Muhammad, in the plain of Karbala, Iraq, in the cause of justice.

19. Quoted in Nassia Hamid, "Near and Far," *Sight and Sound*, Feb. 1997, p. 24.

20. Rashmi Doraiswamy, "Abbas Kiarostami: Life and Much More," *Cinemaya*, 16, 1992, p. 20.

21. For more on the evolution of Banietemad's career and style, see Naficy, *A Social History of Iranian Cinema*, Vol. 4, Ch. 2.

22. Mehrnaz Saeed-Vafa and Jonathan Rosenbaum, *Abbas Kiarostami*, Urbana, IL: University of Illinois Press, 2003, p. 54.

23. Hamid Dabashi, *Close-Up: Iranian Cinema: Past, Present, and Future*, New York, NY: Verso, 2001, p. 155.

24. Phillipe Lejeune, *On Autobiography*, ed. Paul Eakin, Minneapolis, MN: University of Minnesota Press, 1989, p. 5.

25. Mitchell Miller, "Awful Fates: Iranian Cinema, Western Festivals, and the Faltering Art of Conversation," *Drouth*, 5: 4, http://www.thedrouth.org.

26. Quoted in Bertolt Brecht, *Brecht on Theatre: The Development of an Aesthetic*, trans. John Willett, ed., New York, NY: Hill and Wang, 1964, p. 60.

27. Masud Zavarzadeh, *Seeing Films Politically*, Albany, NY: State University of New York Press, 1991, p. 64.

28. Ibid., p. 34.

10. THE RE-EMERGENCE AND EVOLUTION OF POP MUSIC IN THE ISLAMIC REPUBLIC OF IRAN: FROM HEAVENLY TO EARTHLY LOVE

1. Asef Bayat, "Islamism and the Politics of Fun," *Public Culture* 19 (3) (2007): 433–459, p. 455.

2. I draw here on James C. Scott's notion of the "public transcript," which he defines as that which is authorized by the dominant. He writes that "every subordinate group creates, out of its ordeal, a 'hidden transcript' that represents a critique of power spoken behind the back of the dominant", see James C. Scott, *Domination and the Arts of Resistance: Hidden Transcripts*, New Haven, CT; London: Yale University Press, 1990. p. xii. Although the state projects a rather homogeneous "public" transcript in its propaganda, it is fragmented and pluralized by the injections and subversions of the end-receivers. Hence, I believe, it is more appropriate to speak of "transcripts" in the plural, even the public one.

3. As I describe throughout the course of this article, "pop music" in Iran's post-revolutionary context refers to a genre of music that is often similar in its fast tempo, lyrical themes of love and desperation, and general "feel" to *los ānjelesi* pop music. It no longer obliges the Islamic Republic ethos with passages of march or hymn music, has freed itself of that familiar revolutionary somberness, and was recognized at the time of its first appearances in the late 1990s as "new."

4. See Laudan Nooshin, 'Subversion and Counter-subversion: Power, Control and Meaning in the New Iranian Pop Music,' in *Music, Power and Politics*, A. J. Randall (ed.), London: Routledge, 2005. As she charts pop music's trajectory from a genre that, in Pahlavi-era Iran, carried "the symbolic burden of Western cultural imperialism," (p. 239) to its significance as a "statement of resistance in the 1980s" and finally, to "a symbol of post-1997 liberalism, no longer a subversive threat, but domesticated and rendered safe" (p. 251).

5. For more on a history of the problematic of music within Islam see Amnon Shiloah's *Music in the World of Islam*, Aldershot: Scholar Press, 1995, Kristina Nelson's, *The Art of Reciting the Qur'an, Austin: University of Texas Press*, 1985, and William Beeman's, *Iranian Performance Traditions*, Costa Mesa, Calif.: Mazda Publishers, Inc, 2011.

6. See Nahid Siamdoust (Seyedsayamdost), *Iran's Troubled Tunes: Music as Politics in the Islamic Republic.* D.Phil. Thesis: University of Oxford, 2013. As well as Fariba Adelkhah, "'Michael Jackson ne peut absolument rien faire'—Les pratiques musicales en république d'Iran," *Cahiers d'études sur la Mediterranée orientale et le monde turco-iranien* No. 11, janvier–juin 1991, and Ameneh Youssefzadeh, 'The situation of music in Iran since the Revolution: The role of official organizations'. *Ethnomusicology Forum* 9 (2) (2000): 35–61 on publicly promoted music in the 1980s.

7. Nooshin, "Subversion and Counter-subversion: Power, Control and Meaning in the New Iranian Pop Music," p. 241.

8. Ibid.

8. With the exception of Googoosh's work, since she—arguably Iran's most famous pop star of all time—remained in Iran and only emigrated to the US in 2000; see Hadani, "Let Googoosh sing," *Salon*, 18 Sep. 2000, http://www.salon.com/2000/09/18/googoosh/, last accessed on 29 Oct. 2015.

9. Singers who, following the revolution, created their work in Los Angeles are called "*khānandeh-hā-ye los ānjelesi*" in Persian.

10. Nooshin, "Subversion and Counter-subversion: Power, Control and Meaning in the New Iranian Pop Music," p. 251.

11. Arash Nasiri and Azadeh Shahmir-Nuri, "Interview with Fereydun Shahbazian," *Persian Art Music*, 23 Aban 1382 (2003).

12. Babak Bayat was a seminal composer who had written for pre-revolutionary pop stars. He returned to Iran in the 1990s and continued to write music for post-revolutionary musicians, until his death in 2006. Through his music and his personal network, Bayat was uniquely placed to bridge *los ānjelesi* and post-revolutionary pop music. See Bayat, "Islamism and the Politics of Fun."

13. See for example Bijan Bijani, "Parishan," http://www.youtube.com/watch?v=NyEqgHzjCds, last accessed 29 Oct. 2015.

14. See for example Hassan Homayunfal, "Nasim-e Sahari," http://www.youtube.com/watch?v=sgTBTjCbPO8, last accessed on 29 0ct. 2015; the song was often replayed on state media.

15. See Bijan Khavari, "Darya," http://www.youtube.com/watch?v=p2B4vouPHA0, last accessed 29 Oct. 2015.

16. See Kazemi, "Navai Navai," http://www.youtube.com/watch?v=43_3WrI5pqM&feature=results_main&playnext=1&list=PL8B9B451EC7D27943, last accessed 29 Oct. 2015; this is a rendition of the well-known Torbat-e Jām folkloric song.

17. Personal interview with Mohammad Ali Mo'allem-Damghani, Tehran, 2 Aug. 2011.

18. H.E. Chehabi, "From Revolutionary Tasnif to Patriotic Surud: Music and Nation-Building in Pre-World War II Iran," *Iran* 37 (1999): 143–154, p. 147.

19. Ruhollah Khomeini, *Al-Makasib al-Muharrama, vol. 1* (1961), p. 198.

20. Ibid.

21. F. Khosrokhavar, "The New Religiosity in Iran," *Social Compass* 54 (3) (2007):453–463, p. 457.

22. Personal interview with Khashayar Etemadi, 2 Aug. 2011, Tehran. This insight into Etemadi's story was unknown until Apr. 2013, when the singer divulged it in a news conference; see "Khashāyār E'temādi: Beh khāter-e shebāhat-e sedāyam bā yek khānandeh-ye los ānjelesi chand sāl ejāzeh kār nadashtam," *Khabar Online*, 3 Ordibehesht 1392 (2013), http://khabaronline.ir/detail/288644, last accessed on 29 Oct. 2015; he may have been concerned that airing this problem publicly and explicitly linking his voice to that of Dariush would mar his relations with state officials, leading him to keep silence for nearly twenty years. Had this been known at the time, it may have prompted fewer accusations that the state intentionally attempted to produce pop singers with voices similar to *los ānjelesi* stars. Note that "*mobtazal*" is often used in Iran to dismiss music that is thought to be unworthy. As Farzaneh Hemmasi explains, "Encompassing moral, political, and aesthetic values, the term *mobtazal* implies banality, cliché, lack of creativity and worth, and cheapness, but also suggests a cultural form that disorients a listener and can promote disengagement with the world through harmful distraction"; see Farzaneh Hemmasi, *Iranian Popular Music in Los Angeles: Mobilizing Media, Nation, and Politics*. Ph.D. Thesis, Columbia University, New York, 2010.

23. Ibid.

24. At the exchange rate of about 175 tomans per US dollar, 7 million Toman in 1996 amounted to $40,000. For a history of the Iranian rial's exchange rate, see http://www.farsinet.com/toman/exchange.html, last accessed on 29 Oct. 2015. According to Etemadi, the news that someone was investing that much money into an album became the talk of the town. Under Bayat's direction, they employed about fifty musicians, and the studio costs ran very high as they tapped their way forward through trial and error.

25. See Zeinab Mortezayi-Fard, "Gap-e musiqiyā-yi bā khashāyār e'temādi," *Bāshgāh-e Khabarnegārān*, 9 Nov. 2012, http://www.yjc.ir/fa/news/4140123, last accessed on 29 Oct. 2015.

26. *Musiqi-ye fākher*, which translates into fine or sumptuous music, is an oft-repeated term in Iran today. *Fākher* is the opposite of *mobtazal* (trite) and is used by officials to refer to a music that consists of good composition and arrangement, and contains lyrics that are either drawn from poetry or go beyond simplistic, earthly matters. Although often used, it is an ambiguous term, both in aesthetics and ideology.

27. This was confirmed to me in interviews with Khashayar Etemadi, Islamic Iran's "first" post-revolutionary pop singer, 2 Aug 2011, Tehran, Iran, Fereydun Shahbazian, prominent composer, important figure in the revival of state-sanc-

tioned pop music, 2 Mar 2011, Tehran, Iran and Ali Moʻallem Damghani, currently the director of "Farhangestān-e Honar," an institute that was created by the Supreme Council for Cultural Revolution in order to oversee the arts; previously Damghani was the director of the Music Center at IRIB 2 Aug 2011, Tehran, Iran. See also footnote 14.

28. Most singers of the first pop generation were at one point or another found to have similar voices to pre-revolutionary pop stars, or accused of imitating them.

29. Personal interview with Ali Moʻallem-Damghani, Tehran, 2 Aug. 2011. See also footnote 26.

30. The term "occidontosis" or "westoxification" derives from the work of Jalal Al-e-Ahmad titled "Occidontosis: A Plague from the West," published clandestinely in 1962. It encapsulated for many revolutionaries the core of Iran's problems at the time, namely a loss of its own identity in blind adoration of the West.

31. It is said that Moʻallem convinced Khamenei that without homemade pop music Iran's youth would be at greater risk of "cultural invasion" from abroad. Khamenei is then said to have "quietly sought the approval of top Islamic scholars." This is something I heard in conversation about the legitimation of pop music in Iran. See also Daniel Pearl, "Rock Rolls Once More in Iran as Hard-Liners Back Pop Revival," *The Wall Street Journal*, 2 Jun. 2000.

32. Personal interview with Moʻallem-Damghani, Tehran, 2 Aug 2011.

33. "Bu-ye gandom" is one of Dariush's famous political pre-revolutionary pop songs.

34. See "shadmehr-doxdo.ir," http://www.youtube.com/watch?v=MKg31bnWau4& feature=related, last accessed 29 Oct. 2015.

35. See "IRAN SHIA IRANI SONG," http://www.youtube.com/watch?v=wtxOm 5aySUk&feature=related, last accessed on 29 Oct. 2015.

36. Ibid. This version shows the song being played in a Toronto dance club for a Persian New Year's party in March 2006; at 00:34 a clean recording of the song is superimposed on the video.

37. See "Agham, imam zaman, (benyamin)," http://www.youtube.com/watch?v=iIc Fi83dU3k&feature=related, last accessed on 29 Oct. 2015.

38. See "Benyamin Bahadori," MySpace, http://myspace.com/benyamin85, last accessed 29 Oct. 2015.

39. Babak Jahanbakhsh, 2009, single

40. Hamid Askari, *Komā 3*, album, 2013.

41. Farzad Farzin, *Khāss*, album, 2011.

42. Mohsen Yeganeh, *Tah-e Khat*, album.2008.

43. See "Mohammad Mir-Zamani az modire-kolli-ye daftar-e musiqi esteʻfā dād," Musiqi-ye Mā, 8 Dey 1391 (Dec. 2012), http://www.musicema.com/node/171254, last accessed 29 Oct. 2015.

44. See Hamid Naficy, "Islamizing Film Culture in Iran" in *Political Culture in the Islamic Republic*, edited by Samih K. Farsoun and Mehrdad Mashayekhi. London,

New York: Routledge, 1992. See also Hamid Naficy, *A Social History of Iranian Cinema*. 4 vols. Durham, NC; London: Duke University Press, 2011.

45. See Richard Tapper, "Introduction" in *The New Iranian Cinema: Politics, Representation and Identity*, edited by Richard Tapper. London: I. B.Tauris, 2002.

46. For a discussion of this process in Soviet socialism, see Sorce Marcello Keller, "Why is Music So Ideological, and Why Do Totalitarian States Take It So Seriously? A Personal View from History and the Social Sciences," *The Journal of Musicological Research* 26 (2–3) (2007): 91–122. For a discussion of this change in Islamic Iran see Hamid Naficy, "Islamizing film culture in Iran: a post-Khatami update," in Richard Tapper, "Introduction," in *The New Iranian Cinema: Politics, Representation and Identity*, edited by R. Tapper. London: I.B.Tauris, 2007.

47. This was relayed to me by Dr Hassan Riahi, at the time director of the music program at Tehran's Azad University (which he established), as well as a high-ranking member of various governing and oversight boards at IRIB, 29 Sep. 2010, Tehran.

48. Data obtained from Ershād's Music Office. The ministry issued 133 pop concert permits, with each permit corresponding to an average of 2.5 performances (for example, Alireza Assar received one permit for a particular concert, valid for six nights of performances).

49. For a report on the concert, see http://www.musicema.com/module-pagesetter-viewpub-tid-1-pid-5942.html, last accessed on 29 Oct. 2015.

50. This is the *Vezārat-e Keshvar* hall, which is not a professional concert hall. The most modern purpose-built hall in Tehran is the *Borj-e Milād* concert hall, which has about 1,600 seats, 400 of which are "useless," as Tutunchian, Manager of Qoqnus Music Institute and Ticketing Agency, put it, because they don't offer a view of the stage unless one stands. Personal interview, Tehran, 21 July 2011.

51. Personal attendance, Reza Sadeghi concert, 22 Feb. 2011, Borj-e Milād, Tehran.

52. Bezad Yaghmaian, *Social Change in Iran: an Eyewitness Account of dissent, defiance, and new movements for rights*, Albany: State University of New York Press, 2002. Behzad Yaghmaian writes about what he calls "The rise of a new social movement for joy".

53. In my presentation "The counterpublic of love in Iran" at the 2014 Middle East Studies Association Conference in Washington, DC, I argued that the large crowds marking the funeral of the young pop singer Morteza Pashaei in Nov. 2014 was another manifestation of what I call the "counterpublic of love."

54. Bayat, "Islamism and the Politics of Fun," p. 459.

11. THE ECONOMIC AND POLITICAL ROLE OF BONYADS (PARASTATAL FOUNDATIONS) IN THE ISLAMIC REPUBLIC

1. Manochehr Dorraj, *From Zarathustra to Khomeini: Populism and Dissent in Iran*, Boulder, CO: Lynne Rienner Publishers, 1990.

2. Nikki R. Keddie, *Roots of Revolution*, New Haven, CT: Yale University Press, 1981; Nikki R. Keddie, *Religion and Politics in Iran: Shi'ism from Quietism to Revolution*, New Haven, CT: Yale University Press, 1983.

3. Manochehr Dorraj, "Populism and corporatism in post-revolutionary Iranian political culture," in Samih K. Farsoun and Mehrdad Mashayekhi, eds, *Iran: Political Culture in the Islamic Republic*, London: Routledge, 1992, pp. 214–33; Valentine Moghadam, "Islamic populism, class, and gender in post-revolutionary Iran," in John Foran, ed., *A Century of Revolution: Social Movements in Iran*, Minneapolis, MN: University of Minnesota Press, 1994, pp. 189–222.

4. Ervand Abrahamian, *Iran Between two Revolutions*, Princeton, NJ: Princeton University Press, 1982; Said Amir Arjomand, *The Turban for the Crown: The Islamic Revolution in Iran*, London: Oxford University Press, 1989.

5. Suzanne Maloney, "Islamism and Iran's post-revolutionary economy: the case of the Bonyads," in Mary Ann Tétreault and Robert A. Denemark, eds, *Gods, Gun & Globalization: Religious Radicalism and International Political Economy*, Vol. 13, Boulder, CO: Lynne Rienner, 2004, p. 200.

6. Ibid., p. 201.

7. *The New Owners of Corporate Iran*, Tehran: Atieh Bahar Consulting, 2010, pp. 33–4.

8. Ibid., pp. 32–3.

9. See Kimteh-e Emdad-e Imam Khomeini at http://emdad.ir/index_en.asp, Faghr Zodaei Komiteh Emdad Ba Chehl Onvan-e Khedmat (Poverty Reduction of Emdadad Committee through provision of 40 Services). 25 January 2007. Accessed on 24 May 2014.

10. Ali A. Saeidi, "The accountability of para-governmental organizations (Bonyads): the case of Iranian foundations," *Iranian Studies*, 37: 3, Sep. 2004, p. 489.

11. Ibid., p. 488.

12. Bank-e Markazi-e Jomhuri-e Islami-e Iran, *Baresi-e Tahavvolat-e Eqtessadi-e Keshvar Tey-e Salha-e 1361–1369* (*Iran's Economic Development, 1982–1990*), Tehran: Iranian Central Bank, 1994, p. 817, as cited by Saeidi, "The accountability," p. 488.

13. Atieh Bahar Consulting, *The New Owners*, pp. 45–7.

14. Andrew Higgins, "Inside Iran's holy money machine," *Wall Street Journal*, 2 June 2007, pp. 1–2.

15. Atieh Bahar Consulting, *The New Owners*, pp. 12–16.

16. Shaul Bakhash, *The Reign of Ayatollahs*, New York, NY: Basic Books, 1984, pp. 188–9.

17. Saeidi, "The accountability," p. 489.

18. Djavad Salehi-Esfahani, "Iran: poverty and inequality since the Revolution," Brookings, http://www.brookings.edu/research/opinions/2009/01/29-iran-salehi-isfahani, last accessed 15 Oct. 2012.

19. Djavad Salehi-Esfahani, "Poverty, inequality, and populist politics in Iran," *Journal of Economic Inequality*, 7: 5, 2009, p. 28.

20. Mohammad Ali Moradi, "Oil resources abundance, economic growth, and income distribution in Iran," presented at the International Conference on Policy Modeling, Ottawa, Canada, June 2009, pp. 1–21.

21. See United Nations Development Program, *Human Development Report, 2009: Islamic Republic of Iran*, New York, NY: United Nations, 2009.

22. Homy Lafayette, "Iran's cities a sea of poverty," PBS Tehran Bureau, 4 Mar. 2011, http://www.pbs.org/wgbh/pages/frontline/tehranbureau/2011/03/irans-cities-a-sea-of-poverty.html, last accessed 28 Oct 2015.

23. Mir Saeed Moosavi, "An introduction to the socio-spatial consequences of urban poverty in Iran," in *Re-mixing the City: Towards Sustainability and Resilience*, 14–16 May 2012, pp. 1125–9, http://programm.corp.at/cdrom2012/papers 2012/CORP2012_119.pdf, last accessed 28 Oct 2015.

24. Shirin Mirzeyer, "Iran's economy: on the background of the new sanctions," Center for Economic and Social Development, 24 July 2012, pp. 28–39.

25. Djavad Salehi-Isfahani, "Iran's economy after devaluation," *LobeLog Foreign Policy*, 7 Feb. 2013, p. 1.

26. Rick Gladstone, "IMF study details perils of Iranian economy", *The New York Times*, 12 Feb. 2014.

27. Kenneth Katzman, "Iran's Bonyads: economic strengths and weaknesses," Emirates Center for Strategic Studies and Research, 15 Oct. 2012, pp. 1–3; there are other estimates that assess the value of holdings of Bonyads by the end of 1980s to be half of the Iranian government's budget. See for example, Jahangir Amuzegar, *Iran's Economy Under the Islamic Republic*, London: I. B. Tauris, 1993, p. 100.

28. Saeidi, "The accountability," p. 493 sums up the Bonyads' participation in the process of privatization in the 1990s and the attempt to streamline and rationalize their operations: "The foundations sold only some of their assets to the value of 62.2 billion rials in 1992. When the government decided to increase the interest rates on their bank borrowing, they used political pressure to obtain subsidies and financial credit from the national budget."

29. Ibid.

30. Ibid., p. 497.

31. Sohrab Behdad and Farhad Nomani, "What a Revolution: thirty years of social class reshuffling in Iran," *Comparative Studies of South Asia, Africa and the Middle East*, 29: 1, 2009, p. 103.

32. Atieh Bahar Consulting, *The New Owners*, pp. 6–7.

33. Hadi Salehi Esfahani, "Alternative public service delivery mechanism in Iran," *The Quarterly Review of Economics and Finance*, 45, 2005, pp. 521–4.

34. Maloney, "Islamism and Iran's post-revolutionary economy," p. 203.

35. Saeidi, "The Accountability," pp. 490–8.

36. Maloney, "Islamism and Iran's post-revolutionary economy," p. 195.

37. Ibid., p. 208.

38. Ibid., p. 198.

39. Hamid Naficy, *A Social History of Iranian Cinema. Vol. 4: Globalizing Era, 1984–2010*, Durham and London: Duke University Press, 2012, pp. 5–12.

40. Ibid., pp. 14–15.

41. Ibid., pp. 242–311.

42. Suzanne Maloney, "Agents or obstacles? Parastatal foundations and the challenges for Iranian development," in Parvin Alizadeh, ed., *The Economy of Iran: Dilemmas of an Islamic State*, London: I. B. Tauris, 2000, pp. 150–69.

43. Atieh Bahar Consullting, *The New Owners*, p. 37.

44. Eva Patricia Rakel, "Conglomerates in Iran: the political economy of Iranian foundations," in Alex Fernandez Jilberto and Barbara Hogenboom, eds, *Conglomerates and Economic Groups in Developing Countries and Transition Economies*, London: Routledge, 2006, pp. 121–3.

45. Crane Brinton, *The Anatomy of Revolution*, New York: Vintage, 1965.

12. RE-MAPPING OF THE CORPORATE LANDSCAPE IN IRAN

1. Purchasing Power Parity.

2. IndexMundi, "Iran GDP," http://www.indexmundi.com/iran/gdp_(purchasing_power_parity).html, last accessed on 14 Nov. 2015.

3. Payvand News, 29 Dec. 2012.

4. This term will be used throughout this chapter as a reference to the business and enterprise sector of the economy.

5. The terms semi-state and semi-governmental will be used representing the same meaning: institutions that are neither controlled by the government nor by the private sector.

6. Iran's current foreign investment law (the so-called Foreign Investment Promotion and Protection Act or FIPPA) was drafted and passed during President Khatami's term and laid the grounds for a more effective attraction of foreign investment.

7. "Revival of the Management and Planning Organization," IRNA, http://www.irna.ir/fa/News/81381415/, last accessed on 14 November 2015.

8. A detailed account of the objectives of the various FYPs as well as the actual privatization performance can be found on the official website of the Iran Privatization Organization at: http://www.en.ipo.ir/

9. For a more detailed account of the obstacles to privatization, see Bijan Khajehpour, "Domestic Political Reforms and Private Sector Activity in Iran," in *Social Research: Iran since the Revolution*, Vol. 67, No. 2, Summer 2000, pp. 577–98.

10. Ibid.

11. "Doing Business in Iran," The World Bank, http://www.doingbusiness.org/data/exploreeconomies/iran/, last accessed 14 Nov. 2015.

12. "Islamic Republic of Iran Constitution," Iran Online, http://www.iranonline. com/iran/iran-info/government/constitution.html, last accessed 14 Nov. 2015.

13. This emerged in a 2004 decree signed by Supreme Leader Ayatollah Khamenei. The implementation of the decree was debated in the Iranian Parliament and became law in July 2008. For the Persian text of the law, please refer to the website of the Iranian Parliament, www.majlis.ir

14. "General Policies of Article 44 of the Constitution of the Islamic Republic of Iran," Iran Privatization Organization, http://www.en.ipo.ir/index.aspx?siteid=83& pageid=822, last accessed 14 Nov. 2015.

15. Ibid.

16. For a detailed analysis of the approach by the Ahmadinejad administration, please look at: Kevan Harris, "Pseudo-privatization in the Islamic Republic: beyond the headlines on Iran's economic transformation," Muftah, 15 Oct. 2010, http://muftah.org/pseudo-privatization-in-the-islamic-republic-beyond-the-headlines-on-iran%E2%80%99s-economic-transformation-by-kevan-harris/

17. Iran's Ministry of Finance and Economic Affairs has set up a specific website for the ongoing reporting on the implementation of the law on privatization performance; see http://asl44.mefa.ir/Portal/Home

18. For a detailed analysis of the 20-Year Prospect Document, see Jahangir Amuzegar, "Iran's 20-year economic perspective: promises and pitfalls," Middle East Policy Council, http://www.mepc.org/journal/middle-east-policy-archives/irans-20-year-economic-perspective-promises-and-pitfalls

19. Ibid.

20. For a detailed description of the processes, please refer to www.ipo.ir

21. The IPO was established in 2001 within the framework of the 3rd FYP in order to coordinate the government's efforts to privatize state companies.

22. The High Council of Ceding was formed to coordinate, supervise and control the privatization process. It is headed by the minister of economic affairs and finance, and its other members are: the vice president for strategic planning, the governor of the Central Bank, the minister in charge of the relevant sector for privatization, the minister of justice and parliamentary representatives of the economics and planning and budget commissions as observers.

23. "Privatization has been a source of income for the government," Tabnak News, www.tabnak.ir/fa/news/295662

24. This entity is affiliated with the Iranian Parliament and is responsible for auditing all governmental affairs.

25. "Report by the State Audit Organization," Shargh, 3 July 2012.

26. Iranian years start on 21 March and end on 20 March of the following year. The statistics described in this graph reflect Iranian years, so 2011 means the period 21 Mar. 2011 to 20 Mar. 2012. The figure for 2012 reflects a period of 10 months, 21 Mar. 2012 to 20 Jan. 2013.

27. "Performance and Records," Iran Privatization Organization, http://www.en.ipo.ir/index.aspx?siteid=83&pageid=800

28. These shares are managed centrally by a division within the Iran Privatization Organization.

29. "Interview with Mohsen Khalili," Bourse News, http://www.boursenews.ir/fa/pages/?cid=59849

30. The statements in this segment are the results of a study carried out by Atieh Bahar Consulting in 2010.

31. The figures in this table have been derived based on an ongoing analysis of the role of each of the categories in various economic sectors and the role of each sector in Iran's overall GDP. The matrix has been developed by the author based on sector contributions to Iran's GDP as calculated by the Iran Statistical Center.

32. For a detailed analysis of the overall process of privatization, see Kevan Harris, "The rise of the subcontractor state: politics of pseudo-privatization in the Islamic Republic of Iran," *International Journal of Middle East Studies*, 45, 2013, pp. 45–70.

33. Kourosh Avaei, "Will Iran's Revolutionary Guards reduce economic role?" Al-Monitor, http://www.al-monitor.com/pulse/originals/2013/09/rouhani-asks-revolutionary-guard-scale-back.html

34. One of the revolutionary foundations that was set up after the 1979 Revolution to manage the confiscated wealth of the Pahlavi family.

35. For further analysis see Bijan Khajehpour, "Reading the Iranian economy," in Konrad Adenauer Stiftung, *Iran Reader 2012*, available http://www.kas.de/wf/doc/kas_32068-544-1-30.pdf

36. As a result of the country's young demography, Iran needs to generate some 1 million new jobs every year.

37. Jahangir Amuzegar, "Iran's Fourth Plan: A Partial Assessment", *Middle East Policy Council*, http://www.mepc.org/journal/middle-east-policy-archives/irans-fourth-plan-partial-assessment

38. Pari Namazie and Philip Frame, "Developments in Human Resource Management in Iran," *International Journal of Human Resource Management*, 18: 1, 2007, pp. 159–71.

39. "Interim nuclear agreement between Iran and six powers", Reuters, http://www.reuters.com/article/2013/11/24/us-iran-nuclear-agreement-text-idUSBRE9AN0FS20131124

40. For a good summary of the JCPOA, see Gary G. Sick, "Iran After the Deal", Foreign Affairs, 7 September 2015.

41. For a detailed outline of the decree, see Bijan Khajehpour, "Decoding Iran's resistance economy," Al-Monitor, http://www.al-monitor.com/pulse/originals/2014/02/decoding-resistance-economy-iran.html

42. Iran introduced an extensive subsidy reform program in Dec. 2010 that has led to an increase in energy costs for Iranian families and businesses.

43. "Automotive industry at the crossroads of closure or change," Tabnak News, http://www.tabnak.ir/fa/news/315828/

44. For an analysis of this issue, see Pari Namazie, "The effect of sanctions on human resources management in Iran," *International Journal of HRM*, 2014.

45. For a comprehensive analysis of the impact of sanctions, see Bijan Khajehpour, Reza Marashi and Trita Parsi, "Never give in and never give up—the impact of sanctions on Tehran's nuclear calculations," NIAC Report, Mar. 2013.

46. See the official website of the Headquarters to Combat Smuggling, which is part of the Presidential Office: http://www.epe.ir/Home/Single/3472

47. "Economic Indicators," *Iran Economics (Eqtessade Iran) Magazine*, Issue 188, Oct. 2014, p. 74.

48. "Never give in and never give up—the impact of sanctions on Tehran's nuclear calculations", NIAC Report March 2013.

49. *Tehran Times*, 12 Feb. 2013.

50. Dr. Mohammad Nahavandian, "How to Manage the Iranian Economy," HAND Research Foundation, http://handresearch.org/pages/edo_list.php?id=18

51. For a more detailed view of the private sector on sanctions relief, see Bijan Khajehpour, "Iran's private sector eager for nuclear deal" Al-Monitor, http://www.al-monitor.com/pulse/originals/2014/11/iran-private-sector-business-nuclear-talks-economic-growth.html

52. See the Statistical Center of Iran website, www.amar.org.ir

53. "Youth Unemployment Approaching 26%," Hamshahri Online, http://hamshahrionline.ir/details/180751

54. See http://www.transparency.org/country#IRN

55. Survey carried out by the author through interviews with Iranian businesspeople.

56. For more details, see Arash Karami, "Rouhani criticizes consolidation of power in government," Al-Monitor, http://www3.al-monitor.com/pulse/originals/2014/12/rouhani-criticizes-revolutionary-guard-power.html#

57. Iran now has two official rates: a) Official currency exchange rate of approximately Rial 28,000 to the US$ and b) Free market rate of about Rial 35,000 to the US$.

58. In Sep. 2011, it was disclosed that the managing directors of Bank Melli and Bank Saderat—the country's two largest state banks—were involved in the embezzlement of some $3 billion. The most recent case of political accusation was made by President Ahmadinejad against the Larijani brothers during a Parliamentary impeachment session on 3 Feb. 2013.

59. Nasir al-Hassoun, "Iran-Iraq trade reached $12 billion in 2013," Al-Monitor, http://www.al-monitor.com/pulse/business/2014/07/iraq-iran-trade-increase-crisis-border-syria-jordan-turkey.html

60. A militia organization that is affiliated with the IRGC, but structured around local mosques.

CONCLUSION

1. Robin Wright, *The Last Great Revolution: Turmoil and Transformation in Iran*, New York: Alfred A. Knopf, 2000, p. 284.

2. Sandra Mackey, *The Iranians: Persia, Islam and the Soul of a Nation*, New York: Dutton, 1996, p. 368.

3. Arang Keshavarzian, "Iran," in Michele Penner Angrist, ed., *Politics & Society in the Contemporary Middle East*, Second Edition, Boulder, CO: Lynne Rienner Publishers, 2013, pp. 251–83; see p. 252.

4. Sasan Fayazmanesh, *The United States and Iran: Sanctions, Wars and the Policy of Dual Containment*, New York: Routledge, 2008, p. 228.

5. Nader Hashemi and Danny Postel, eds, *The People Reloaded: The Green Movement and the Struggle for Iran's Future*, New York: Melville House, 2010.

6. Barbara Ann Rieffer-Flanagan, *Evolving Iran: An Introduction to Politics and Problems in the Islamic Republic*, Washington, DC: Georgetown University Press, 2013, p. 198.

7. Mehrzad Boroujerdi, "Iran," in Ellen Lust, ed., *The Middle East*, Thirteenth Edition, Thousand Oaks, CA: CQ Press, 2014, pp. 478–506; see p. 487.

8. Ibid., p. 488.

9. Mark Gasiorowski, "Islamic Republic of Iran," in Mark Gasiorowski, ed., *The Government and Politics in the Middle East and North Africa*, Boulder, CO: Westview Press, 2014, pp. 51–89; see p. 71.

10. Mahmood Monshipouri, *Democratic Uprisings in the New Middle East: Youth, Technology, Human Rights, and US Foreign Policy*, Boulder, CO: Paradigm Publishers, 2014, p. 27.

11. "WDR 2009: Urbanization and narrowing rural-urban disparities in the Islamic Republic of Iran," World Development Report, http://web.worldbank.org/WBSITE/EXTERNAL/EXTDEC/EXTRESEARCH/EXTWDRS/0,,contentMDK:23080427~pagePK:478093~piPK:477627~theSitePK:477624,00.html, last accessed 1 Jan. 2015.

12. Ibid.

13. "President Rouhani Confronts Iran's Hardliners on Corruption," *YaLibnan*, 9 Dec. 2014, http://yalibnan.com/2014/12/09/president-rouhani-confronts-irans-hard-liners-on-corruption/, last accessed 2 Jan. 2015.

14. Ali M. Ansari, "Iran and international politics," in Karl Yambert, ed., *The Contemporary Middle East: A Westview Reader*, Second Edition, Boulder, CO: Westview Press, 2010, pp. 283–93; see p. 283.

15. Anoushiravan Ehteshami, "The foreign policy of Iran," in Raymond Hinnebusch and Anoushiravan Ehteshami, eds, *The Foreign Policies of Middle East States*, Second Edition, Boulder, CO: Lynne Rienner Publishers, 2014, pp. 261–88; see p. 277.

16. Ibid., p. 287.

17. "Iran's Rouhani Cancels Visit to Italy and France over Paris Attacks," Reuters, 14 November 2015, available at http://in.reuters.com/article/2015/11/14/france-shooting-iran-syria-idINKCN0T30DU20151114, last accessed on 14 November 2015.

18. Michael Jansen, "Clouds of uncertainty," *Gulf Today: Panorama*, 26 Dec. 2014—1 Jan. 2015, pp. 56–7.

INDEX